SCHOOL-LIVE! ⑦

SADORU CHIBA
NORIMITSU KAIHOU
(Nitroplus)

Translation: Leighann Harvey

Lettering: Alexis Eckerman

GAKKOU GURASHI! Vol. 7
©Nitroplus / Norimitsu Kaihou, Sadoru Chiba, Houbunsha. All rights reserved. First published in Japan in 2016 by HOUBUNSHA CO., LTD., Tokyo. English translation rights in United States, Canada, and United Kingdom arranged with HOUBUNSHA CO., LTD through Tuttle-Mori Agency, Inc., Tokyo.

Yen Press
1290 Avenue of the Americas
New York, NY 10104

Visit us at yenpress.com
facebook.com/yenpress
twitter.com/yenpress
yenpress.tumblr.com
instagram.com/yenpress

First Yen Press Edition: June 2017

Yen Press is an imprint of Yen Press, LLC.
The Yen Press name and logo are trademarks of Yen Press, LLC.

The publisher is not responsible for websites (or their content) that are not owned by the publisher.

Library of Congress Control Number: 2015952613

ISBNs: 978-0-316-47172-5 (paperback)
       978-0-316-55966-9 (ebook)

10 9 8 7 6 5 4 3

BVG

Printed in the United States of America

Translation Notes

Common Honorifics:

no honorific: Indicates familiarity or closeness; if used without permission or reason, addressing someone in this manner would constitute an insult.

-san: The Japanese equivalent of Mr./Mrs./Miss. If a situation calls for politeness, this is the fail-safe honorific.

-kun: Used most often when referring to boys, this indicates affection or familiarity. Occasionally used by older men among their peers, but it may also be used by anyone referring to a person of lower standing.

-chan: An affectionate honorific indicating familiarity used mostly in reference to girls; also used in reference to cute persons or animals of either gender.

-senpai: A suffix used to address upperclassmen or more experienced coworkers.

-sensei: A respectful term for teachers, artists, or high-level professionals.

-nee: Honorific derived from onee-san/-sama ("big sister"). When used alone after a name, -nee can mean closeness.

Page 31
The titles of the Japanese movies, much like the English ones, are parodies of popular films. The movies being referenced in the Japanese titles are *Frankenstein's Army* and *Return of the Living Dead 3*.

Page 79
Semi is the Japanese word for cicada.

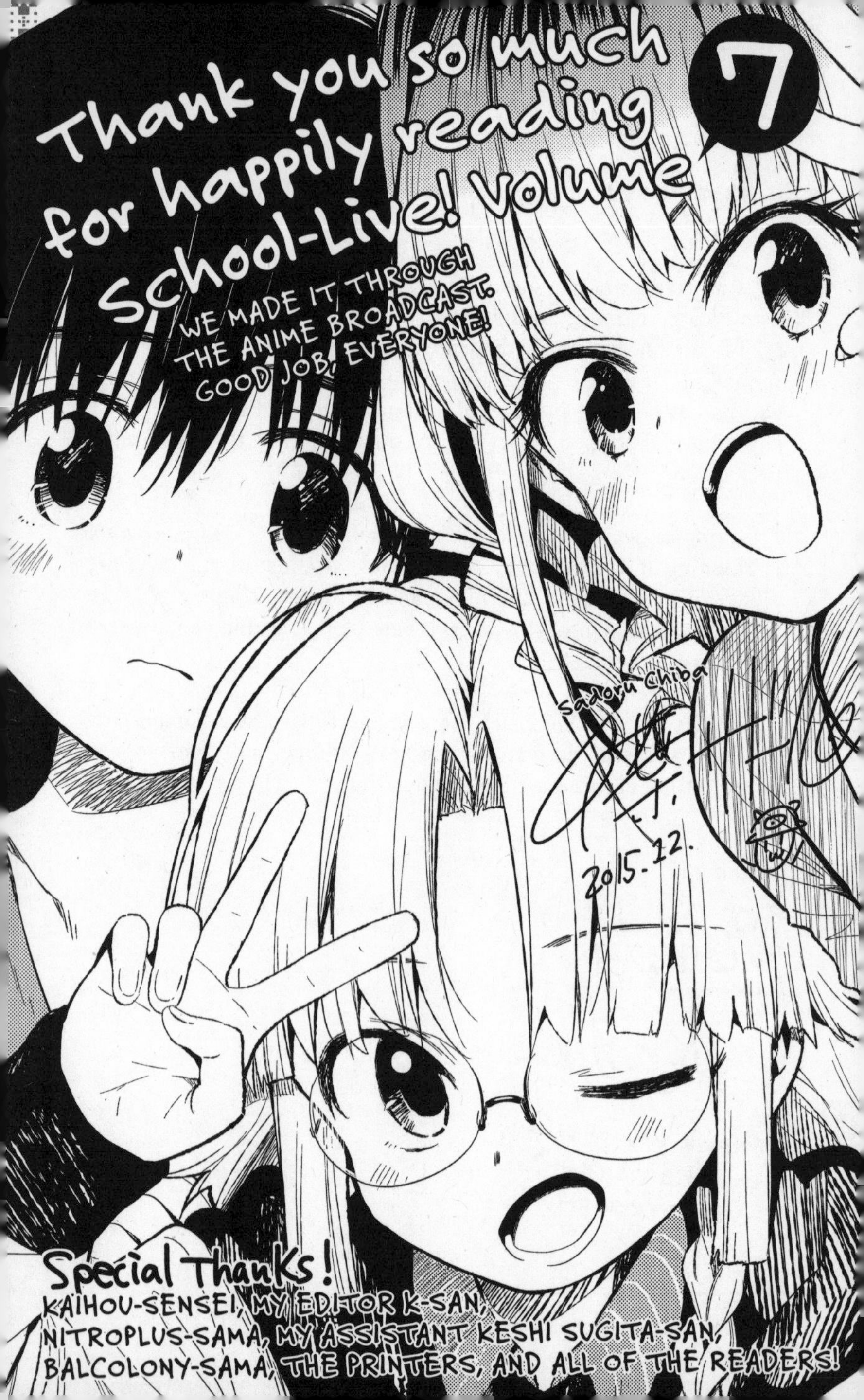
Thank you so much for happily reading School-Live! volume 7
WE MADE IT THROUGH THE ANIME BROADCAST. GOOD JOB, EVERYONE!
Sadoru Chiba
2015.12.
Special Thanks!
KAIHOU-SENSEI, MY EDITOR K-SAN, NITROPLUS-SAMA, MY ASSISTANT KESHI SUGITA-SAN, BALCOLONY-SAMA, THE PRINTERS, AND ALL OF THE READERS!

When I started college, I felt like I had been left all alone in this huge place.

I was given a book—the course catalogue. I had to pick out my own classes from it, arrange my own schedule, and calculate my credits all on my own. I had no idea what to do. Through high school, if I didn't come to class, I stood out and people would get mad at me. But in college, no one cared, and they didn't say anything if I skipped class. In exchange, I'd have to stay another year.

Having to decide everything for myself like that was incredibly frightening at first. In a way, that was just an illusion, and there are plenty of people, both in college and in the working world, who will offer to help you. However, it may be that you have to realize that on your own.

College life for Yuki and the gang is full of such brand-new challenges. Please do wait for the next volume, with more of the school living club's dazzling campus life.

Thank you.

Norimitsu Kaihou

Thank you so much for the wonderful anime reception!!

Special Thanks:
Itsuka Yamada (Circle Notebook design)

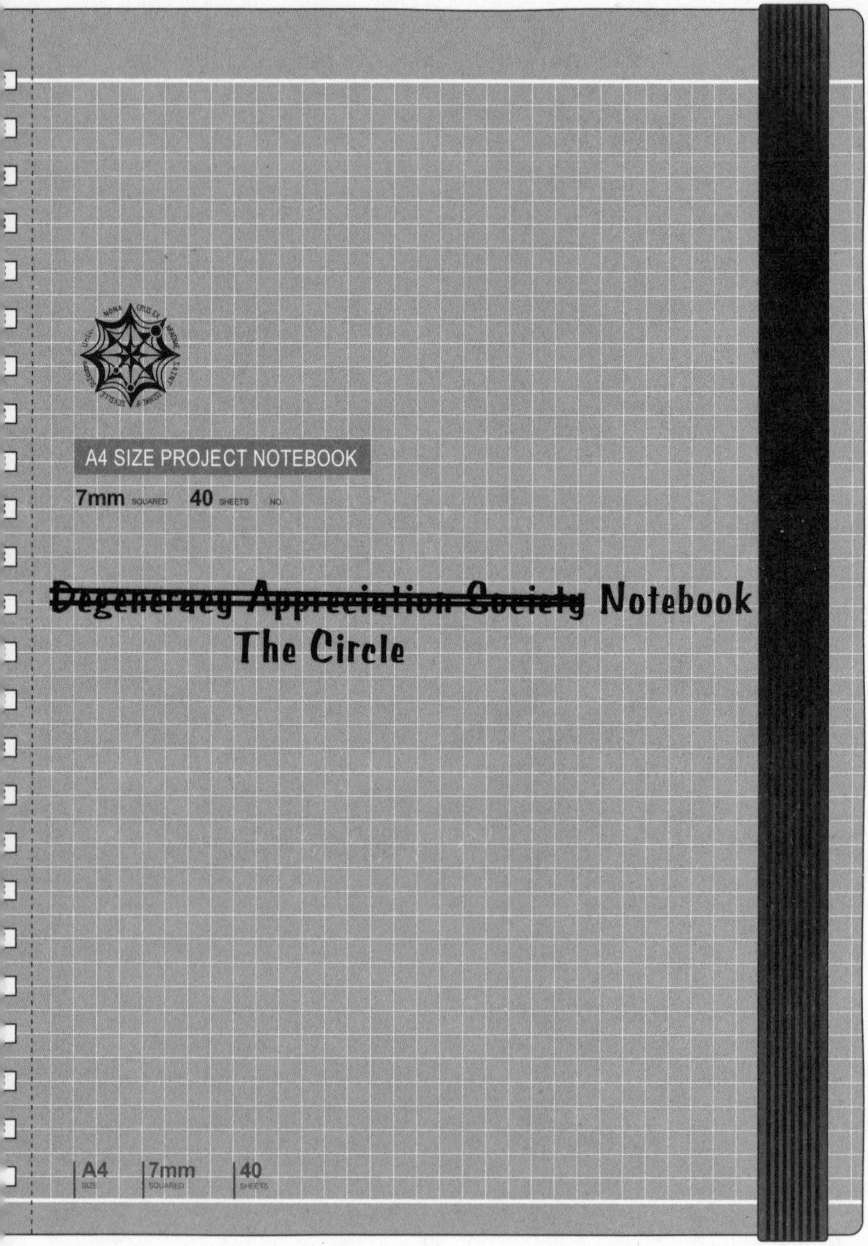
A4 SIZE PROJECT NOTEBOOK
7mm SQUARED 40 SHEETS NO.
~~Degeneracy Appreciation Society~~ Notebook
The Circle
A4 SIZE
7mm SQUARED
40 SHEETS

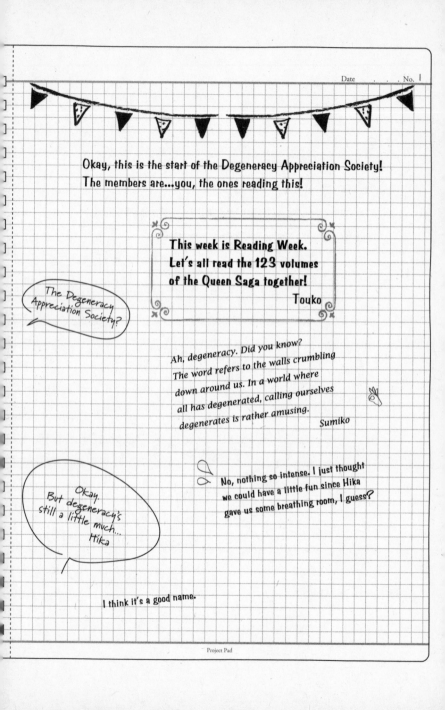

Okay, this is the start of the Degeneracy Appreciation Society!
The members are...you, the ones reading this!

> **This week is Reading Week.**
> **Let's all read the 123 volumes**
> **of the Queen Saga together!**
> Touko

The Degeneracy Appreciation Society?

Ah, degeneracy. Did you know?
The word refers to the walls crumbling
down around us. In a world where
all has degenerated, calling ourselves
degenerates is rather amusing.
Sumiko

Okay.
But degeneracy's
still a little much...
Hika

No, nothing so intense. I just thought
we could have a little fun since Hika
gave us some breathing room, I guess?

I think it's a good name.

The power of light to change night to day.

However, the power of humans is but a fraction of that of the

stars in the night sky. Still, I cannot help but see the arrogance

of man fondly, as a young child standing on tiptoes.

Sumiko

It's solar power, so please don't overuse it.

With power, we can start doing cultural stuff again. Thanks so much, Hika!

You're welcome.

All right! The GS4 is working too!

★ **Looking for participants** ★
★ **in a forty-eight hour** ★
★ **Ballout 3 marathon!** ★

That's cultural stuff?

Thank you from the library.

Who are you?

Ahhh, I really want to go to Akihabara!
They should have some imported
copies of BO4 in the shops there.

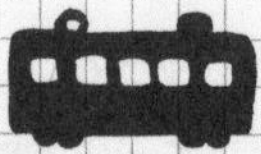

Right?

Touko

If you go to Akihabara,
I'd really like some
electronics and manuals.

Hika

But I'm not really going.
That's a bit too far away.

Akihabara is like the birthplace of your soul, is it not, Touko? But people can never truly return to their birthplaces, since the birthplace you return to is not the same birthplace that you set out from. And thus, you lose it once again. Longing for the birthplace that you can never see again may just be a sort of karma.

I miss it too.

Sumiko

Date . . No. 4

To whomever it was who borrowed the manga "My Maidenly Circumstances," volumes 1–17 from the library, when you check out books, please write which books you are taking down at the front desk, and when you bring them back, please put them back in their proper places.

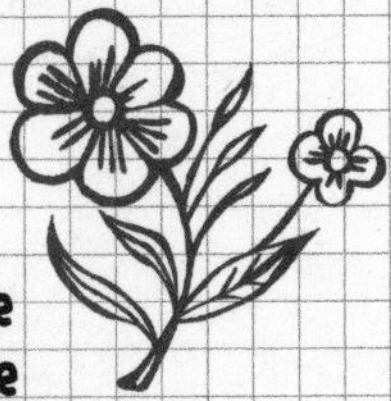

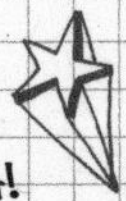

It's the hidden character!
It's the arrival of the hidden character!
Since you're here, please do introduce yourself.

I offer my respects to the mistress of the library, the storehouse of never-ending knowledge. Please do guide we who are living in these Second Dark Ages on the path toward the wisdom of the ancients.

Sumiko

I'm Rise Ryougawara from the cultural anthropology department. I'm usually in the library, but I come over here from time to time. If you have any questions about books, just ask me.
Rise

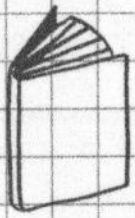

Sorry. I'll be sure to put them back right next time.
Hika

I'm Aki. I'm going to be joining you guys
from now on. Nice to meet you.

Welcome to the Degeneracy Appreciation Society!

Aki was living with the militants,
but things got a little awkward
over there, so she came to us...
That's okay, right?

The Degeneracy
Appreciation
Society?

Was that you guys' name? I mean, you
did say that you like to take it easy.
Yeah.

We really have a bad
reputation, don't we?
Then, how about the Idle Living
Friendship Society?

A name is an expression of the body and a restriction of the heart.

That is the law. It is the origin, but also the demise. The snake eating

its tail. The never-ending change. That is the proper name for us.

The title of a
notebook!?

Sumiko

It's not so bad.

Agreed.

I agree.

~~~~~~~~~~~~~~~~~~~~~~~~~~~~~~

After last month, which was Robot Anime Month,
this month is Foreign Drama Month!

Week one is a 72-hour marathon!

"Inflation Model"

Seasons 1-6 in one go!

We'll be waiting!   Touko

~~~~~~~~~~~~~~~~~~~~~~~~~~~~~~

I'll be there.
Hika

Watching them's good and all,
but make sure you clean up, okay?   Aki

Okay!

Let it not be said that indulging in temporary fantasies is a foolish endeavor.

Living is but another vain dream of glory.

We shall retake our forms after dreaming, and the dreams shall disappear into the ether.

Sumiko ✌

Okay, so you're coming.

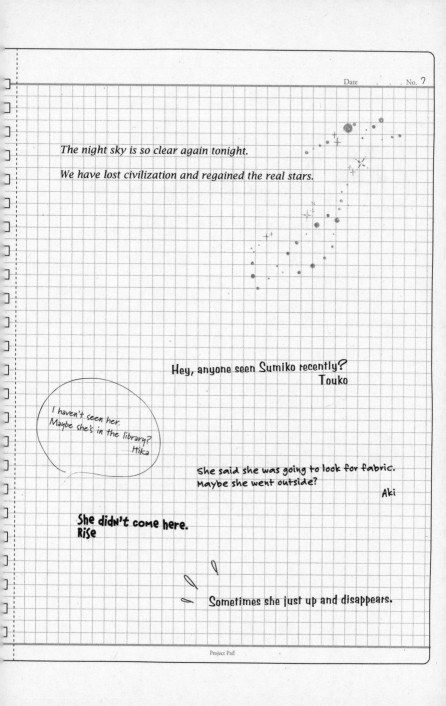

The night sky is so clear again tonight.

We have lost civilization and regained the real stars.

Hey, anyone seen Sumiko recently?
Touko

I haven't seen her.
Maybe she's in the library?
Hika

She said she was going to look for fabric.
Maybe she went outside?
Aki

She didn't come here.
Rise

Sometimes she just up and disappears.

Project Pad

Date . . No. 8

BIG NEWS!

New people arrived.
We might just finally have new members

for the Degeneracy Appreciation Society, I mean, the Circle!

Project Pad

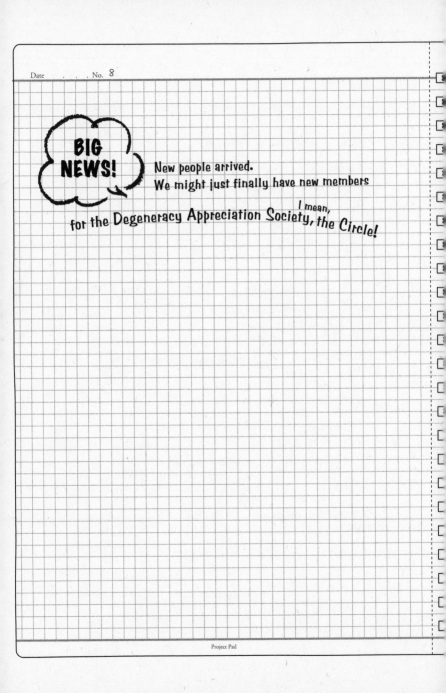

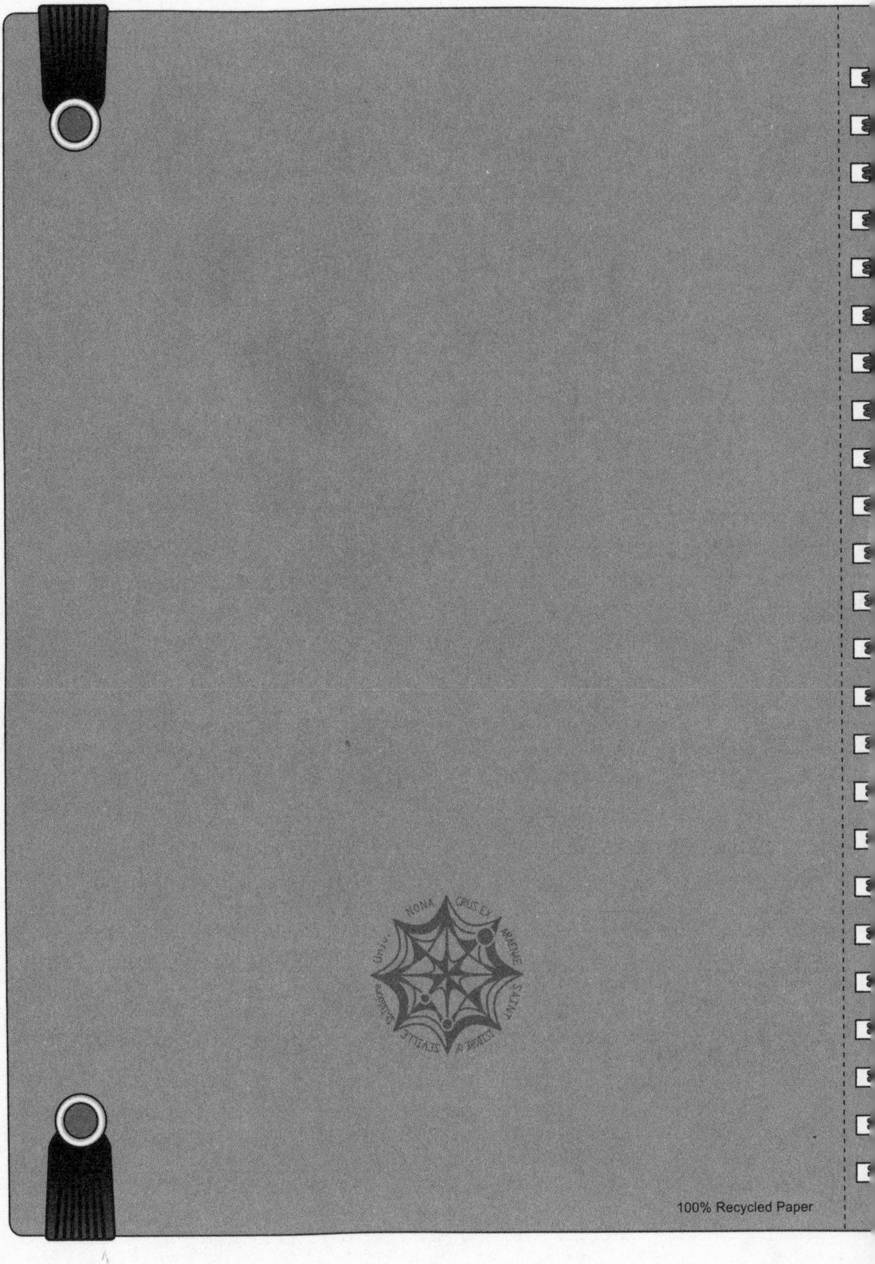
NONA
CRUS EX
SAINT
SEVILLE
Univ.
100% Recycled Paper

SCHOOL-LIVE!

Six Stars

Effects vary from
person to person,
but smoking nicotine
causes addiction.

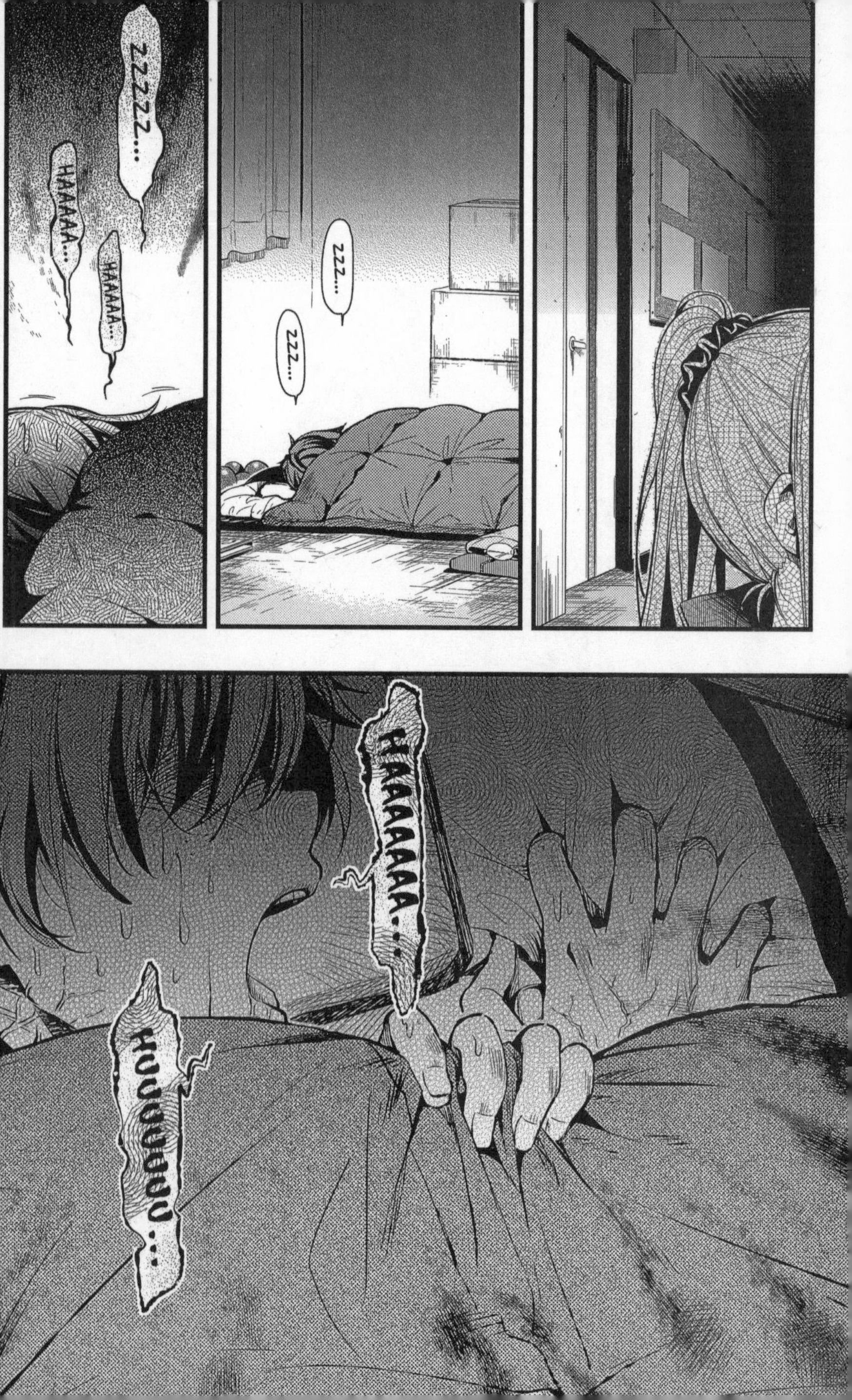
ZZZ...
ZZZ...
ZZZZZ...
HAAAAA...
HAAAAA...
HAAAAAAAA...
HUUUUUUU...

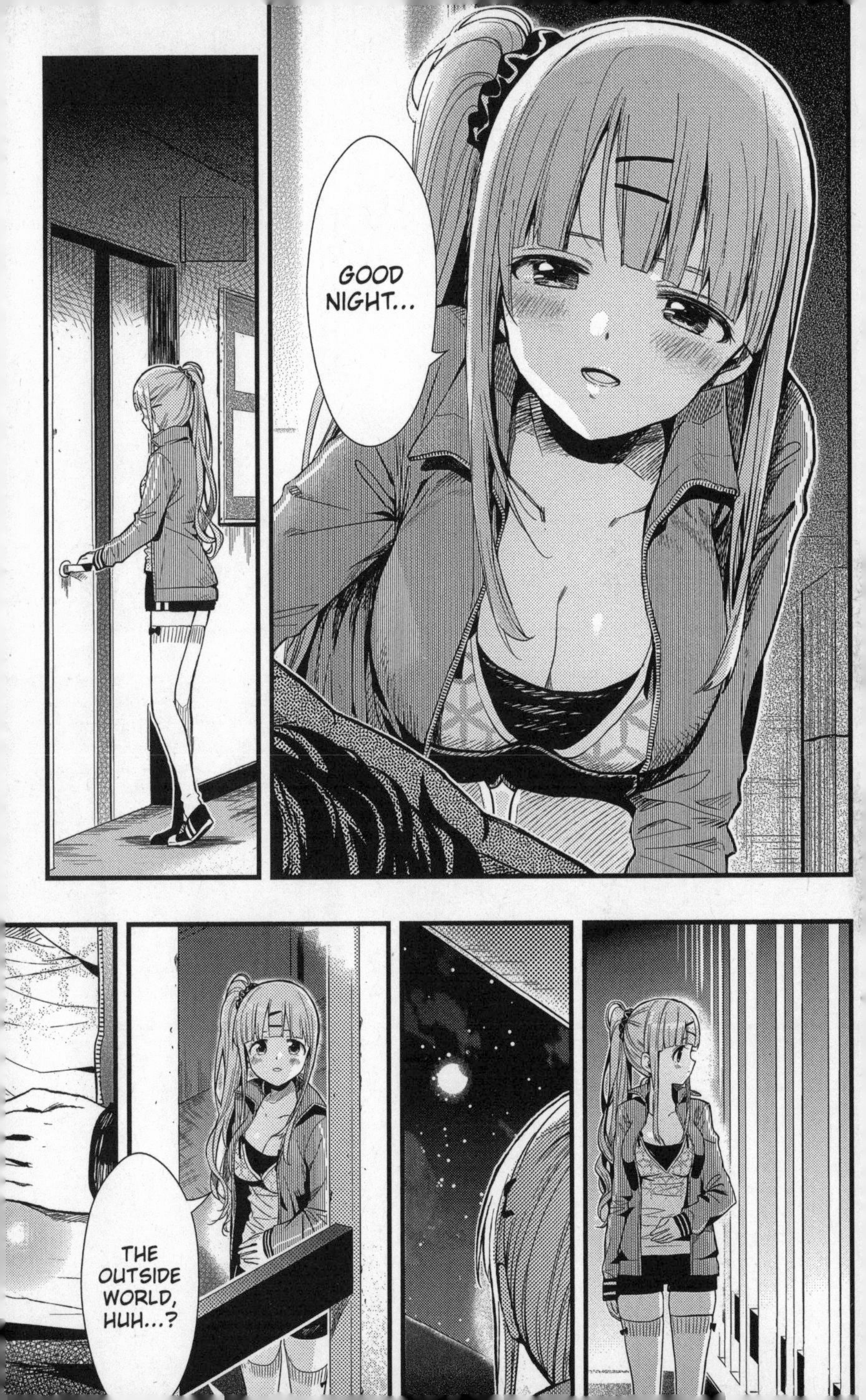
GOOD NIGHT...
THE OUTSIDE WORLD, HUH...?

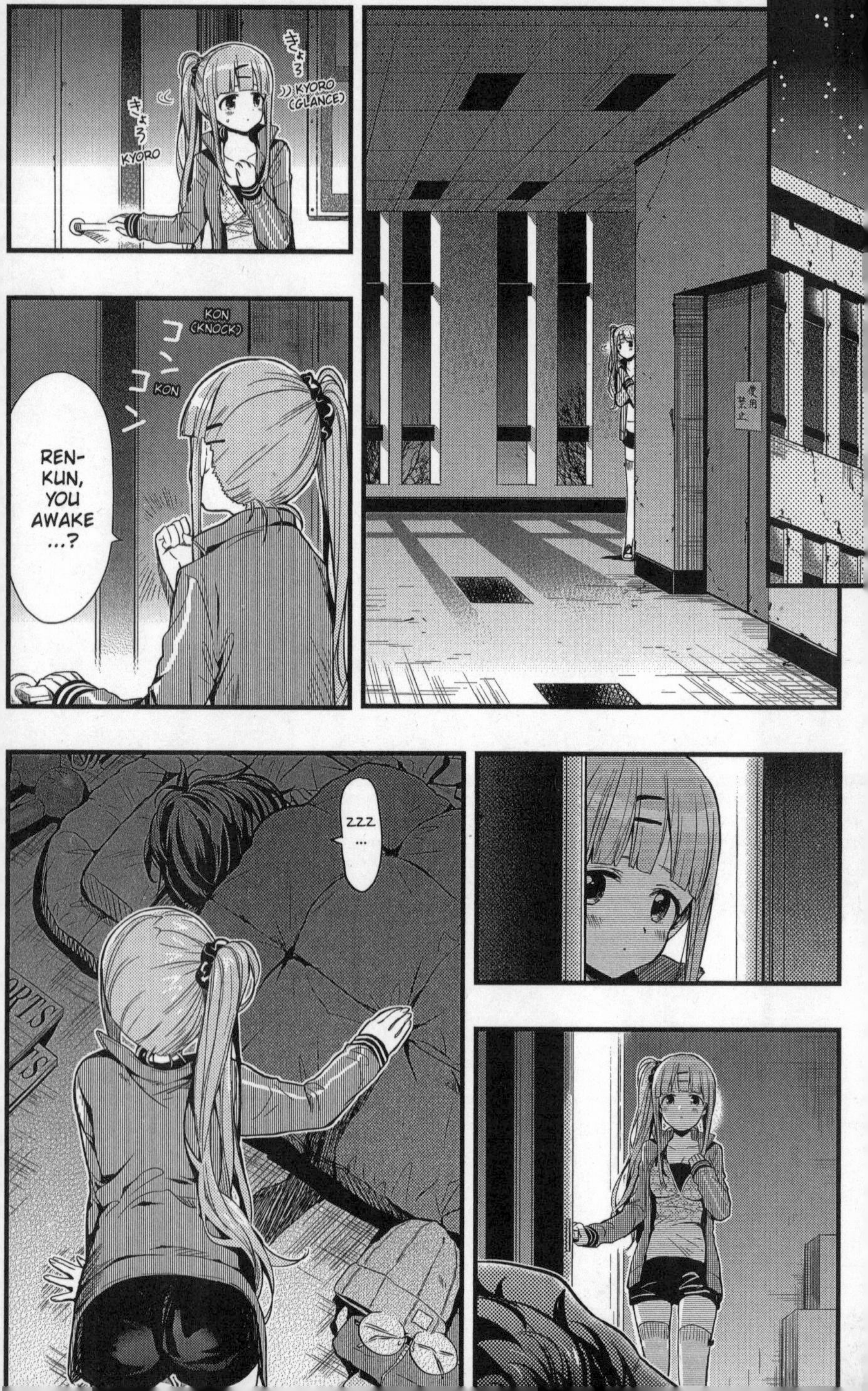
きょろ
KYORO (GLANCE)
きょろ
KYORO
コン
KON (KNOCK)
コン
KON
REN-KUN, YOU AWAKE ...?
ZZZ ...

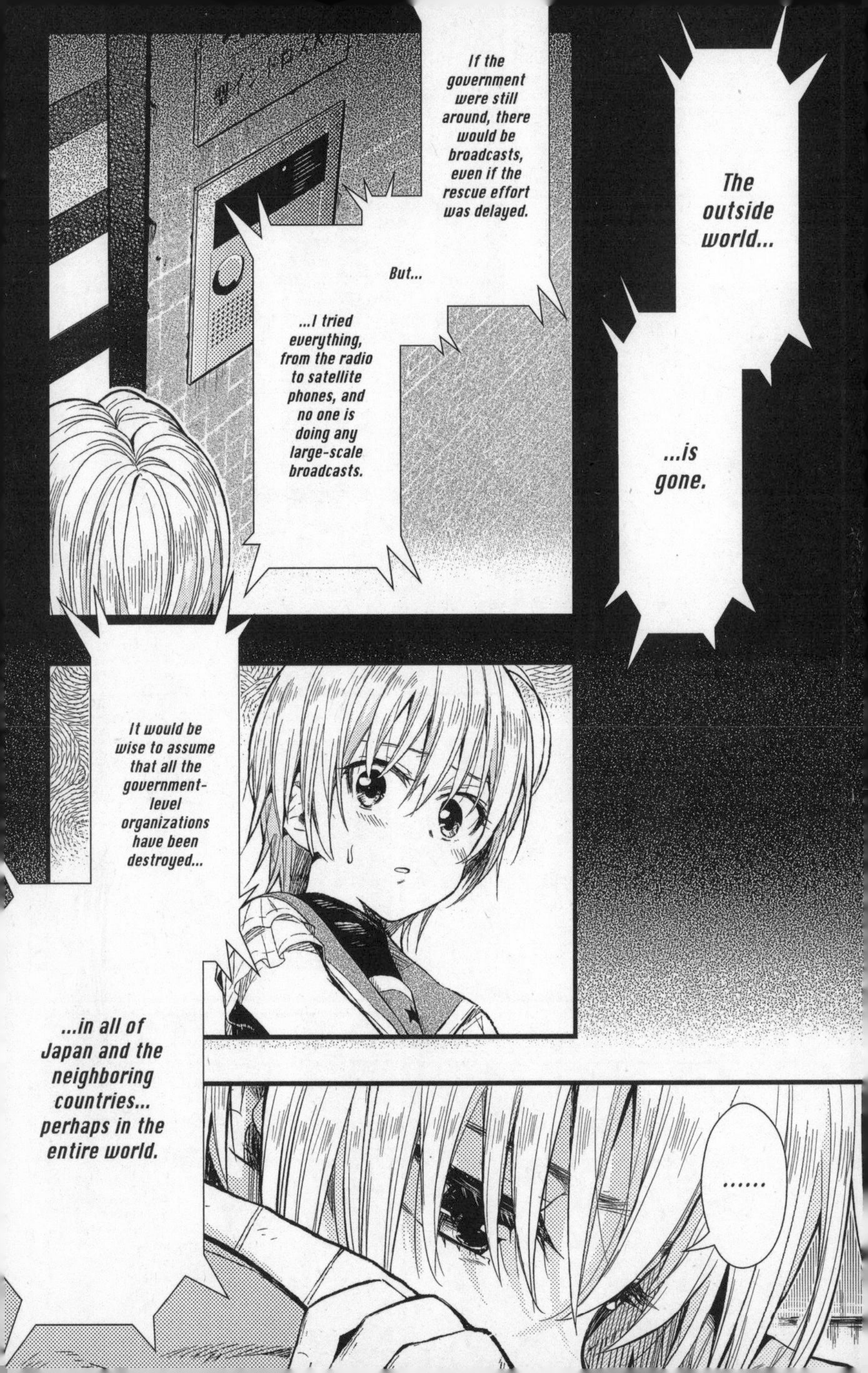
The outside world...
...is gone.
If the government were still around, there would be broadcasts, even if the rescue effort was delayed.
But...
...I tried everything, from the radio to satellite phones, and no one is doing any large-scale broadcasts.
It would be wise to assume that all the government-level organizations have been destroyed...
...in all of Japan and the neighboring countries... perhaps in the entire world.
......

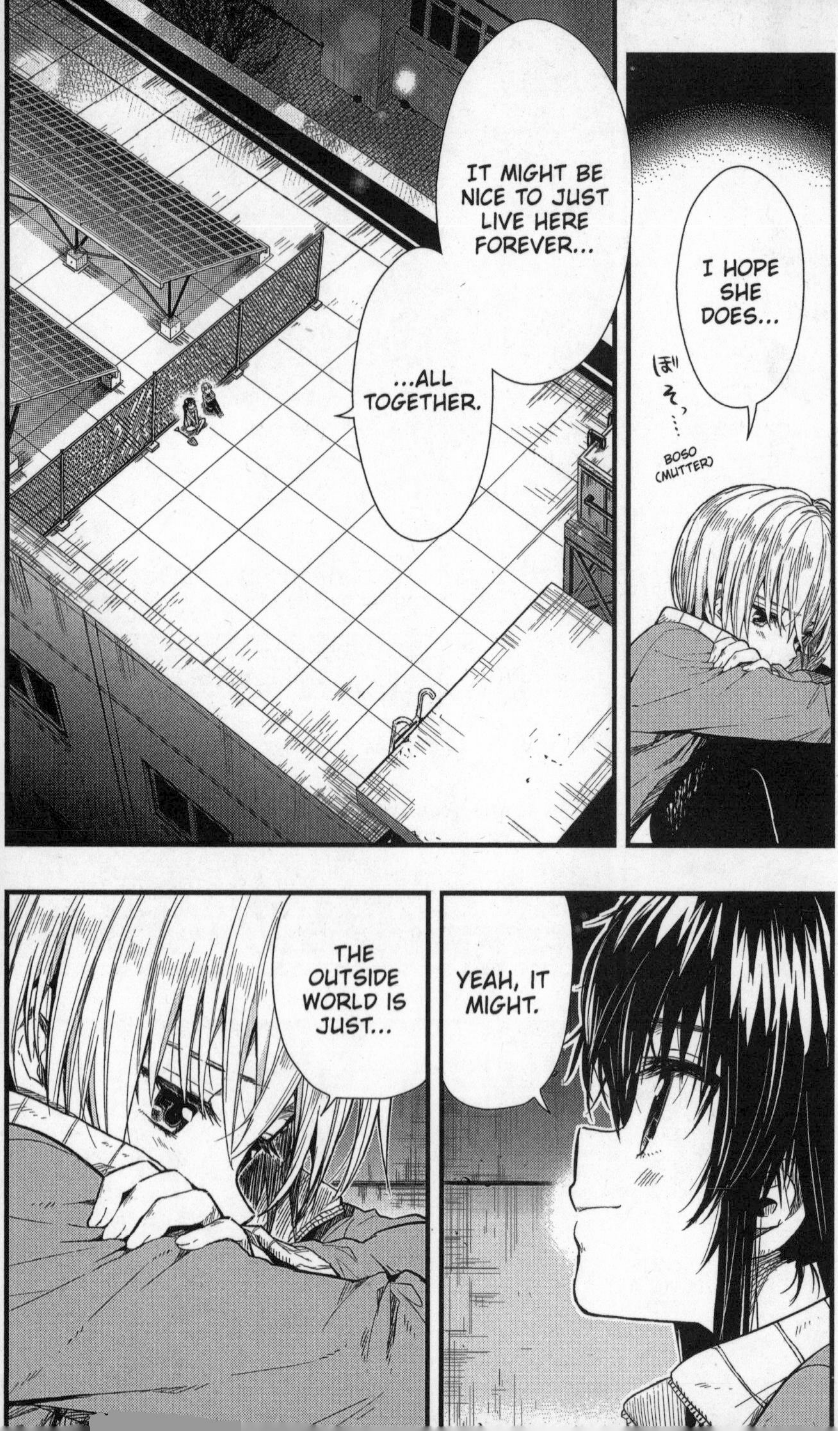
I HOPE SHE DOES...
ぼそっ...
BOSO (MUTTER)
IT MIGHT BE NICE TO JUST LIVE HERE FOREVER...
...ALL TOGETHER.
YEAH, IT MIGHT.
THE OUTSIDE WORLD IS JUST...

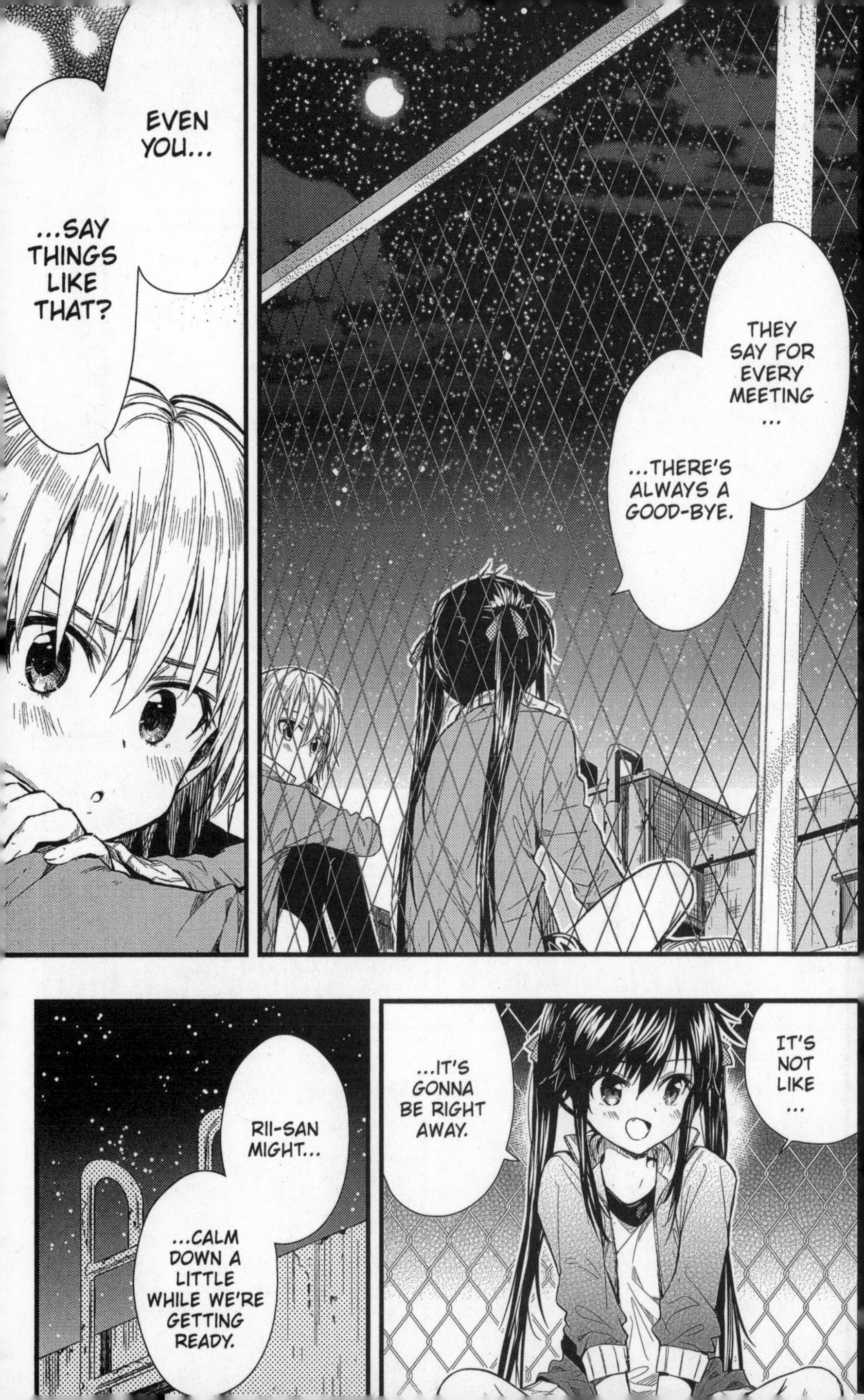
THEY SAY FOR EVERY MEETING...
...THERE'S ALWAYS A GOOD-BYE.
EVEN YOU...
...SAY THINGS LIKE THAT?
IT'S NOT LIKE...
...IT'S GONNA BE RIGHT AWAY.
RII-SAN MIGHT...
...CALM DOWN A LITTLE WHILE WE'RE GETTING READY.

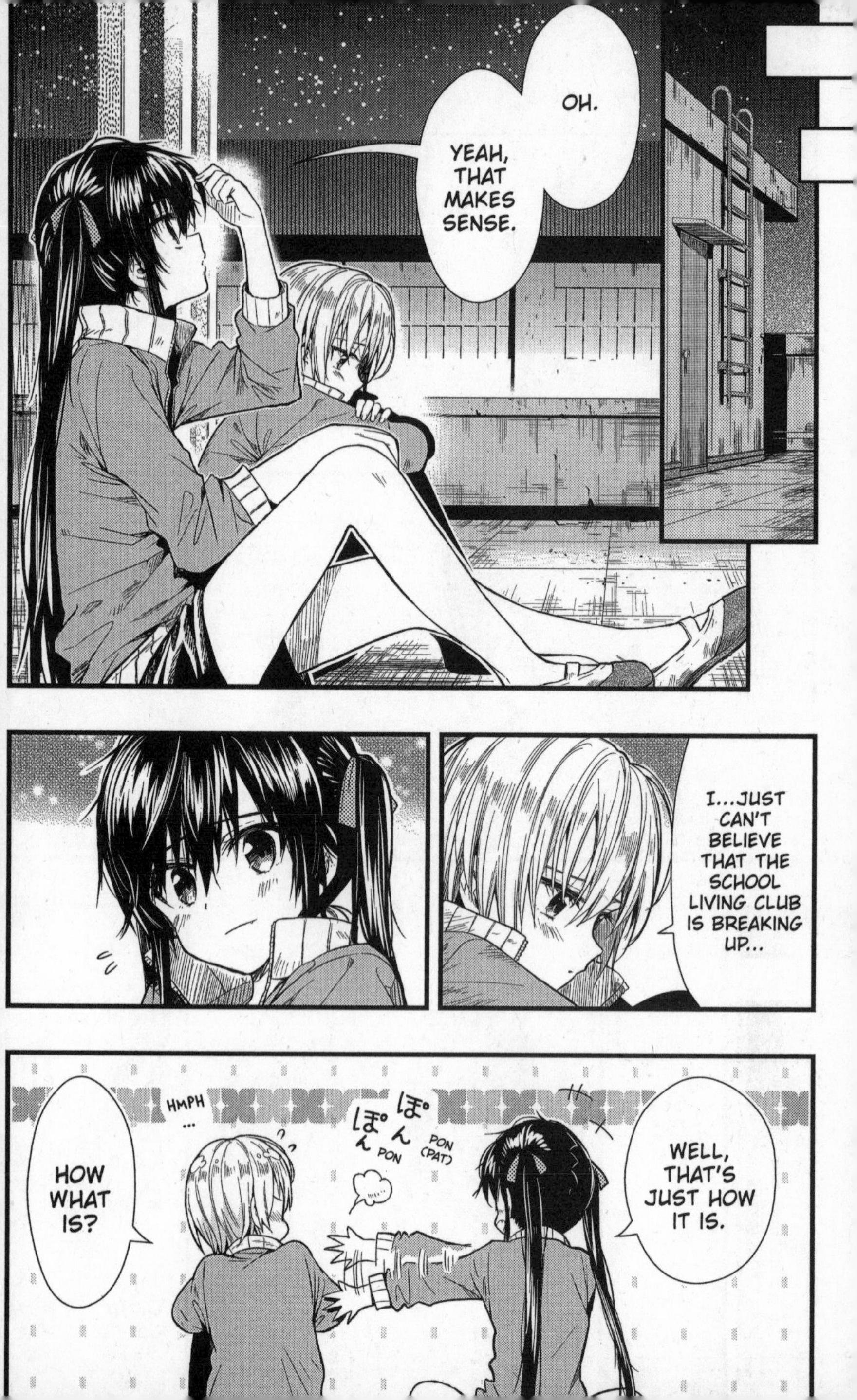
OH.
YEAH, THAT MAKES SENSE.
I...JUST CAN'T BELIEVE THAT THE SCHOOL LIVING CLUB IS BREAKING UP...
WELL, THAT'S JUST HOW IT IS.
ぽんぽん
PON PON (PAT)
HMPH ...
HOW WHAT IS?

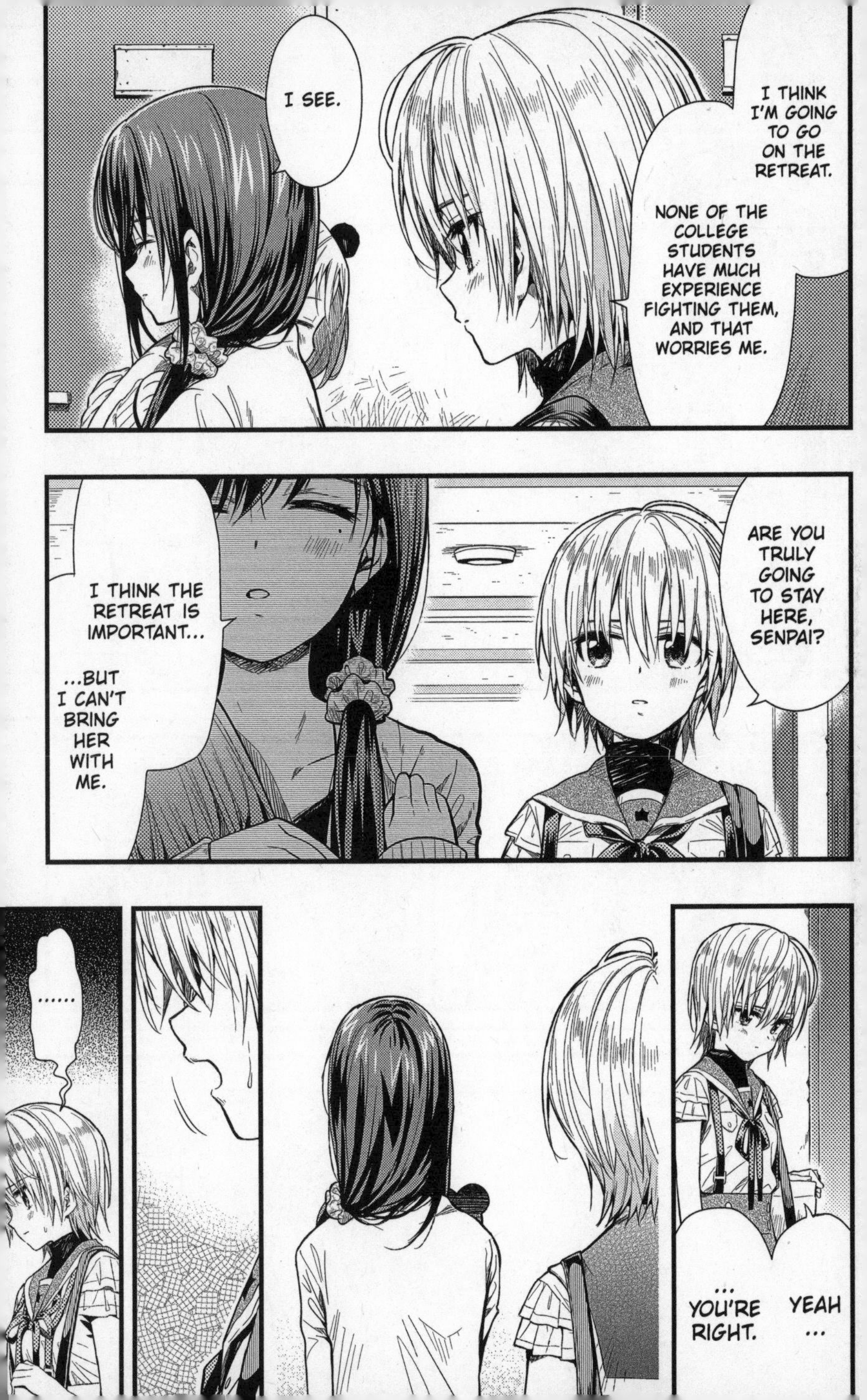
I THINK I'M GOING TO GO ON THE RETREAT.
NONE OF THE COLLEGE STUDENTS HAVE MUCH EXPERIENCE FIGHTING THEM, AND THAT WORRIES ME.
I SEE.
ARE YOU TRULY GOING TO STAY HERE, SENPAI?
I THINK THE RETREAT IS IMPORTANT...
...BUT I CAN'T BRING HER WITH ME.
YEAH...
...YOU'RE RIGHT.
......

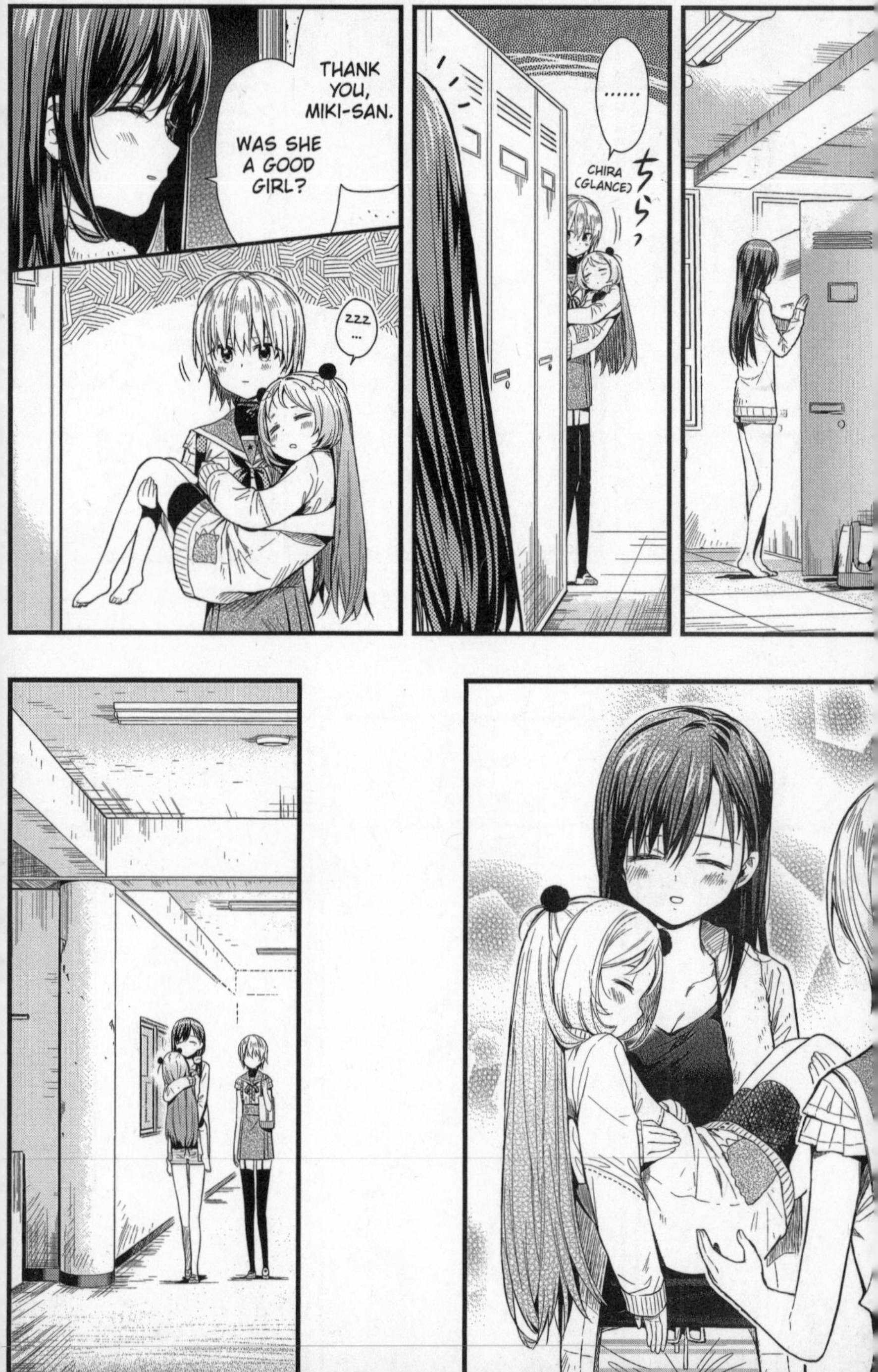
......
CHIRA (GLANCE)
ちらっ
THANK YOU, MIKI-SAN.
WAS SHE A GOOD GIRL?
ZZZ...

HFF!

HFF!

WOW, RII-SAN, YOU BEAT YOUR RECORD!

OKAY, ALL DONE!

TA

POSU
(PLOP)

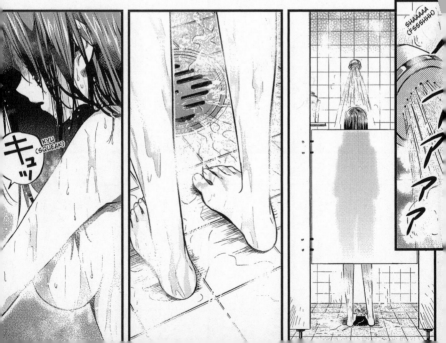

KYU
(SQUEAK)

SHAAAAA
(FSSSHHH)

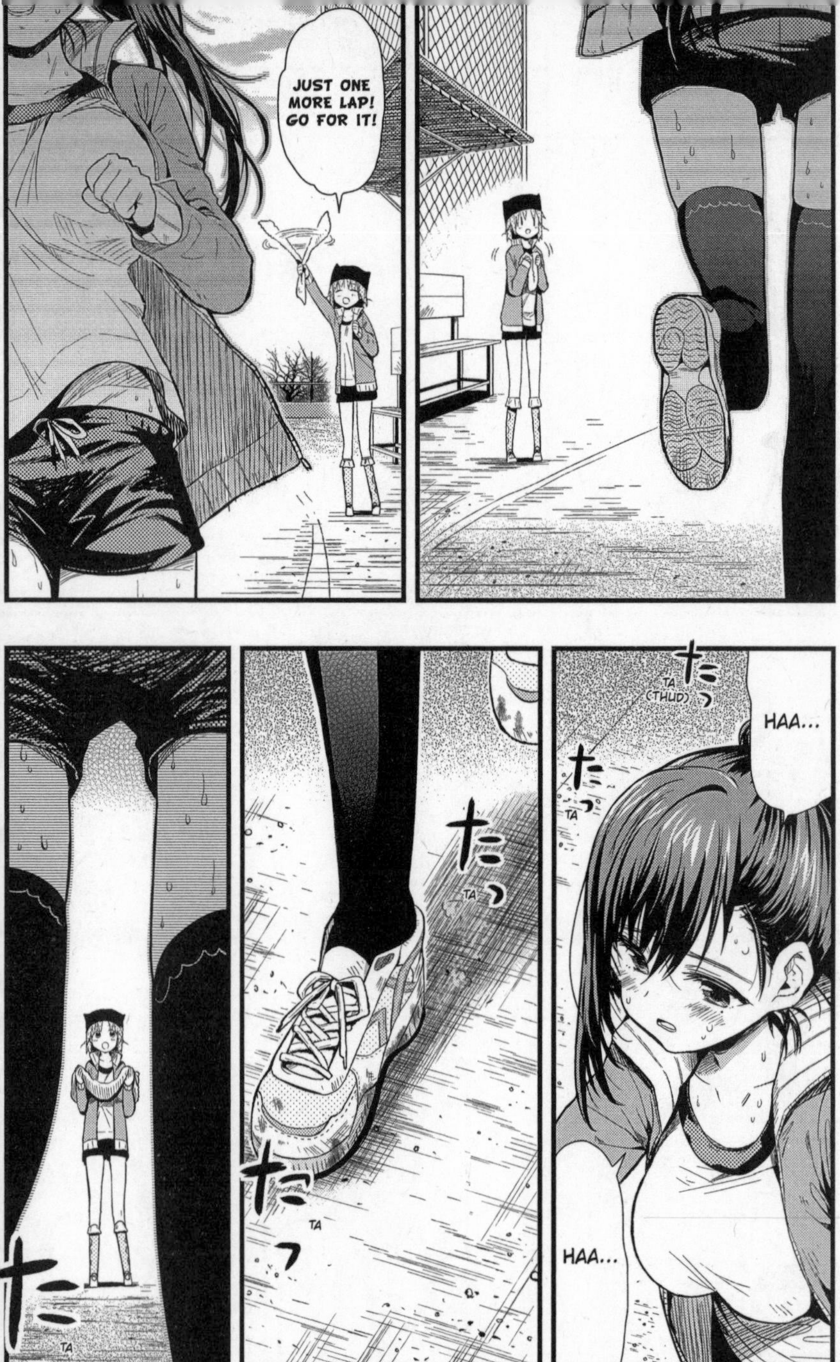
JUST ONE MORE LAP! GO FOR IT!
TA (THUD)
HAA...
TA
HAA...
TA
TA
TA

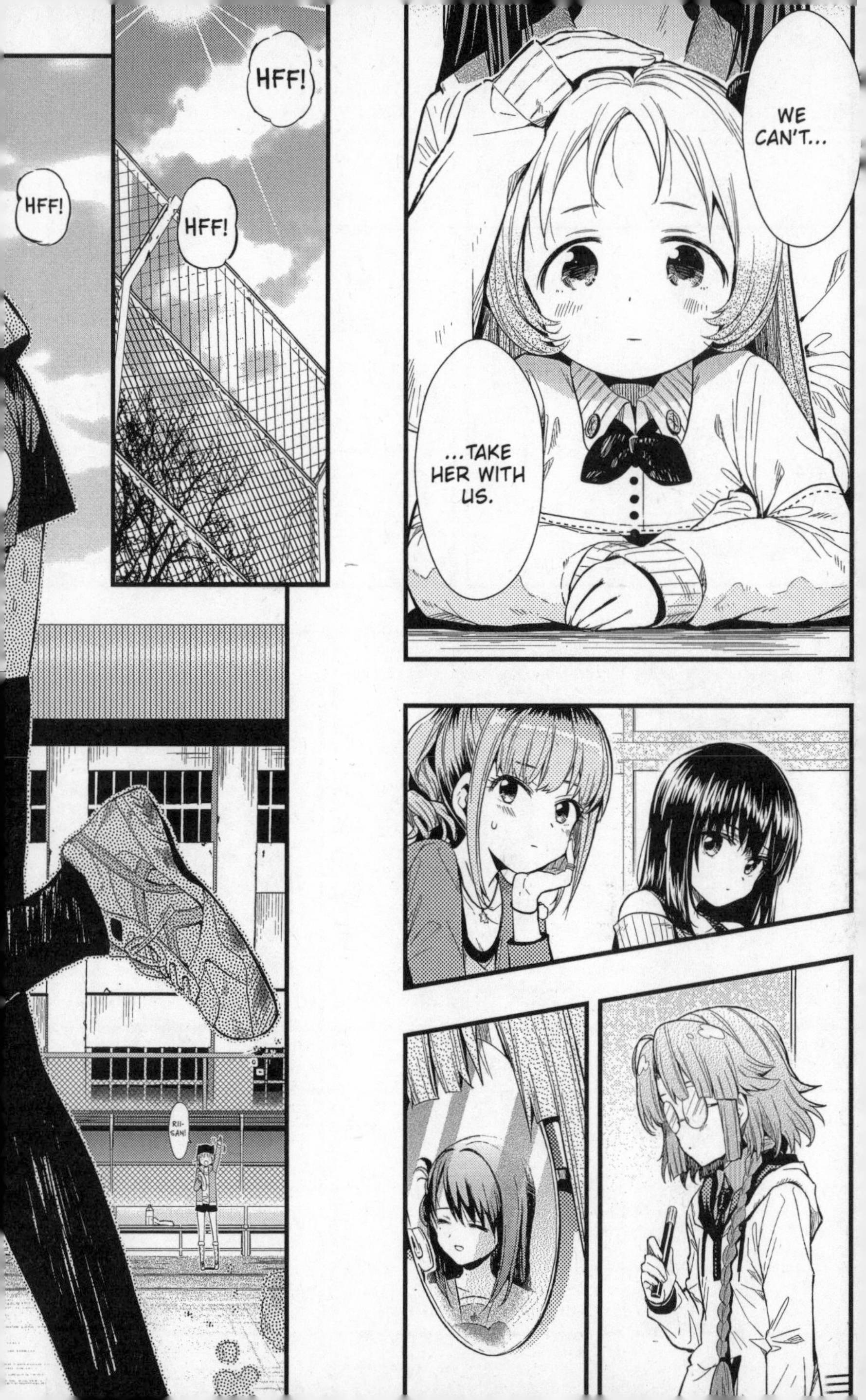
WE CAN'T...
...TAKE HER WITH US.
HFF!
HFF!
HFF!
RII-SAN!

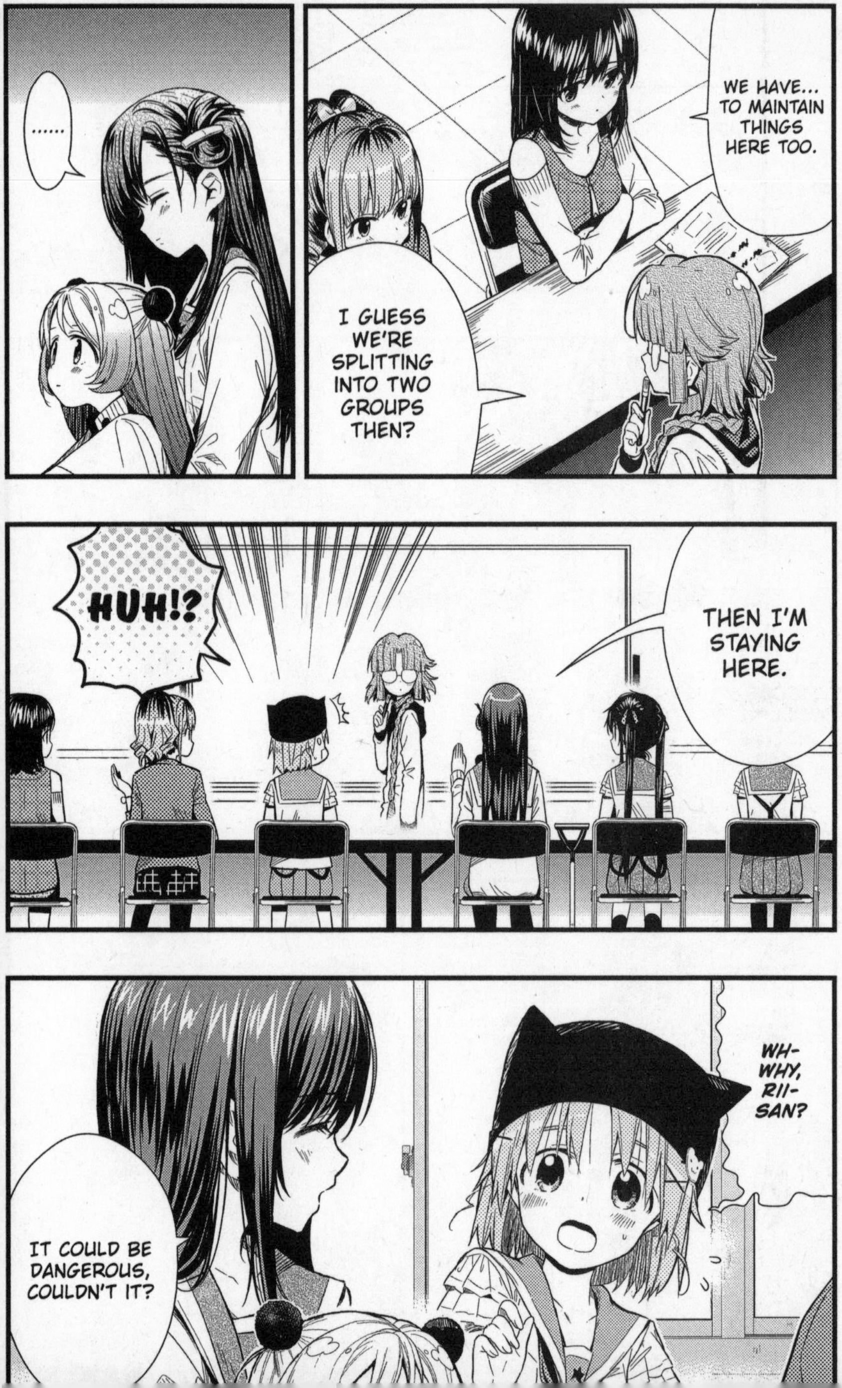
WE HAVE... TO MAINTAIN THINGS HERE TOO.
I GUESS WE'RE SPLITTING INTO TWO GROUPS THEN?
......
THEN I'M STAYING HERE.
HUH!?
WH-WHY, RII-SAN?
IT COULD BE DANGEROUS, COULDN'T IT?

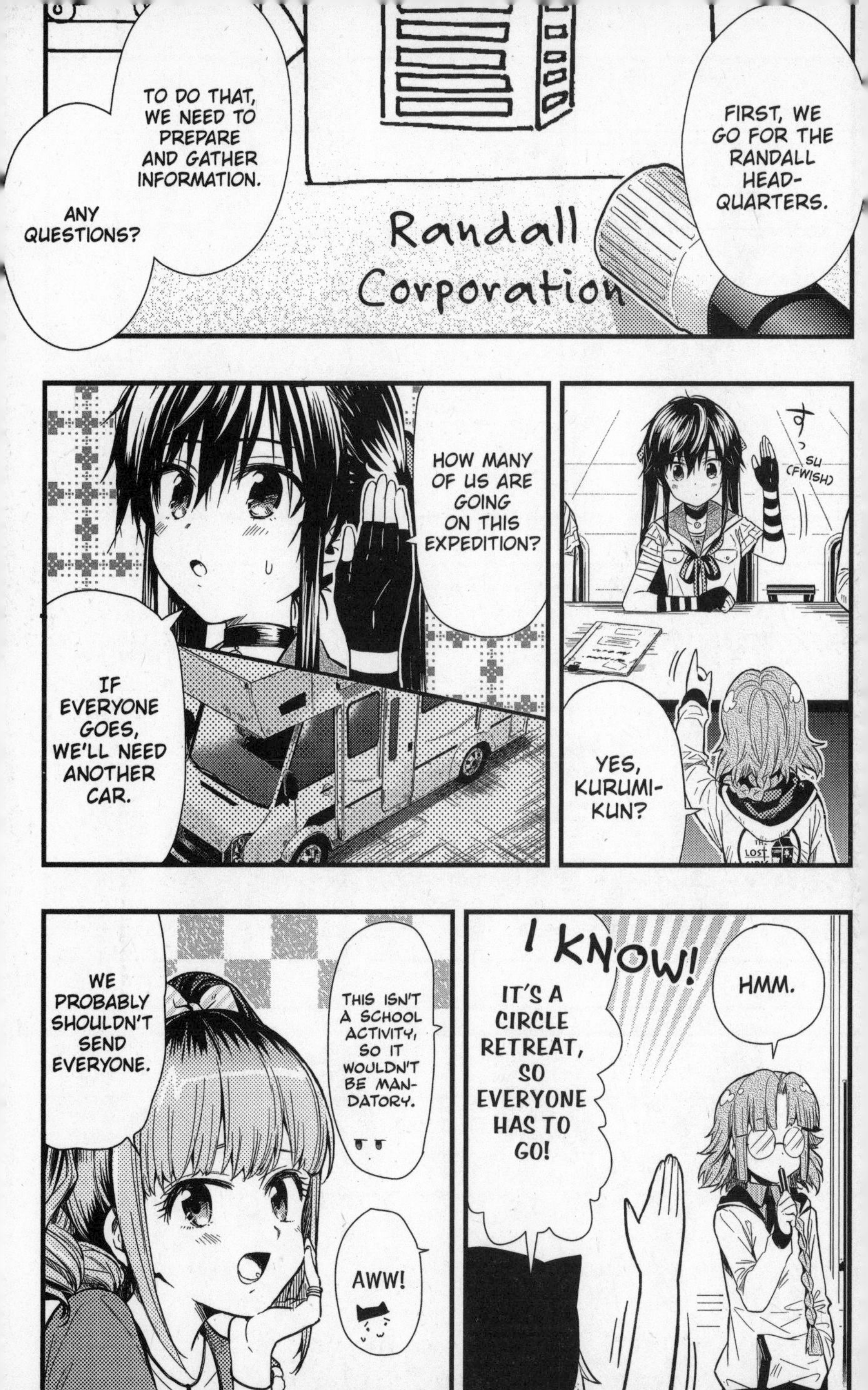
FIRST, WE GO FOR THE RANDALL HEAD-QUARTERS.
Randall Corporation
TO DO THAT, WE NEED TO PREPARE AND GATHER INFORMATION.
ANY QUESTIONS?
す
SU (FWISH)
YES, KURUMI-KUN?
HOW MANY OF US ARE GOING ON THIS EXPEDITION?
IF EVERYONE GOES, WE'LL NEED ANOTHER CAR.
HMM.
I KNOW!
IT'S A CIRCLE RETREAT, SO EVERYONE HAS TO GO!
THIS ISN'T A SCHOOL ACTIVITY, SO IT WOULDN'T BE MAN-DATORY.
AWW!
WE PROBABLY SHOULDN'T SEND EVERYONE.

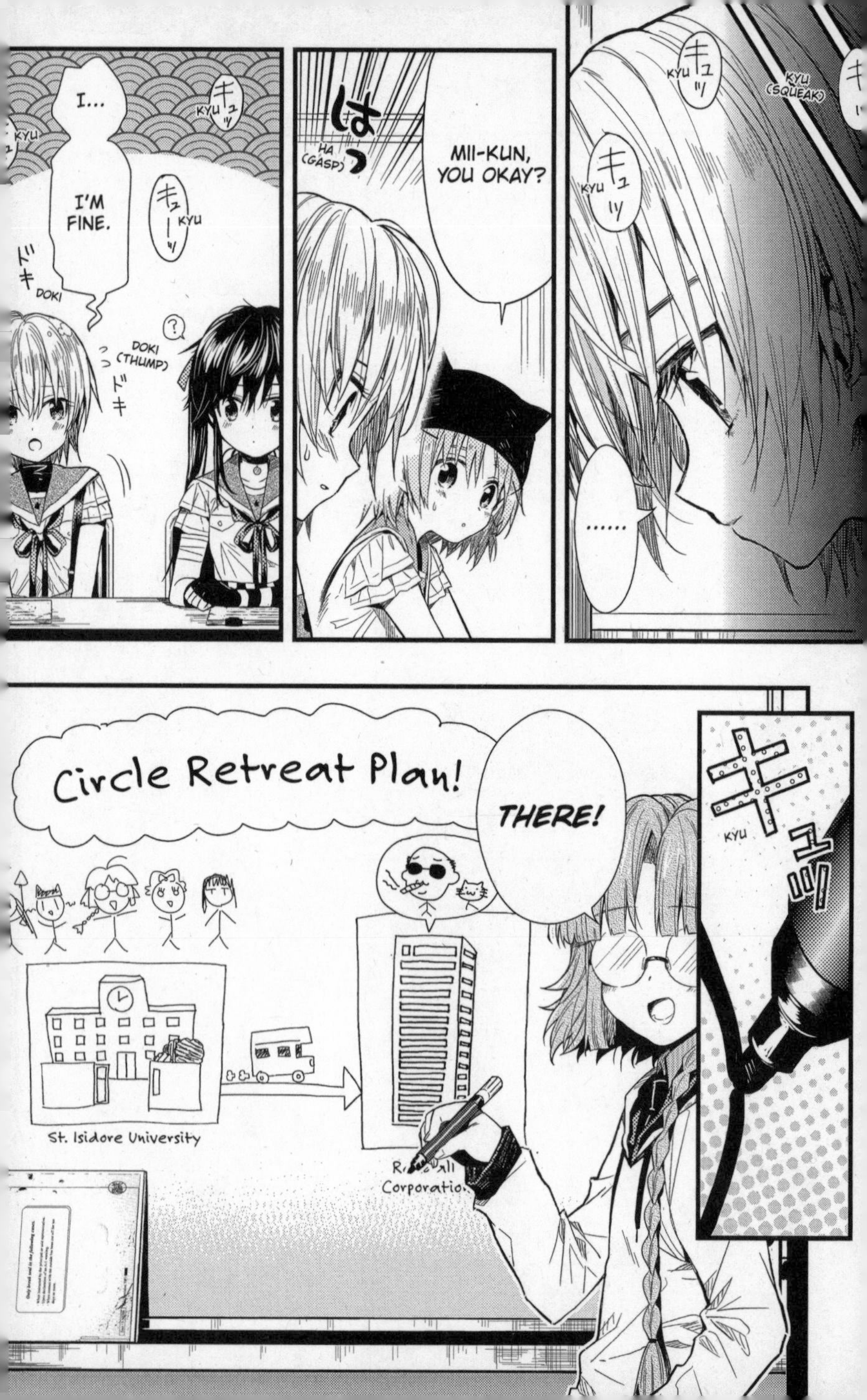

キュ
KYU (SQUEAK)
キュッ
KYU
キュッ
KYU
……
はっ
HA (GASP)
MII-KUN, YOU OKAY?
キュッ
KYU
I...
I'M FINE.
キュ-ッ
KYU
ドキ
DOKI
DOKI (THUMP)
ドキ
?
キュッ
KYU
THERE!
Circle Retreat Plan!
St. Isidore University

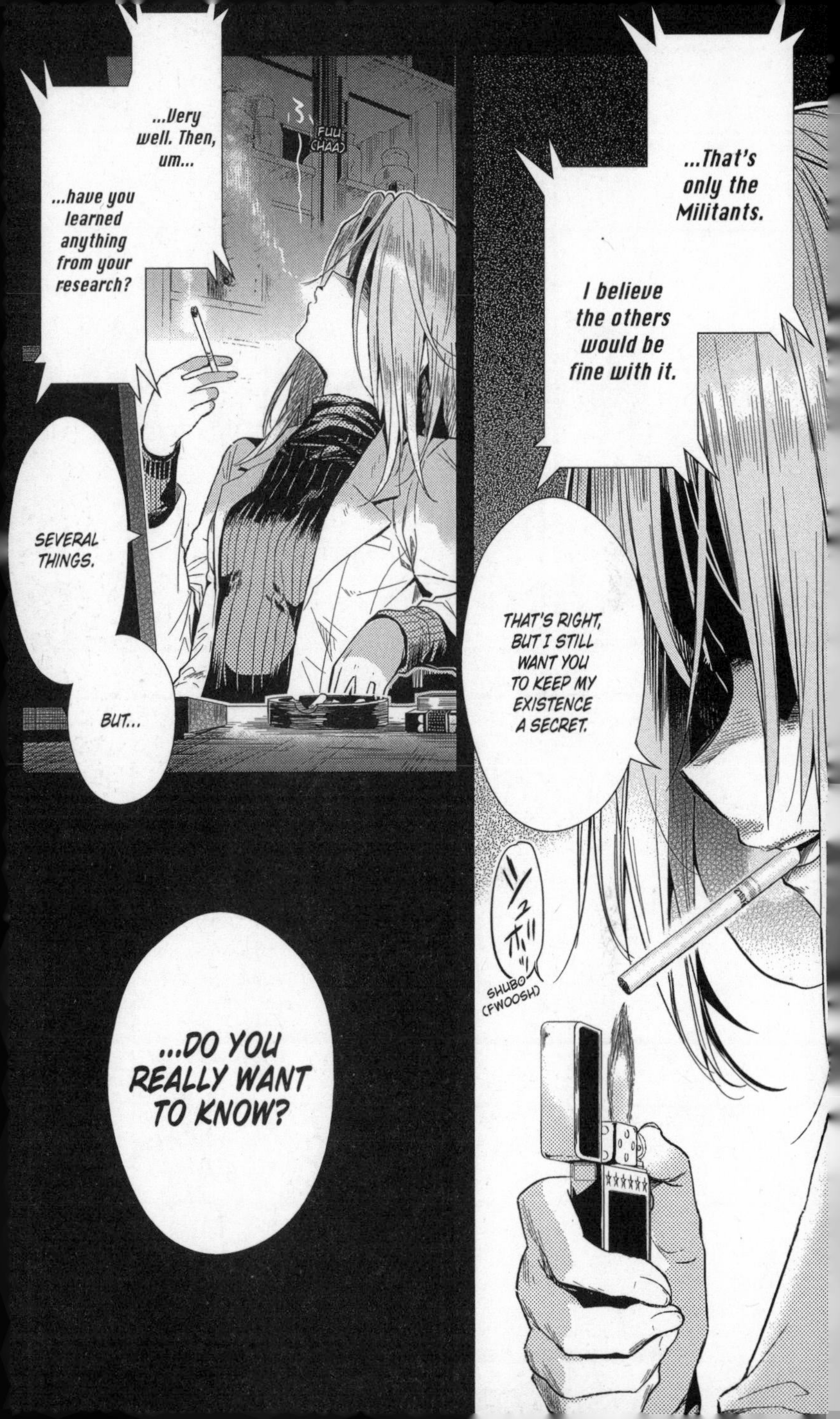
...That's only the Militants.
I believe the others would be fine with it.
THAT'S RIGHT, BUT I STILL WANT YOU TO KEEP MY EXISTENCE A SECRET.
シュボッ
SHUBO (FWOOSH)
...Very well. Then, um...
...have you learned anything from your research?
FUU (CHAA)
SEVERAL THINGS.
BUT...
...DO YOU REALLY WANT TO KNOW?

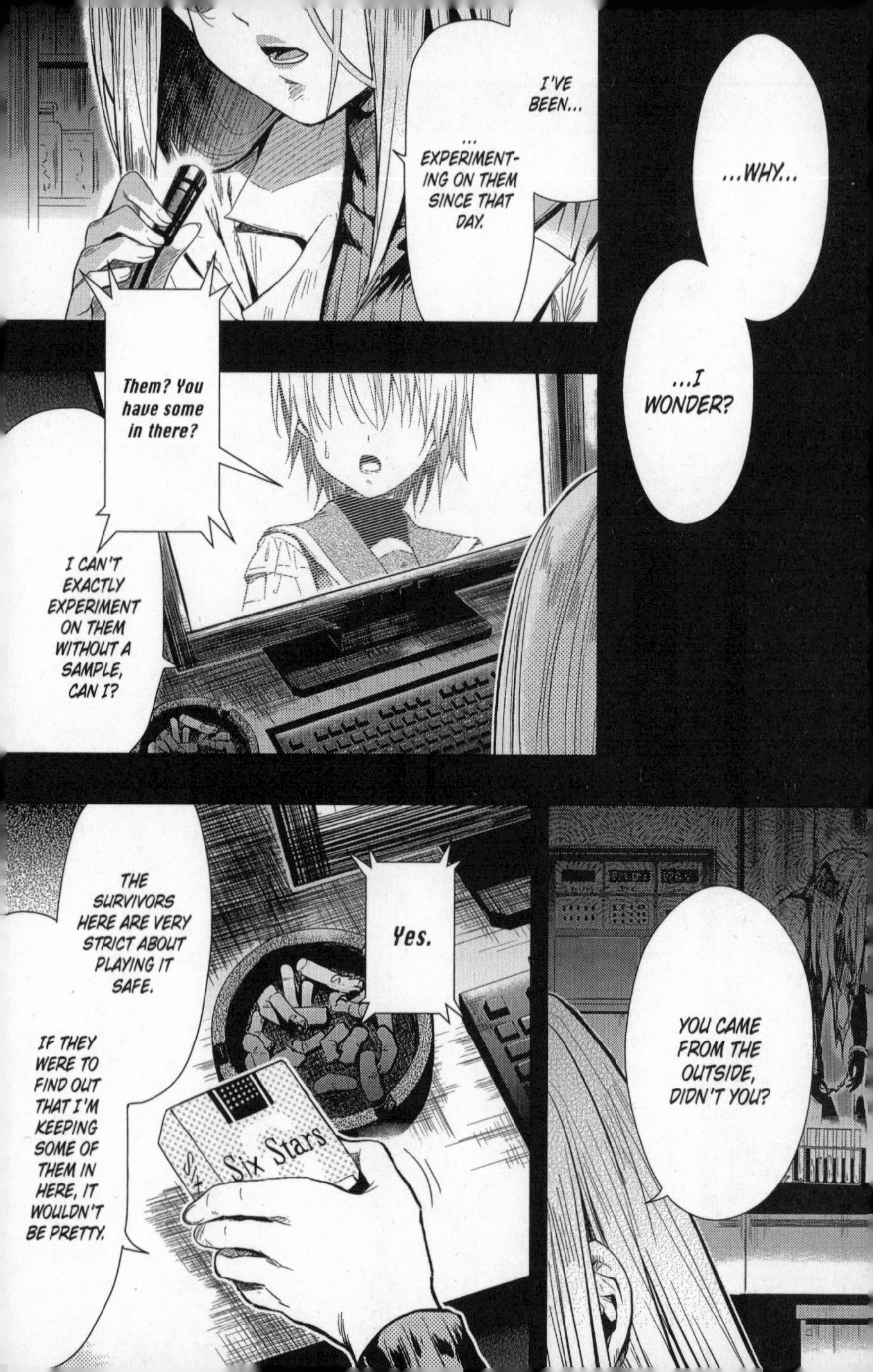
...WHY...
...I WONDER?
I'VE BEEN...
... EXPERIMENT-ING ON THEM SINCE THAT DAY.
Them? You have some in there?
I CAN'T EXACTLY EXPERIMENT ON THEM WITHOUT A SAMPLE, CAN I?
YOU CAME FROM THE OUTSIDE, DIDN'T YOU?
Yes.
THE SURVIVORS HERE ARE VERY STRICT ABOUT PLAYING IT SAFE.
IF THEY WERE TO FIND OUT THAT I'M KEEPING SOME OF THEM IN HERE, IT WOULDN'T BE PRETTY.
Six Stars

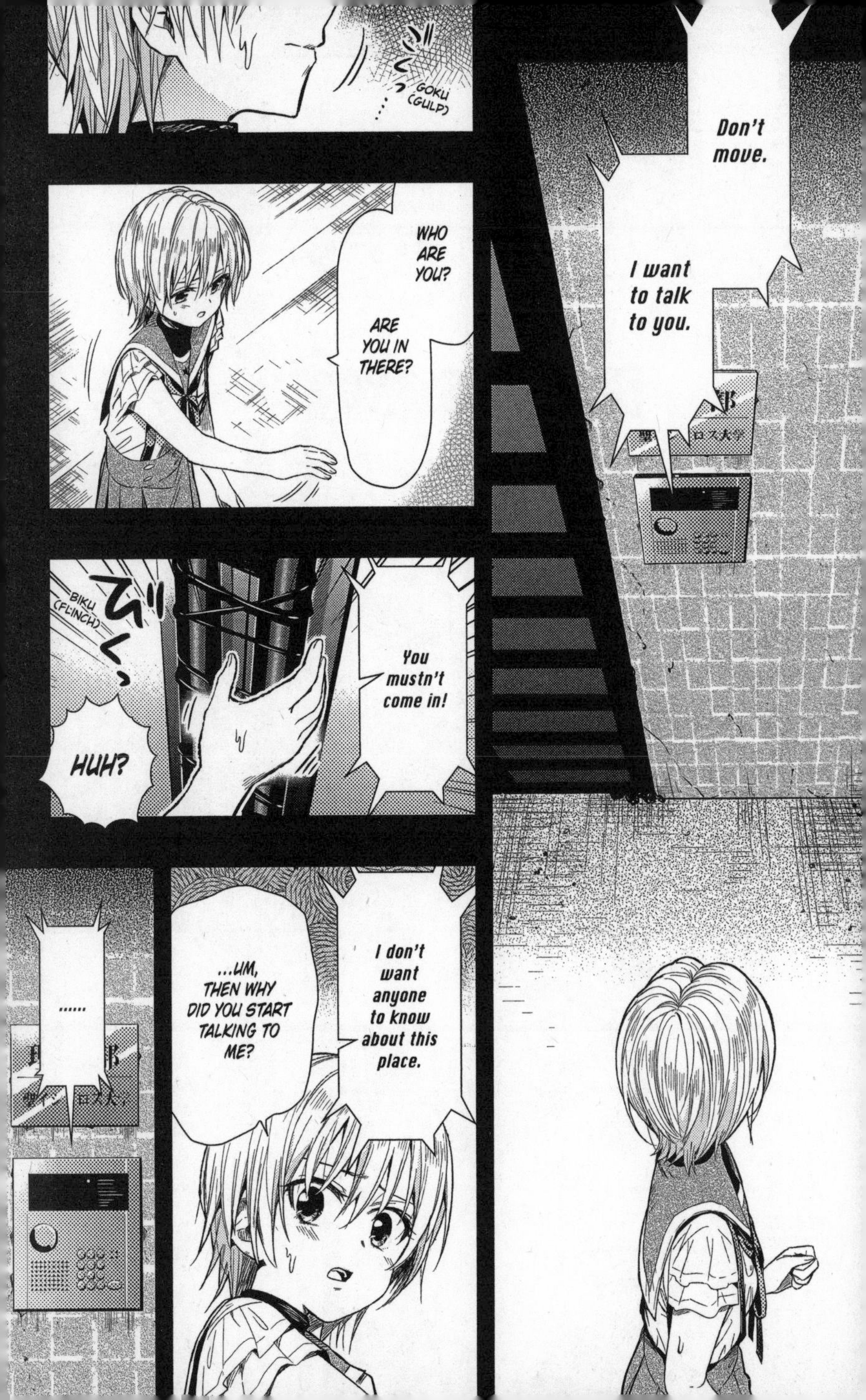

Don't move.
I want to talk to you.
GOKU (GULP)
WHO ARE YOU?
ARE YOU IN THERE?
You mustn't come in!
BIKU (FLINCH)
HUH?
I don't want anyone to know about this place.
...UM, THEN WHY DID YOU START TALKING TO ME?
......

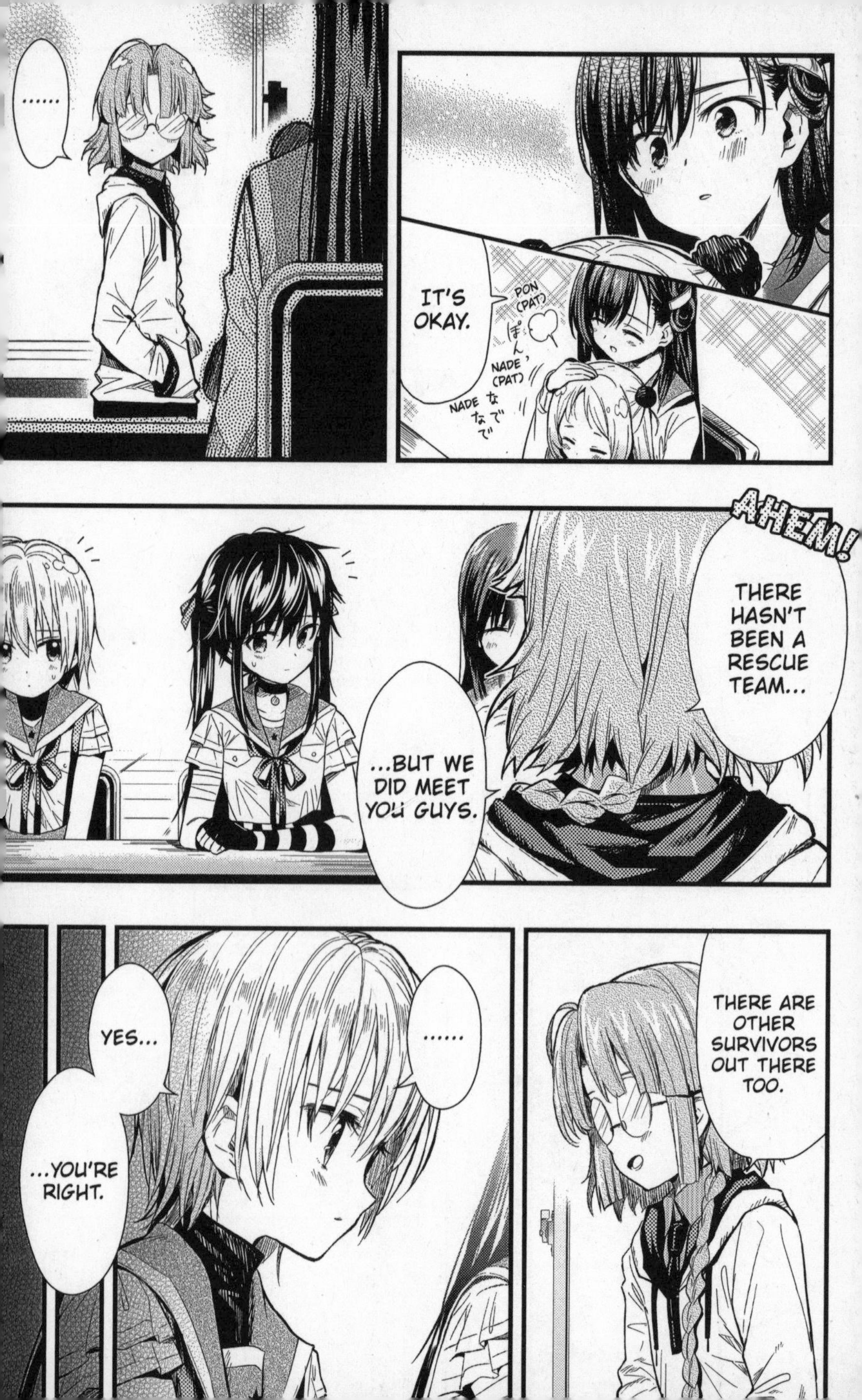
PON (PAT)
ぽん、
NADE (PAT)
なで
NADE
なで
IT'S OKAY.
......
AHEM!
THERE HASN'T BEEN A RESCUE TEAM...
...BUT WE DID MEET YOU GUYS.
THERE ARE OTHER SURVIVORS OUT THERE TOO.
......
YES...
...YOU'RE RIGHT.

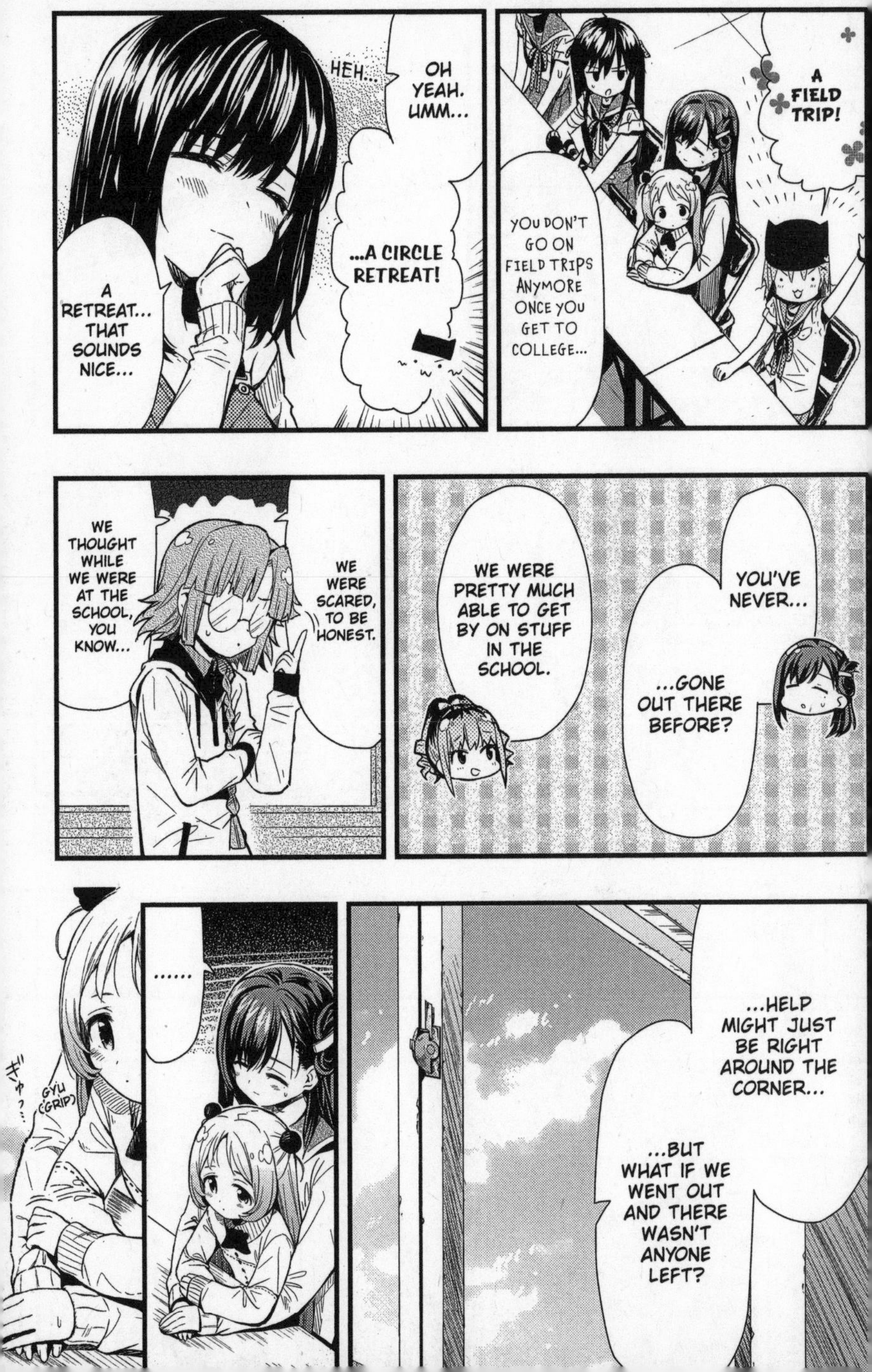
A FIELD TRIP!
YOU DON'T GO ON FIELD TRIPS ANYMORE ONCE YOU GET TO COLLEGE...
OH YEAH. UMM...
HEH...
...A CIRCLE RETREAT!
A RETREAT... THAT SOUNDS NICE...
YOU'VE NEVER...
...GONE OUT THERE BEFORE?
WE WERE PRETTY MUCH ABLE TO GET BY ON STUFF IN THE SCHOOL.
WE WERE SCARED, TO BE HONEST.
WE THOUGHT WHILE WE WERE AT THE SCHOOL, YOU KNOW...
...HELP MIGHT JUST BE RIGHT AROUND THE CORNER...
...BUT WHAT IF WE WENT OUT AND THERE WASN'T ANYONE LEFT?
......
ぎゅっ…
GYU (GRIP)

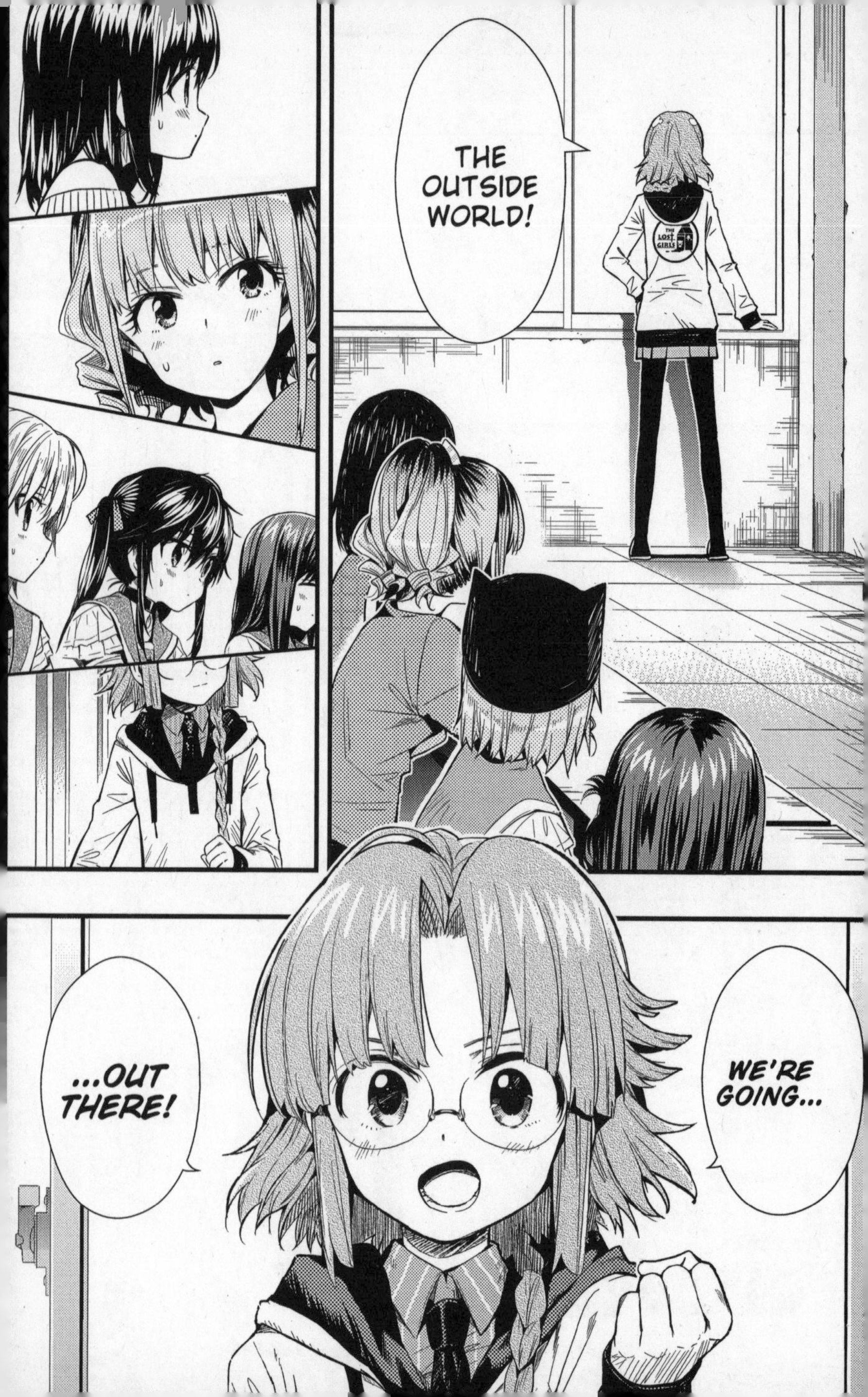
THE OUTSIDE WORLD!
THE LOST GIRLS
WE'RE GOING...
...OUT THERE!

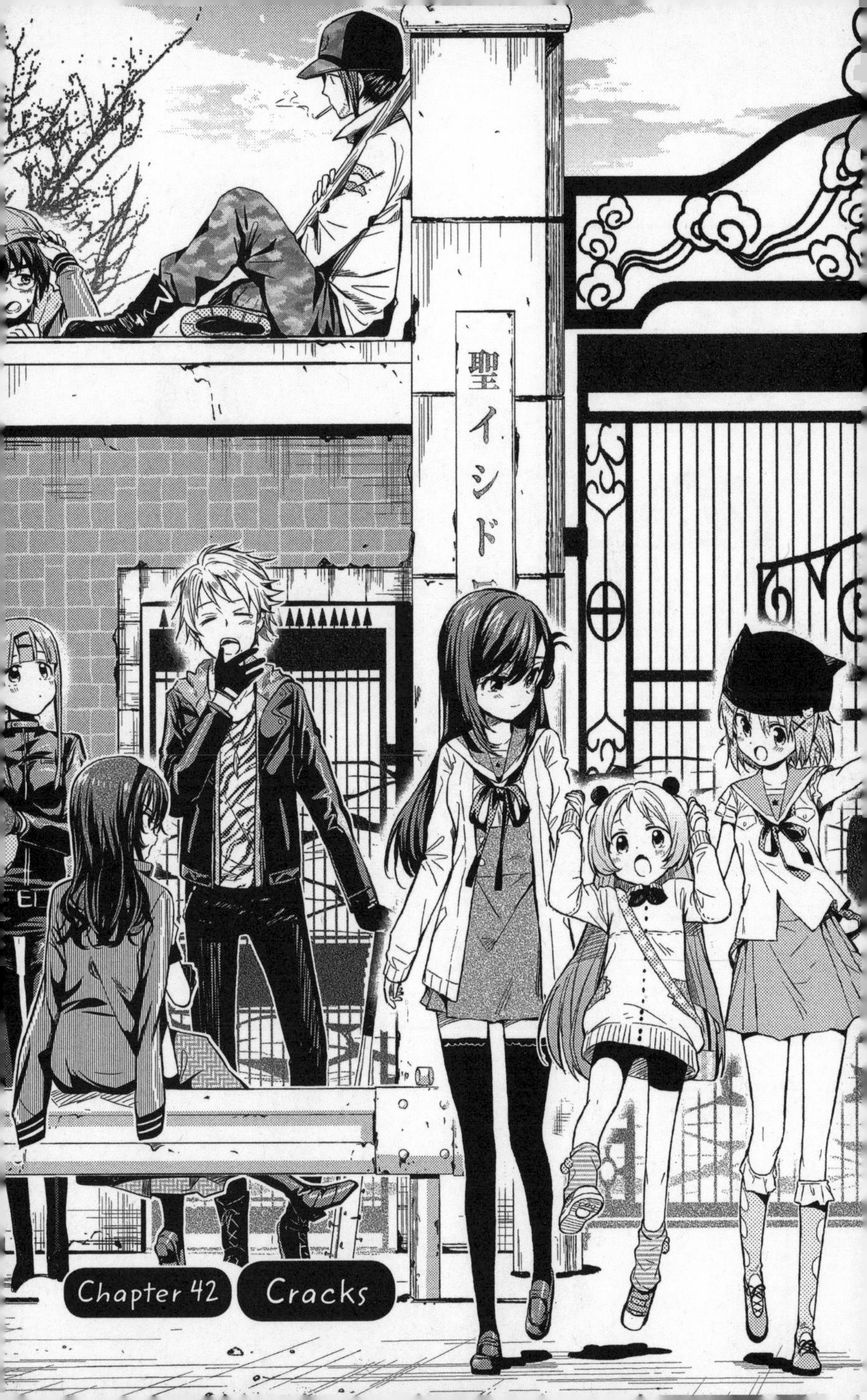
聖イシド
Chapter 42
Cracks

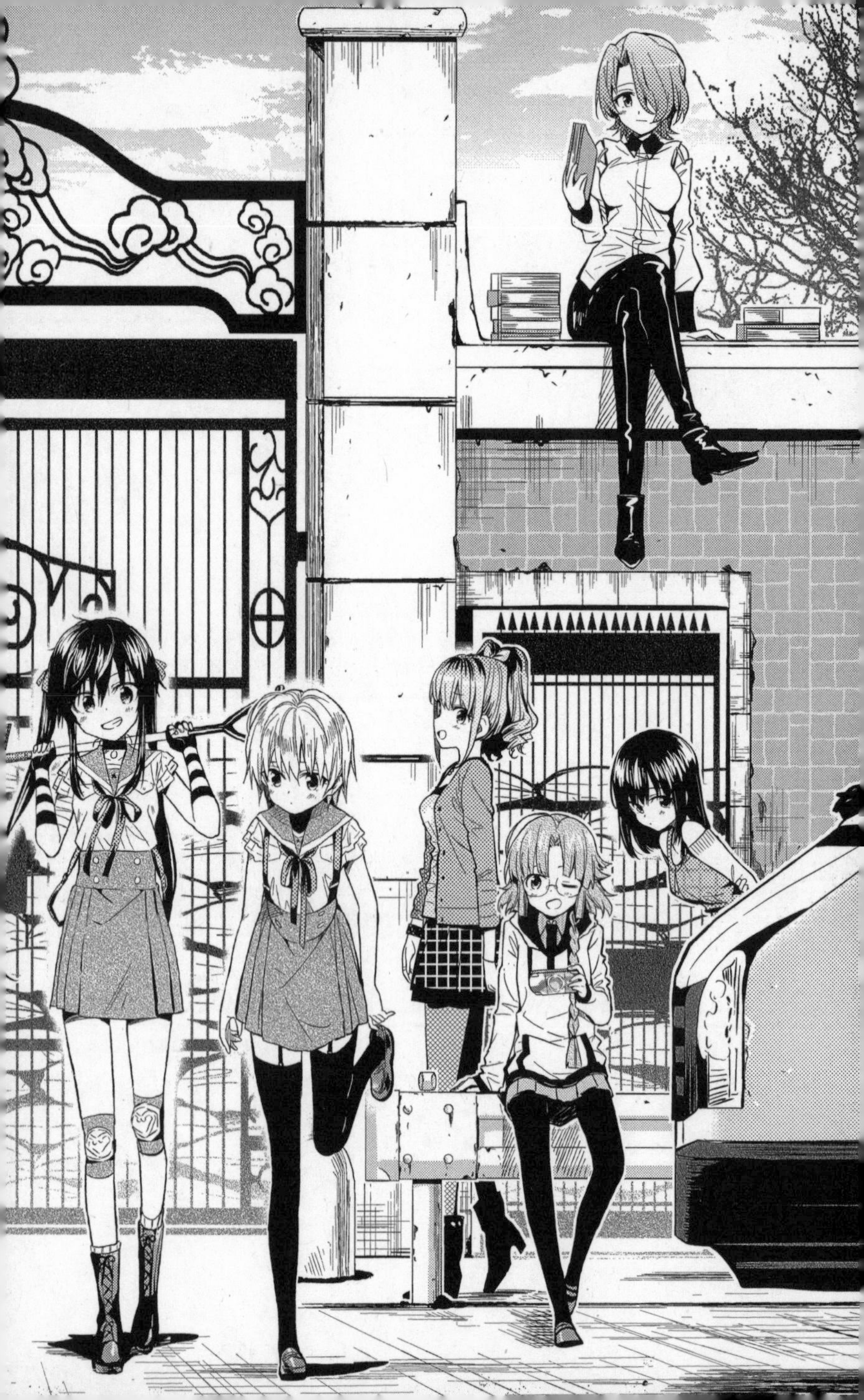

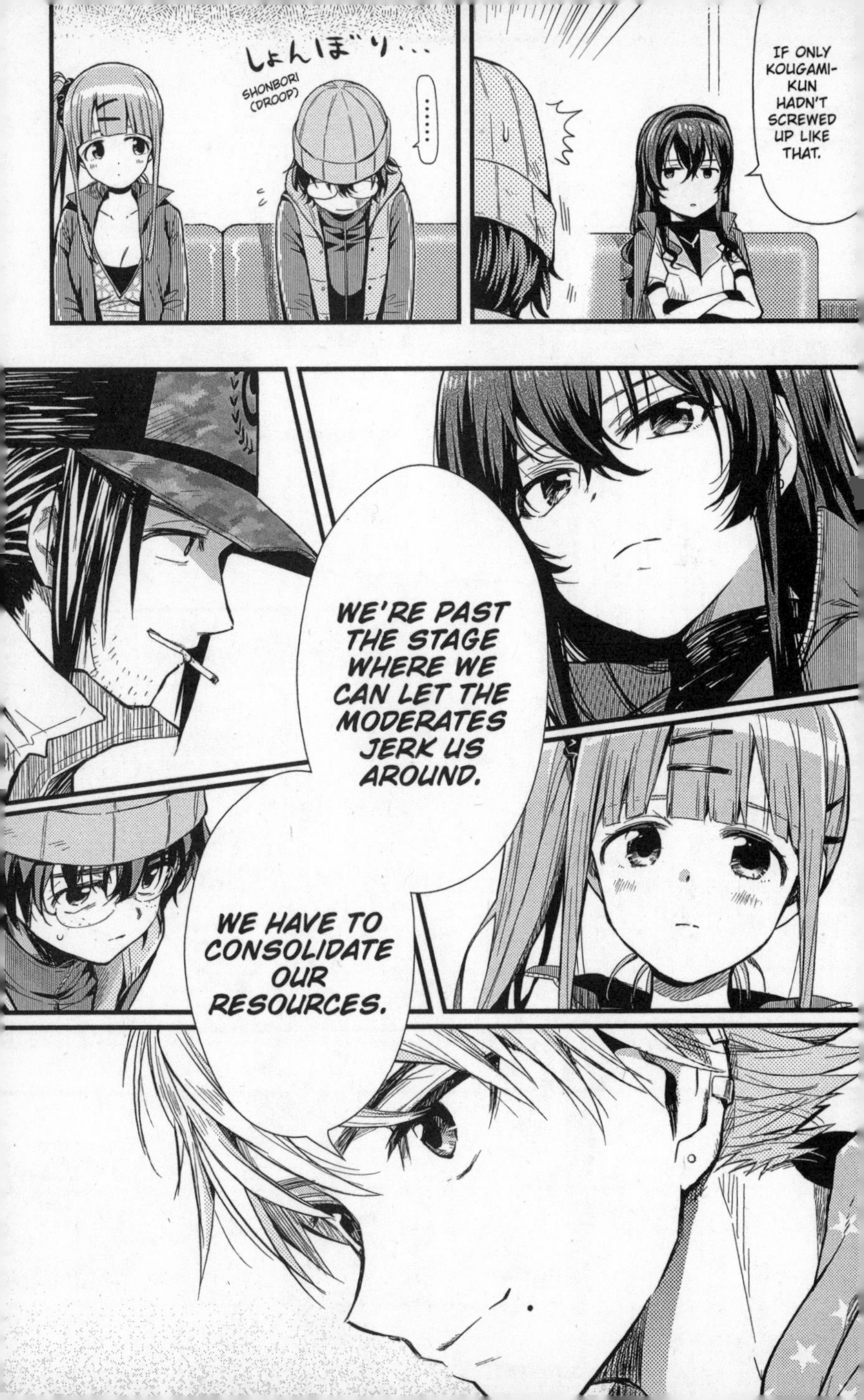
IF ONLY KOUGAMI-KUN HADN'T SCREWED UP LIKE THAT.
しょんぼり…
SHONBORI (DROOP)
……
WE'RE PAST THE STAGE WHERE WE CAN LET THE MODERATES JERK US AROUND.
WE HAVE TO CONSOLIDATE OUR RESOURCES.

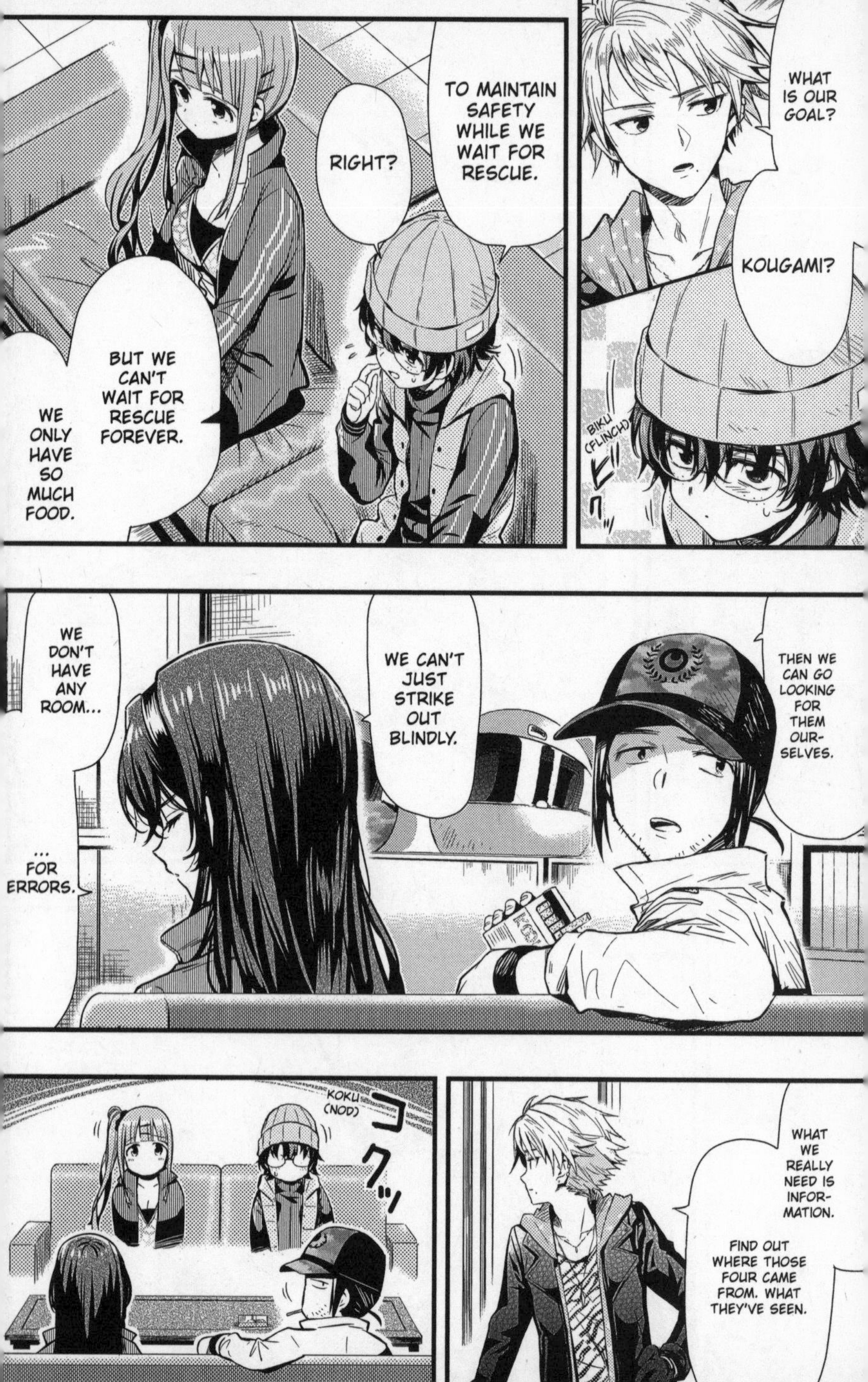
WHAT IS OUR GOAL?
KOUGAMI?
BIKU (FLINCH)
TO MAINTAIN SAFETY WHILE WE WAIT FOR RESCUE.
RIGHT?
BUT WE CAN'T WAIT FOR RESCUE FOREVER.
WE ONLY HAVE SO MUCH FOOD.
THEN WE CAN GO LOOKING FOR THEM OURSELVES.
WE CAN'T JUST STRIKE OUT BLINDLY.
WE DON'T HAVE ANY ROOM...
...FOR ERRORS.
WHAT WE REALLY NEED IS INFORMATION.
FIND OUT WHERE THOSE FOUR CAME FROM. WHAT THEY'VE SEEN.
KOKU (NOD)

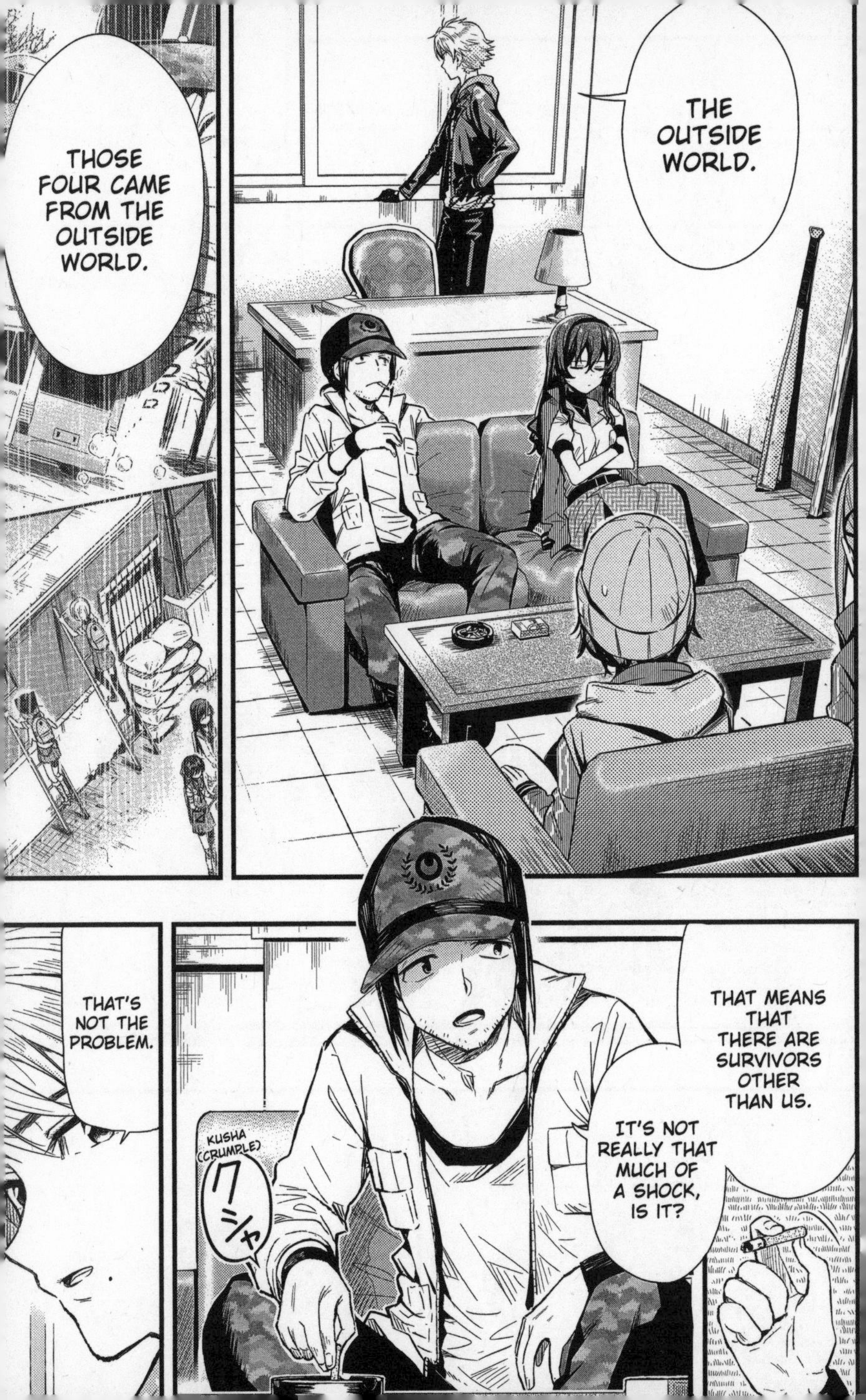
THE OUTSIDE WORLD.
THOSE FOUR CAME FROM THE OUTSIDE WORLD.
THAT MEANS THAT THERE ARE SURVIVORS OTHER THAN US.
IT'S NOT REALLY THAT MUCH OF A SHOCK, IS IT?
KUSHA (CRUMPLE)
クシャ
THAT'S NOT THE PROBLEM.

SCHOOL-LIVE!

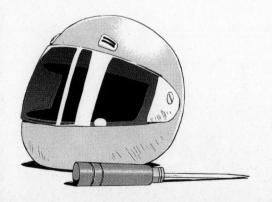

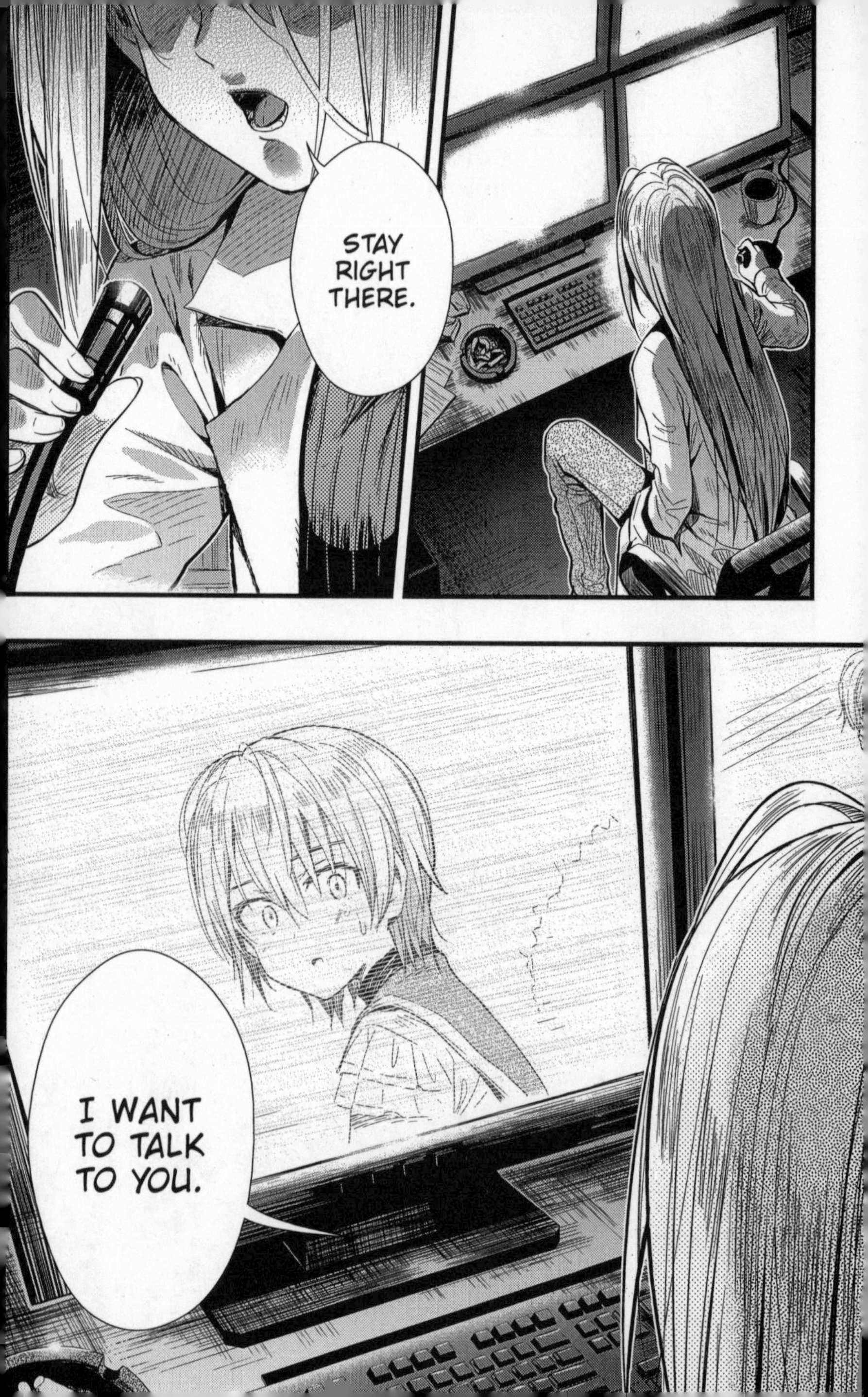
STAY RIGHT THERE.
I WANT TO TALK TO YOU.

理学部
聖バロ大

Don't
move!

......!?

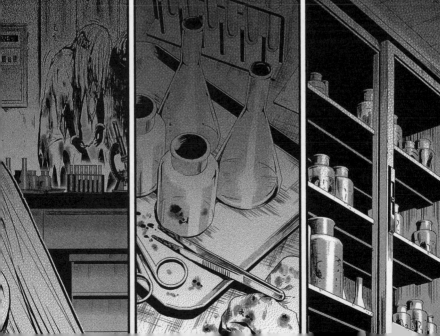

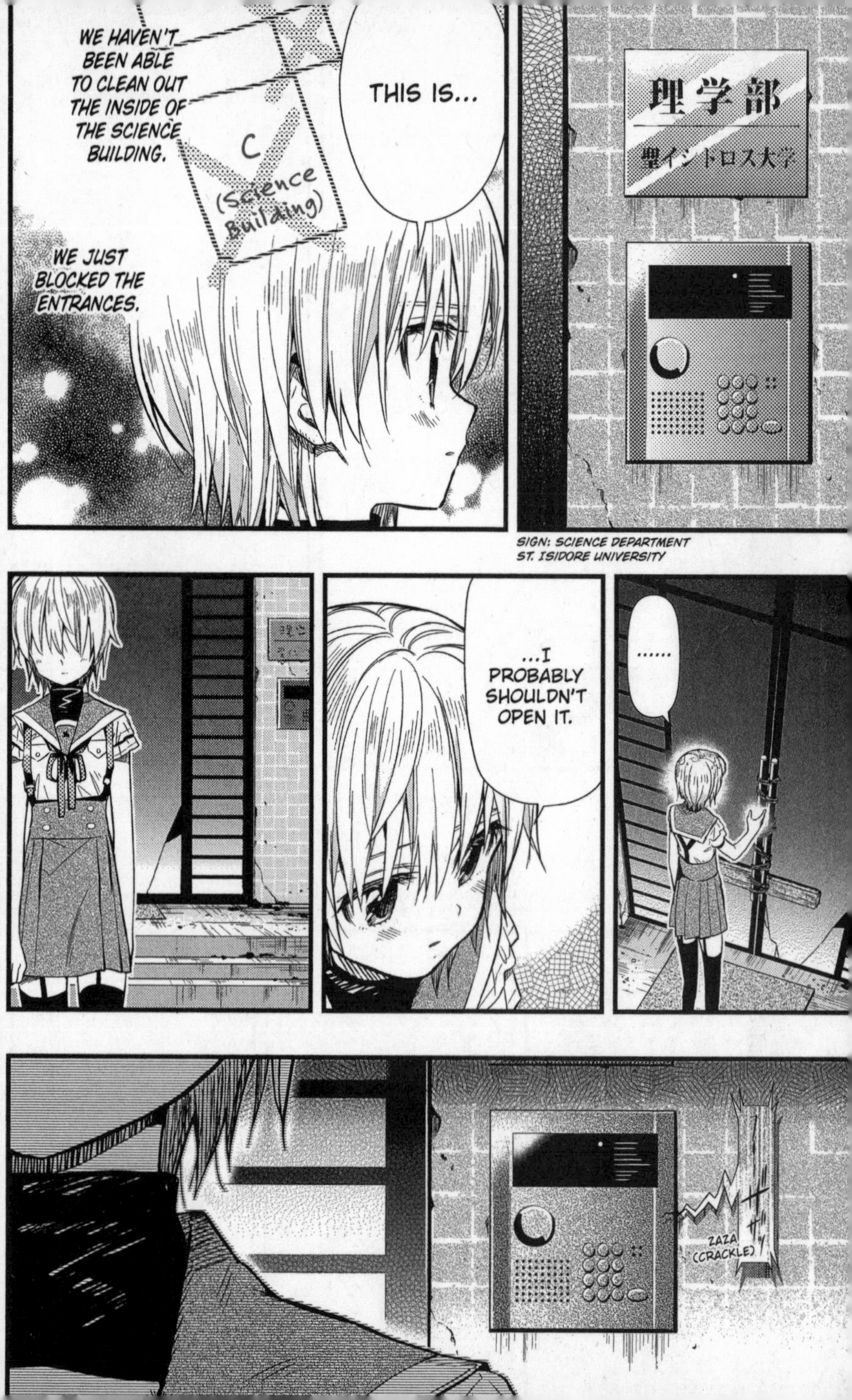
理学部
聖イシドロス大学
THIS IS...
C
(Science Building)
WE HAVEN'T BEEN ABLE TO CLEAN OUT THE INSIDE OF THE SCIENCE BUILDING.
WE JUST BLOCKED THE ENTRANCES.
SIGN: SCIENCE DEPARTMENT ST. ISIDORE UNIVERSITY
......
...I PROBABLY SHOULDN'T OPEN IT.
ザザッ
ZAZA (CRACKLE)

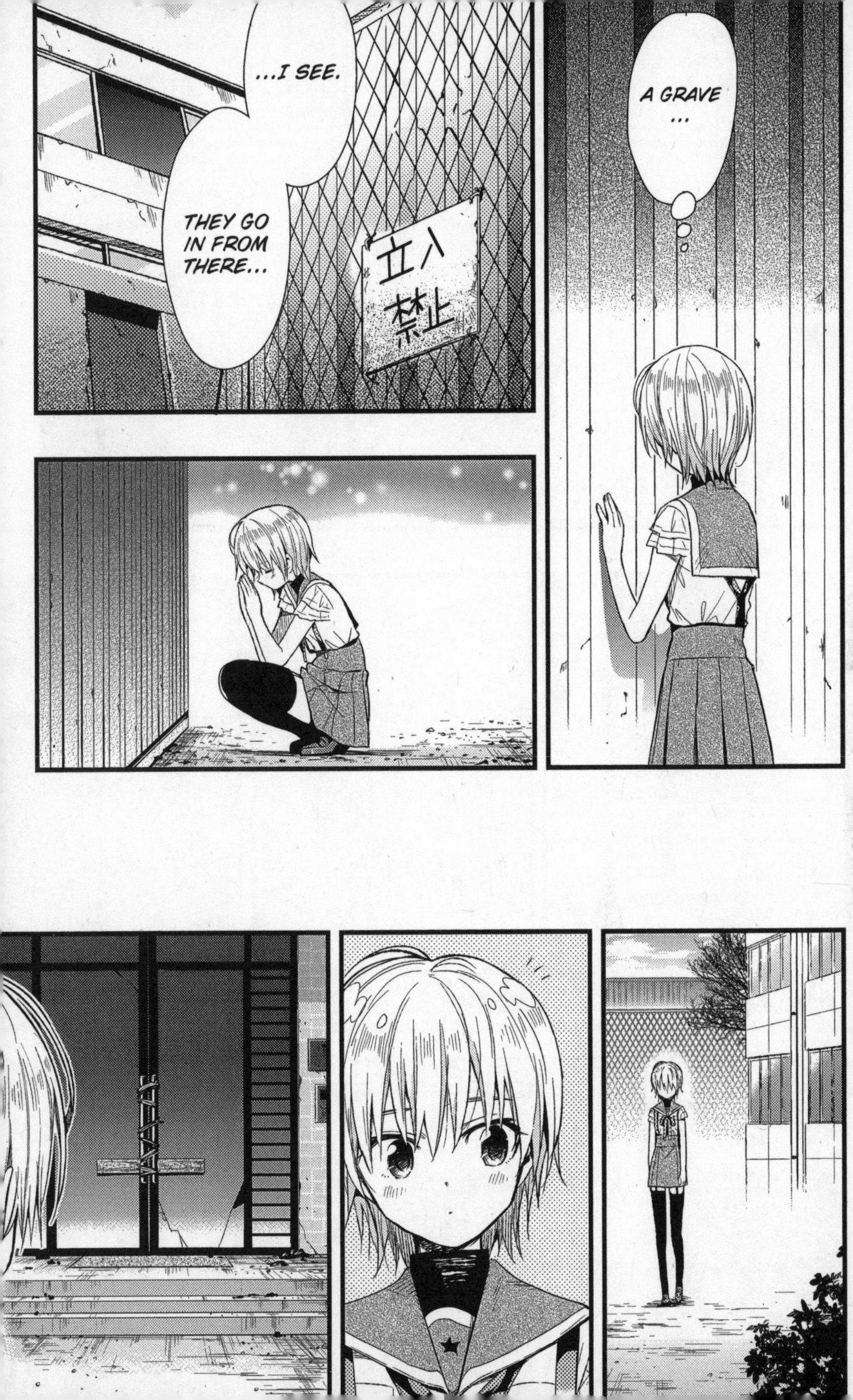
A GRAVE ...
...I SEE.
THEY GO IN FROM THERE...
立入禁止

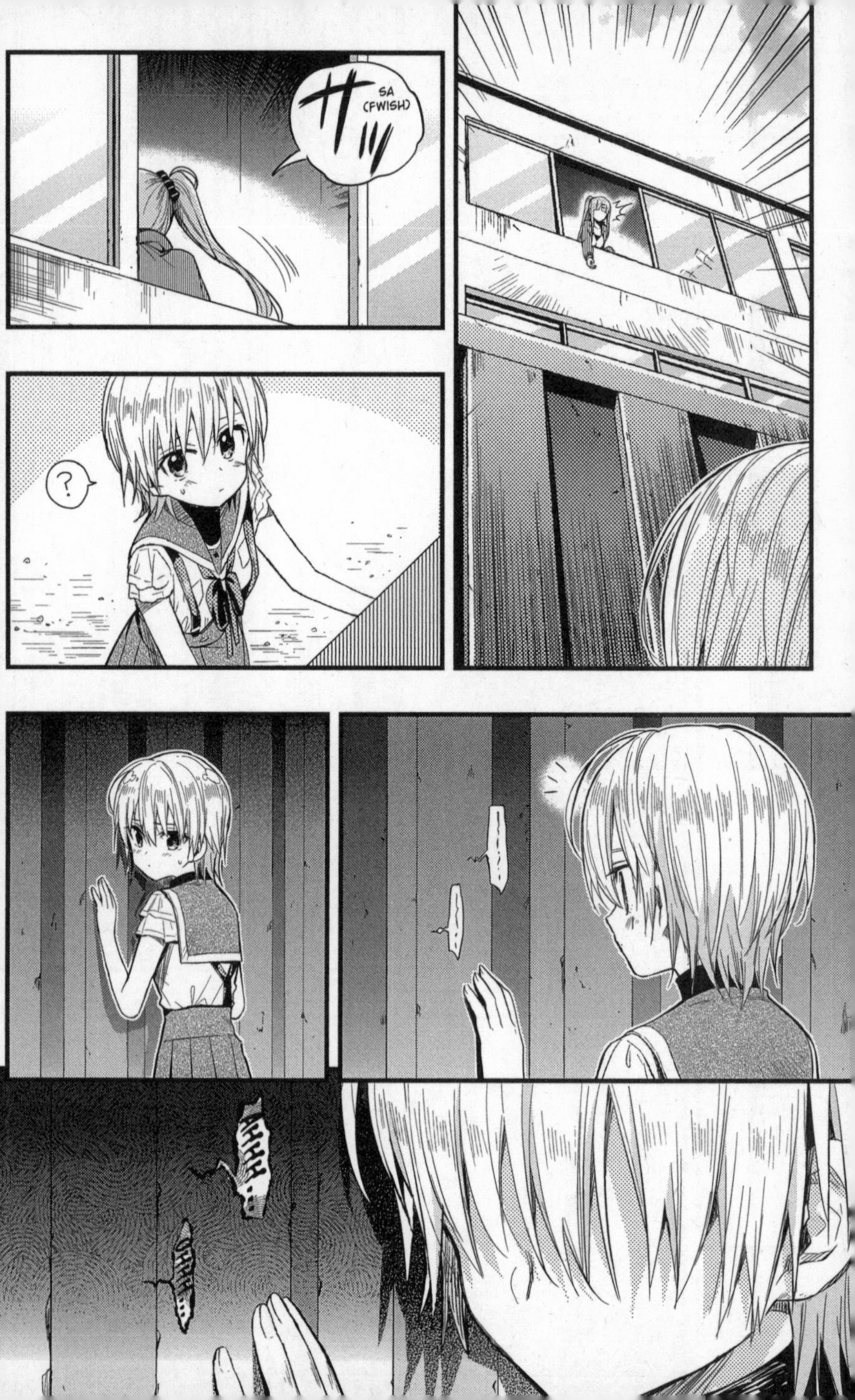
SA (FWISH)
?
AHHHH...
UHHH...

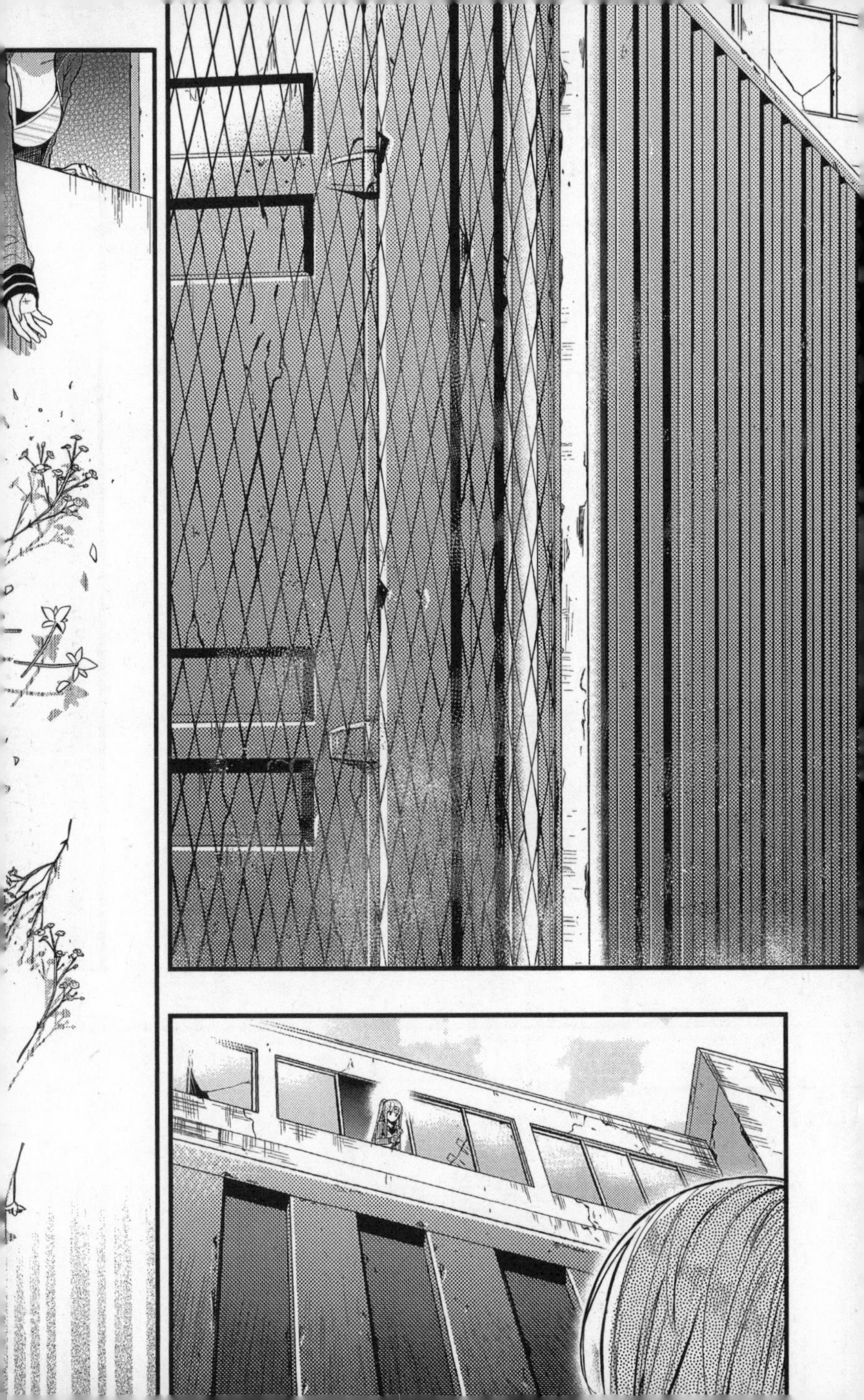

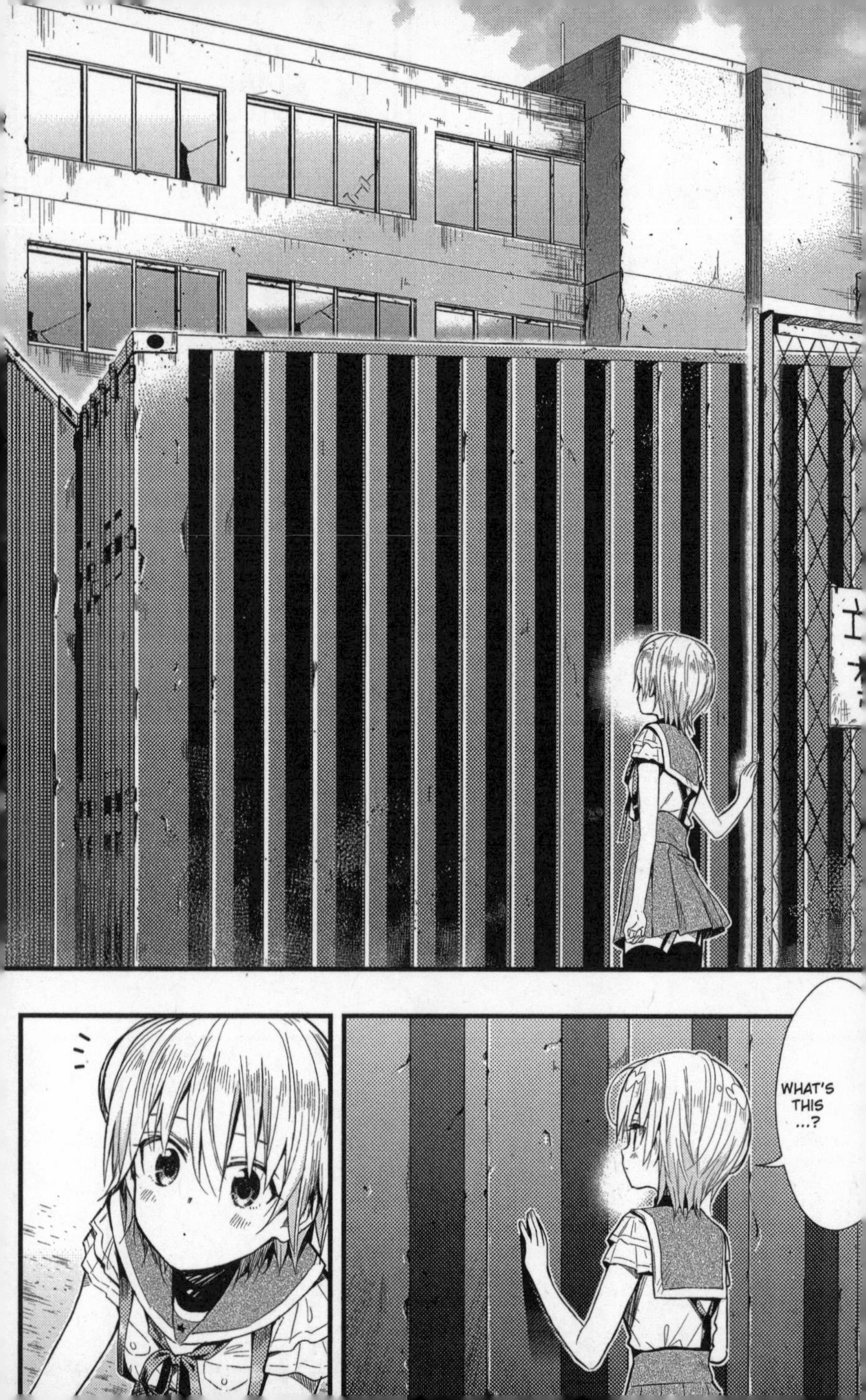
WHAT'S THIS ...?

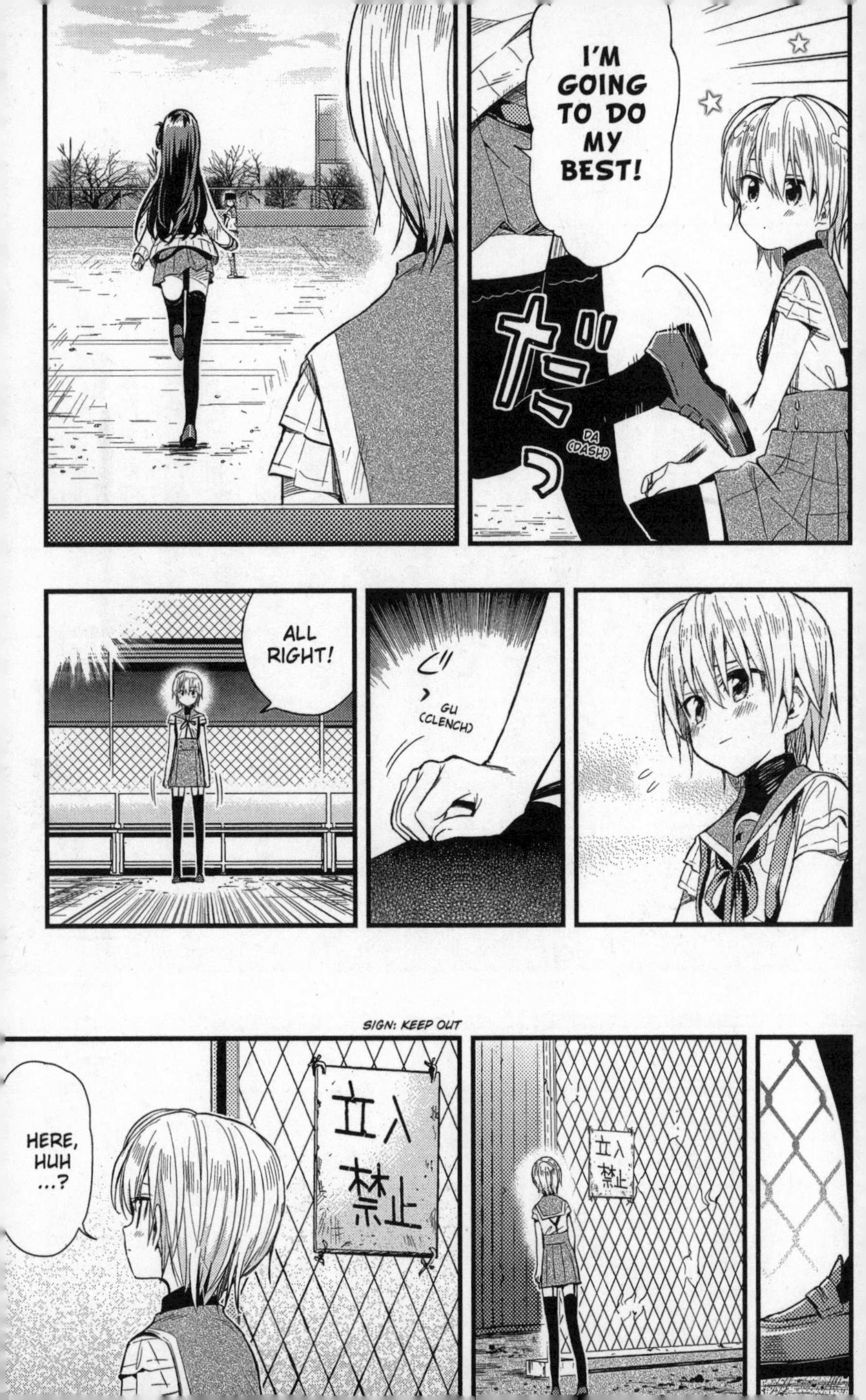
I'M GOING TO DO MY BEST!
DA (DASH)
GU (CLENCH)
ALL RIGHT!
SIGN: KEEP OUT
立入禁止
立入禁止
HERE, HUH ...?

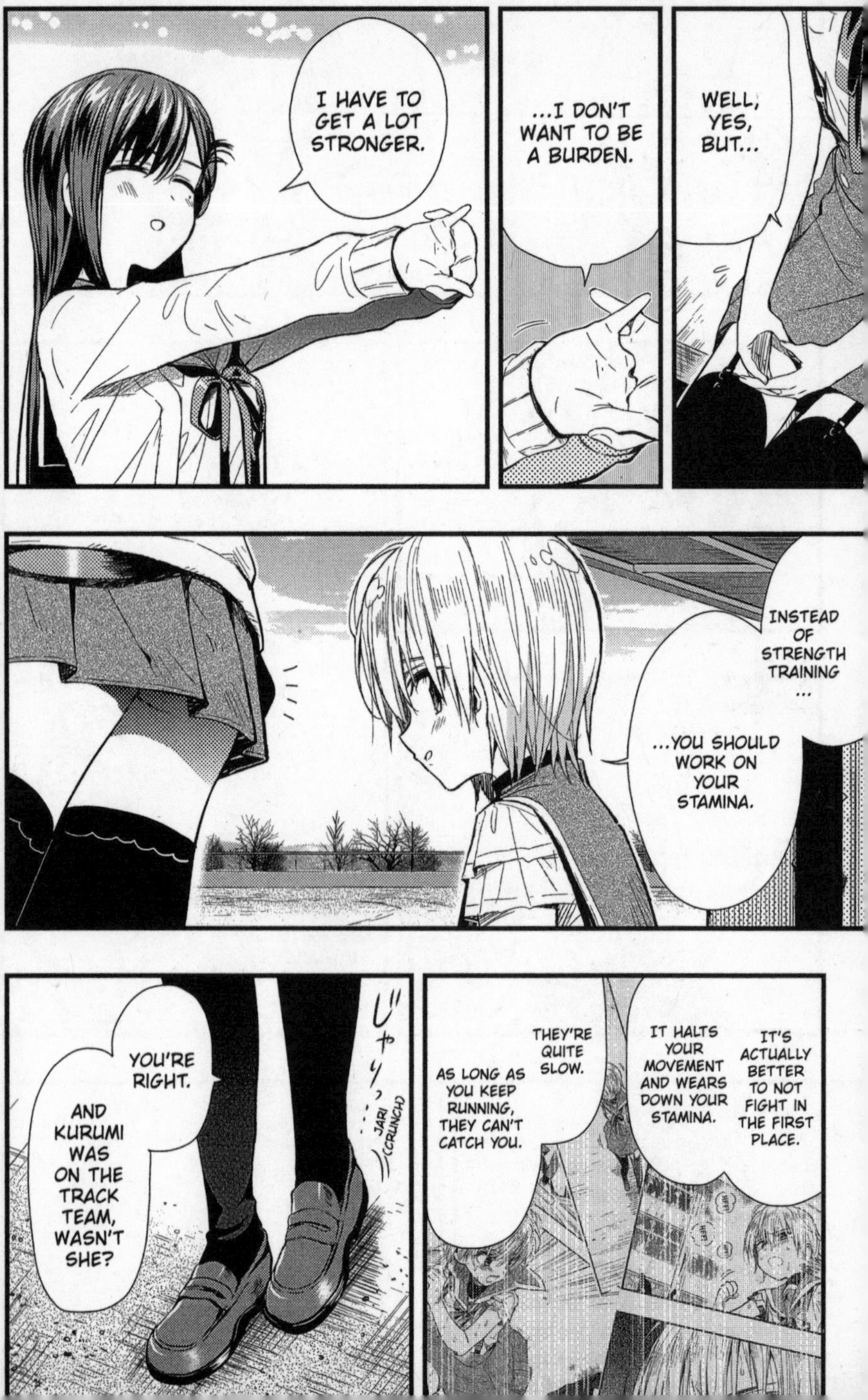
WELL, YES, BUT...
...I DON'T WANT TO BE A BURDEN.
I HAVE TO GET A LOT STRONGER.
INSTEAD OF STRENGTH TRAINING ...
...YOU SHOULD WORK ON YOUR STAMINA.
IT'S ACTUALLY BETTER TO NOT FIGHT IN THE FIRST PLACE.
IT HALTS YOUR MOVEMENT AND WEARS DOWN YOUR STAMINA.
THEY'RE QUITE SLOW.
AS LONG AS YOU KEEP RUNNING, THEY CAN'T CATCH YOU.
じゃり...
JARI (CRUNCH)
YOU'RE RIGHT.
AND KURUMI WAS ON THE TRACK TEAM, WASN'T SHE?

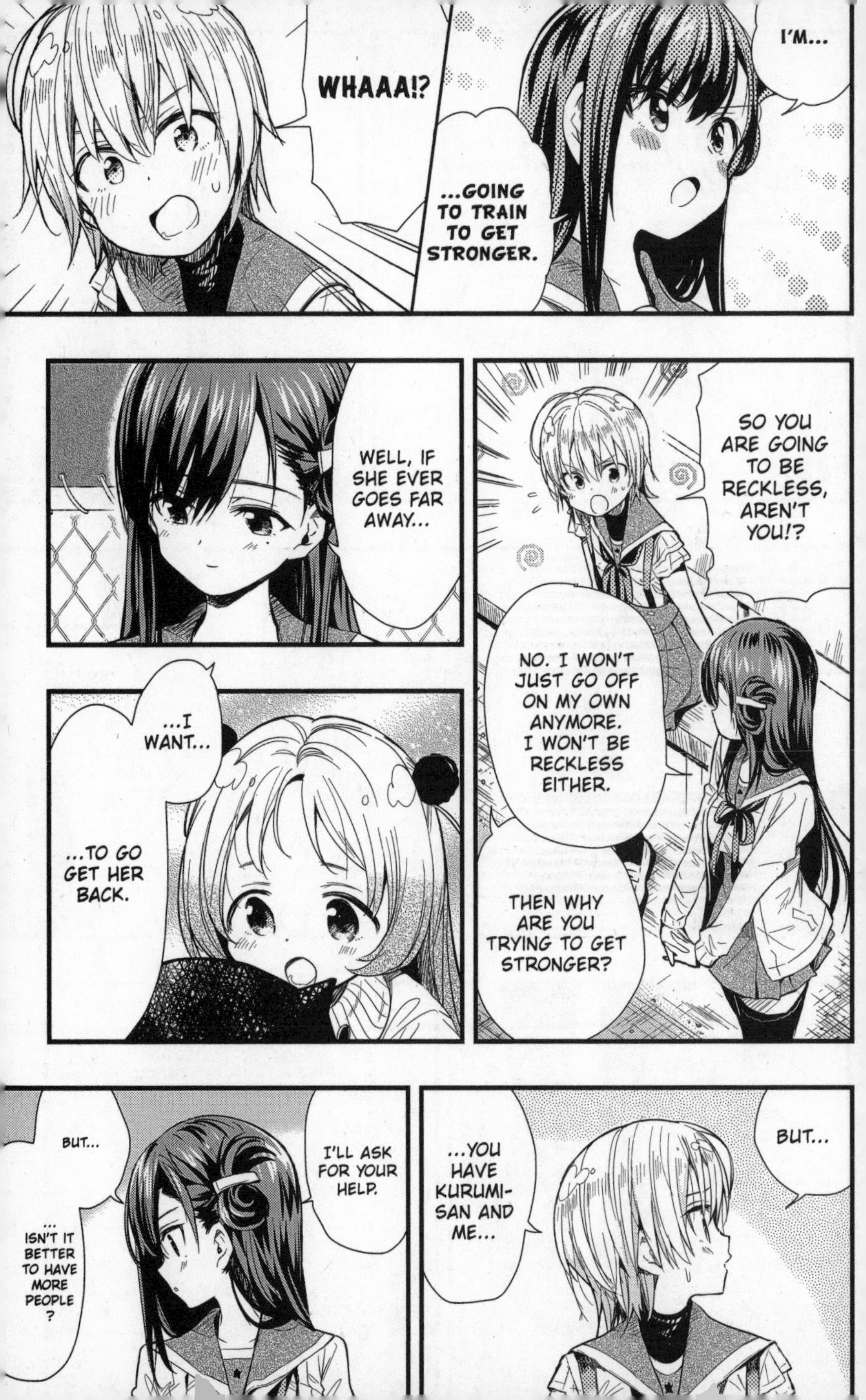
I'M...
...GOING TO TRAIN TO GET STRONGER.
WHAAA!?
SO YOU ARE GOING TO BE RECKLESS, AREN'T YOU!?
NO. I WON'T JUST GO OFF ON MY OWN ANYMORE. I WON'T BE RECKLESS EITHER.
THEN WHY ARE YOU TRYING TO GET STRONGER?
WELL, IF SHE EVER GOES FAR AWAY...
...I WANT...
...TO GO GET HER BACK.
BUT...
...YOU HAVE KURUMI-SAN AND ME...
I'LL ASK FOR YOUR HELP.
BUT...
...ISN'T IT BETTER TO HAVE MORE PEOPLE?

...BUT I REALLY...

GYU (SQUEEZE)

...AM GLAD YOU'RE ALL RIGHT.

YOU'RE ALL RIGHT, SO IT'S NOT A PROBLEM...

I'M SORRY. I SEE.

OH...

SUKU (STAND)

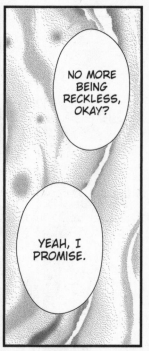

NO MORE BEING RECKLESS, OKAY?

YEAH, I PROMISE.

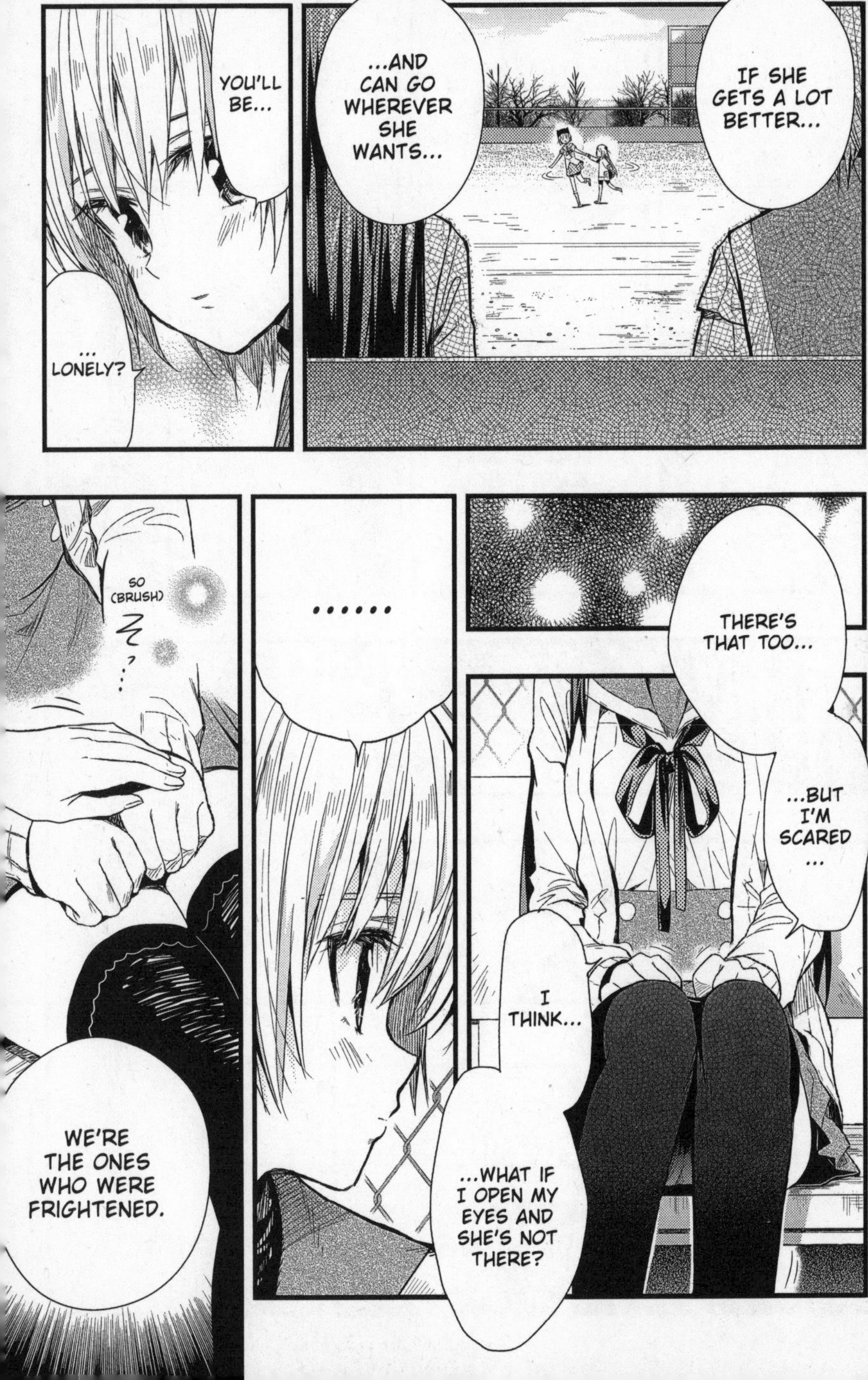
IF SHE GETS A LOT BETTER...
...AND CAN GO WHEREVER SHE WANTS...
YOU'LL BE...
...LONELY?
THERE'S THAT TOO...
...BUT I'M SCARED...
I THINK...
...WHAT IF I OPEN MY EYES AND SHE'S NOT THERE?
......
SO (BRUSH)
WE'RE THE ONES WHO WERE FRIGHTENED.

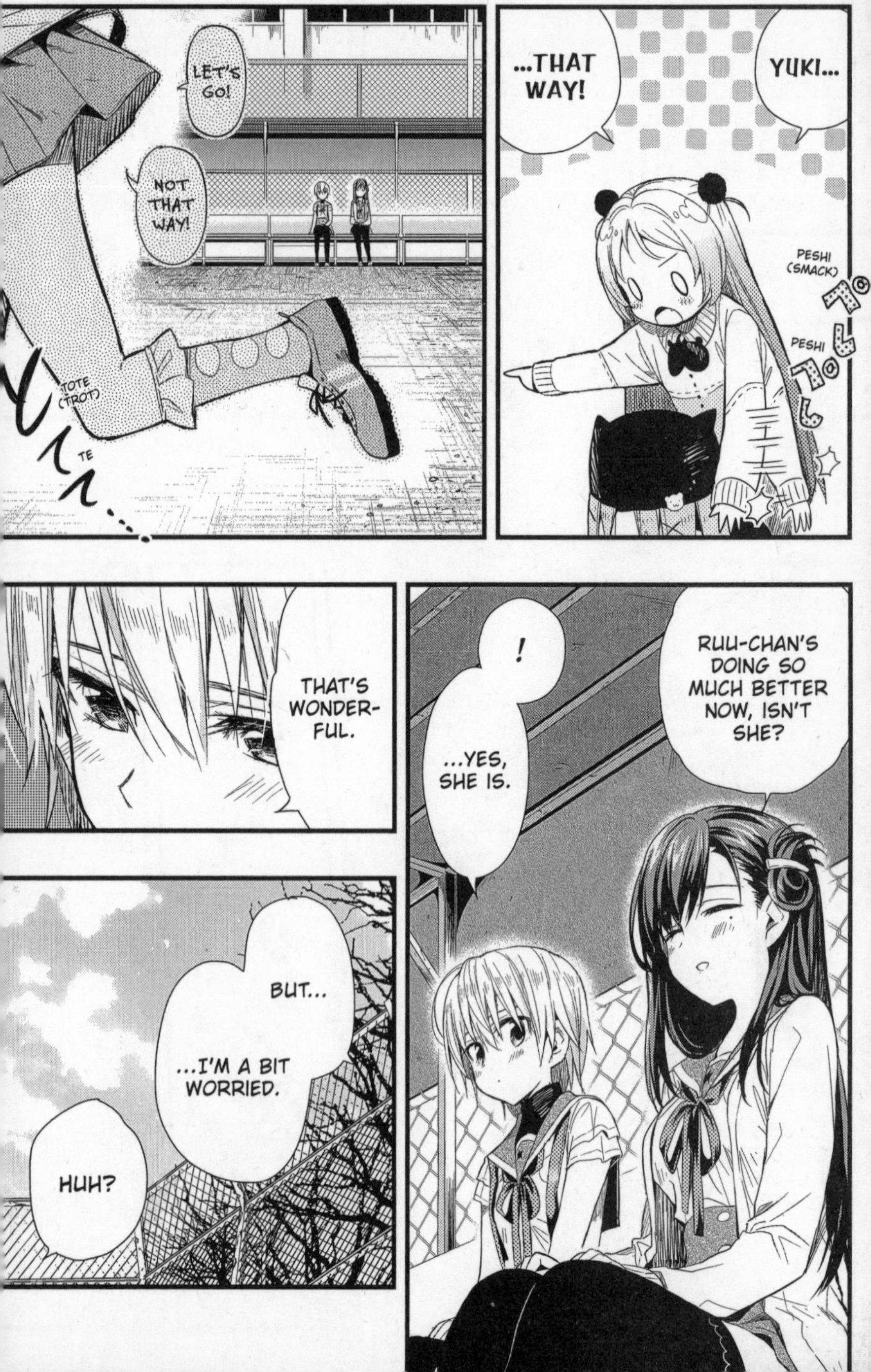
YUKI...
...THAT WAY!
PESHI (SMACK)
PESHI
LET'S GO!
NOT THAT WAY!
TOTE (TROT)
TE
RUU-CHAN'S DOING SO MUCH BETTER NOW, ISN'T SHE?
!
...YES, SHE IS.
THAT'S WONDER-FUL.
BUT...
...I'M A BIT WORRIED.
HUH?

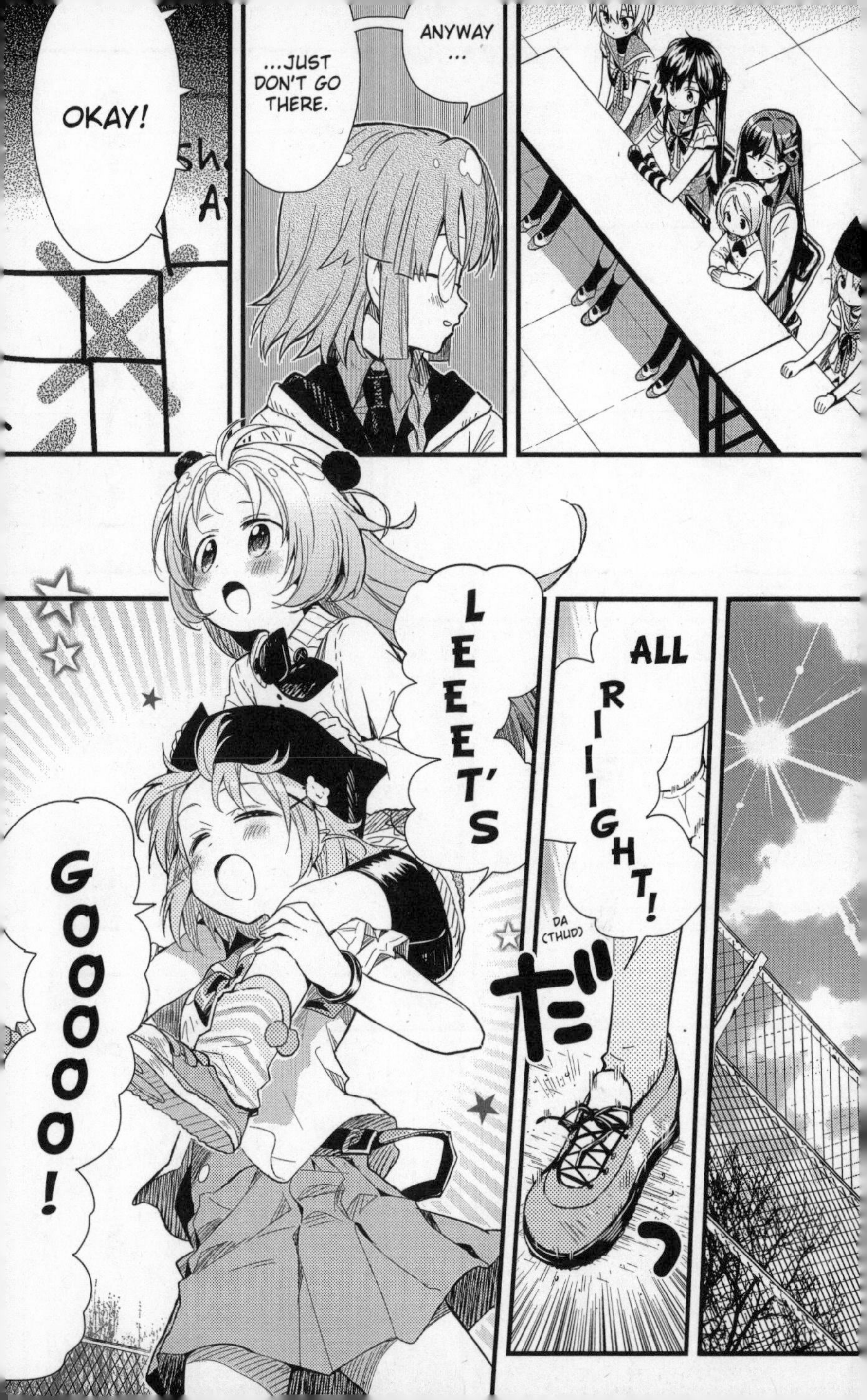

ANYWAY ...
...JUST DON'T GO THERE.
OKAY!
ALL RIIIGHT!
DA (THUD)
だっ
LEEET'S
GOOOOOO!

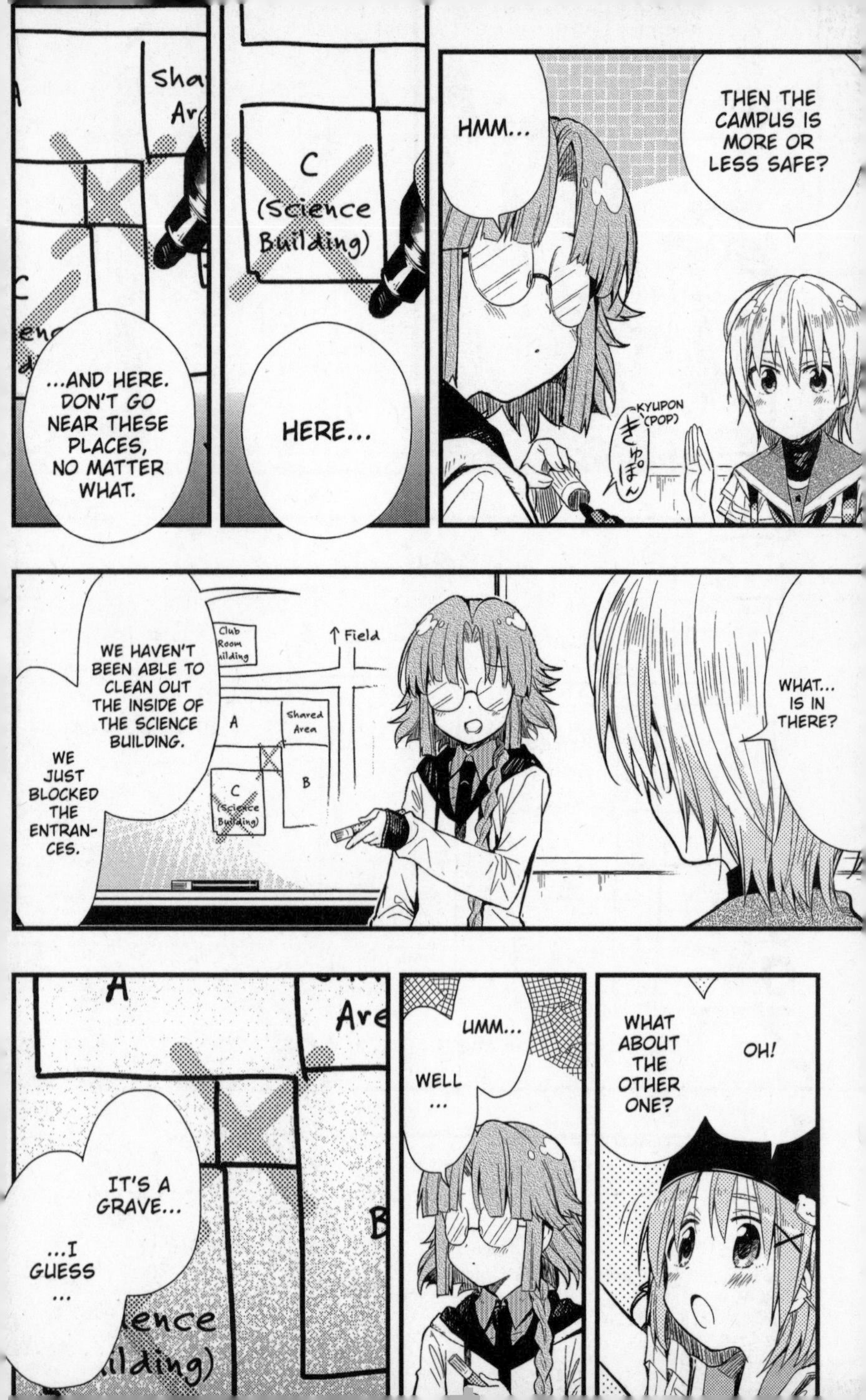
THEN THE CAMPUS IS MORE OR LESS SAFE?
HMM...
KYUPON (POP)
きゅぽん
C (Science Building)
HERE...
...AND HERE. DON'T GO NEAR THESE PLACES, NO MATTER WHAT.
WHAT... IS IN THERE?
↑ Field
Shared Area
A
B
C (Science Building)
WE HAVEN'T BEEN ABLE TO CLEAN OUT THE INSIDE OF THE SCIENCE BUILDING.
WE JUST BLOCKED THE ENTRAN-CES.
OH!
WHAT ABOUT THE OTHER ONE?
UMM...
WELL ...
IT'S A GRAVE...
...I GUESS ...

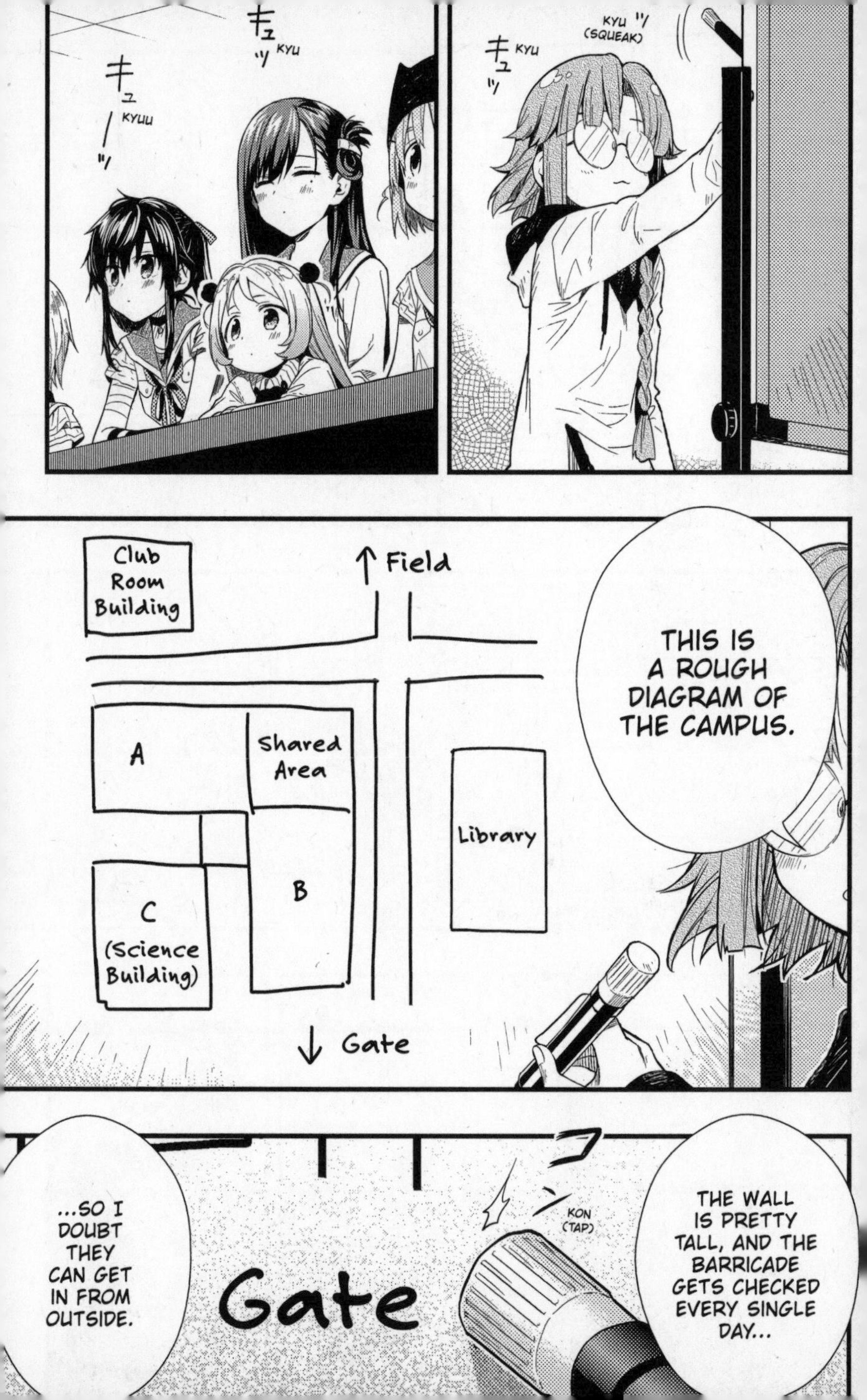

KYU ッ (SQUEAK)
キュッ KYU
キュッ KYU
キュー KYUU ッ
THIS IS A ROUGH DIAGRAM OF THE CAMPUS.
Club Room Building
↑ Field
A
Shared Area
Library
B
C (Science Building)
↓ Gate
THE WALL IS PRETTY TALL, AND THE BARRICADE GETS CHECKED EVERY SINGLE DAY...
コン KON (TAP)
Gate
...SO I DOUBT THEY CAN GET IN FROM OUTSIDE.

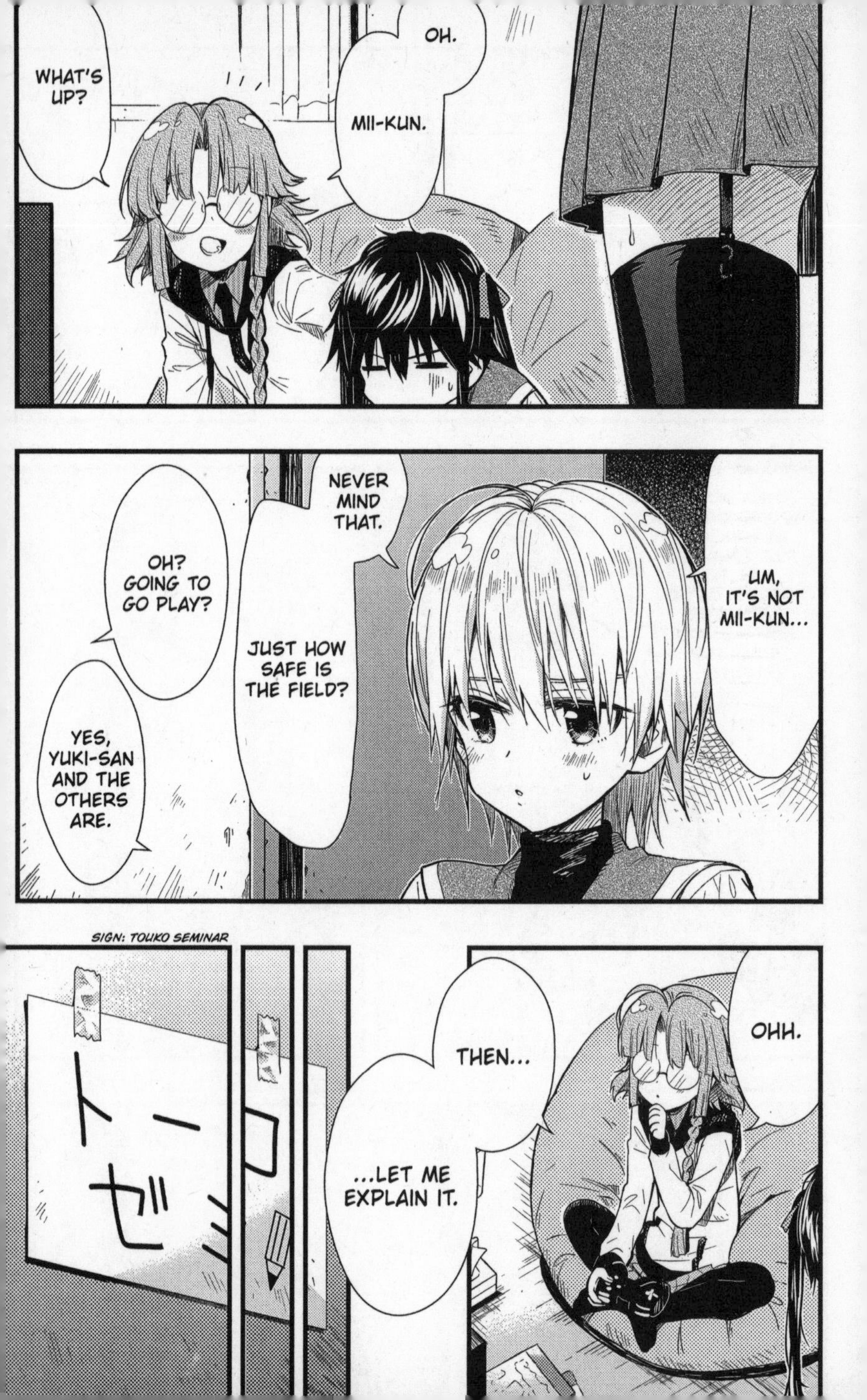
OH. MII-KUN.
WHAT'S UP?
UM, IT'S NOT MII-KUN...
NEVER MIND THAT.
JUST HOW SAFE IS THE FIELD?
OH? GOING TO GO PLAY?
YES, YUKI-SAN AND THE OTHERS ARE.
OHH.
THEN...
...LET ME EXPLAIN IT.
SIGN: TOUKO SEMINAR
トーコゼミ

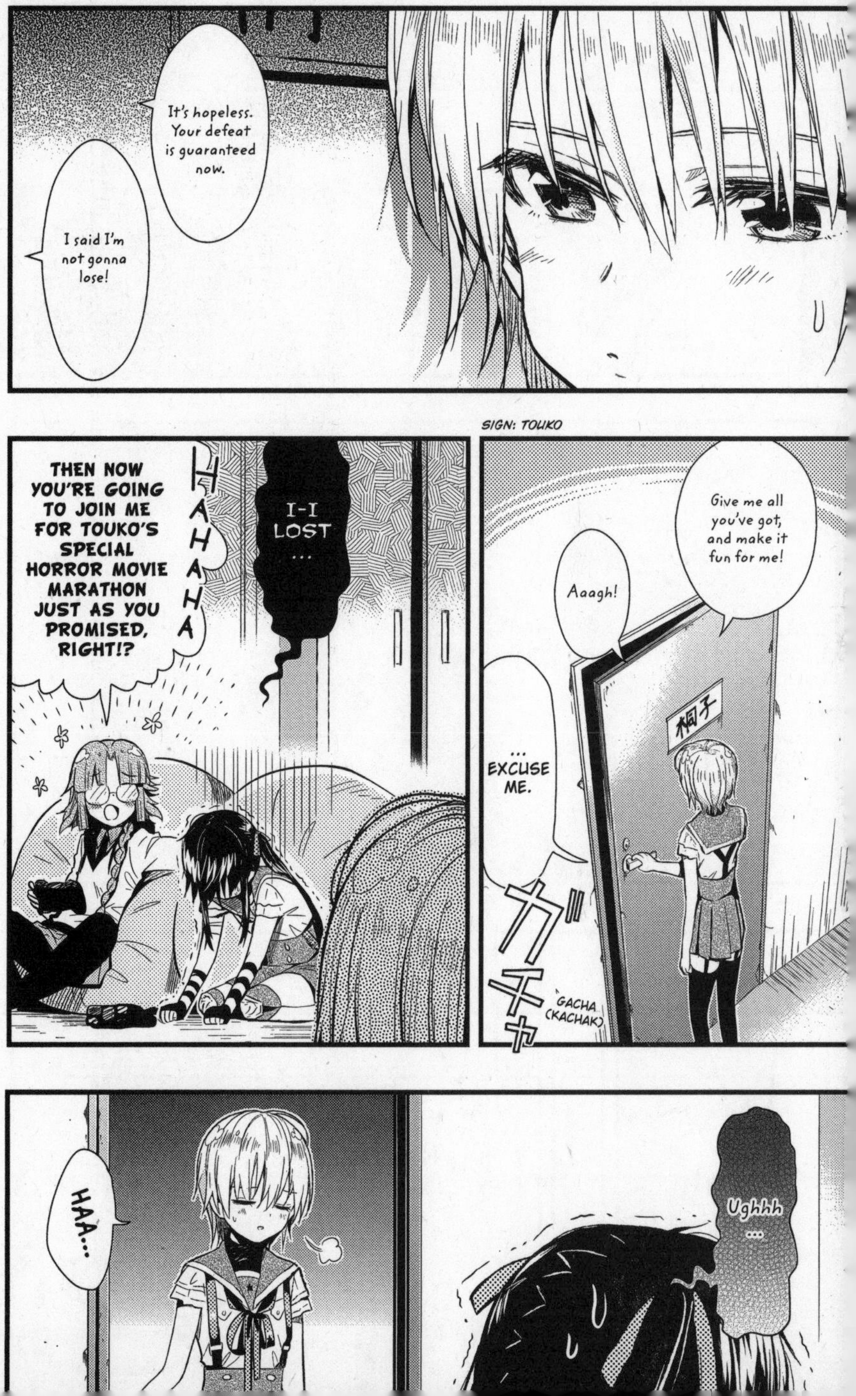
It's hopeless. Your defeat is guaranteed now.
I said I'm not gonna lose!
SIGN: TOUKO
Give me all you've got, and make it fun for me!
Aaagh!
桐子
... EXCUSE ME.
ガチャ
GACHA (KACHAK)
I-I LOST ...
HAHAHAHA
THEN NOW YOU'RE GOING TO JOIN ME FOR TOUKO'S SPECIAL HORROR MOVIE MARATHON JUST AS YOU PROMISED, RIGHT!?
Ughhh ...
HAA...

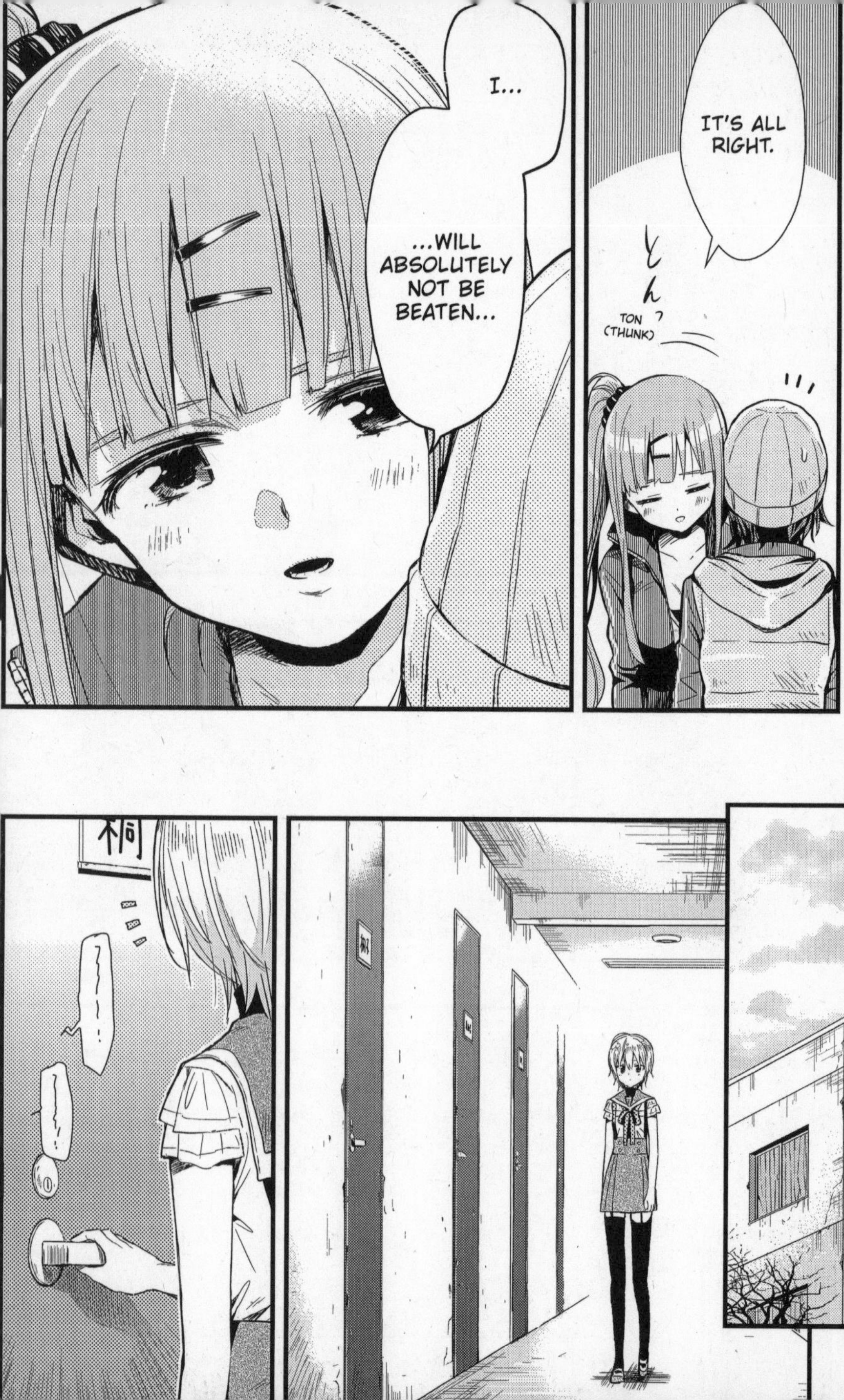
IT'S ALL RIGHT.
とん
TON (THUNK)
I...
...WILL ABSOLUTELY NOT BE BEATEN...
桐

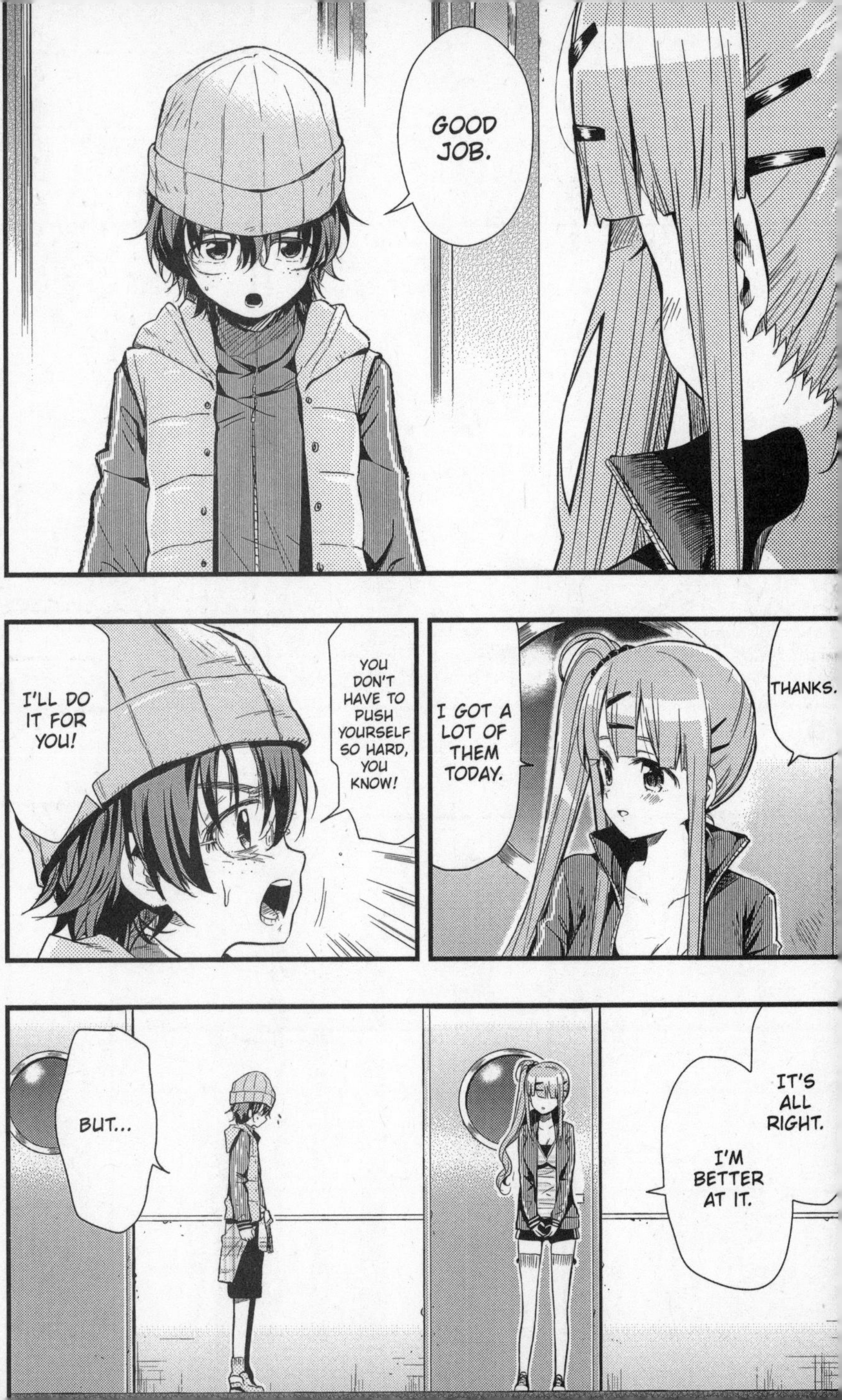
GOOD JOB.
THANKS.
I GOT A LOT OF THEM TODAY.
YOU DON'T HAVE TO PUSH YOURSELF SO HARD, YOU KNOW!
I'LL DO IT FOR YOU!
IT'S ALL RIGHT.
I'M BETTER AT IT.
BUT...

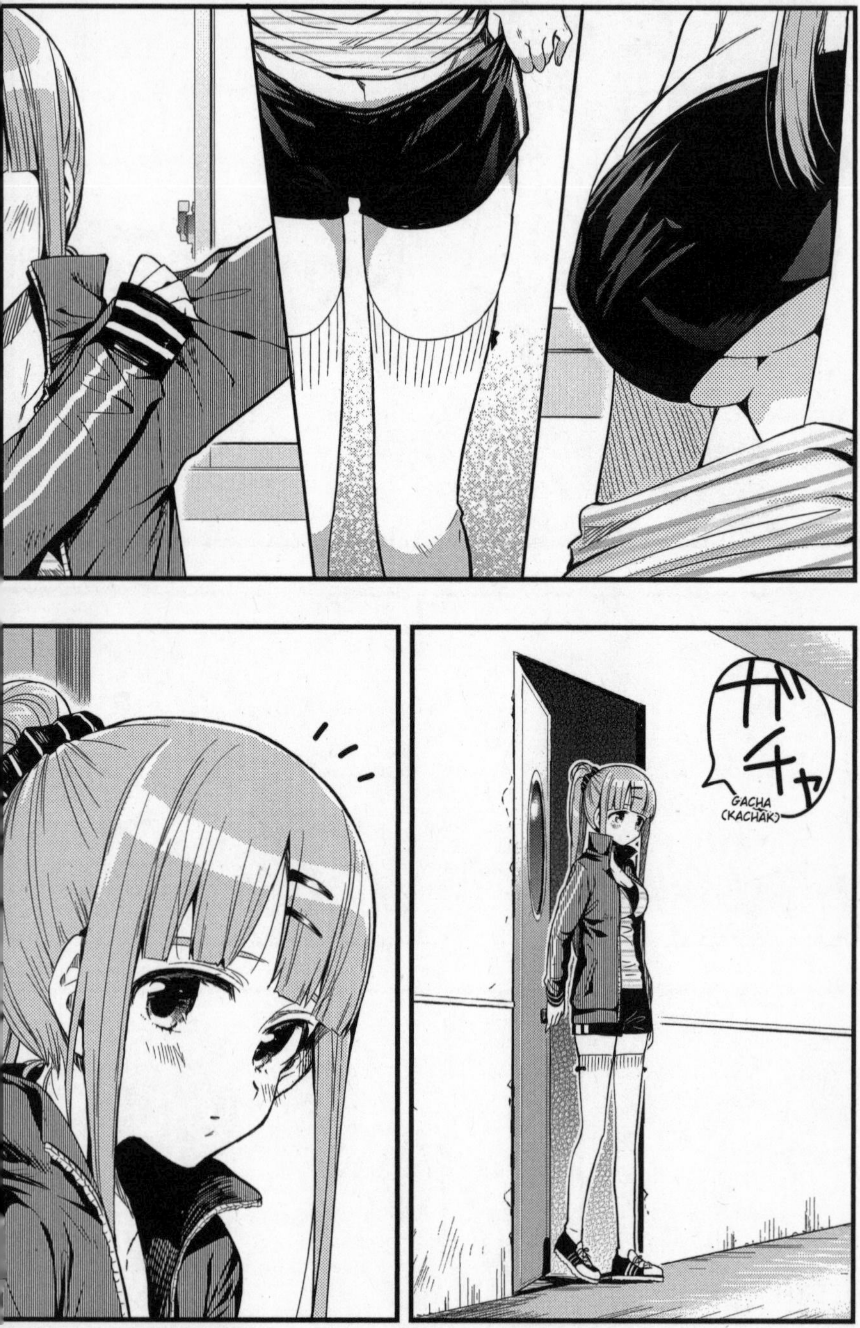
ガチャ
GACHA (KACHAK)

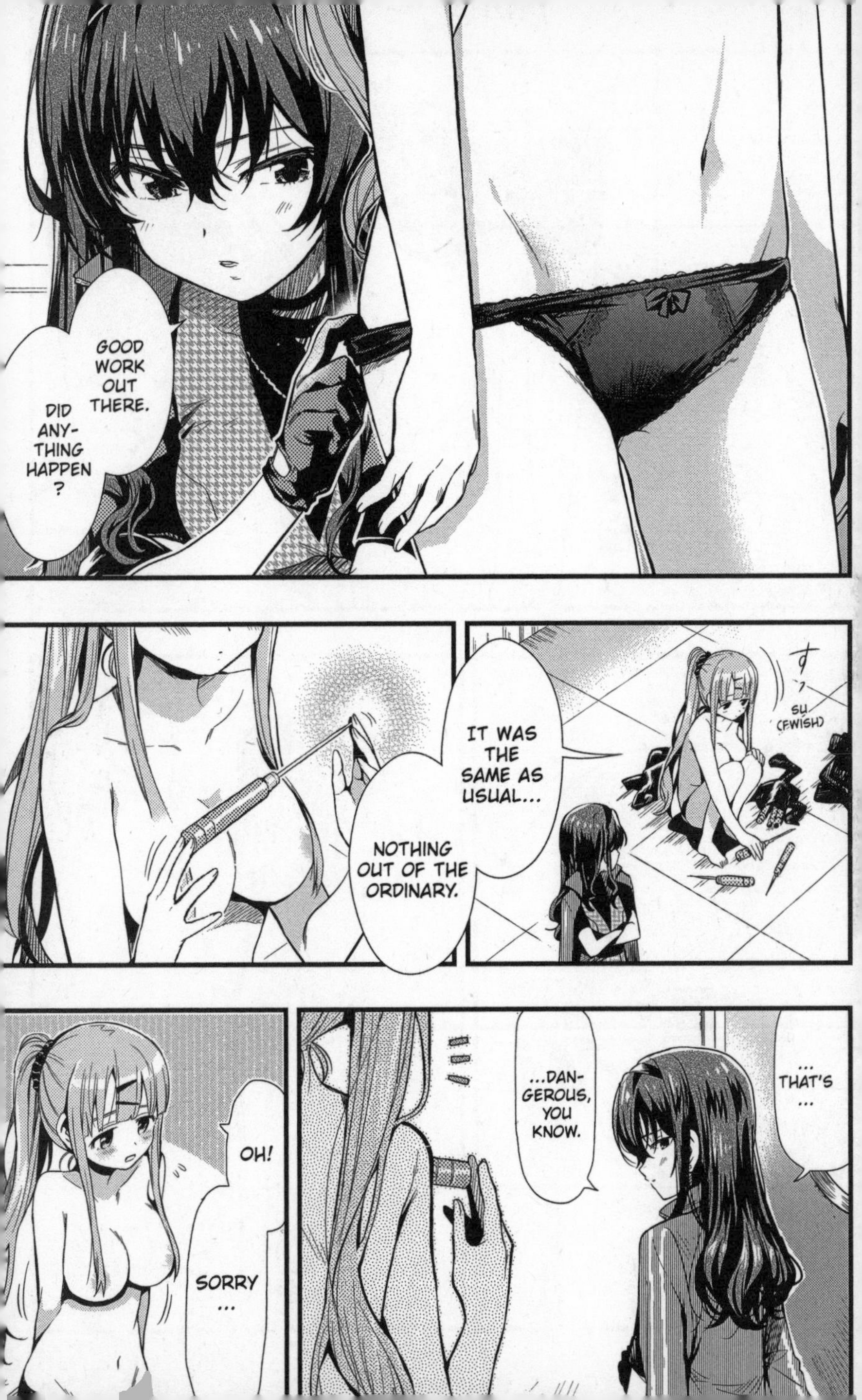
GOOD WORK OUT THERE.
DID ANY-THING HAPPEN?
す
SU (FWISH)
IT WAS THE SAME AS USUAL...
NOTHING OUT OF THE ORDINARY.
...THAT'S...
...DAN-GEROUS, YOU KNOW.
OH!
SORRY...

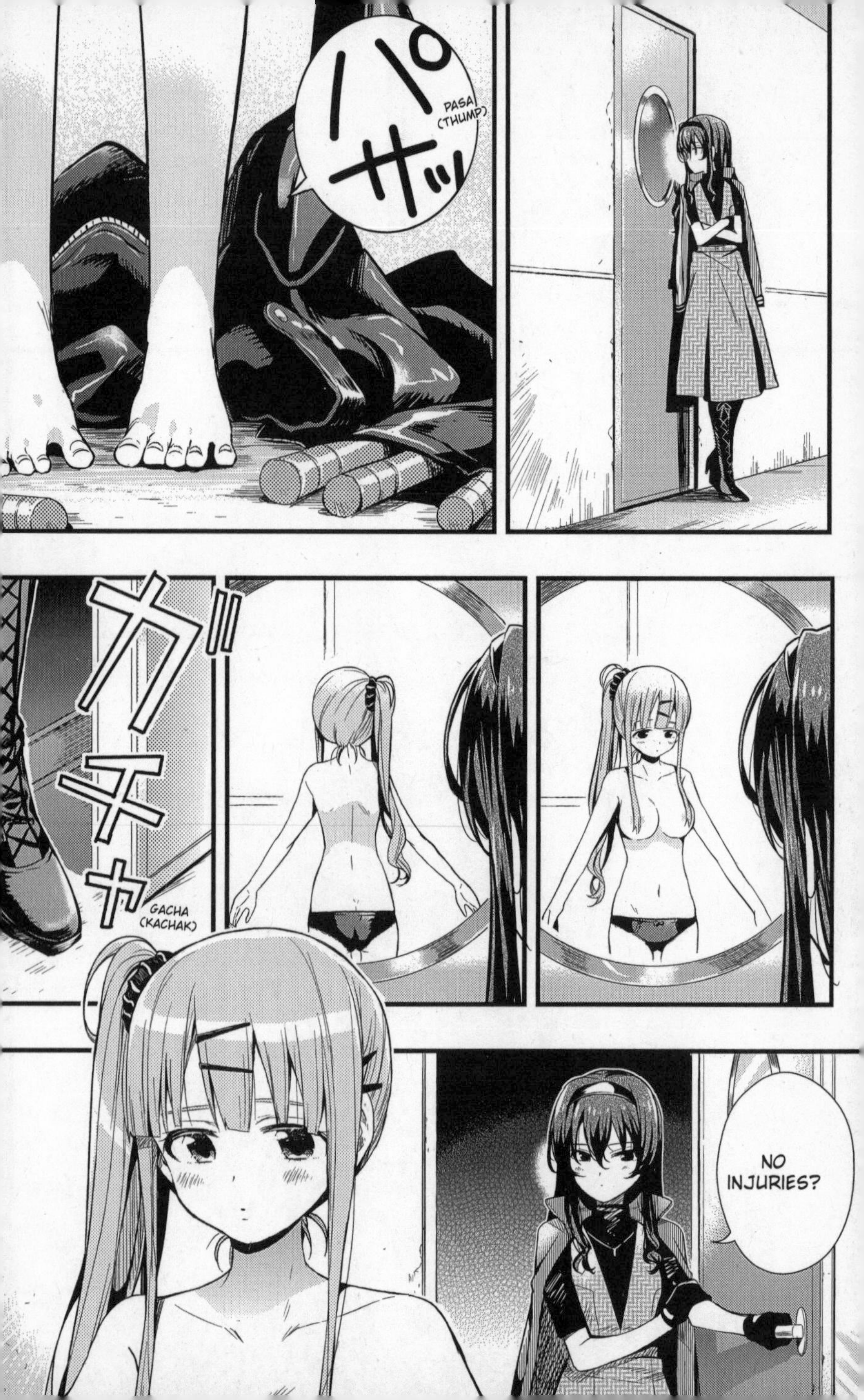
パサッ
PASA (THUMP)
ガチャ
GACHA (KACHAK)
NO INJURIES?

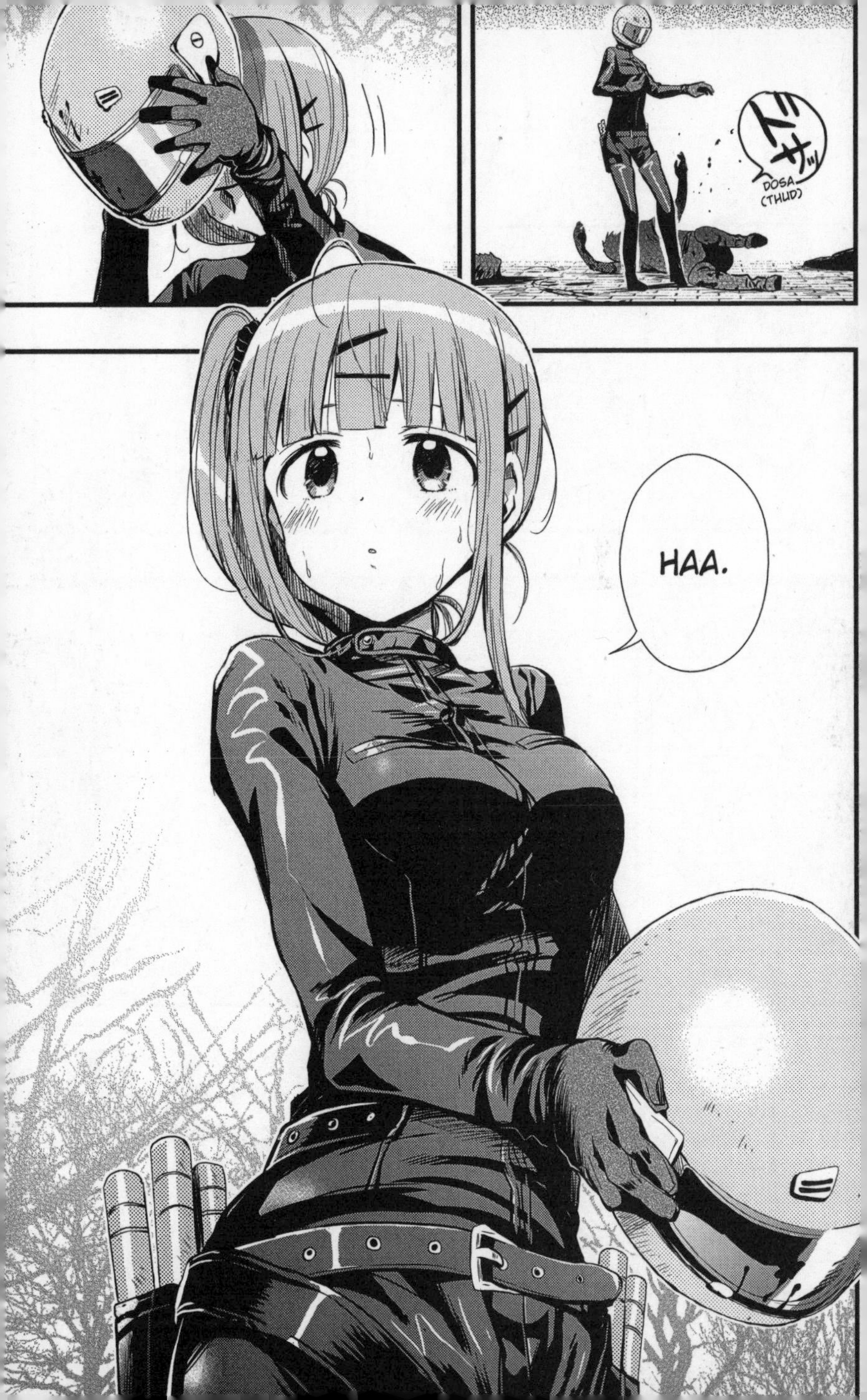
ドサッ
DOSA (THUD)
HAA.

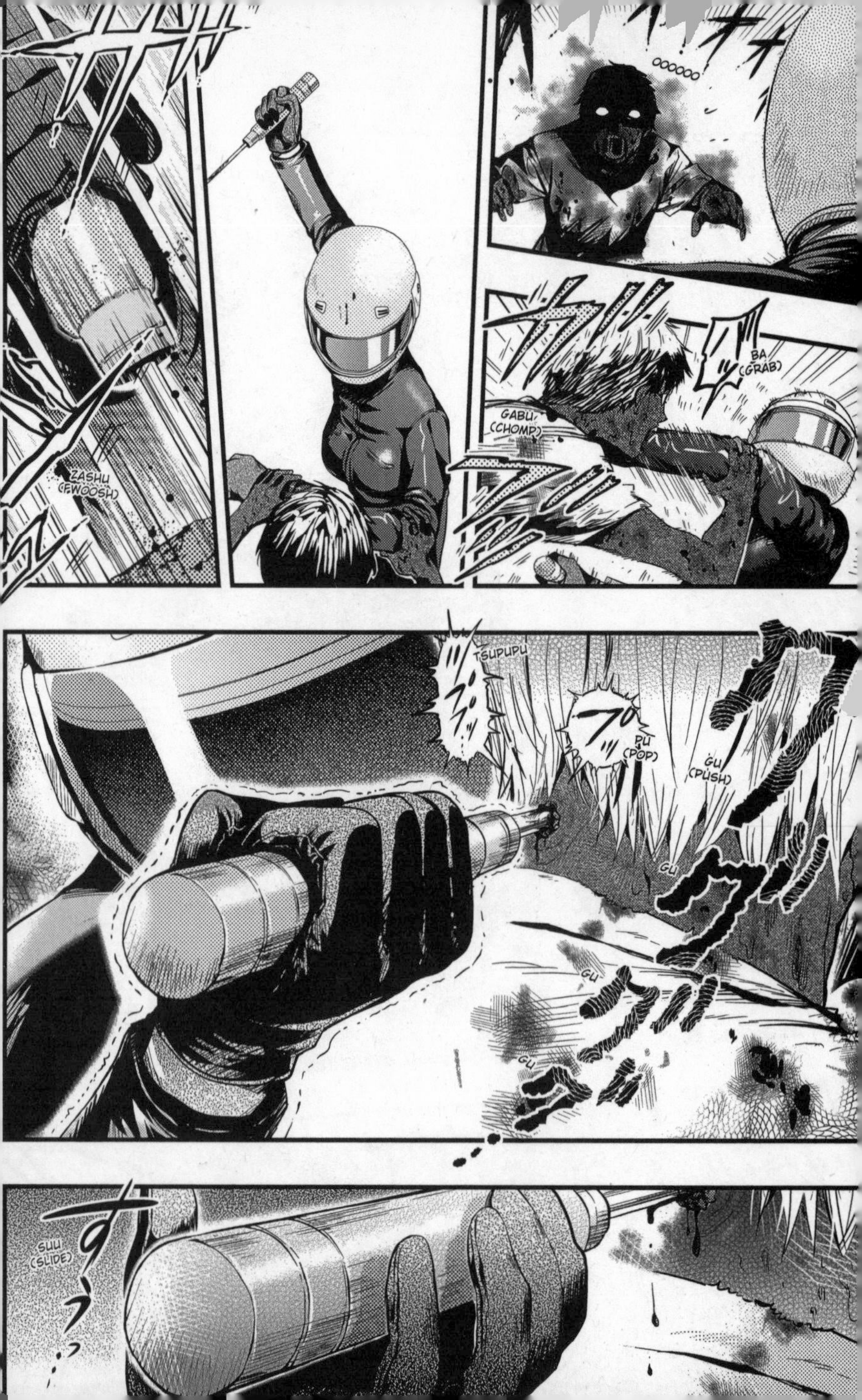
OOOOOO
BA (GRAB)
GABU (CHOMP)
ZASHU (FWOOSH)
TSUPUPU
GU (PUSH)
PU (POP)
GU
GU
GU
SUU (SLIDE)

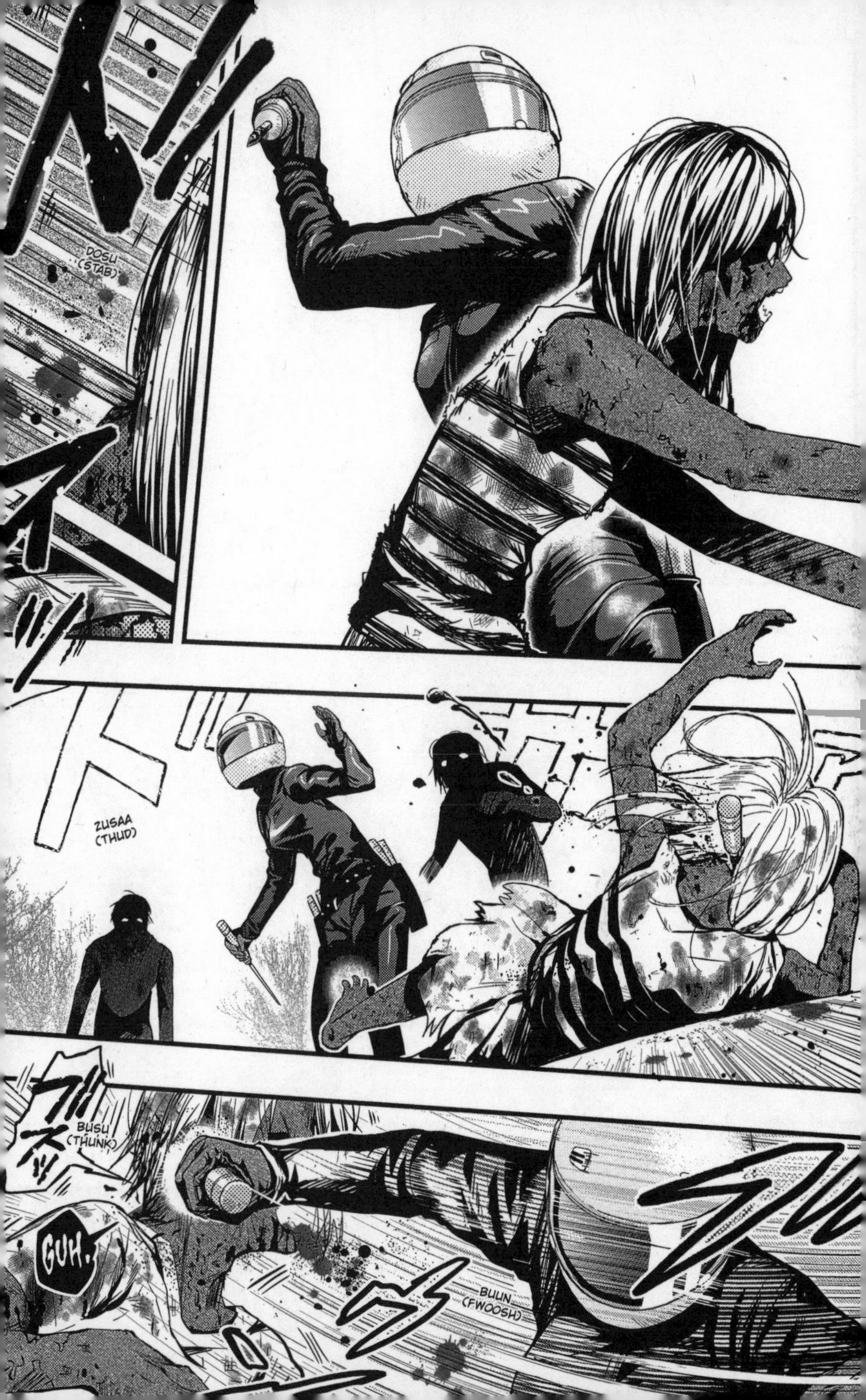
DOSU
(STAB)
ZUSAA
(THUD)
BUUN
(FWOOSH)
BUSU
(THUNK)
GUH.

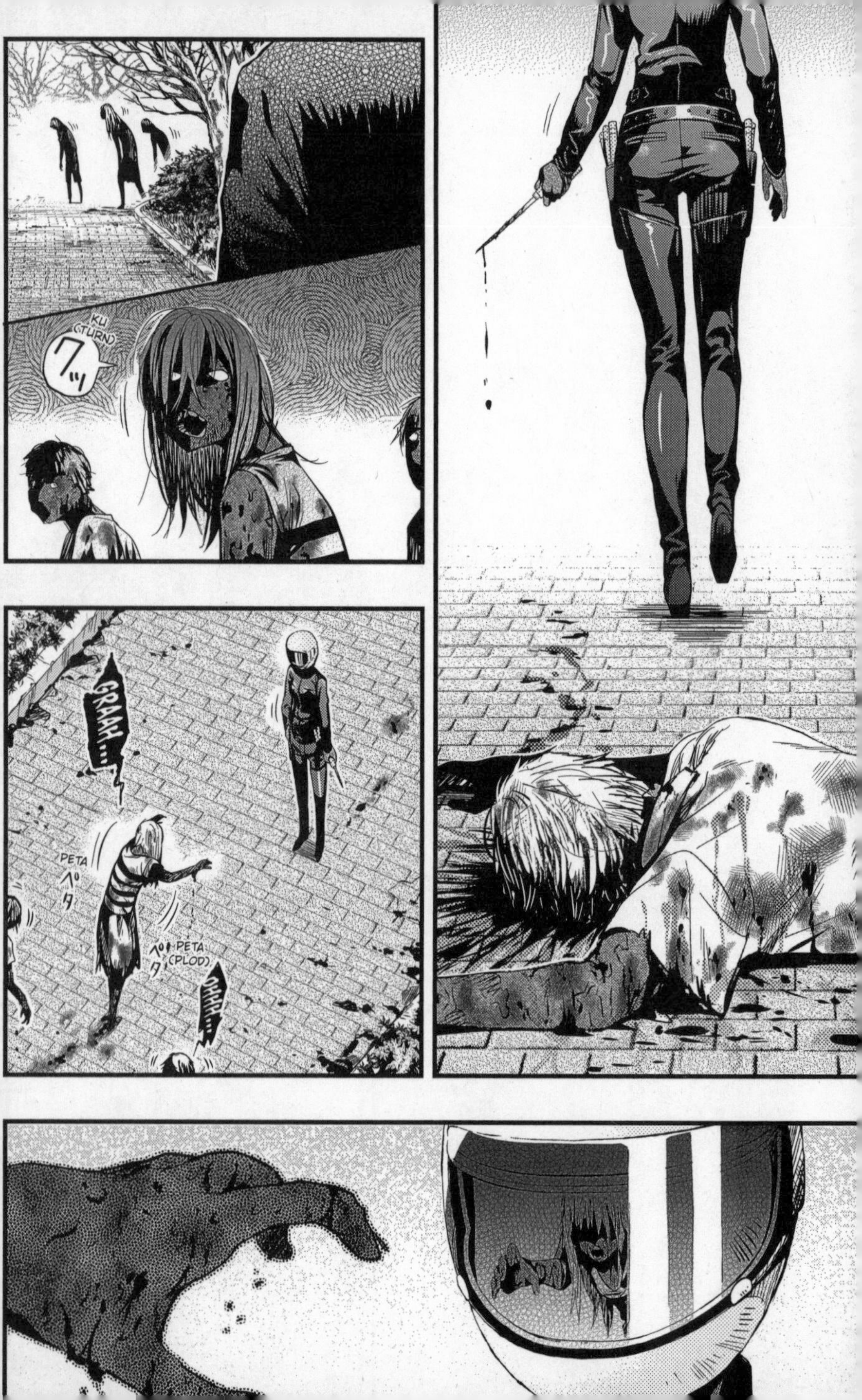
KU (TURN)
ワッ
GRAAH...
PETA
ペタ
PETA (PLOD)
ペタ
OHHH...

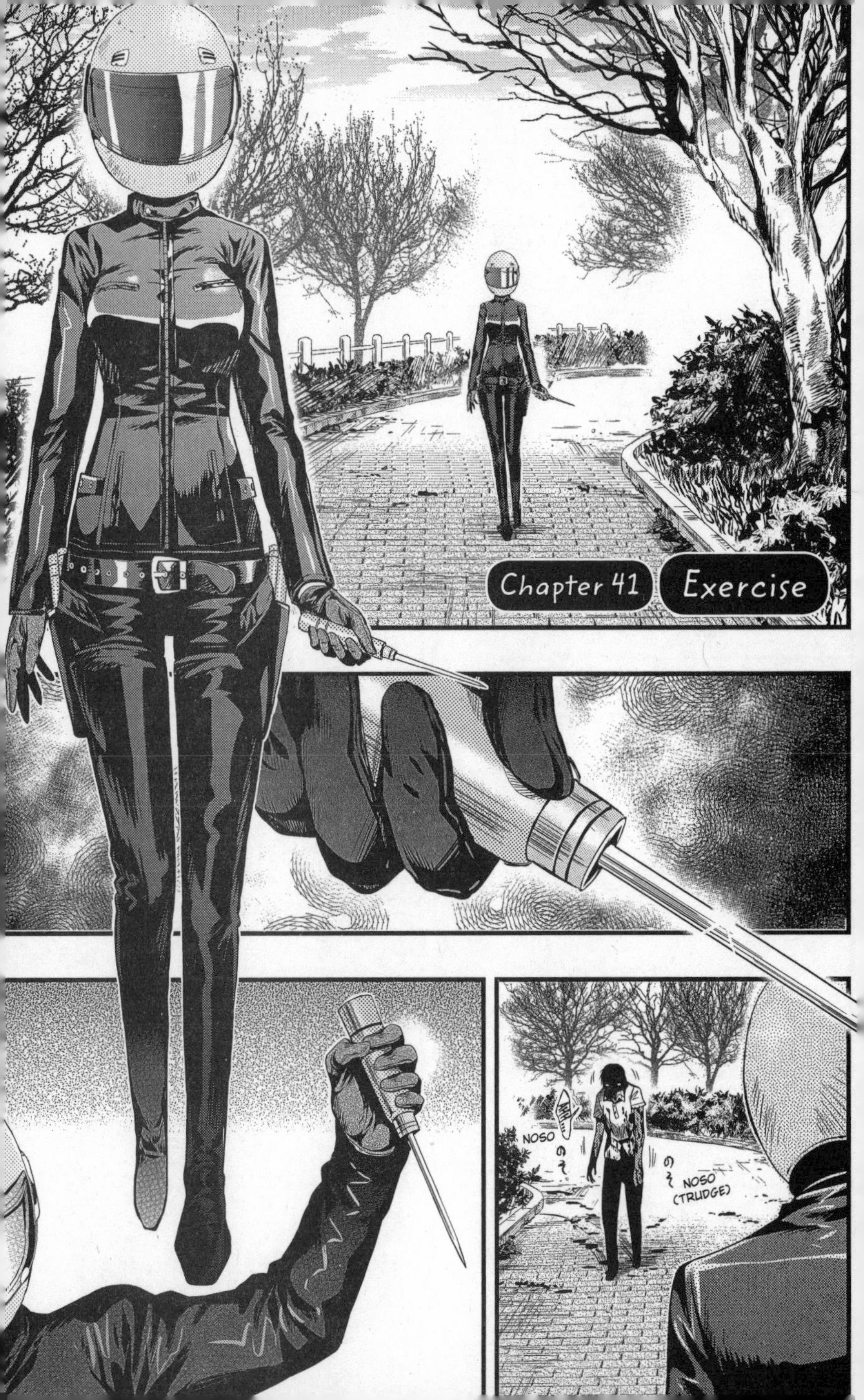
Chapter 41
Exercise
のそ
NOSO (TRUDGE)
のそ
NOSO

SCHOOL-LIVE!

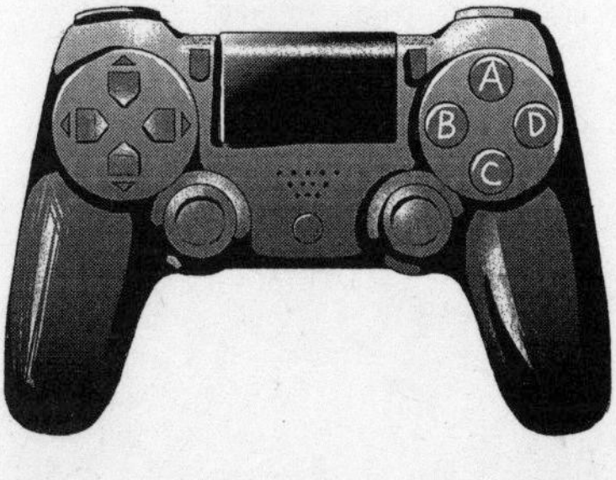
A
B
D
C

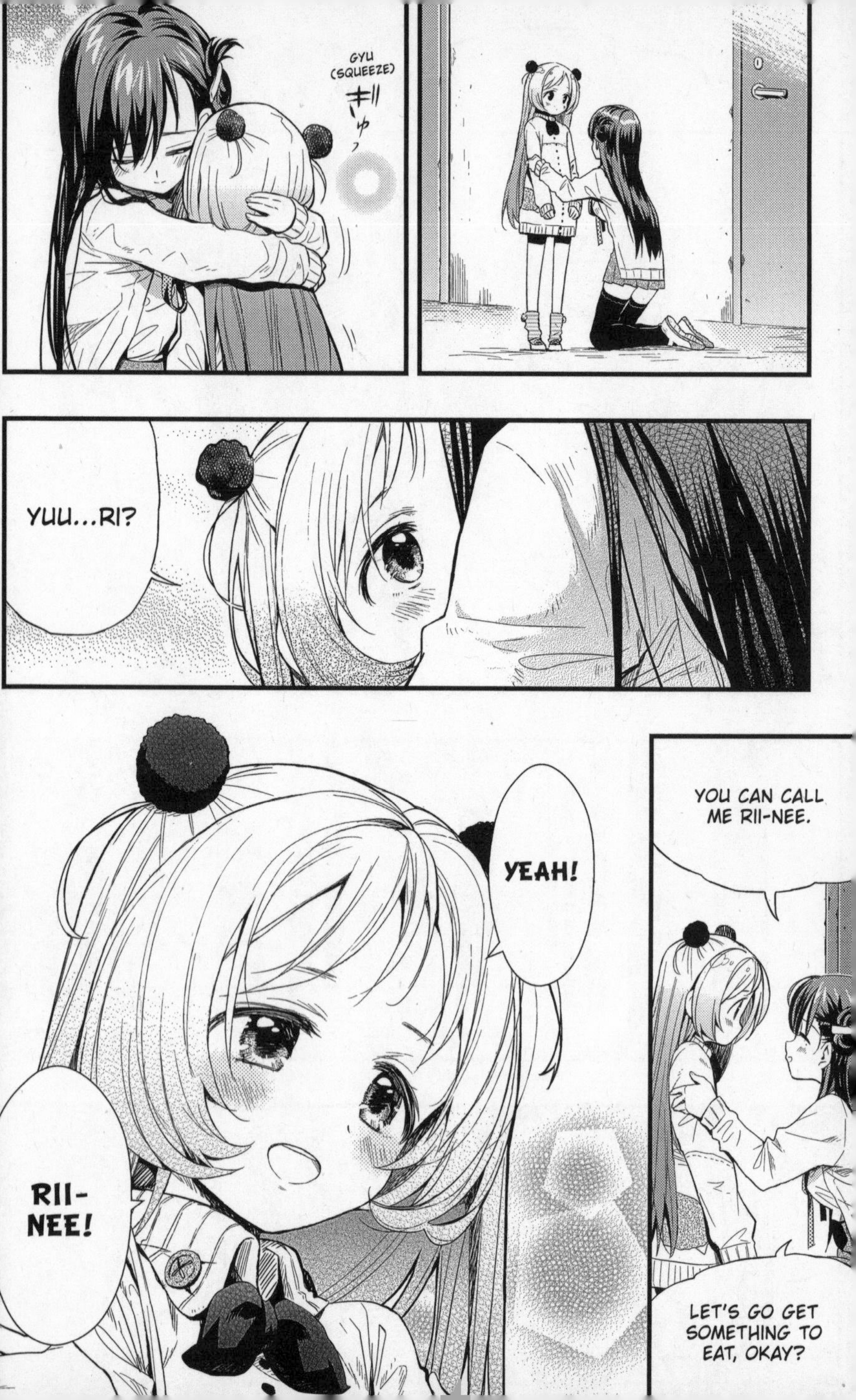
GYU (SQUEEZE)
ぎゅっ
YUU...RI?
YOU CAN CALL ME RII-NEE.
LET'S GO GET SOMETHING TO EAT, OKAY?
YEAH!
RII-NEE!

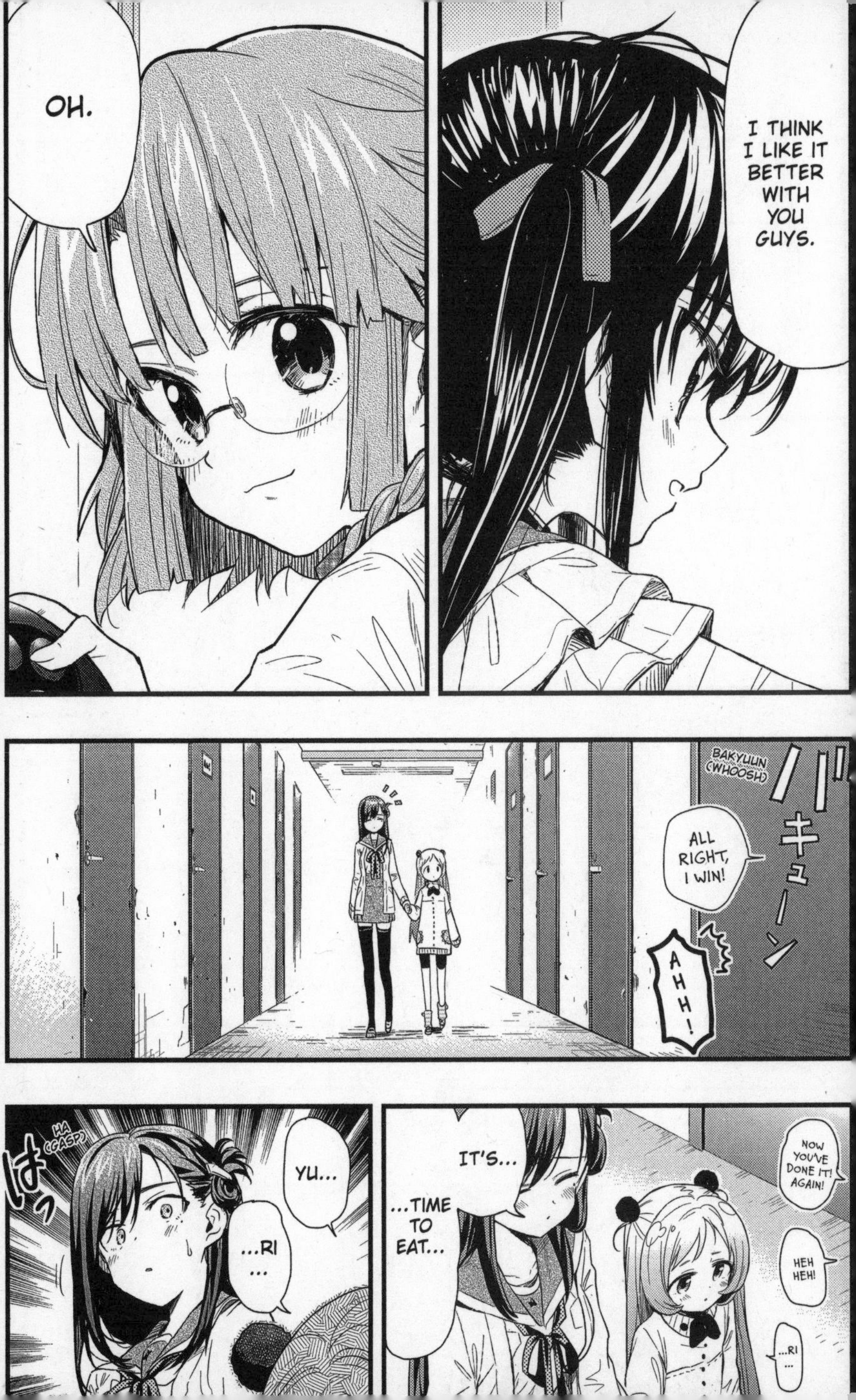
I THINK I LIKE IT BETTER WITH YOU GUYS.
OH.
BAKYUUN (WHOOSH)
バキューン
ALL RIGHT, I WIN!
AHH!
NOW YOU'VE DONE IT! AGAIN!
HEH HEH!
IT'S...
...TIME TO EAT...
...RI ...
HA (GASP)
はっ
YU...
...RI ...

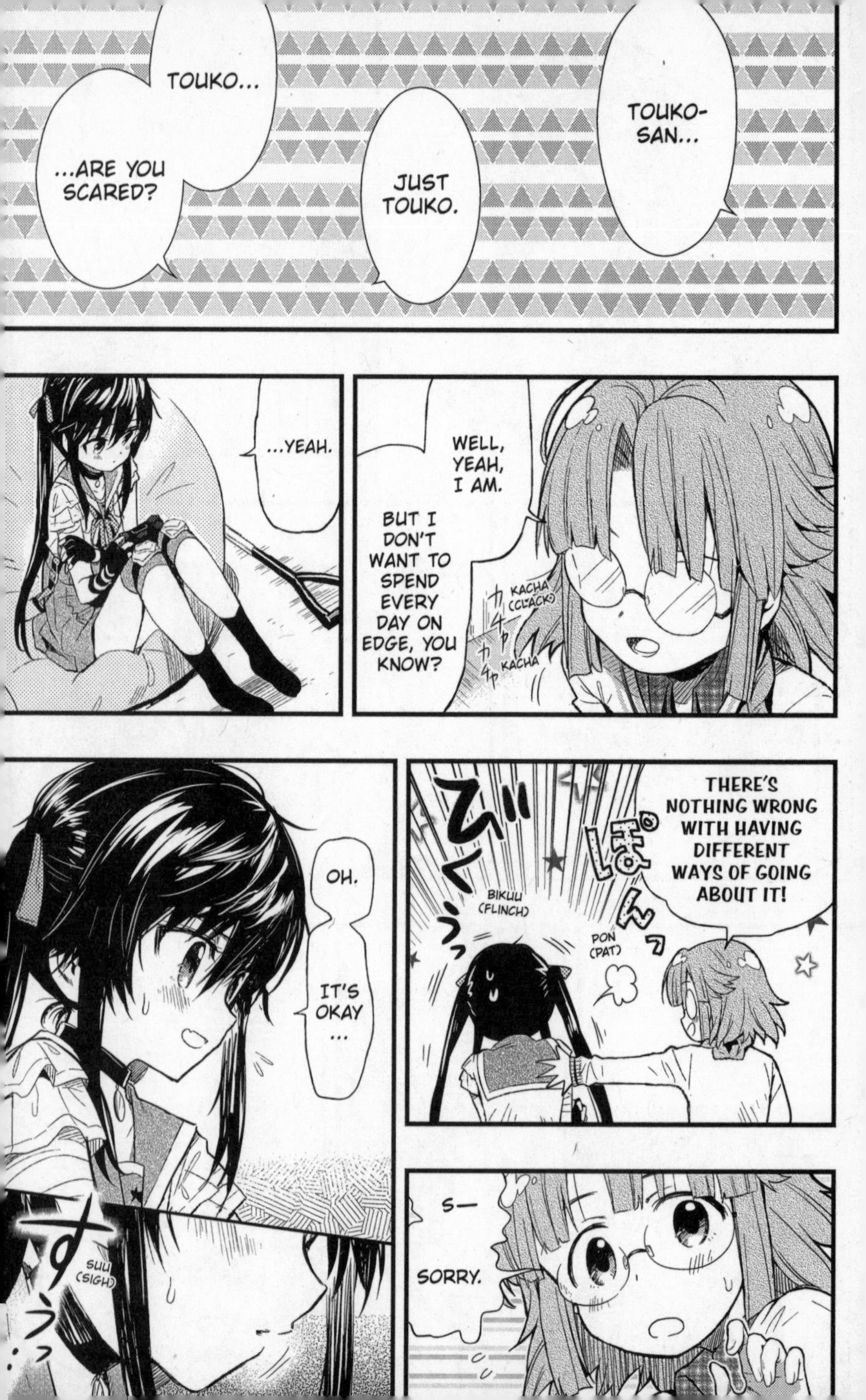
TOUKO-SAN...
JUST TOUKO.
TOUKO...
...ARE YOU SCARED?
WELL, YEAH, I AM.
BUT I DON'T WANT TO SPEND EVERY DAY ON EDGE, YOU KNOW?
KACHA (CLACK)
KACHA
...YEAH.
THERE'S NOTHING WRONG WITH HAVING DIFFERENT WAYS OF GOING ABOUT IT!
PON (PAT)
BIKUU (FLINCH)
S—
SORRY.
OH.
IT'S OKAY...
SUU (SIGH)

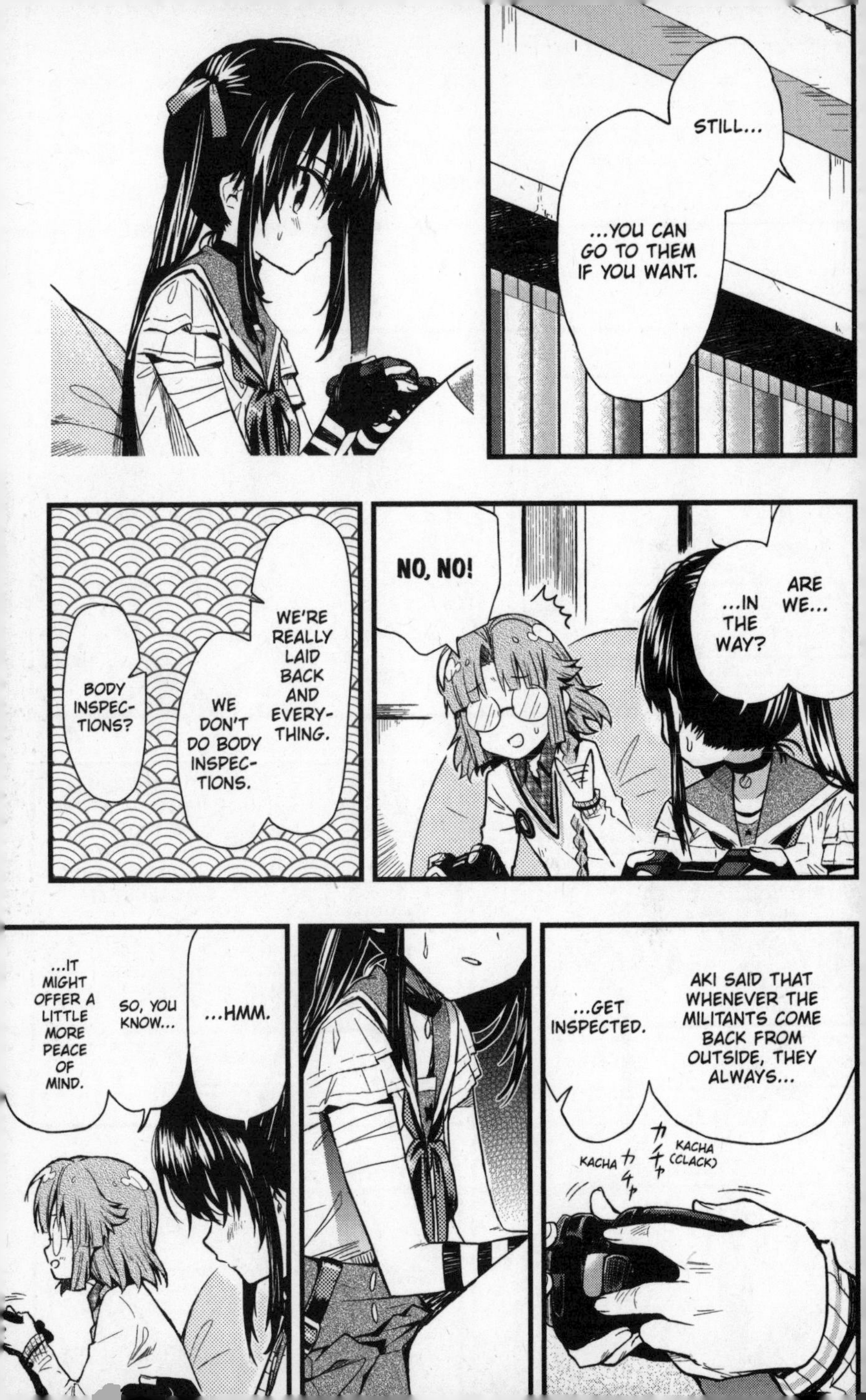
STILL...
...YOU CAN GO TO THEM IF YOU WANT.
ARE WE...
...IN THE WAY?
NO, NO!
WE'RE REALLY LAID BACK AND EVERYTHING.
WE DON'T DO BODY INSPECTIONS.
BODY INSPECTIONS?
AKI SAID THAT WHENEVER THE MILITANTS COME BACK FROM OUTSIDE, THEY ALWAYS...
...GET INSPECTED.
カチャ KACHA (CLACK)
カチャ KACHA
...HMM.
SO, YOU KNOW...
...IT MIGHT OFFER A LITTLE MORE PEACE OF MIND.

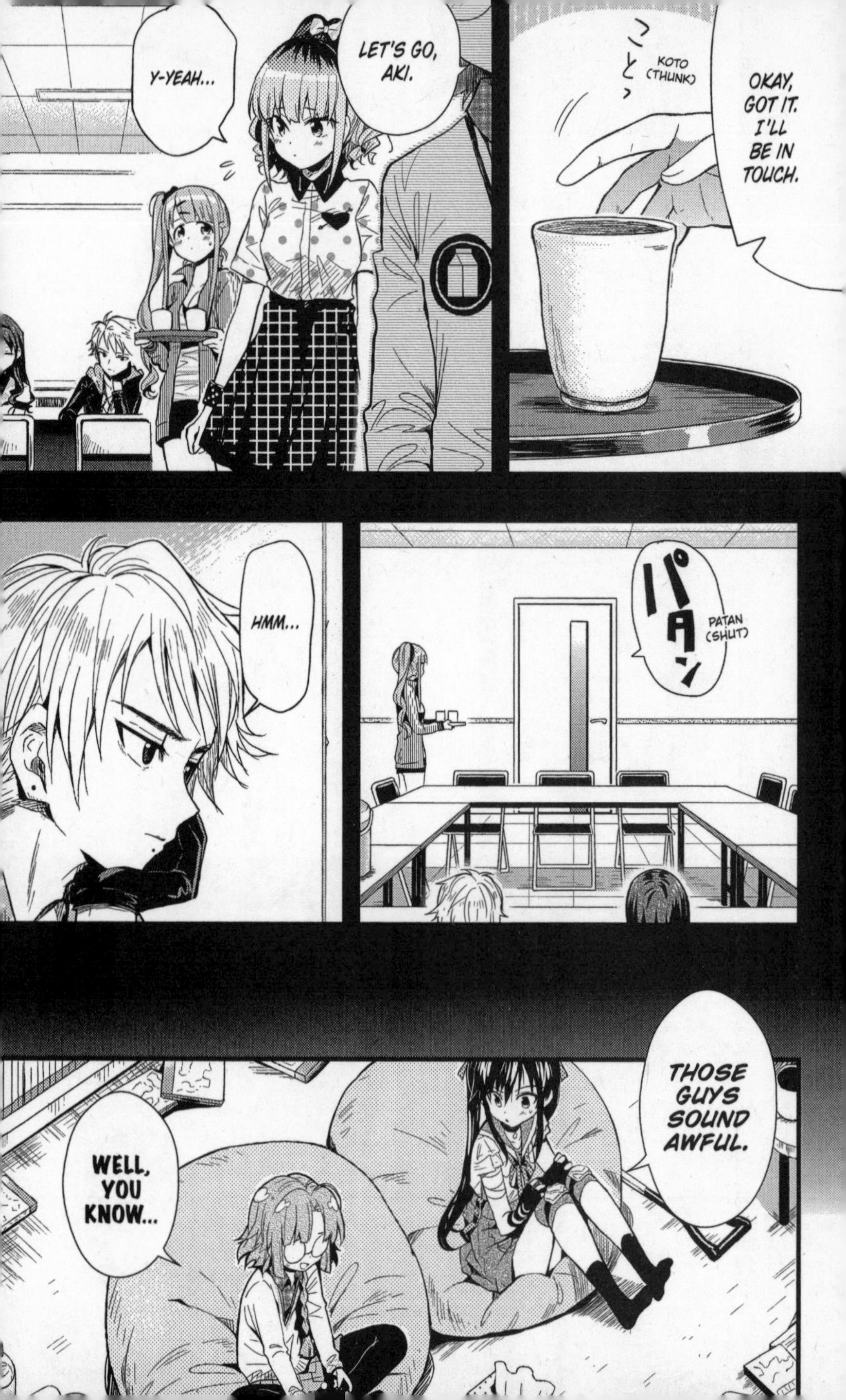
OKAY, GOT IT. I'LL BE IN TOUCH.
ことっ
KOTO (THUNK)
LET'S GO, AKI.
Y-YEAH...
パタン
PATAN (SHUT)
HMM...
THOSE GUYS SOUND AWFUL.
WELL, YOU KNOW...

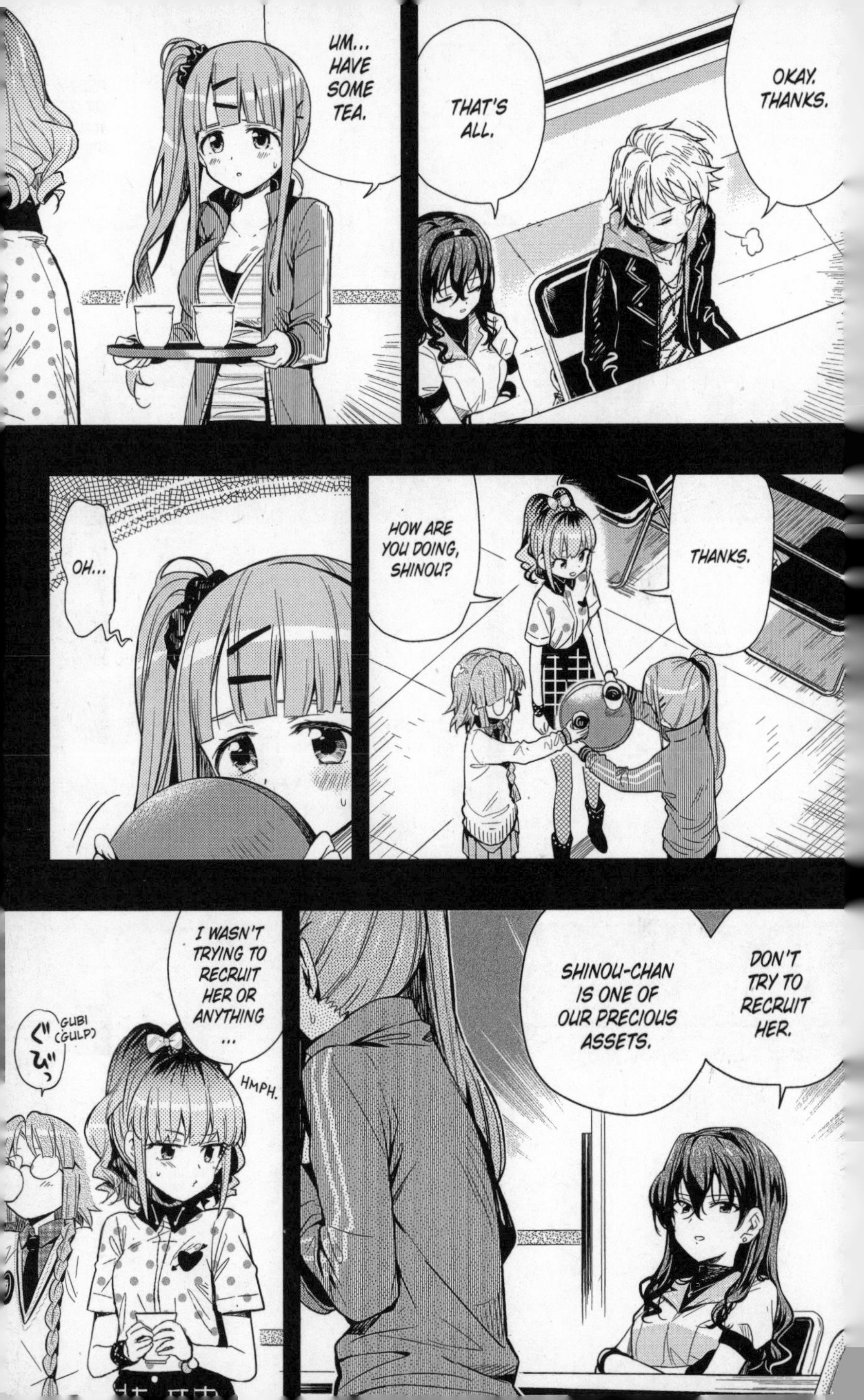
OKAY. THANKS.
THAT'S ALL.
UM... HAVE SOME TEA.
THANKS.
HOW ARE YOU DOING, SHINOU?
OH...
DON'T TRY TO RECRUIT HER.
SHINOU-CHAN IS ONE OF OUR PRECIOUS ASSETS.
I WASN'T TRYING TO RECRUIT HER OR ANYTHING...
HMPH.
ぐびっ
GUBI (GULP)

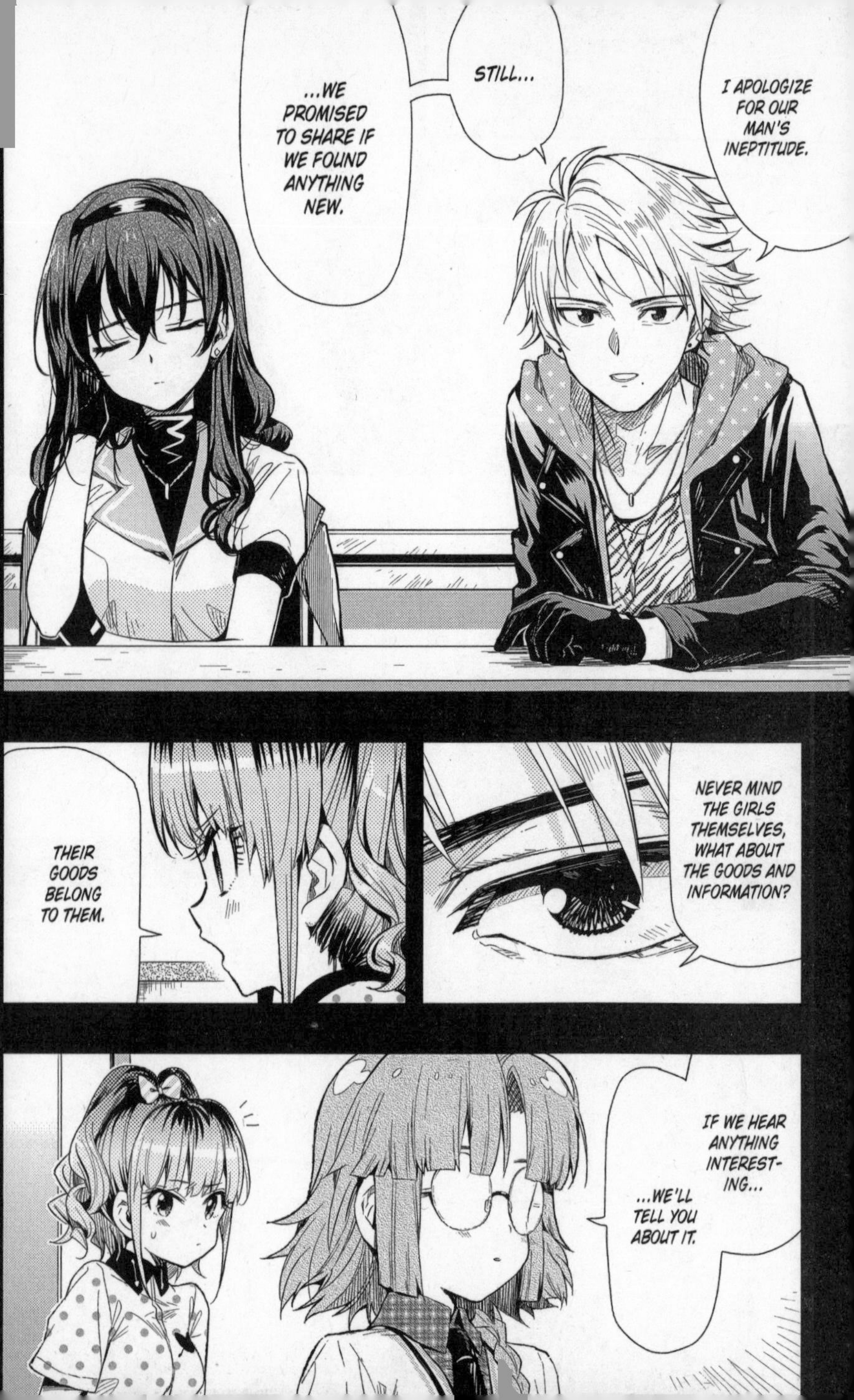
I APOLOGIZE FOR OUR MAN'S INEPTITUDE.
STILL...
...WE PROMISED TO SHARE IF WE FOUND ANYTHING NEW.
NEVER MIND THE GIRLS THEMSELVES, WHAT ABOUT THE GOODS AND INFORMATION?
THEIR GOODS BELONG TO THEM.
IF WE HEAR ANYTHING INTEREST-ING...
...WE'LL TELL YOU ABOUT IT.

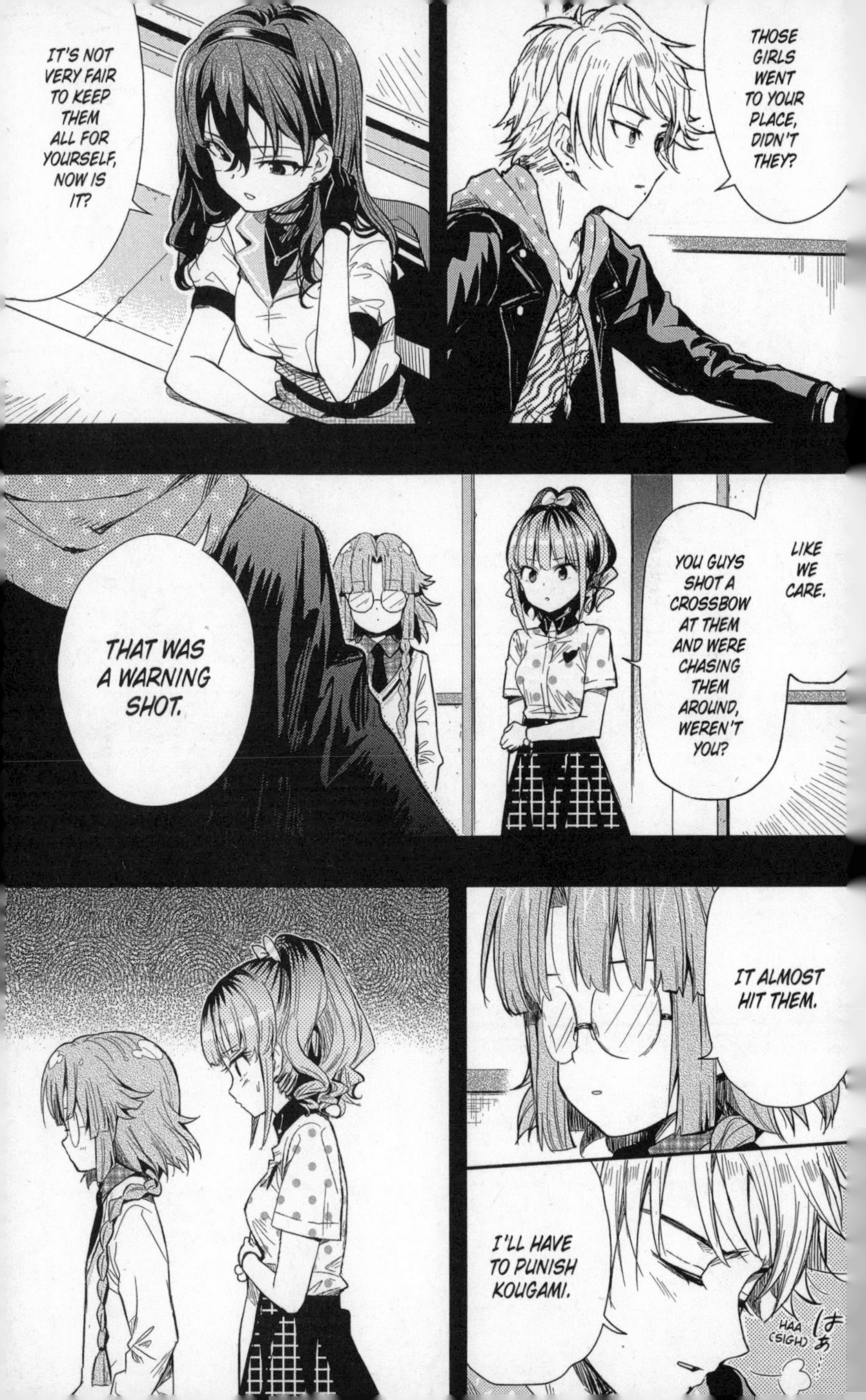
THOSE GIRLS WENT TO YOUR PLACE, DIDN'T THEY?
IT'S NOT VERY FAIR TO KEEP THEM ALL FOR YOURSELF, NOW IS IT?
LIKE WE CARE.
YOU GUYS SHOT A CROSSBOW AT THEM AND WERE CHASING THEM AROUND, WEREN'T YOU?
THAT WAS A WARNING SHOT.
IT ALMOST HIT THEM.
I'LL HAVE TO PUNISH KOUGAMI.
はあ
HAA (SIGH)

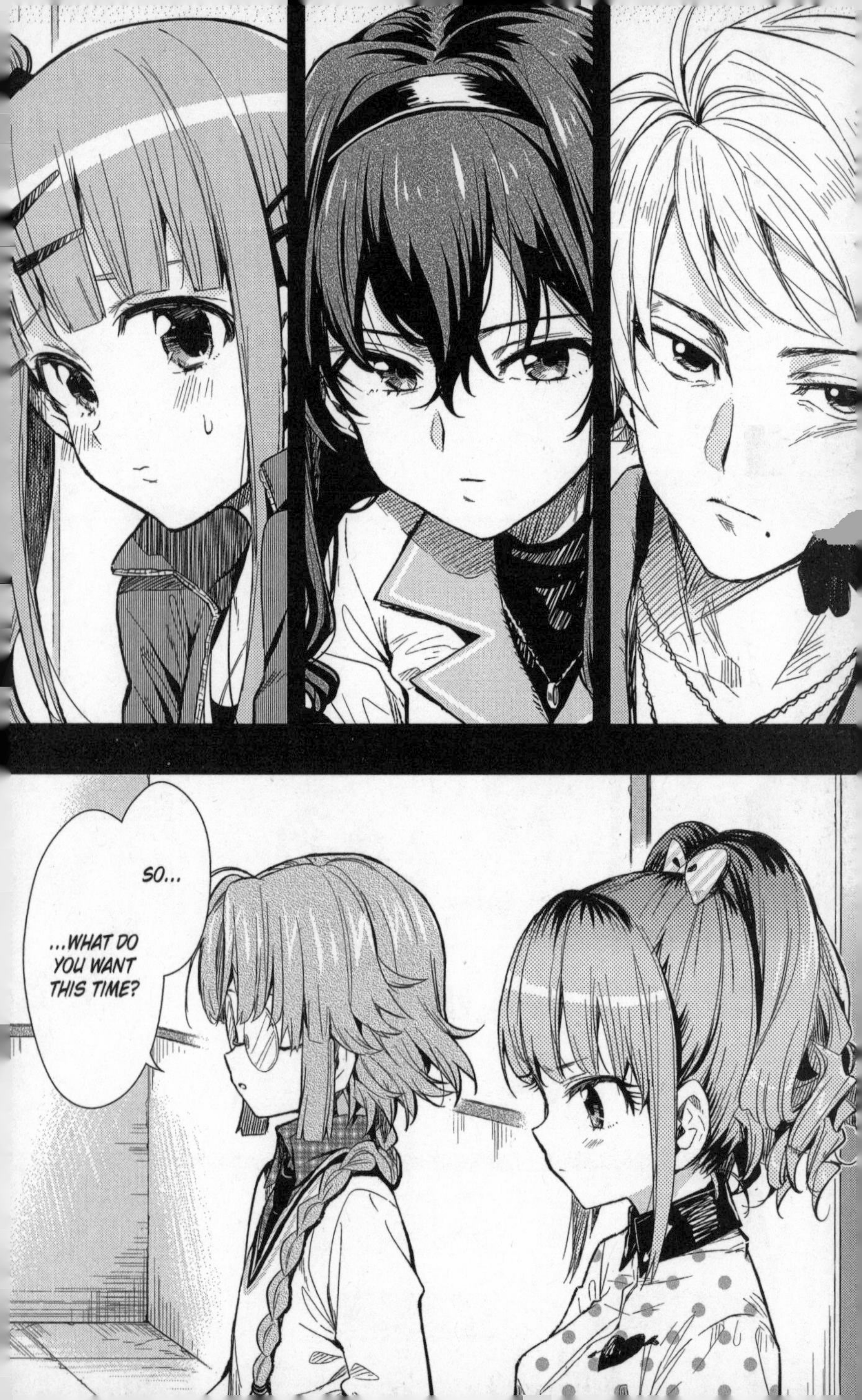
SO...
...WHAT DO YOU WANT THIS TIME?

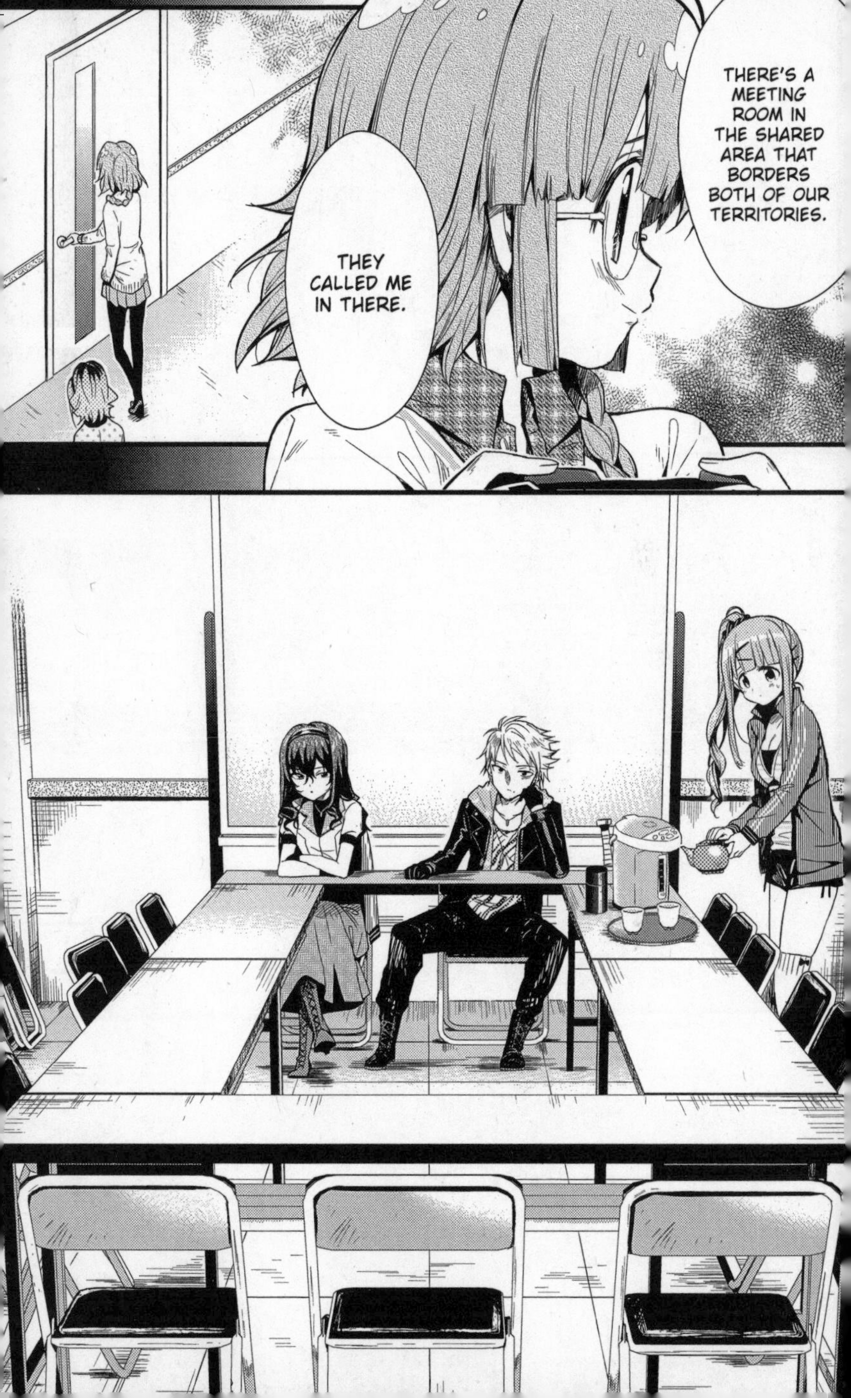
THERE'S A MEETING ROOM IN THE SHARED AREA THAT BORDERS BOTH OF OUR TERRITORIES.
THEY CALLED ME IN THERE.

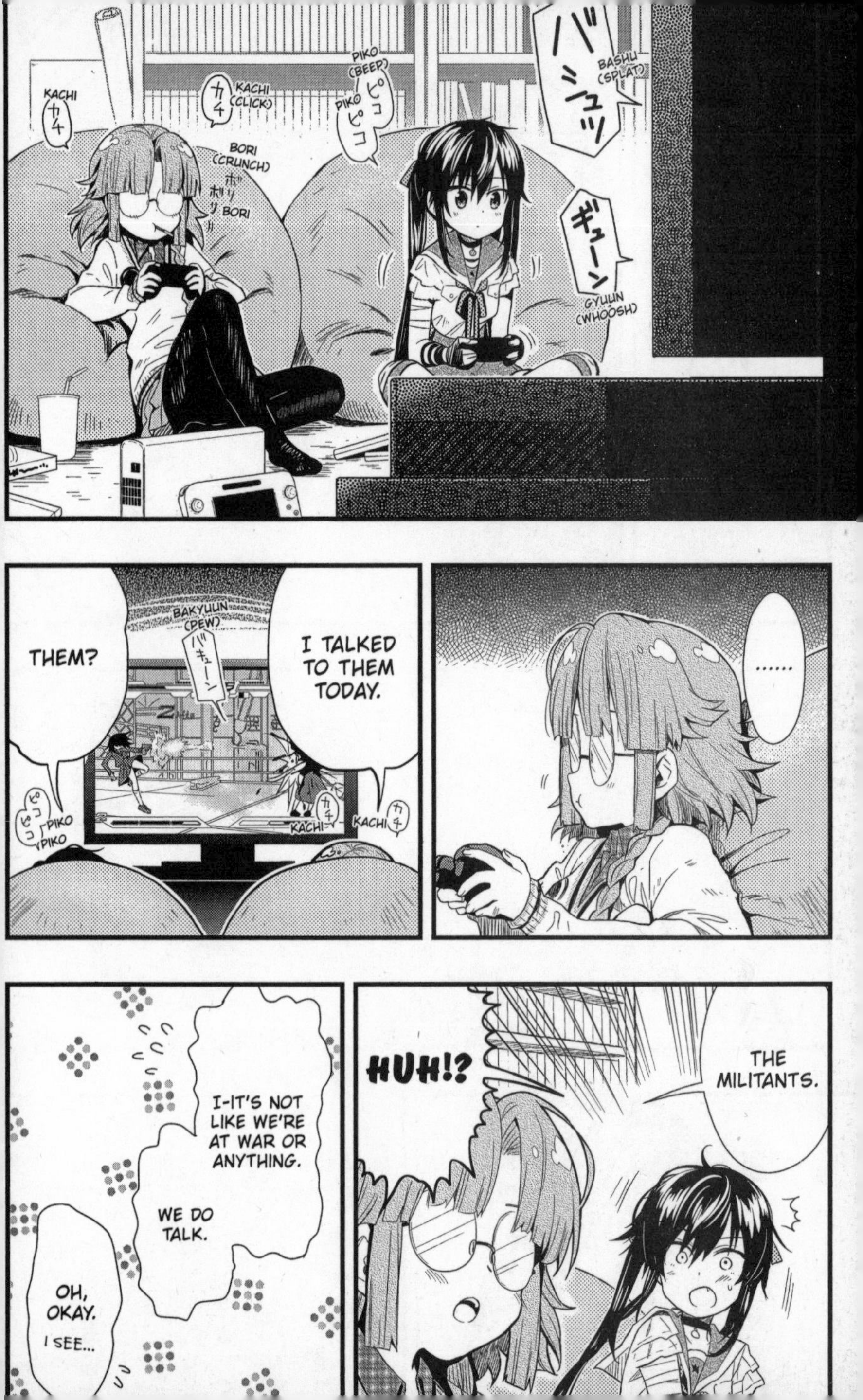

BASHU (SPLAT)
バシュッ
ギューン
GYUUN (WHOOSH)
PIKO (BEEP) PIKO
ピコピコ
KACHI (CLICK)
カチ
BORI (CRUNCH) BORI
ボリボリ
KACHI
カチ
......
I TALKED TO THEM TODAY.
KACHI
カチ
BAKYUUN (PEW)
バキューン
KACHI
カチ
THEM?
PIKO PIKO
ピコピコ
THE MILITANTS.
HUH!?
I-IT'S NOT LIKE WE'RE AT WAR OR ANYTHING.
WE DO TALK.
OH, OKAY.
I SEE...

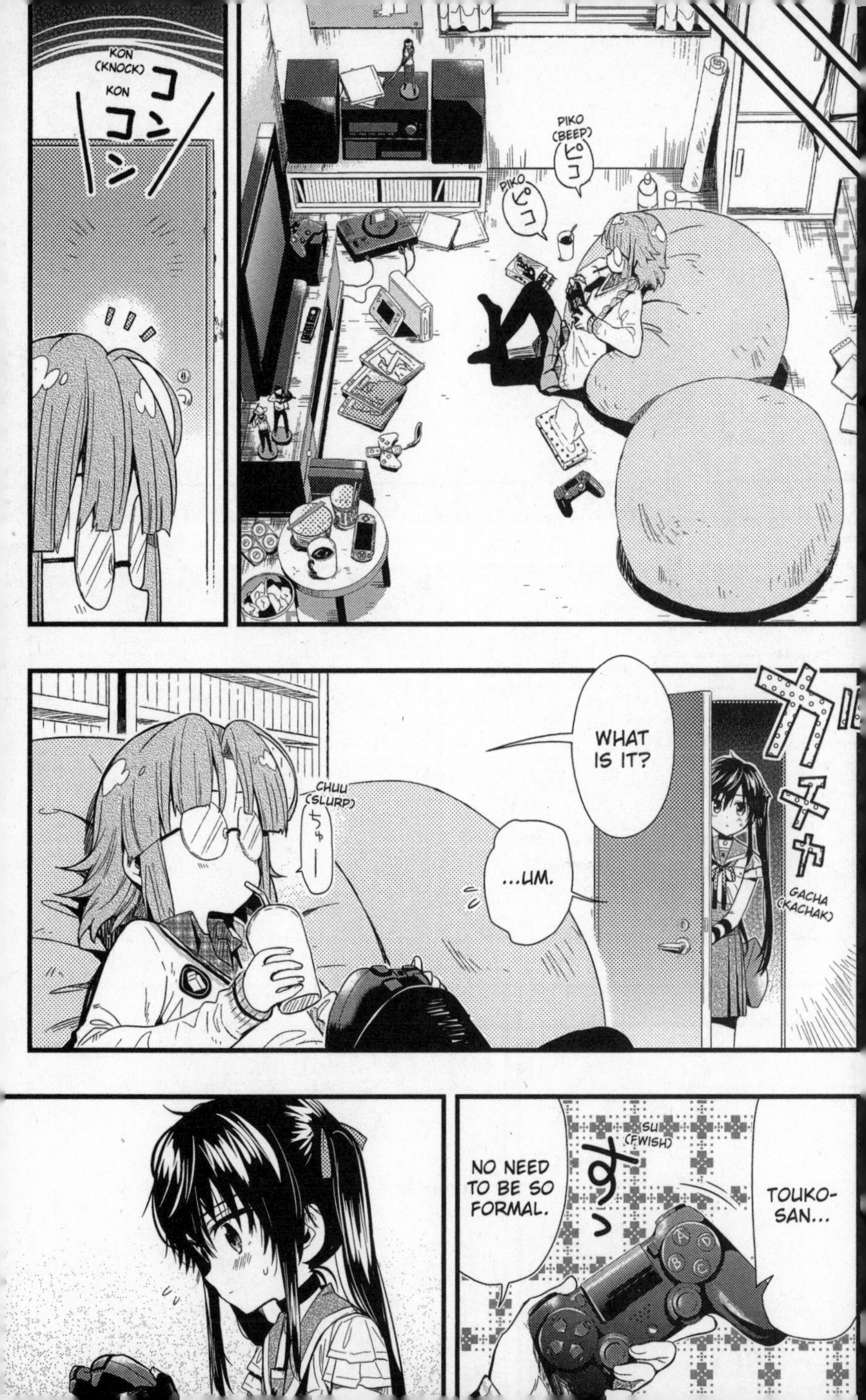
PIKO (BEEP)
ピコ
PIKO
ピコ
KON (KNOCK)
KON
コンコン
GACHA (KACHAK)
ガチャ
WHAT IS IT?
...UM.
CHUU (SLURP)
ちゅー
TOUKO-SAN...
SU (FWISH)
すっ
NO NEED TO BE SO FORMAL.

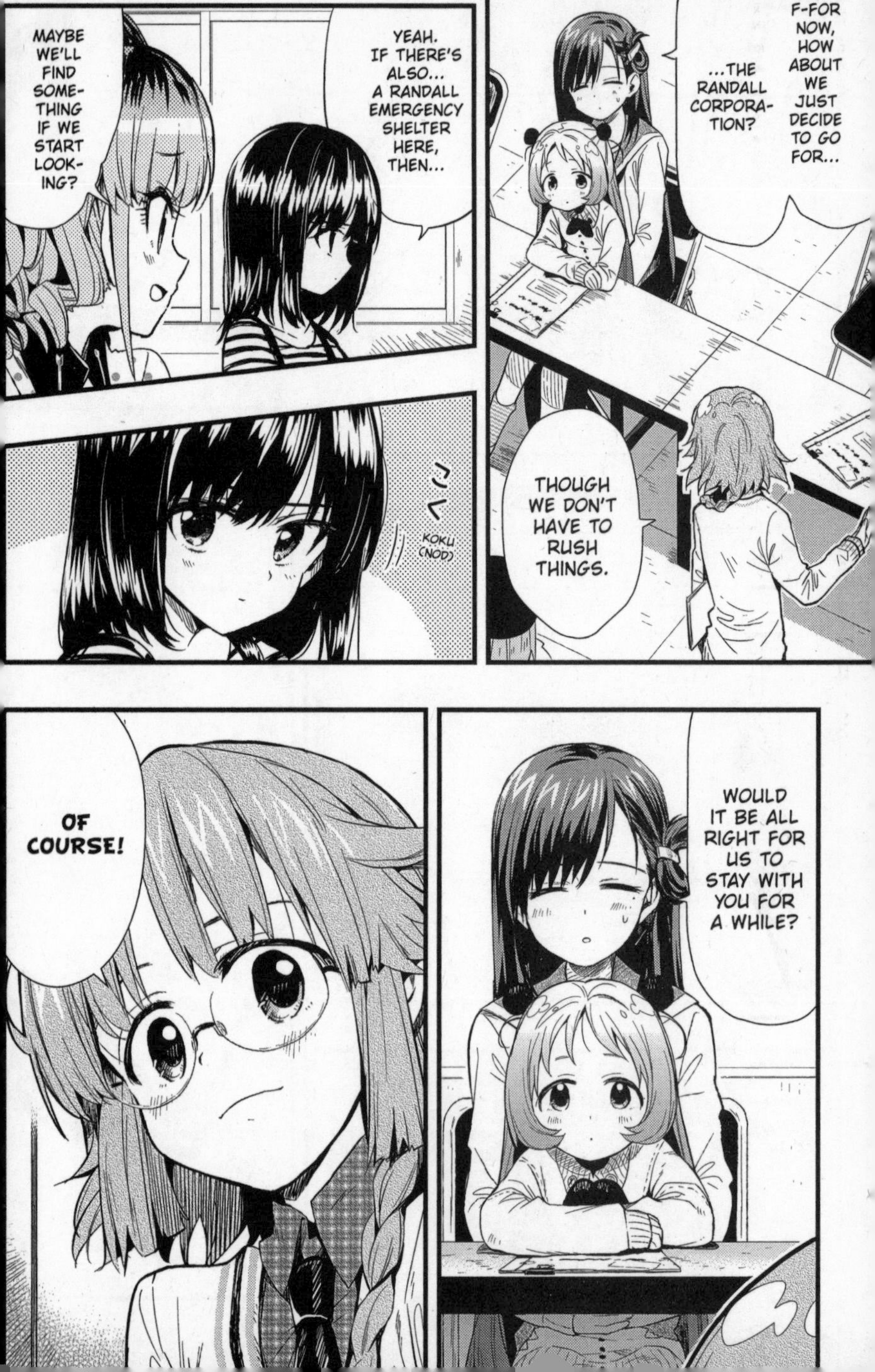
F-FOR NOW, HOW ABOUT WE JUST DECIDE TO GO FOR...
...THE RANDALL CORPORATION?
THOUGH WE DON'T HAVE TO RUSH THINGS.
YEAH. IF THERE'S ALSO... A RANDALL EMERGENCY SHELTER HERE, THEN...
MAYBE WE'LL FIND SOME-THING IF WE START LOOK-ING?
こく
KOKU (NOD)
WOULD IT BE ALL RIGHT FOR US TO STAY WITH YOU FOR A WHILE?
OF COURSE!

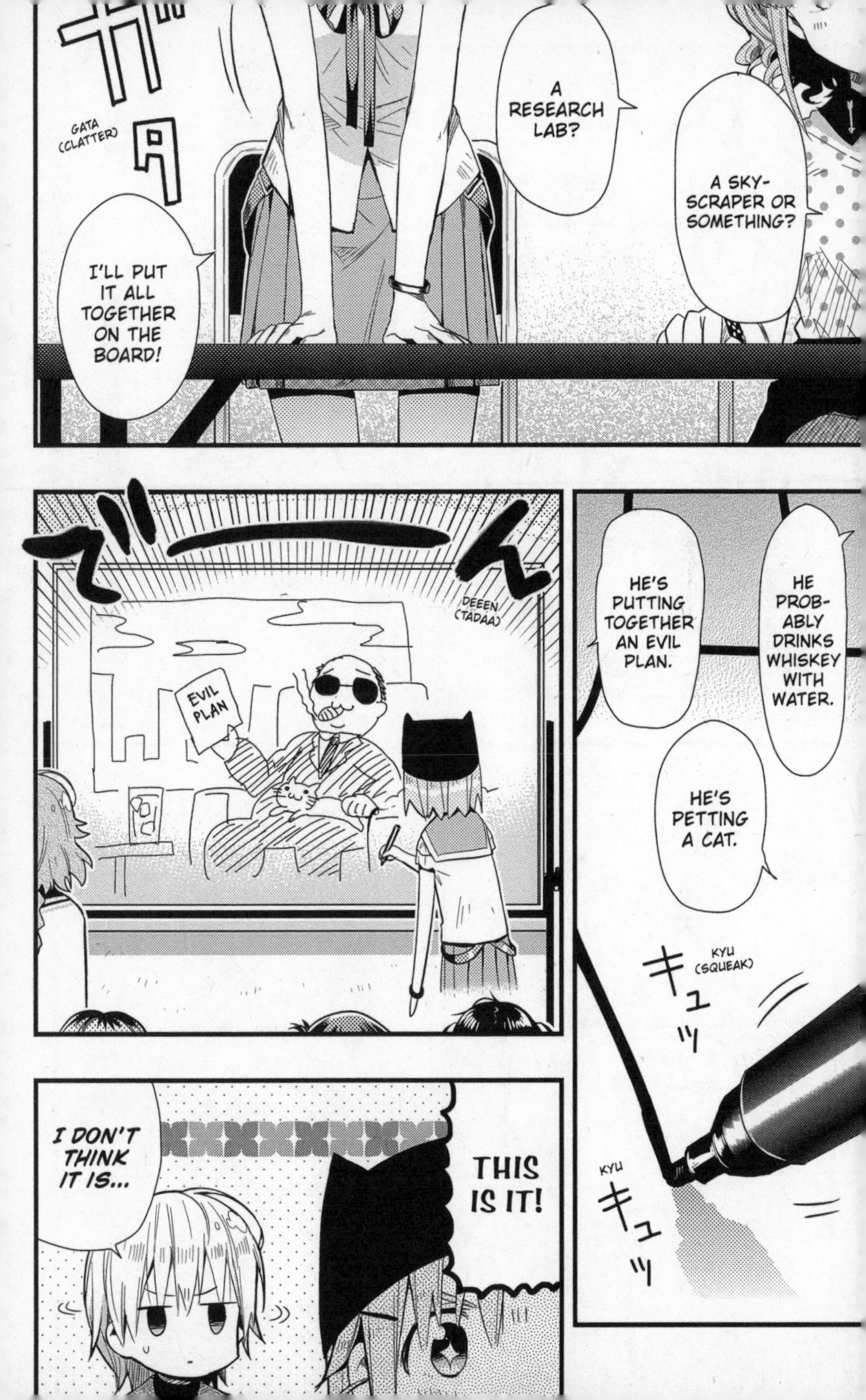
A SKY-SCRAPER OR SOMETHING?
A RESEARCH LAB?
GATA (CLATTER)
I'LL PUT IT ALL TOGETHER ON THE BOARD!
HE PROBABLY DRINKS WHISKEY WITH WATER.
HE'S PUTTING TOGETHER AN EVIL PLAN.
HE'S PETTING A CAT.
KYU (SQUEAK)
KYU
DEEEN (TADAA)
EVIL PLAN
THIS IS IT!
I DON'T THINK IT IS...

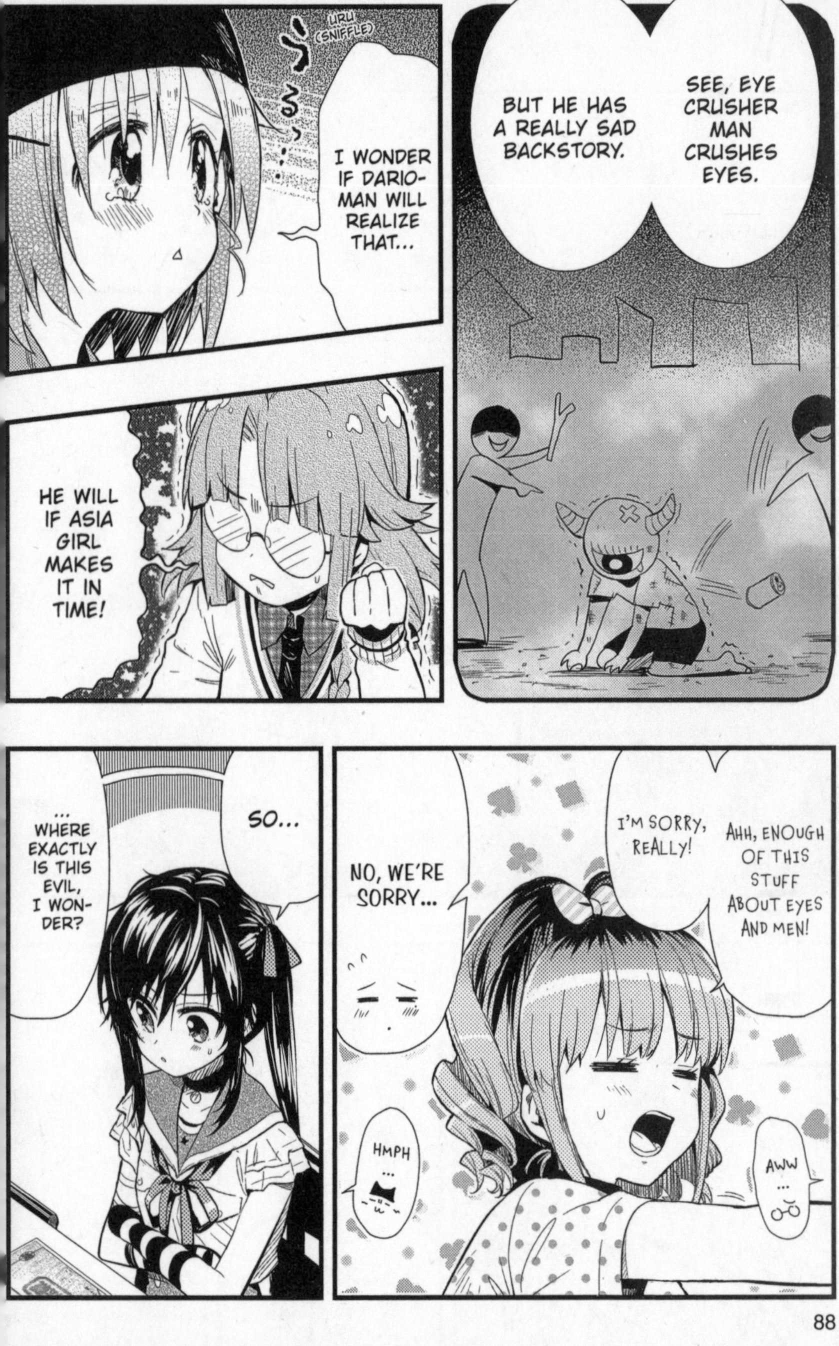
SEE, EYE CRUSHER MAN CRUSHES EYES.
BUT HE HAS A REALLY SAD BACKSTORY.
URU (SNIFFLE)
うる…
I WONDER IF DARIO-MAN WILL REALIZE THAT...
HE WILL IF ASIA GIRL MAKES IT IN TIME!
AHH, ENOUGH OF THIS STUFF ABOUT EYES AND MEN!
I'M SORRY, REALLY!
NO, WE'RE SORRY...
AWW ...
HMPH ...
SO...
... WHERE EXACTLY IS THIS EVIL, I WONDER?

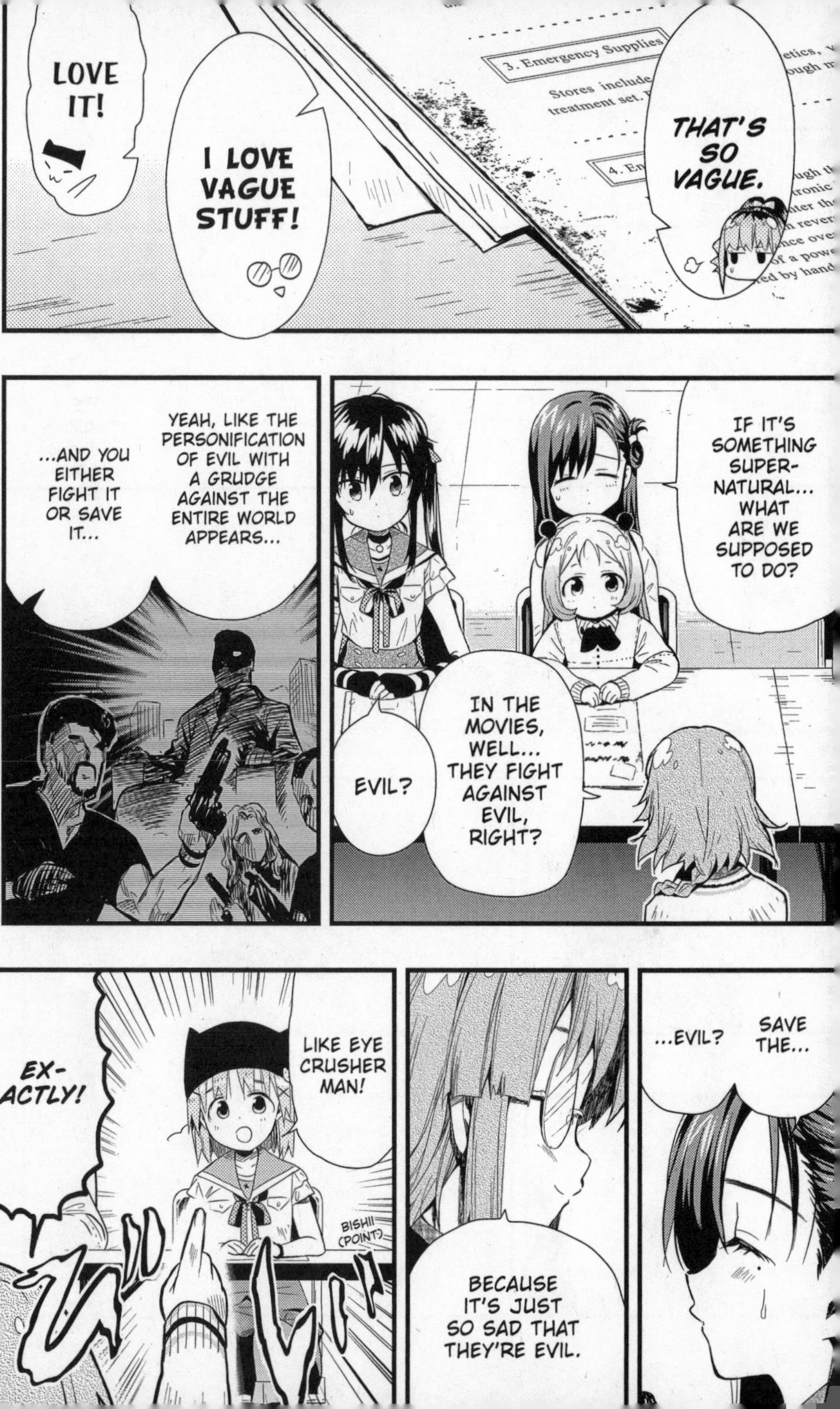
3. Emergency Supplies
THAT'S SO VAGUE.
I LOVE VAGUE STUFF!
LOVE IT!
IF IT'S SOMETHING SUPER-NATURAL... WHAT ARE WE SUPPOSED TO DO?
IN THE MOVIES, WELL... THEY FIGHT AGAINST EVIL, RIGHT?
EVIL?
YEAH, LIKE THE PERSONIFICATION OF EVIL WITH A GRUDGE AGAINST THE ENTIRE WORLD APPEARS...
...AND YOU EITHER FIGHT IT OR SAVE IT...
SAVE THE...
...EVIL?
BECAUSE IT'S JUST SO SAD THAT THEY'RE EVIL.
LIKE EYE CRUSHER MAN!
EX-ACTLY!
BISHI! (POINT)

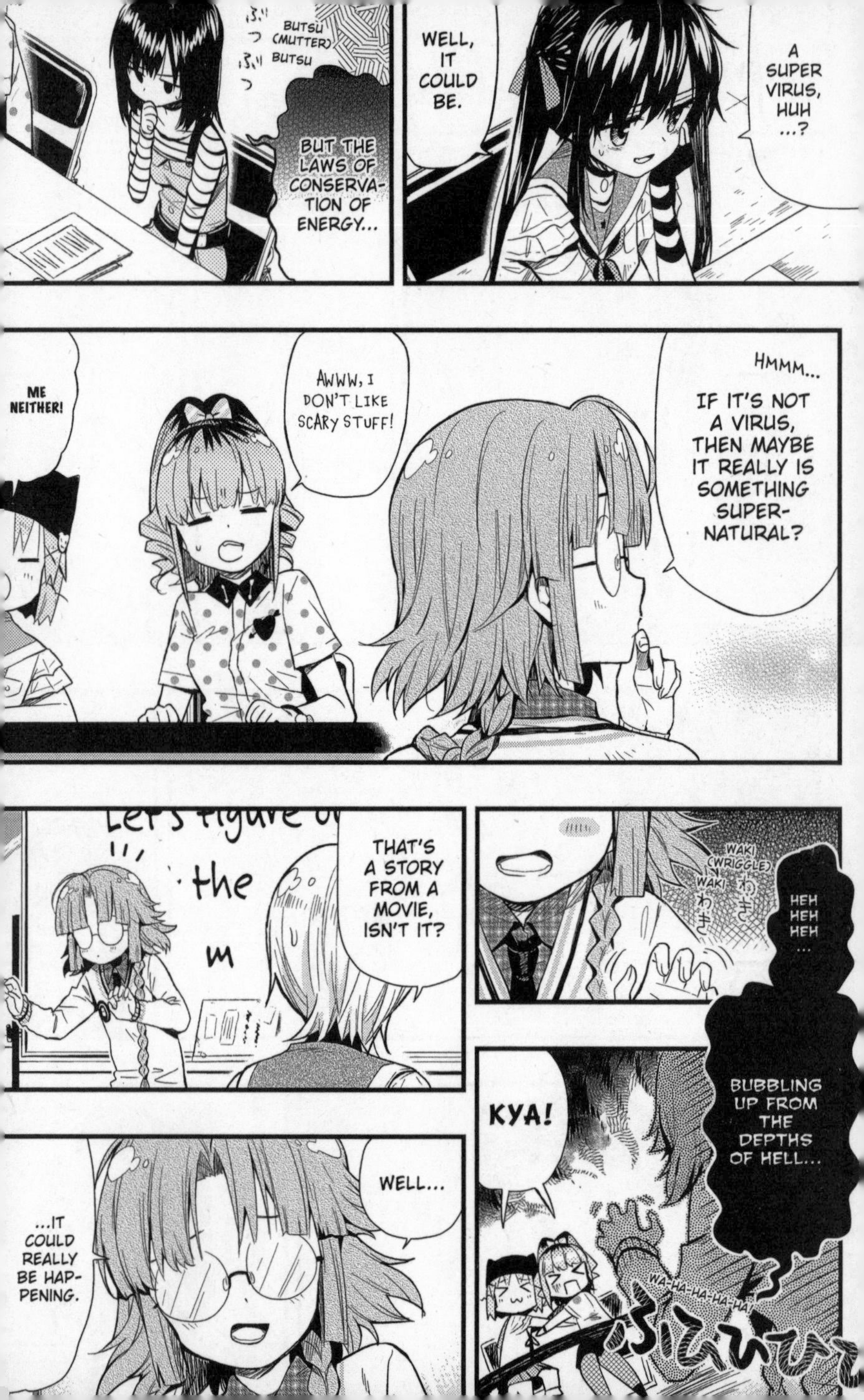
A SUPER VIRUS, HUH ...?
WELL, IT COULD BE.
ぶつぶつ
BUTSU (MUTTER) BUTSU
BUT THE LAWS OF CONSERVATION OF ENERGY...
HMMM... IF IT'S NOT A VIRUS, THEN MAYBE IT REALLY IS SOMETHING SUPER-NATURAL?
AWWW, I DON'T LIKE SCARY STUFF!
ME NEITHER!
わきわき
WAKI (WRIGGLE) WAKI
HEH HEH HEH ...
BUBBLING UP FROM THE DEPTHS OF HELL...
KYA!
WA-HA-HA-HA-HA!
THAT'S A STORY FROM A MOVIE, ISN'T IT?
WELL...
...IT COULD REALLY BE HAP-PENING.

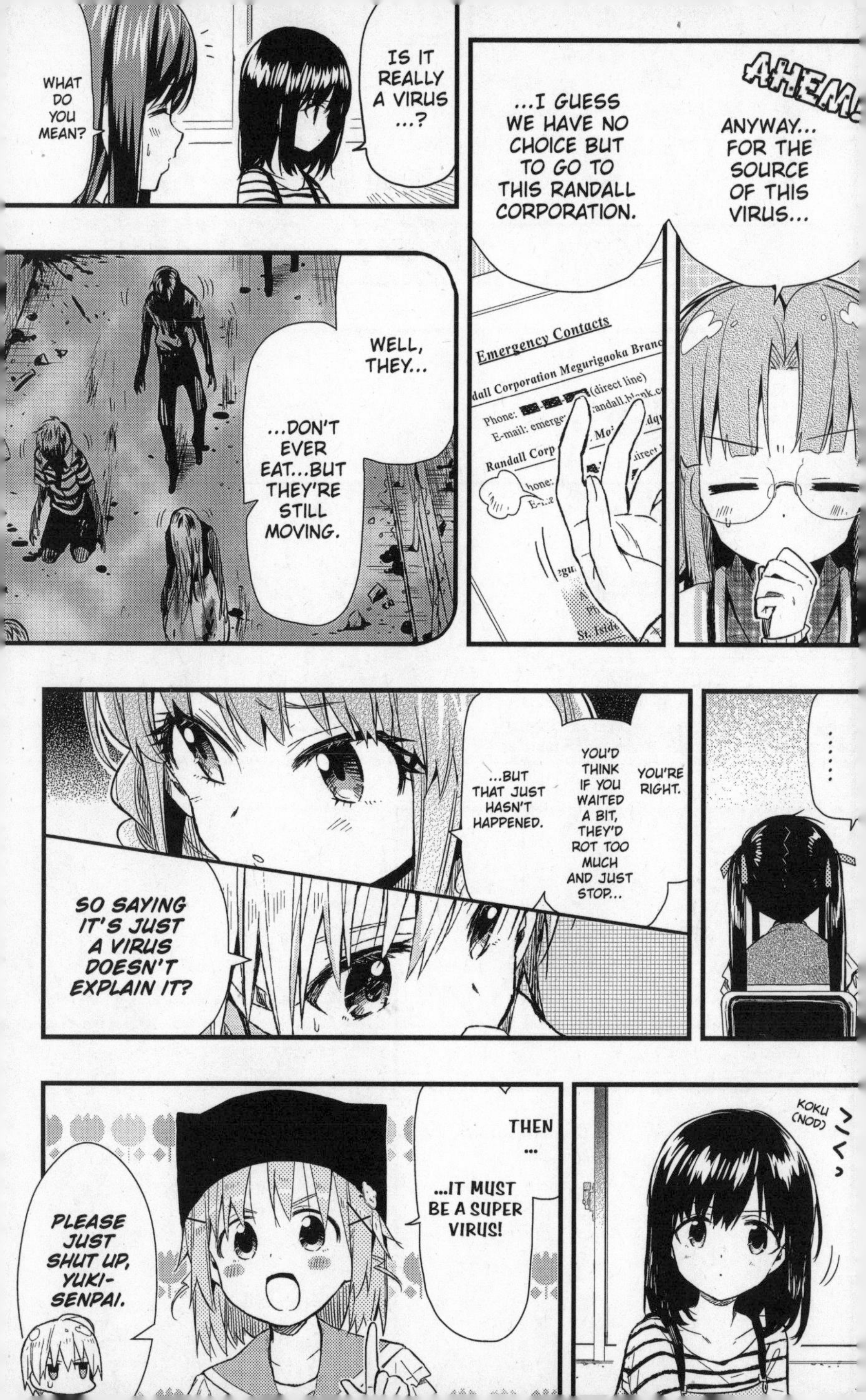
AHEM!
ANYWAY... FOR THE SOURCE OF THIS VIRUS...
...I GUESS WE HAVE NO CHOICE BUT TO GO TO THIS RANDALL CORPORATION.
Emergency Contacts
dall Corporation Megurigaoka Branc
Phone: [redacted](direct line)
IS IT REALLY A VIRUS ...?
WHAT DO YOU MEAN?
WELL, THEY...
...DON'T EVER EAT...BUT THEY'RE STILL MOVING.
......
YOU'RE RIGHT.
YOU'D THINK IF YOU WAITED A BIT, THEY'D ROT TOO MUCH AND JUST STOP...
...BUT THAT JUST HASN'T HAPPENED.
SO SAYING IT'S JUST A VIRUS DOESN'T EXPLAIN IT?
KOKU (NOD)
THEN ...
...IT MUST BE A SUPER VIRUS!
PLEASE JUST SHUT UP, YUKI-SENPAI.

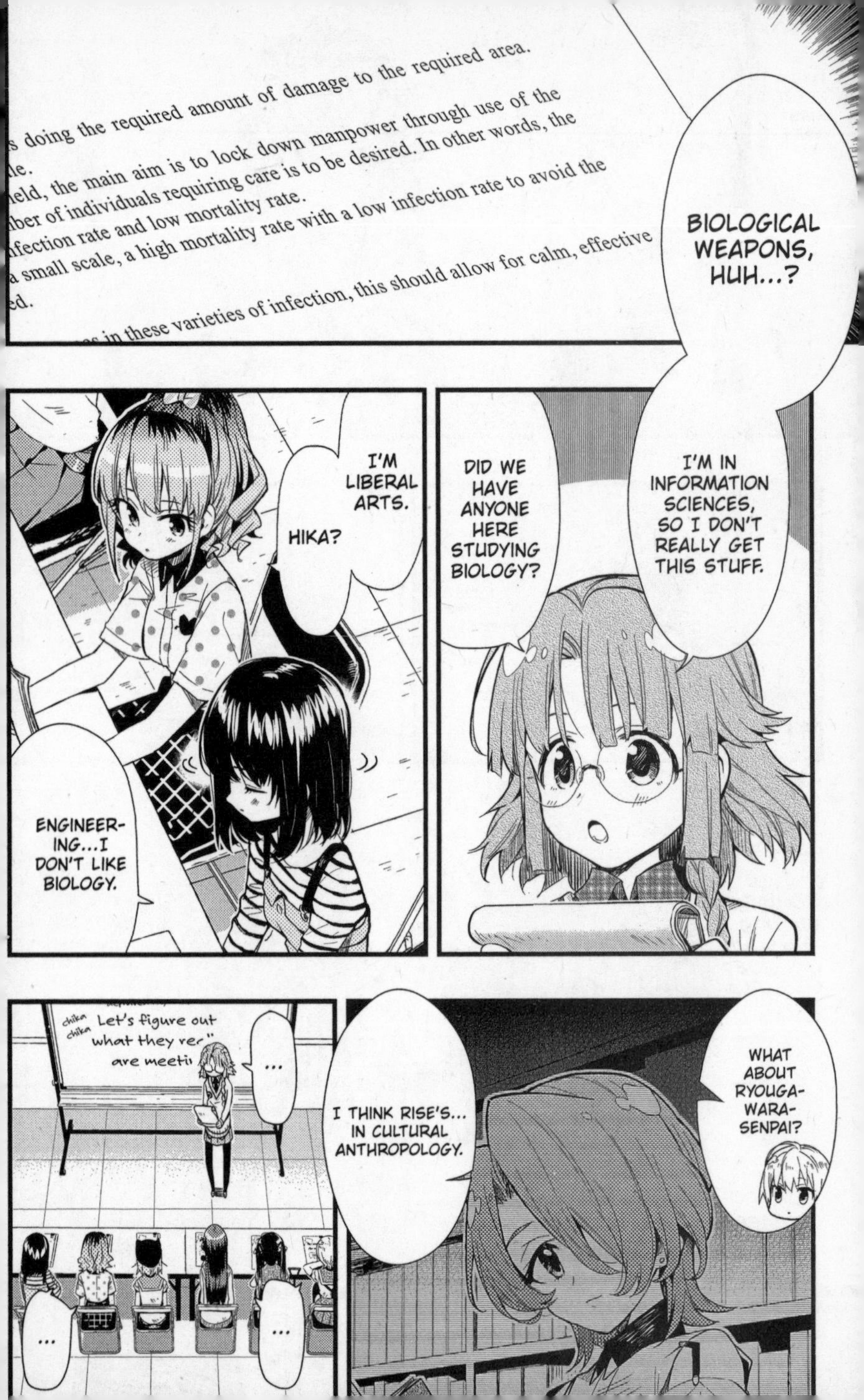
s doing the required amount of damage to the required area.
ne.
neld, the main aim is to lock down manpower through use of the
nber of individuals requiring care is to be desired. In other words, the
nfection rate and low mortality rate.
a small scale, a high mortality rate with a low infection rate to avoid the
ed.
in these varieties of infection, this should allow for calm, effective
BIOLOGICAL WEAPONS, HUH...?
I'M IN INFORMATION SCIENCES, SO I DON'T REALLY GET THIS STUFF.
DID WE HAVE ANYONE HERE STUDYING BIOLOGY?
I'M LIBERAL ARTS.
HIKA?
ENGINEERING...I DON'T LIKE BIOLOGY.
WHAT ABOUT RYOUGAWARA-SENPAI?
I THINK RISE'S... IN CULTURAL ANTHROPOLOGY.
chika chika
Let's figure out
what they re
are meeti
...
...
...

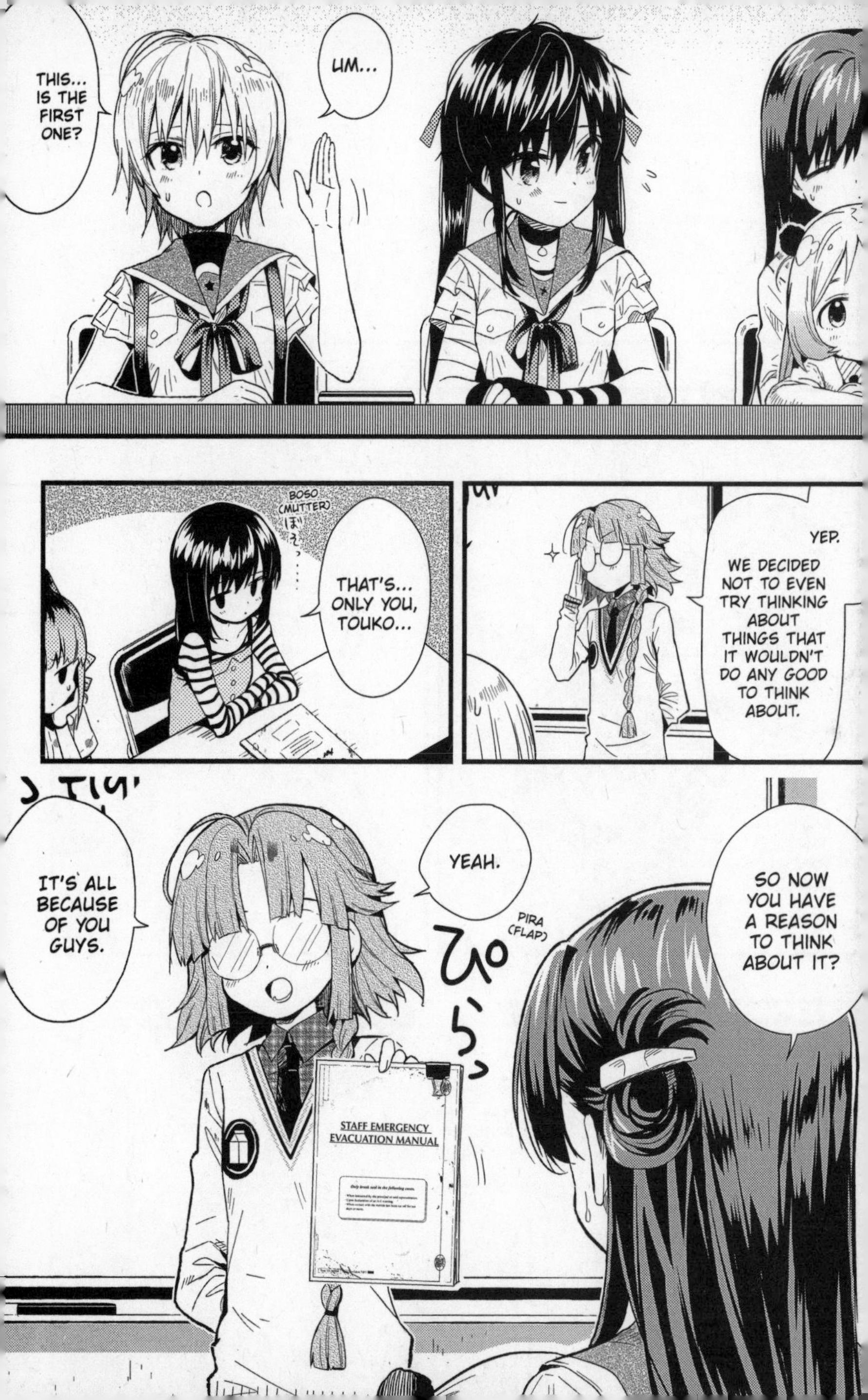
UM...
THIS... IS THE FIRST ONE?
YEP.
WE DECIDED NOT TO EVEN TRY THINKING ABOUT THINGS THAT IT WOULDN'T DO ANY GOOD TO THINK ABOUT.
BOSO (MUTTER)
ぼそっ…
THAT'S... ONLY YOU, TOUKO...
SO NOW YOU HAVE A REASON TO THINK ABOUT IT?
PIRA (FLAP)
ぴらっ
YEAH.
IT'S ALL BECAUSE OF YOU GUYS.
STAFF EMERGENCY EVACUATION MANUAL

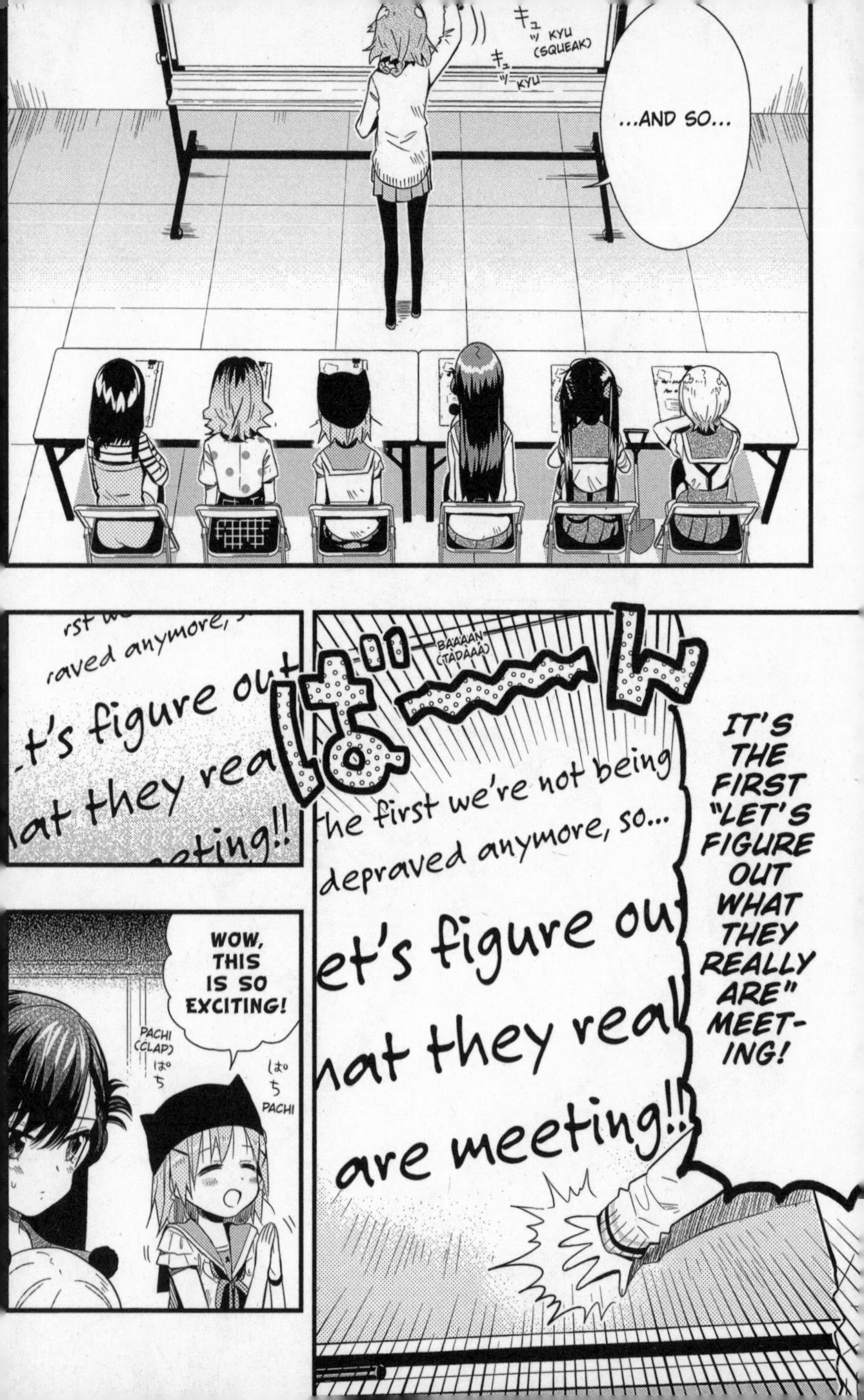
...AND SO...
キュッ
KYU (SQUEAK)
キュッ
KYU
BAAAAN (TADAAA)
IT'S THE FIRST "LET'S FIGURE OUT WHAT THEY REALLY ARE" MEETING!
he first we're not being
depraved anymore, so...
et's figure ou
hat they real
are meeting!!
rst we
raved anymore, s
t's figure ou
at they rea
eting!!
WOW, THIS IS SO EXCITING!
PACHI (CLAP)
ぱち
ぱち
PACHI

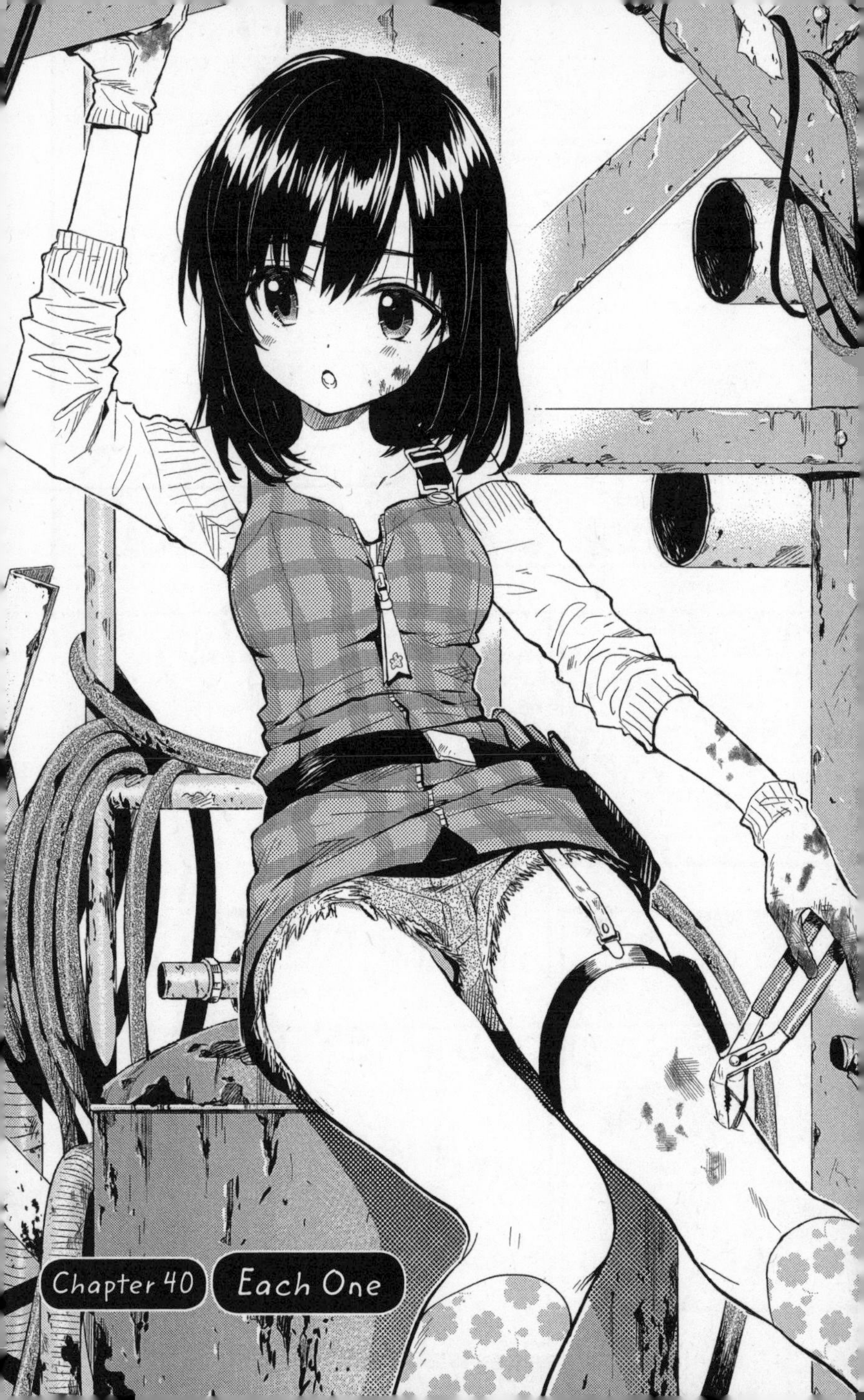
Chapter 40
Each One

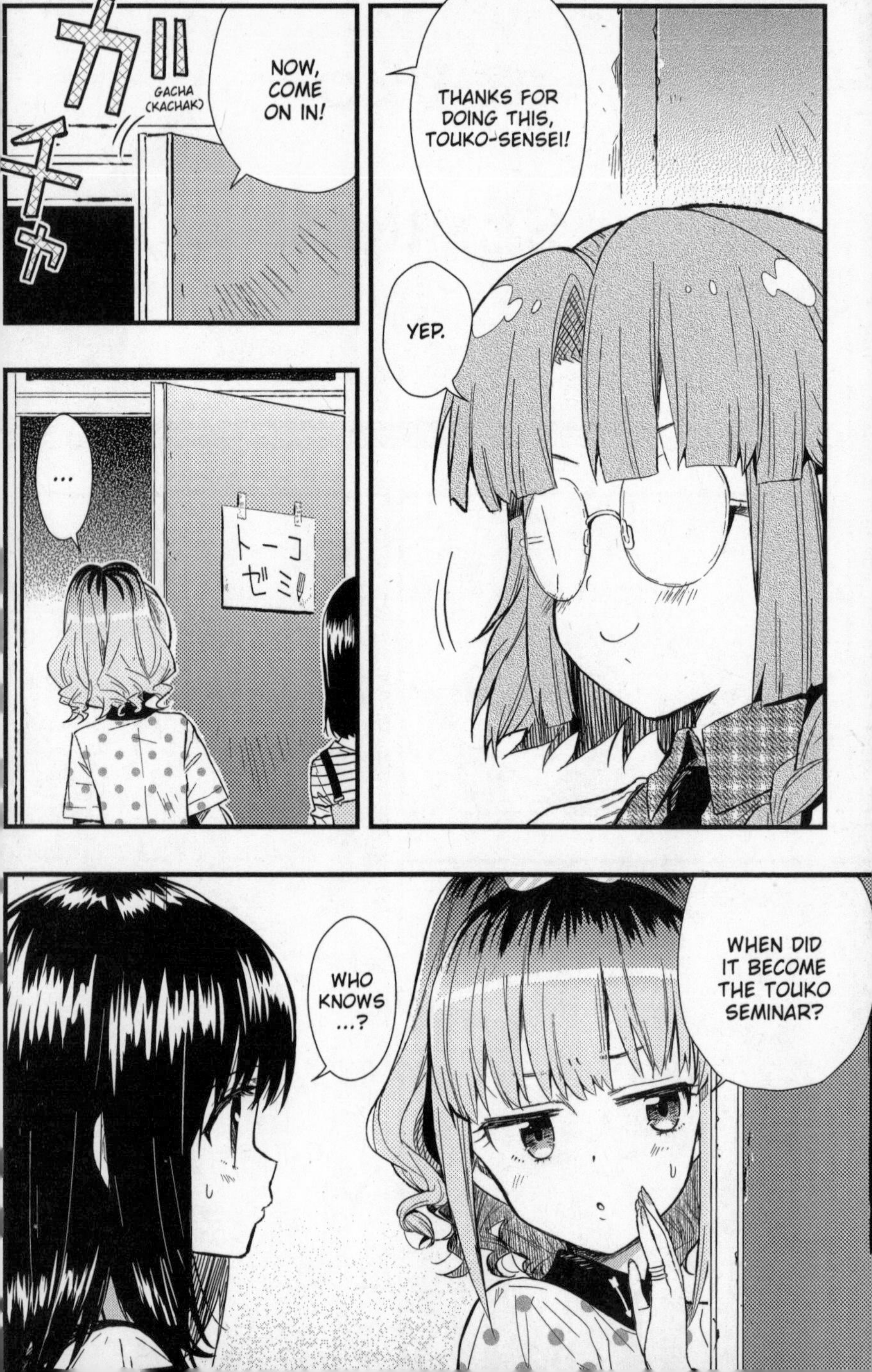
THANKS FOR DOING THIS, TOUKO-SENSEI!
YEP.
カチャ
GACHA (KACHAK)
NOW, COME ON IN!
...
トーコゼミ
WHEN DID IT BECOME THE TOUKO SEMINAR?
WHO KNOWS ...?

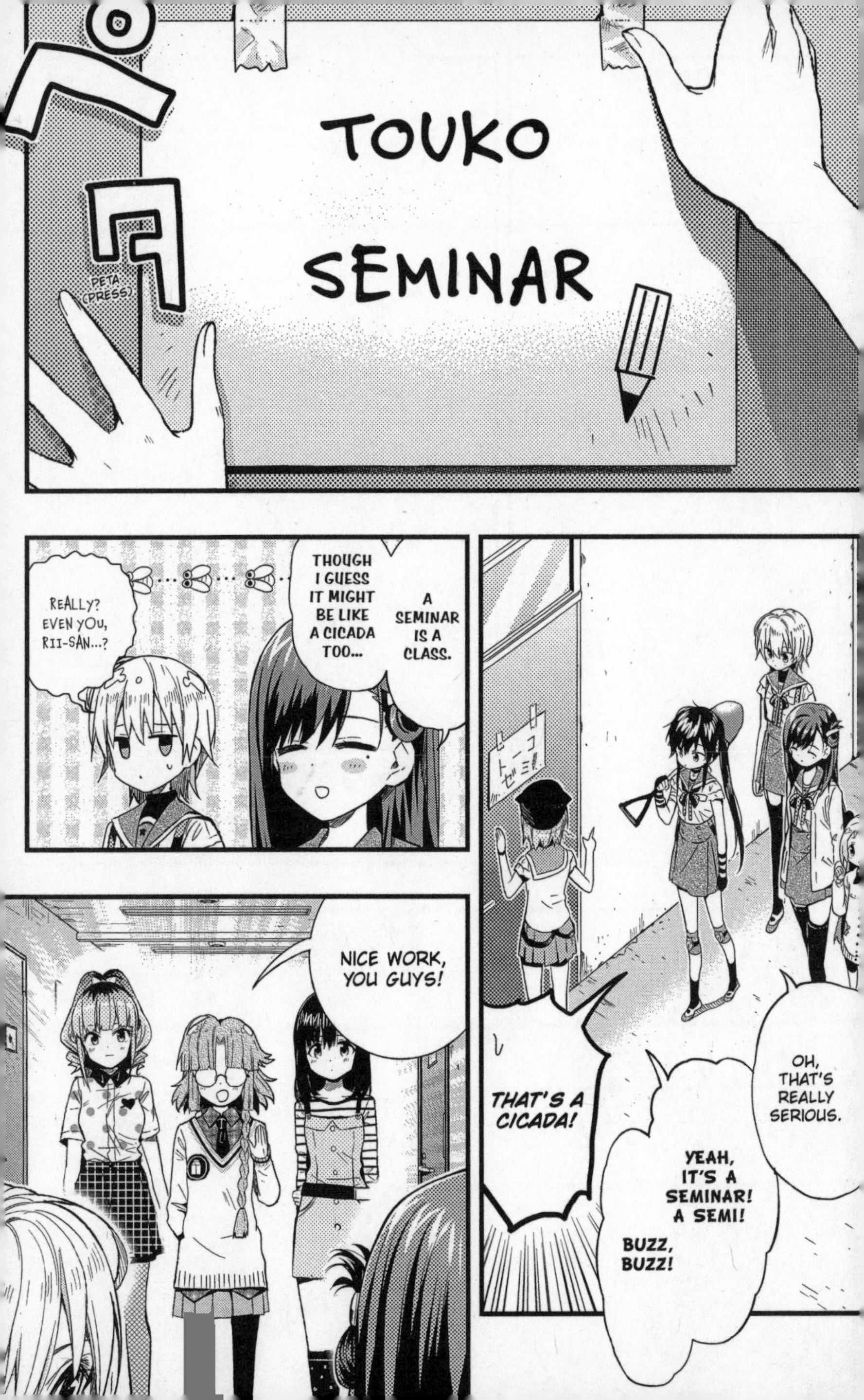

TOUKO SEMINAR
PETA (PRESS)
OH, THAT'S REALLY SERIOUS.
YEAH, IT'S A SEMINAR! A SEMI!
BUZZ, BUZZ!
THAT'S A CICADA!
A SEMINAR IS A CLASS.
THOUGH I GUESS IT MIGHT BE LIKE A CICADA TOO...
REALLY? EVEN YOU, RII-SAN...?
NICE WORK, YOU GUYS!

SCHOOL-LIVE!

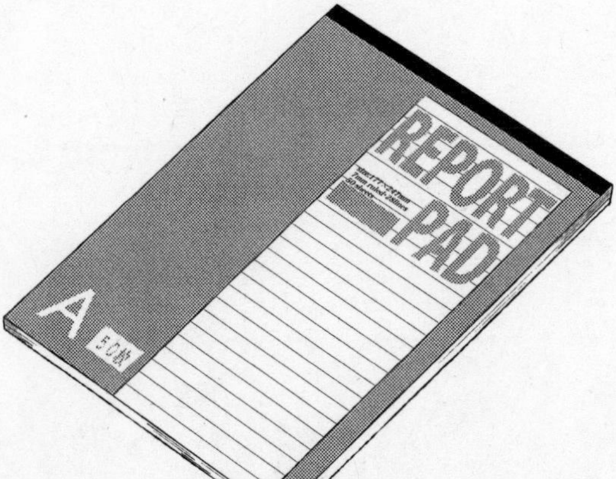
REPORT
PAD
A

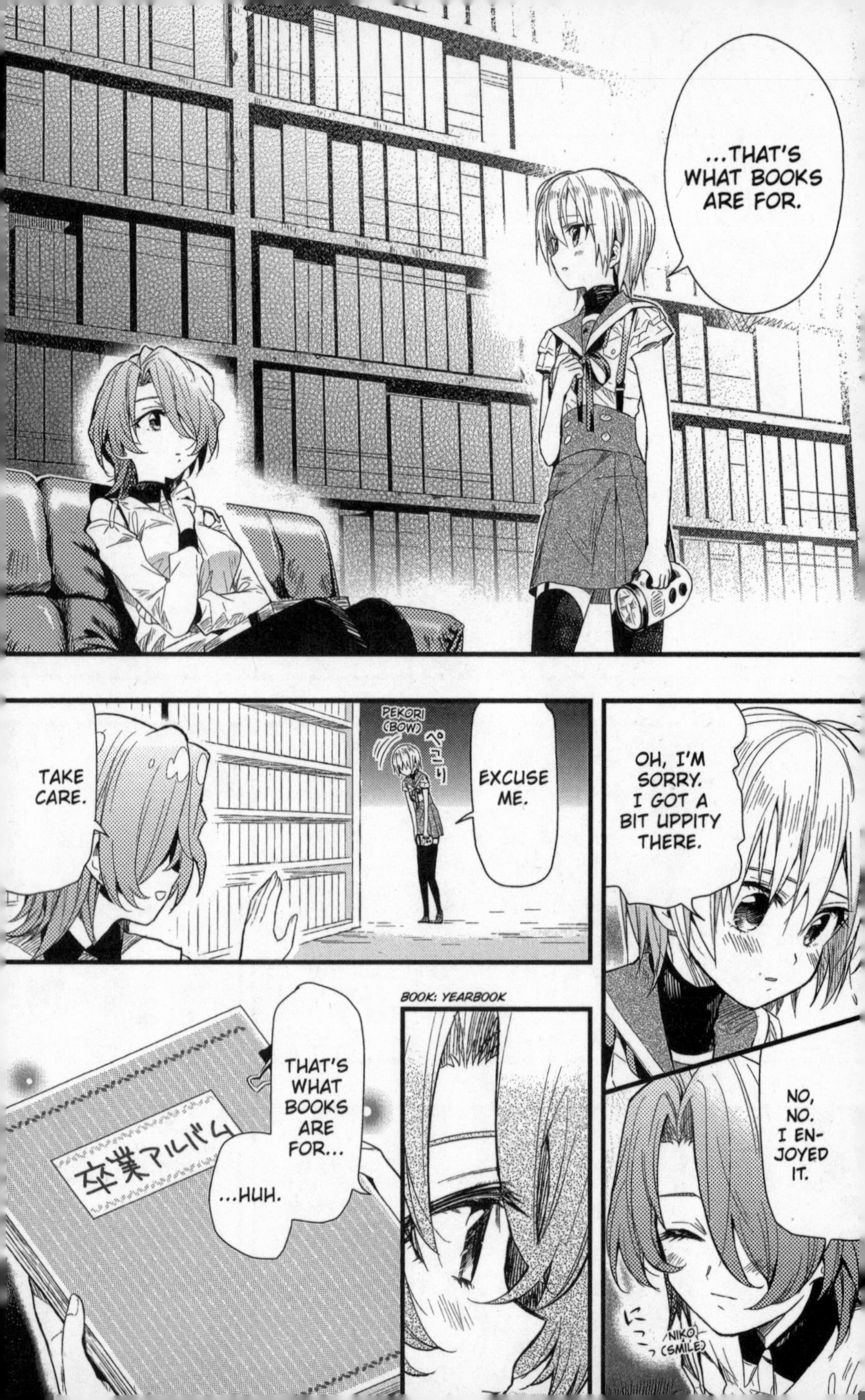
...THAT'S WHAT BOOKS ARE FOR.
OH, I'M SORRY. I GOT A BIT UPPITY THERE.
NO, NO. I ENJOYED IT.
にこっ
NIKO (SMILE)
ぺこり
PEKORI (BOW)
EXCUSE ME.
TAKE CARE.
BOOK: YEARBOOK
卒業アルバム
THAT'S WHAT BOOKS ARE FOR...
...HUH.

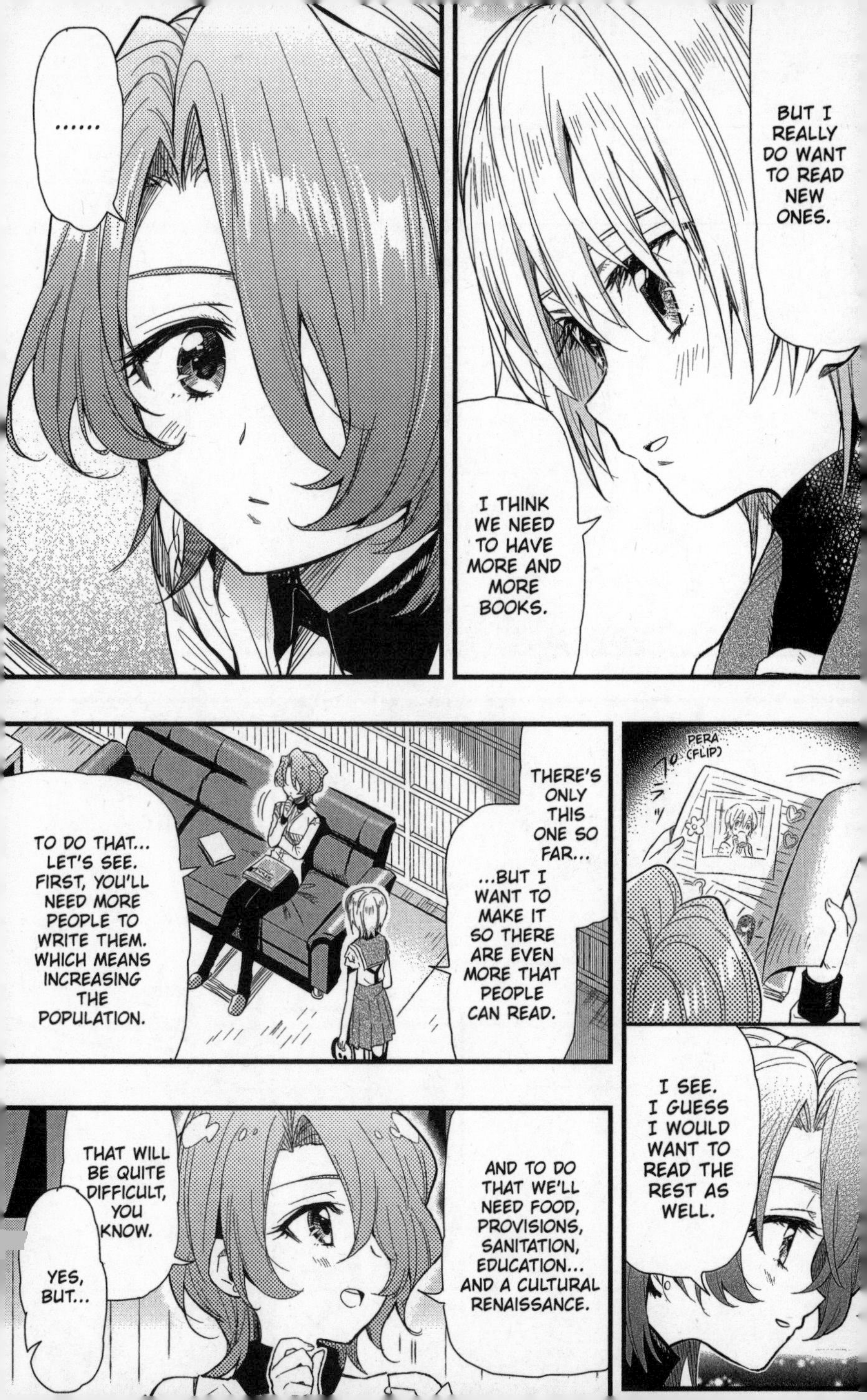
BUT I REALLY DO WANT TO READ NEW ONES.
I THINK WE NEED TO HAVE MORE AND MORE BOOKS.
......
PERA (FLIP)
THERE'S ONLY THIS ONE SO FAR...
...BUT I WANT TO MAKE IT SO THERE ARE EVEN MORE THAT PEOPLE CAN READ.
TO DO THAT... LET'S SEE. FIRST, YOU'LL NEED MORE PEOPLE TO WRITE THEM. WHICH MEANS INCREASING THE POPULATION.
I SEE. I GUESS I WOULD WANT TO READ THE REST AS WELL.
AND TO DO THAT WE'LL NEED FOOD, PROVISIONS, SANITATION, EDUCATION... AND A CULTURAL RENAISSANCE.
THAT WILL BE QUITE DIFFICULT, YOU KNOW.
YES, BUT...

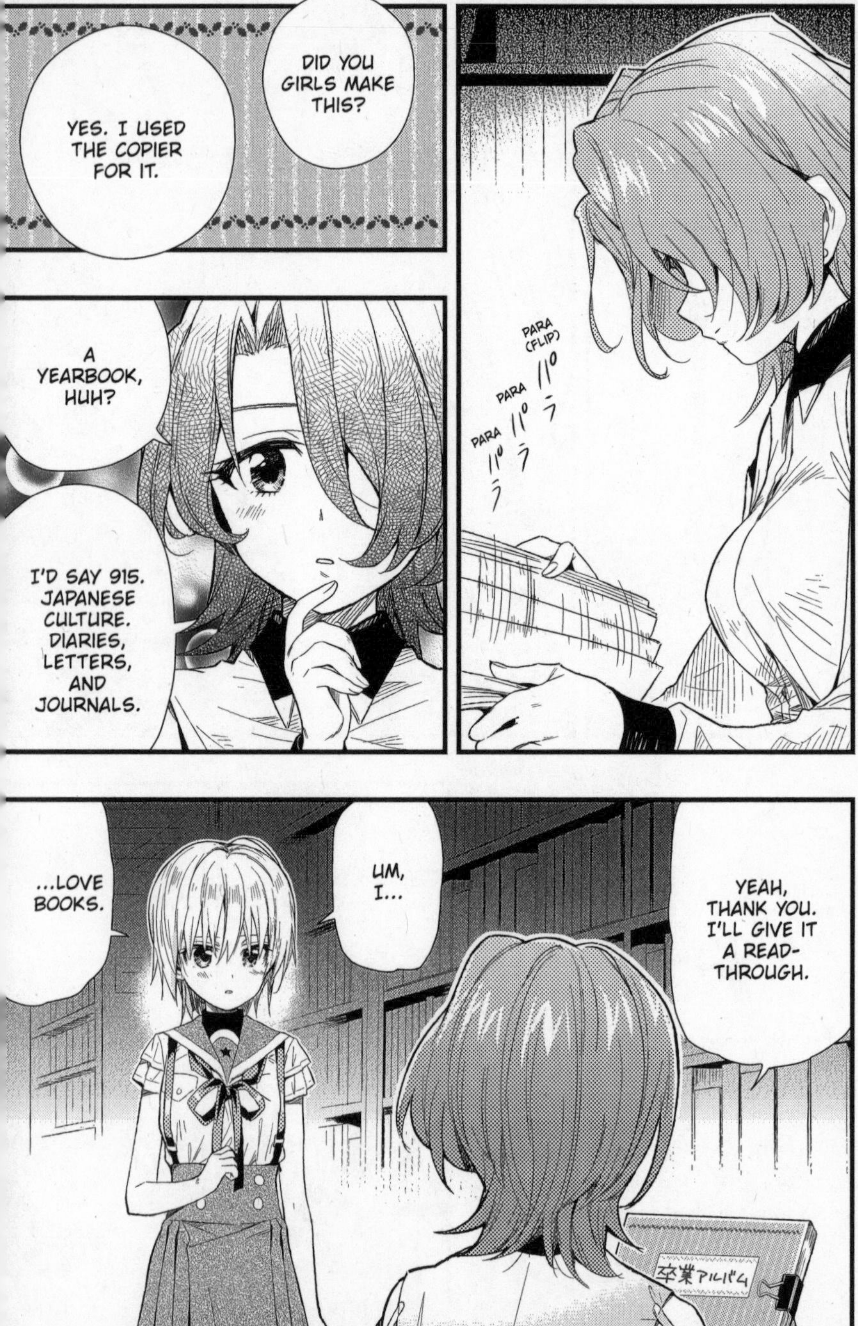
PARA (FLIP)
パラ
PARA
パラ
PARA
パラ
DID YOU GIRLS MAKE THIS?
YES. I USED THE COPIER FOR IT.
A YEARBOOK, HUH?
I'D SAY 915. JAPANESE CULTURE. DIARIES, LETTERS, AND JOURNALS.
YEAH, THANK YOU. I'LL GIVE IT A READ-THROUGH.
卒業アルバム
UM, I...
...LOVE BOOKS.

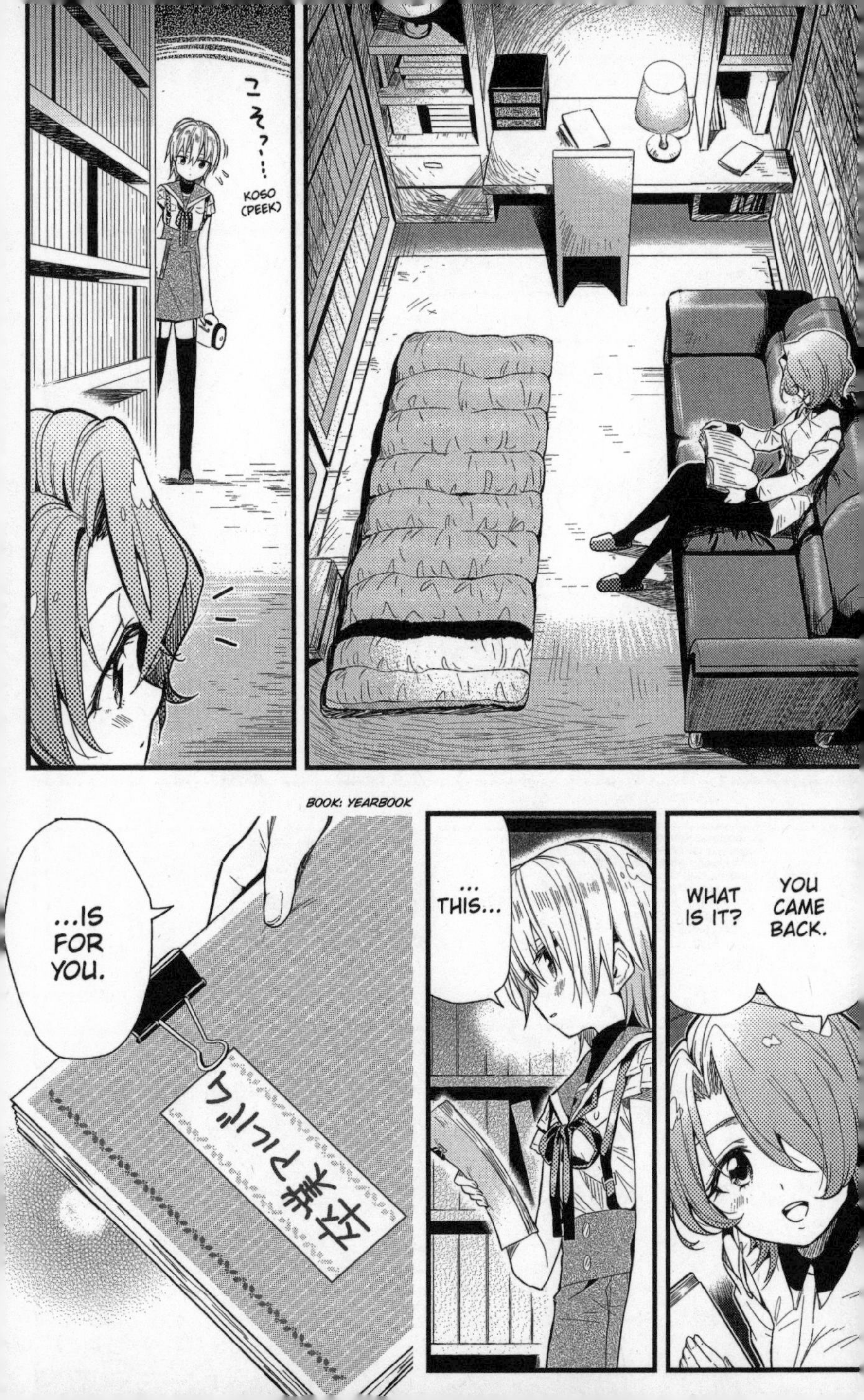
こそっ…
KOSO (PEEK)
BOOK: YEARBOOK
YOU CAME BACK.
WHAT IS IT?
... THIS...
...IS FOR YOU.
卒業アルバム

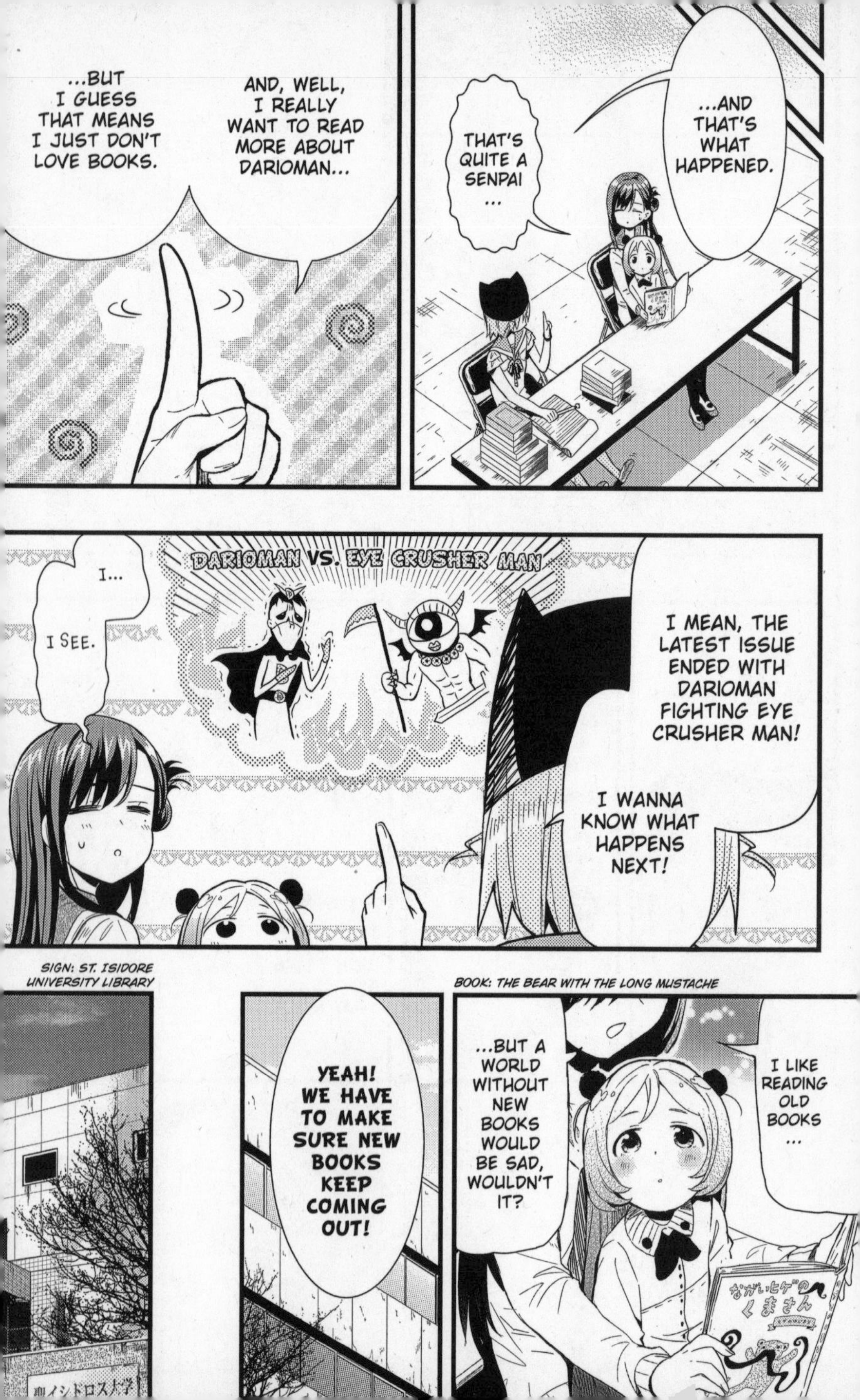
...AND THAT'S WHAT HAPPENED.
THAT'S QUITE A SENPAI ...
AND, WELL, I REALLY WANT TO READ MORE ABOUT DARIOMAN...
...BUT I GUESS THAT MEANS I JUST DON'T LOVE BOOKS.
I MEAN, THE LATEST ISSUE ENDED WITH DARIOMAN FIGHTING EYE CRUSHER MAN!
I WANNA KNOW WHAT HAPPENS NEXT!
DARIOMAN VS. EYE CRUSHER MAN
I... I SEE.
BOOK: THE BEAR WITH THE LONG MUSTACHE
I LIKE READING OLD BOOKS ...
...BUT A WORLD WITHOUT NEW BOOKS WOULD BE SAD, WOULDN'T IT?
ながいヒゲのくまさん
YEAH! WE HAVE TO MAKE SURE NEW BOOKS KEEP COMING OUT!
SIGN: ST. ISIDORE UNIVERSITY LIBRARY
イシドロス大学

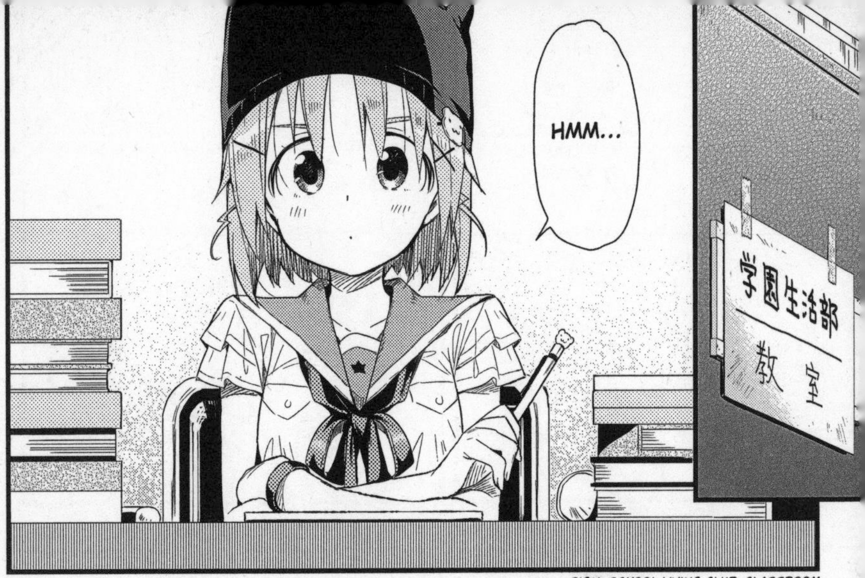
HMM...
学園生活部
教室

SIGN: SCHOOL LIVING CLUB, CLASSROOM

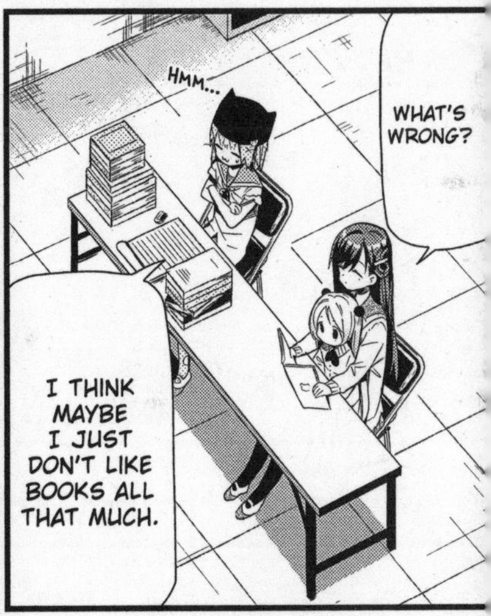
WHAT'S WRONG?
HMM...
I THINK MAYBE I JUST DON'T LIKE BOOKS ALL THAT MUCH.

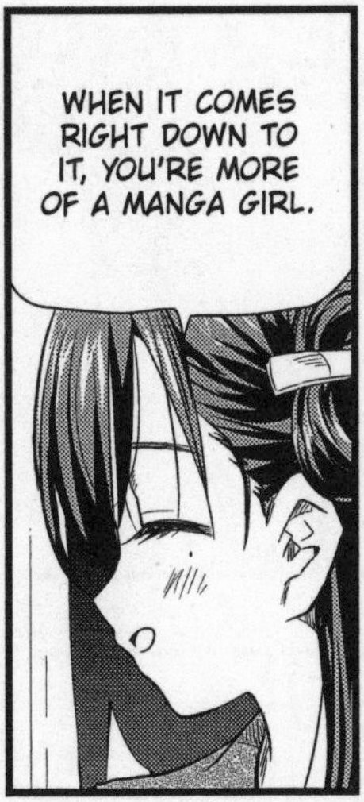
WHEN IT COMES RIGHT DOWN TO IT, YOU'RE MORE OF A MANGA GIRL.

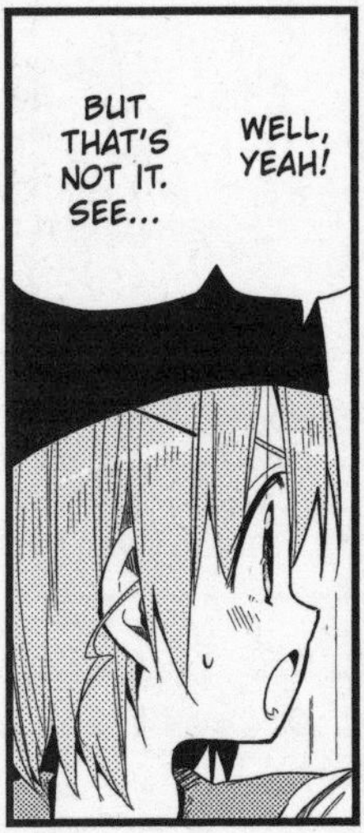
WELL, YEAH!
BUT THAT'S NOT IT. SEE...

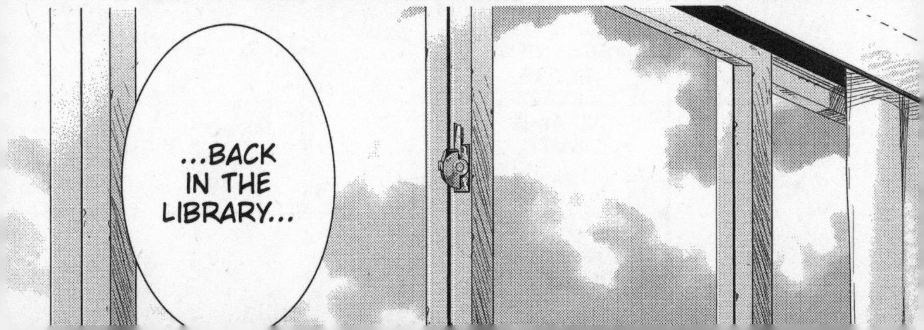
...BACK IN THE LIBRARY...

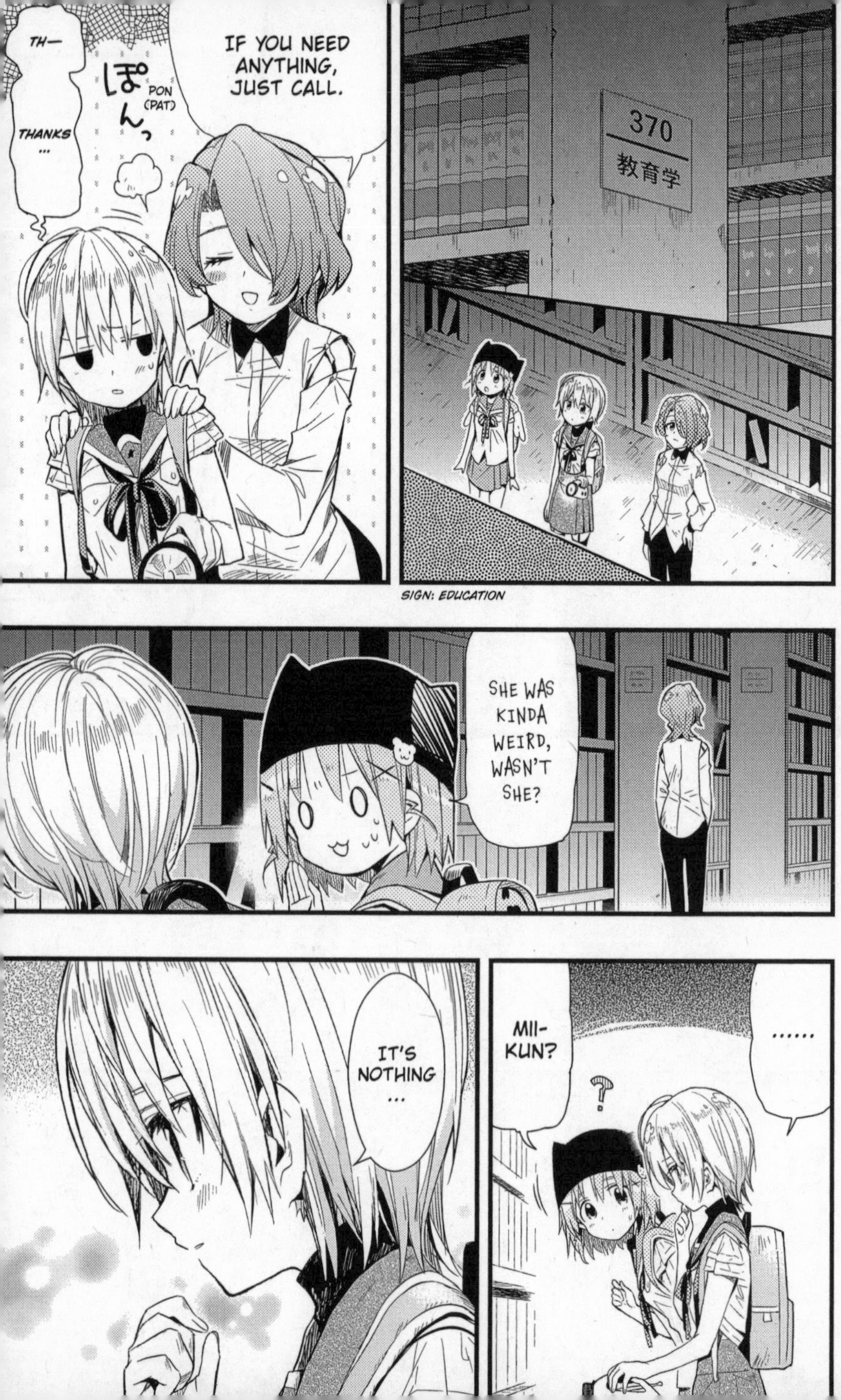
370
教育学
SIGN: EDUCATION
IF YOU NEED ANYTHING, JUST CALL.
ぽんっ PON (PAT)
TH— THANKS...
SHE WAS KINDA WEIRD, WASN'T SHE?
......
MII-KUN?
?
IT'S NOTHING...

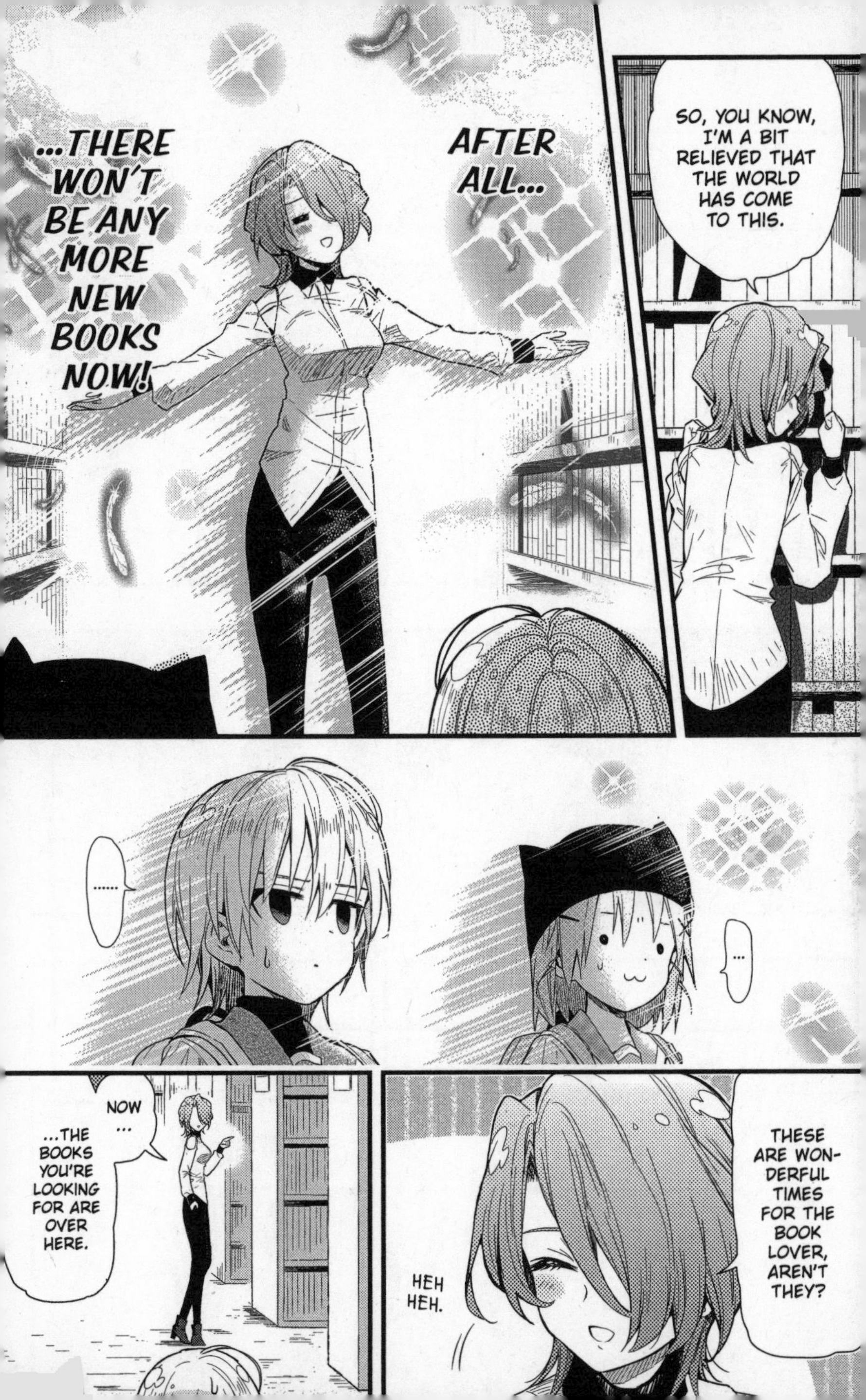
SO, YOU KNOW, I'M A BIT RELIEVED THAT THE WORLD HAS COME TO THIS.
AFTER ALL...
...THERE WON'T BE ANY MORE NEW BOOKS NOW!
...
......
THESE ARE WON-DERFUL TIMES FOR THE BOOK LOVER, AREN'T THEY?
HEH HEH.
NOW...
...THE BOOKS YOU'RE LOOKING FOR ARE OVER HERE.

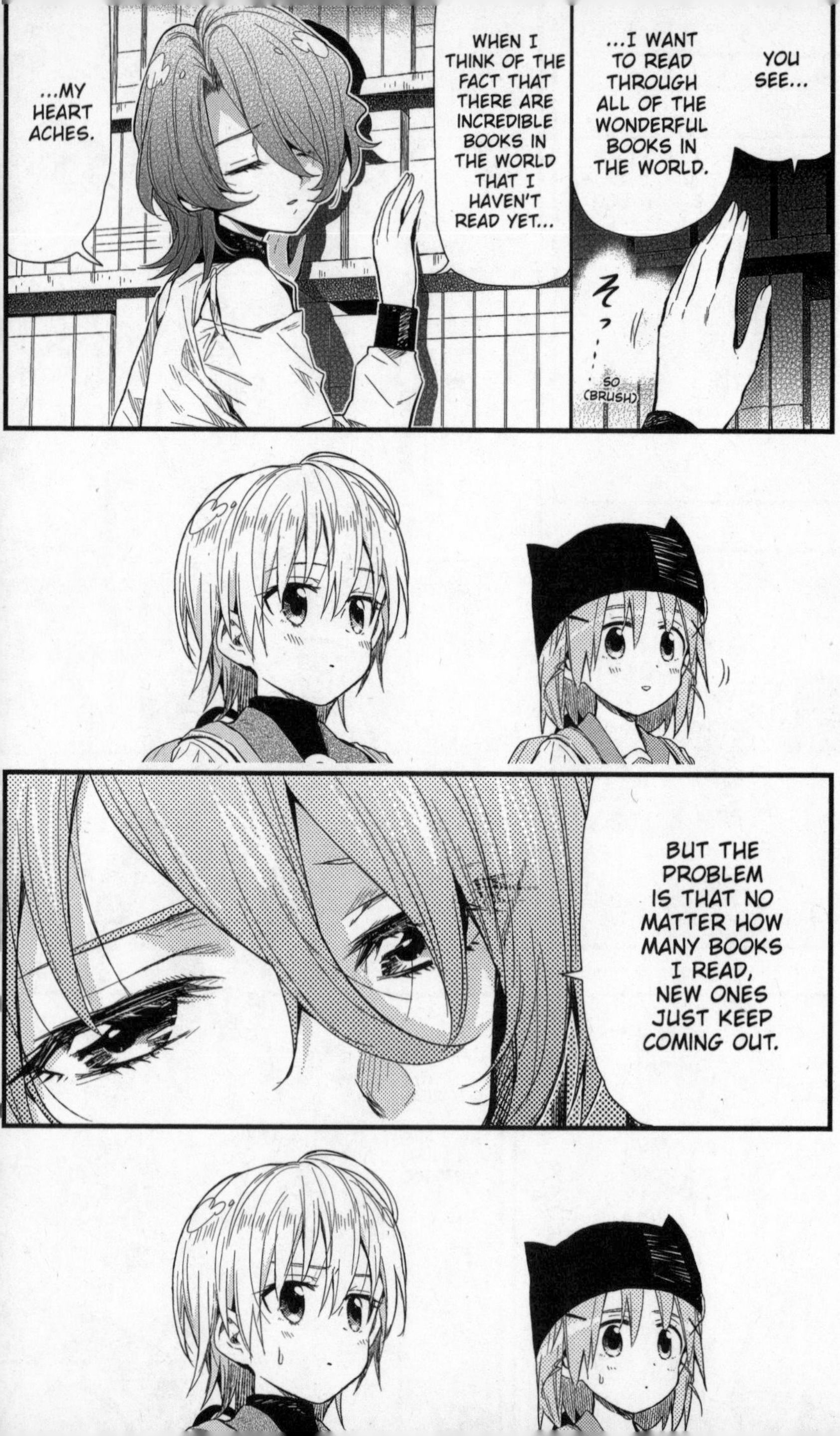
YOU SEE...
...I WANT TO READ THROUGH ALL OF THE WONDERFUL BOOKS IN THE WORLD.
SO (BRUSH)
WHEN I THINK OF THE FACT THAT THERE ARE INCREDIBLE BOOKS IN THE WORLD THAT I HAVEN'T READ YET...
...MY HEART ACHES.
BUT THE PROBLEM IS THAT NO MATTER HOW MANY BOOKS I READ, NEW ONES JUST KEEP COMING OUT.

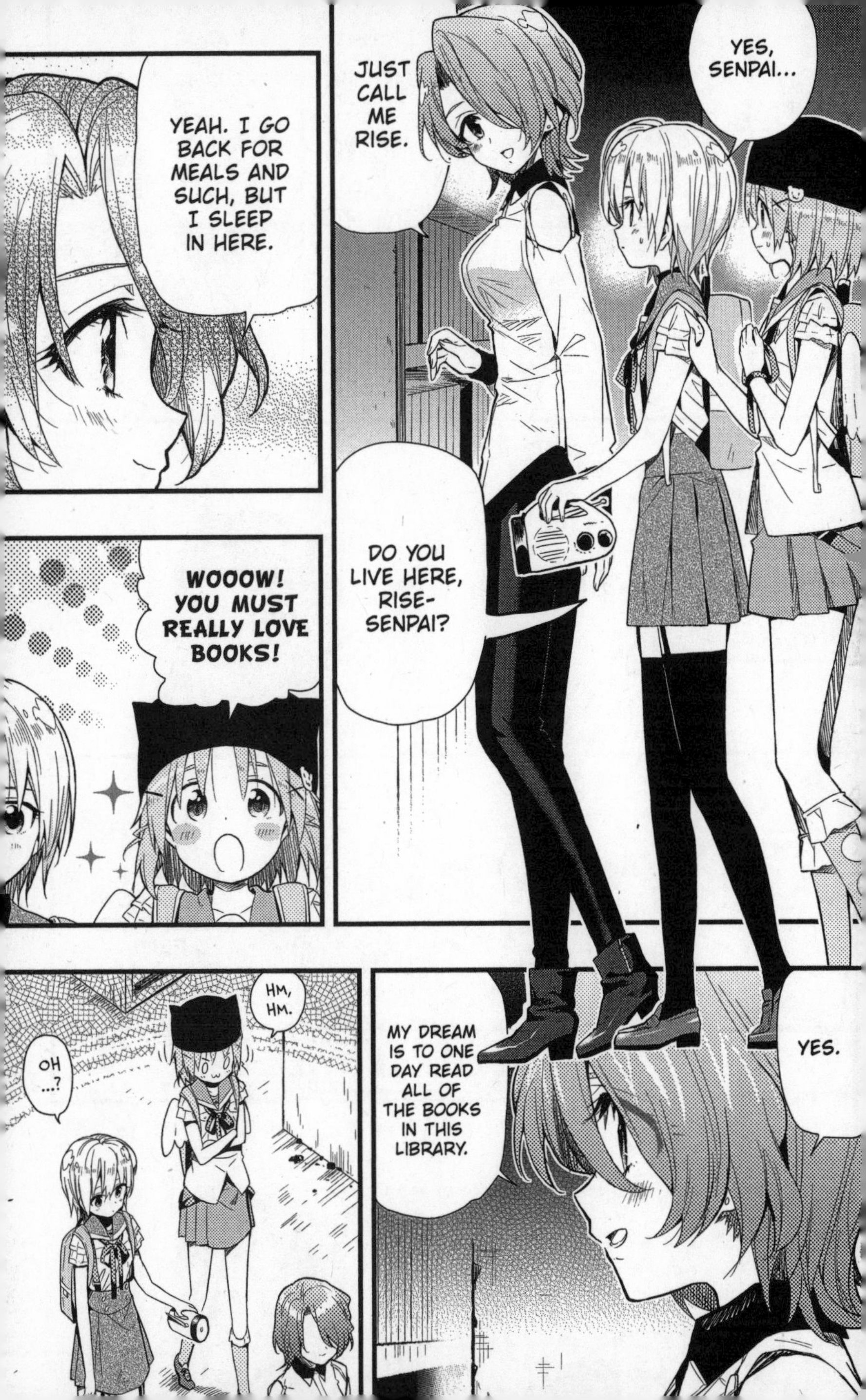
JUST CALL ME RISE.
YES, SENPAI...
DO YOU LIVE HERE, RISE-SENPAI?
YEAH. I GO BACK FOR MEALS AND SUCH, BUT I SLEEP IN HERE.
WOOOW! YOU MUST REALLY LOVE BOOKS!
YES.
MY DREAM IS TO ONE DAY READ ALL OF THE BOOKS IN THIS LIBRARY.
HM, HM.
OH ...?

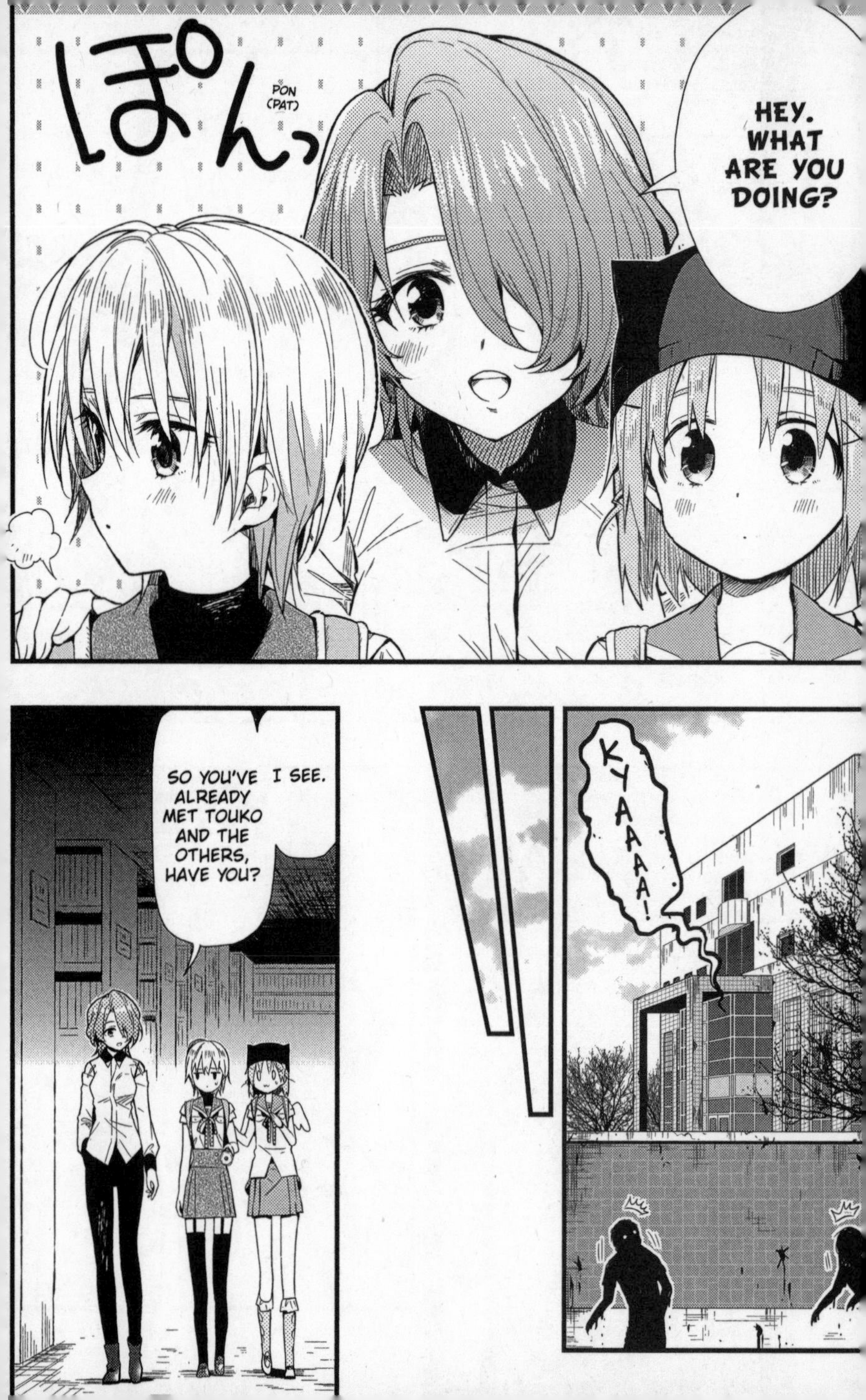
HEY. WHAT ARE YOU DOING?
ぽんっ
PON (PAT)
KYAAAAA!
I SEE. SO YOU'VE ALREADY MET TOUKO AND THE OTHERS, HAVE YOU?

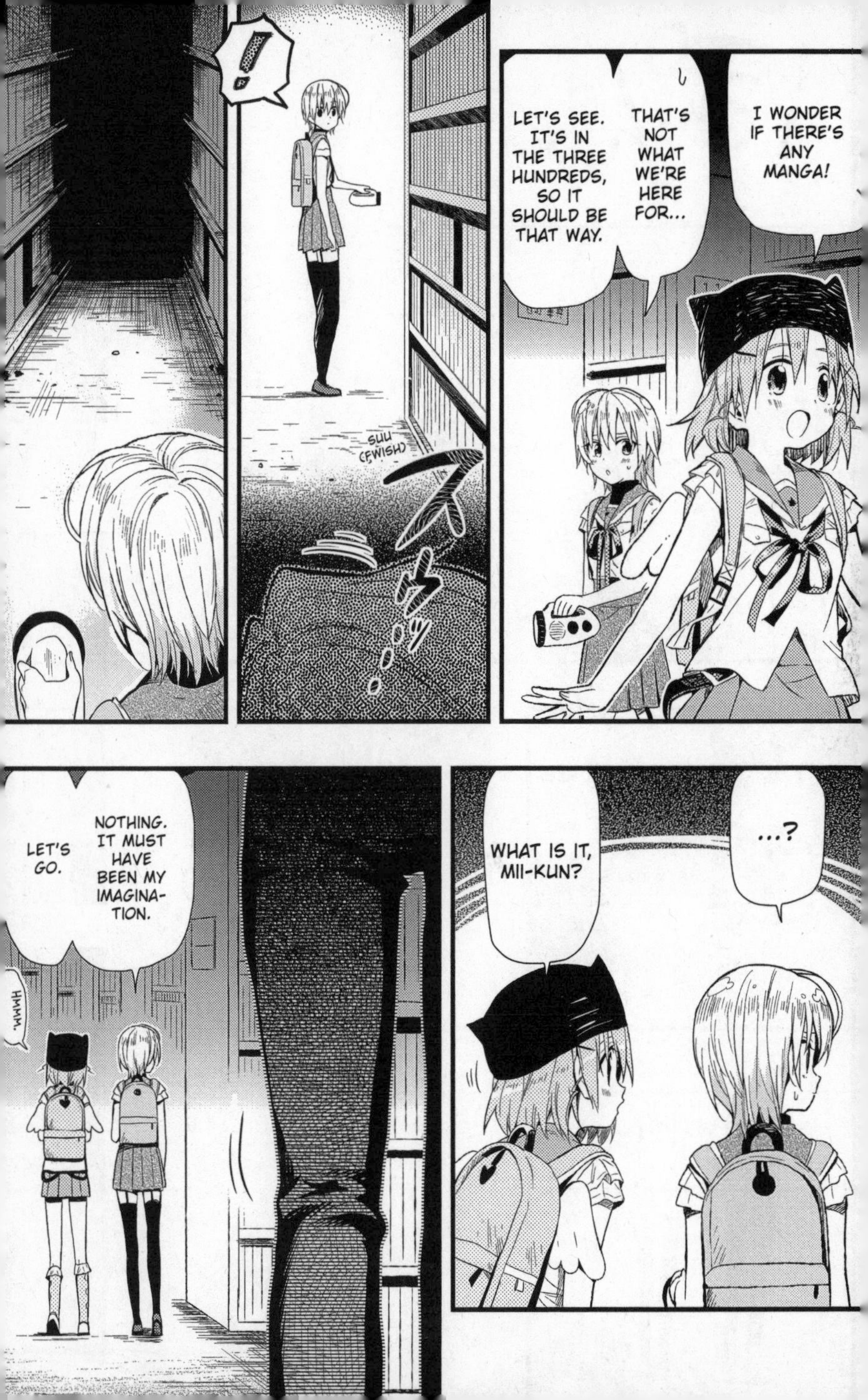
I WONDER IF THERE'S ANY MANGA!
THAT'S NOT WHAT WE'RE HERE FOR...
LET'S SEE. IT'S IN THE THREE HUNDREDS, SO IT SHOULD BE THAT WAY.
!
SUU (FWISH)
...?
WHAT IS IT, MII-KUN?
NOTHING. IT MUST HAVE BEEN MY IMAGINATION.
LET'S GO.
HMMM.

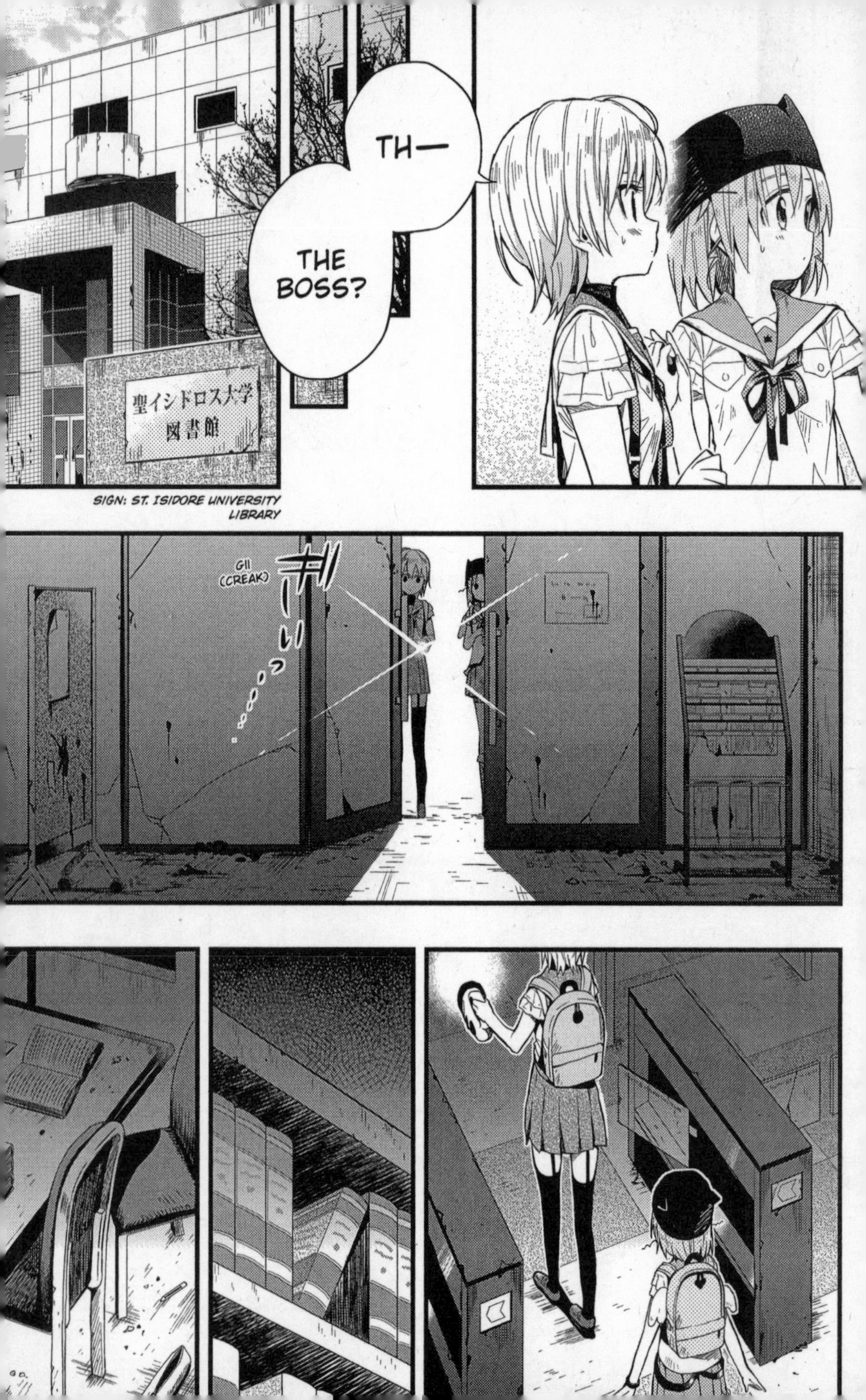
TH—
THE BOSS?
聖イシドロス大学
図書館
SIGN: ST. ISIDORE UNIVERSITY LIBRARY
GII (CREAK)

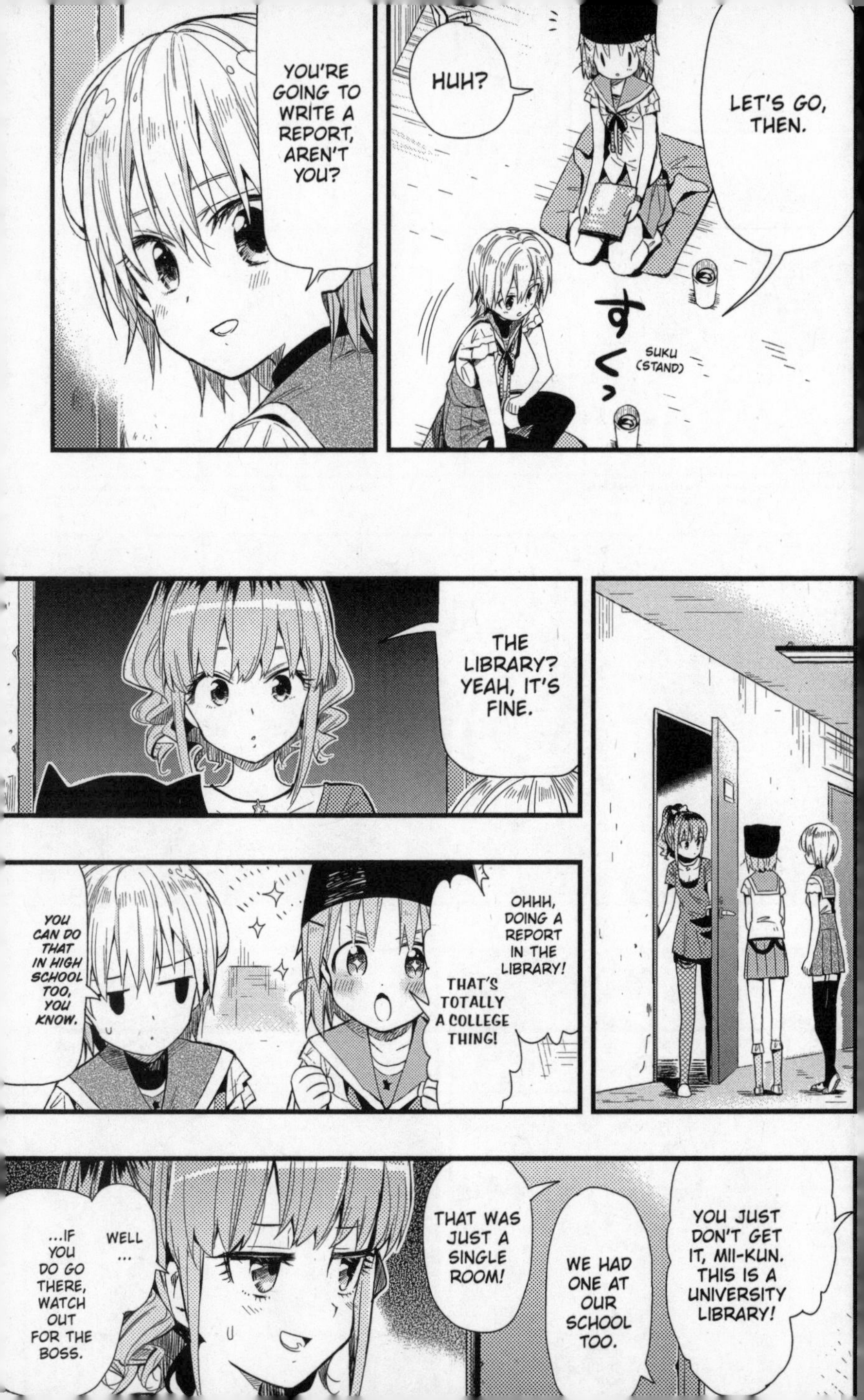
LET'S GO, THEN.
HUH?
すくっ
SUKU (STAND)
YOU'RE GOING TO WRITE A REPORT, AREN'T YOU?
THE LIBRARY? YEAH, IT'S FINE.
OHHH, DOING A REPORT IN THE LIBRARY!
THAT'S TOTALLY A COLLEGE THING!
YOU CAN DO THAT IN HIGH SCHOOL TOO, YOU KNOW.
YOU JUST DON'T GET IT, MII-KUN. THIS IS A UNIVERSITY LIBRARY!
WE HAD ONE AT OUR SCHOOL TOO.
THAT WAS JUST A SINGLE ROOM!
WELL...
...IF YOU DO GO THERE, WATCH OUT FOR THE BOSS.

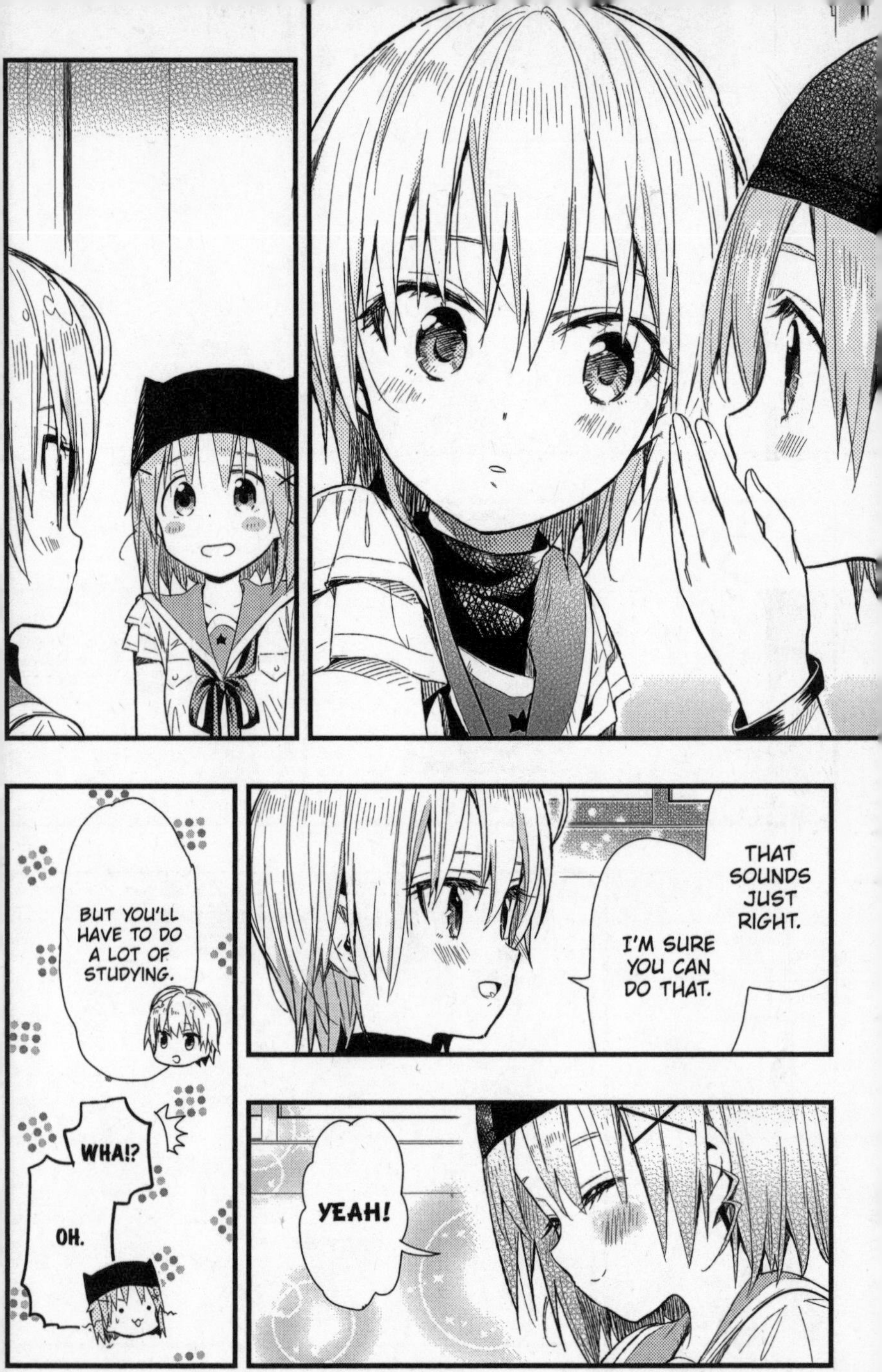

THAT SOUNDS JUST RIGHT.
I'M SURE YOU CAN DO THAT.
YEAH!
BUT YOU'LL HAVE TO DO A LOT OF STUDYING.
WHA!?
OH.

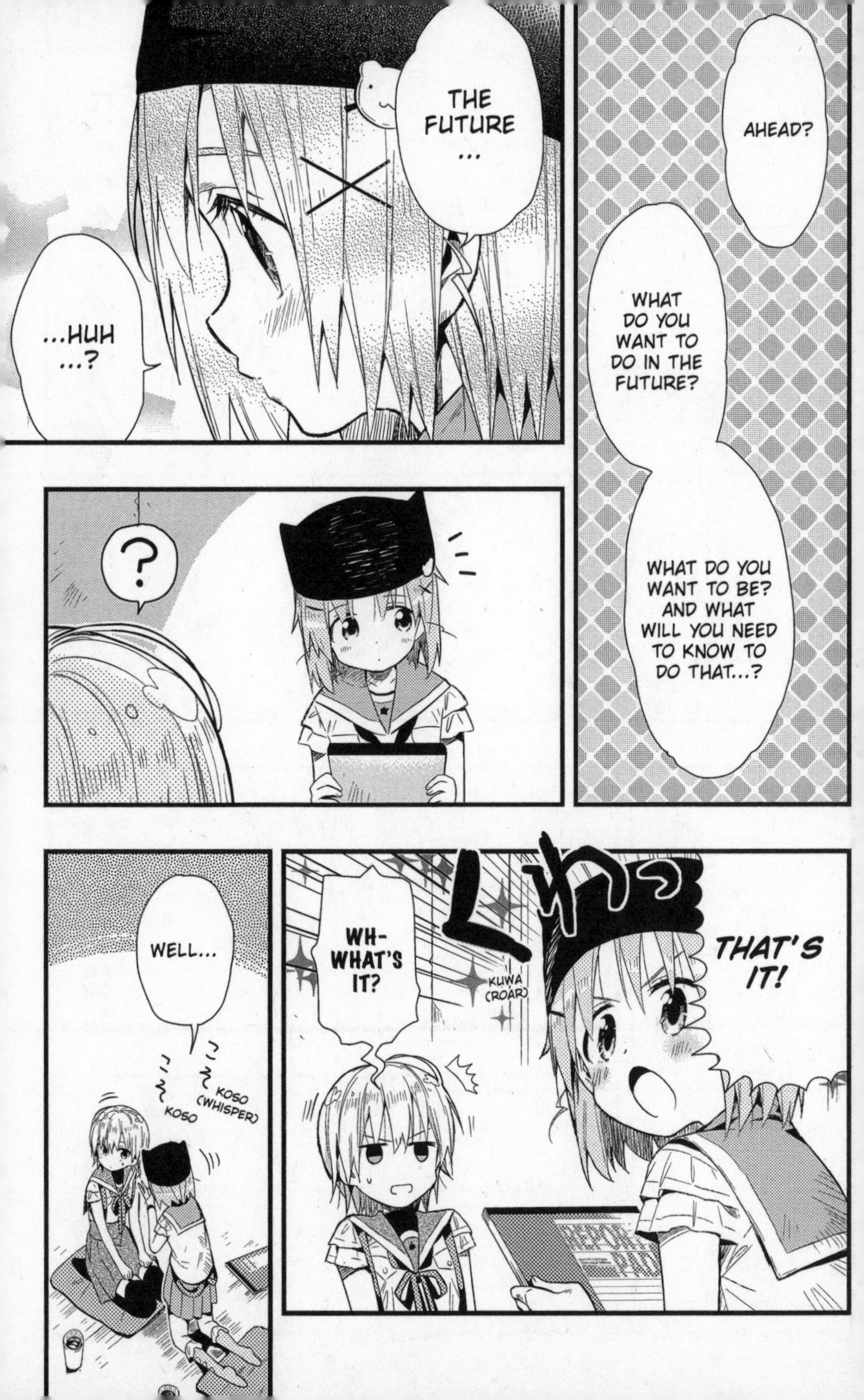
AHEAD?
WHAT DO YOU WANT TO DO IN THE FUTURE?
WHAT DO YOU WANT TO BE? AND WHAT WILL YOU NEED TO KNOW TO DO THAT...?
THE FUTURE ...
...HUH ...?
?
THAT'S IT!
KUWA (ROAR)
WH- WHAT'S IT?
WELL...
こそ
KOSO (WHISPER)
こそ
KOSO

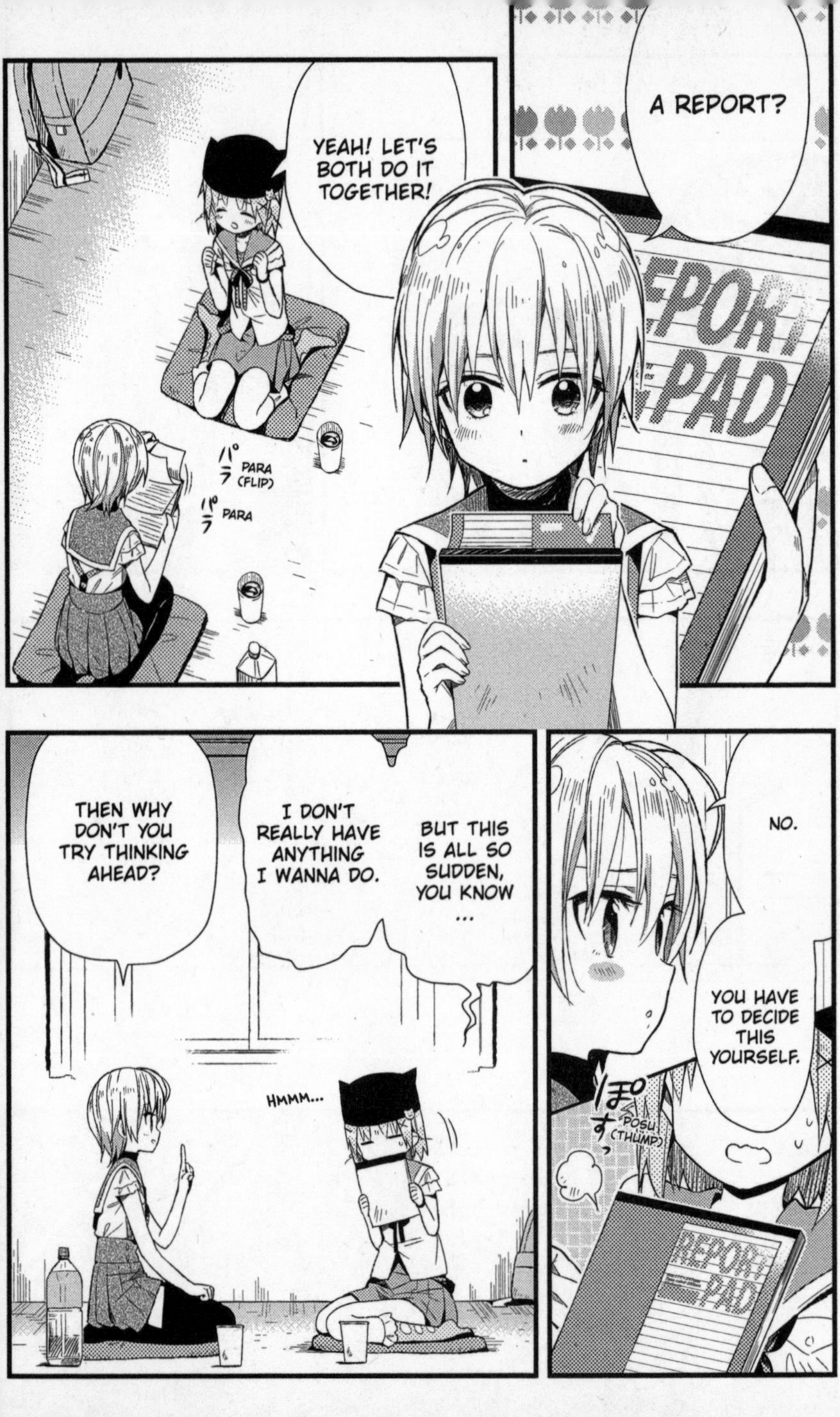
A REPORT?
YEAH! LET'S BOTH DO IT TOGETHER!
パラ PARA (FLIP)
パラ PARA
NO.
YOU HAVE TO DECIDE THIS YOURSELF.
ぽすっ POSU (THUMP)
BUT THIS IS ALL SO SUDDEN, YOU KNOW...
I DON'T REALLY HAVE ANYTHING I WANNA DO.
THEN WHY DON'T YOU TRY THINKING AHEAD?
HMMM...

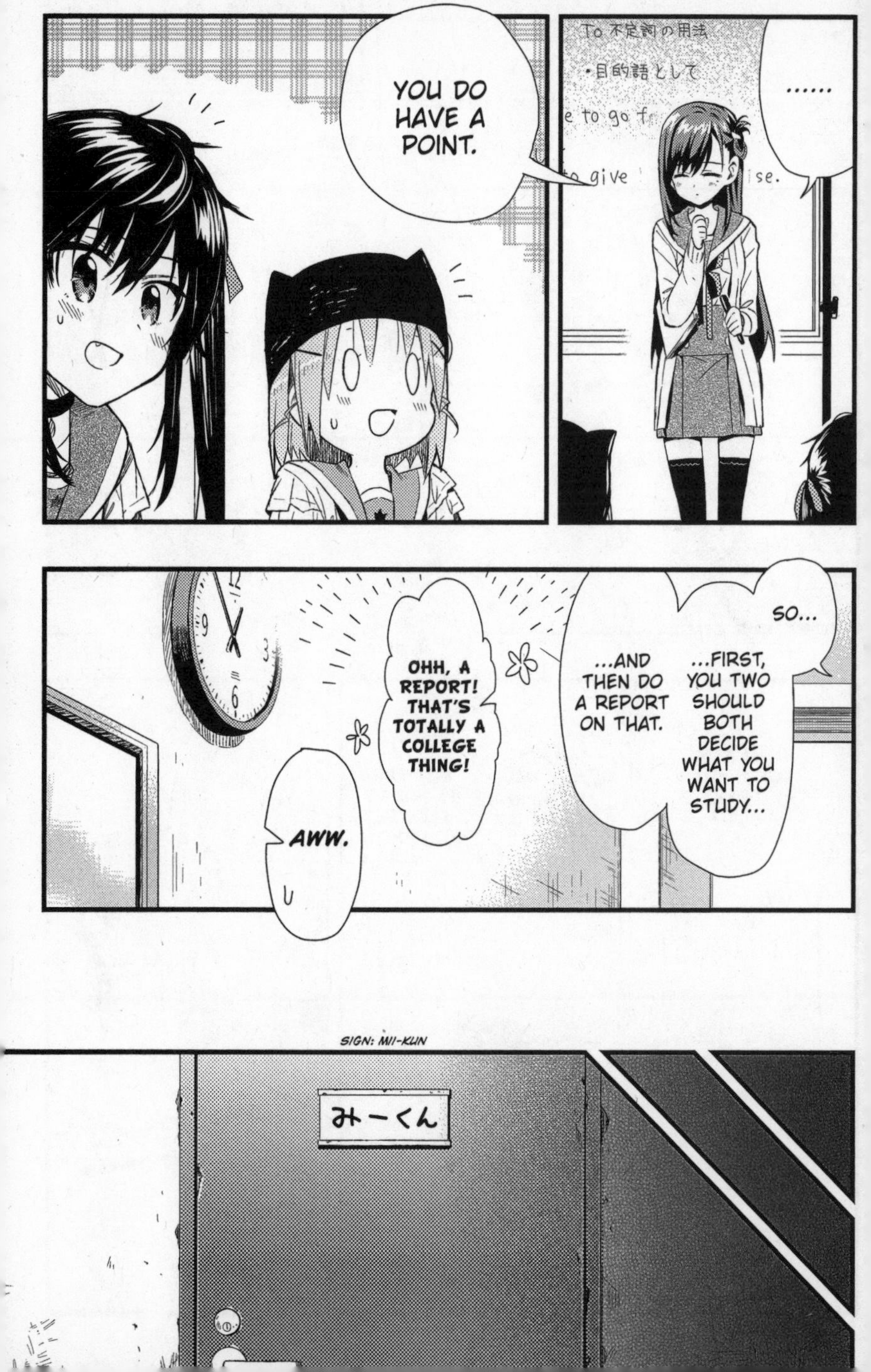
To 不定詞の用法
・目的語として
......
YOU DO HAVE A POINT.
SO...
...FIRST, YOU TWO SHOULD BOTH DECIDE WHAT YOU WANT TO STUDY...
...AND THEN DO A REPORT ON THAT.
OHH, A REPORT! THAT'S TOTALLY A COLLEGE THING!
AWW.
SIGN: MII-KUN
みーくん

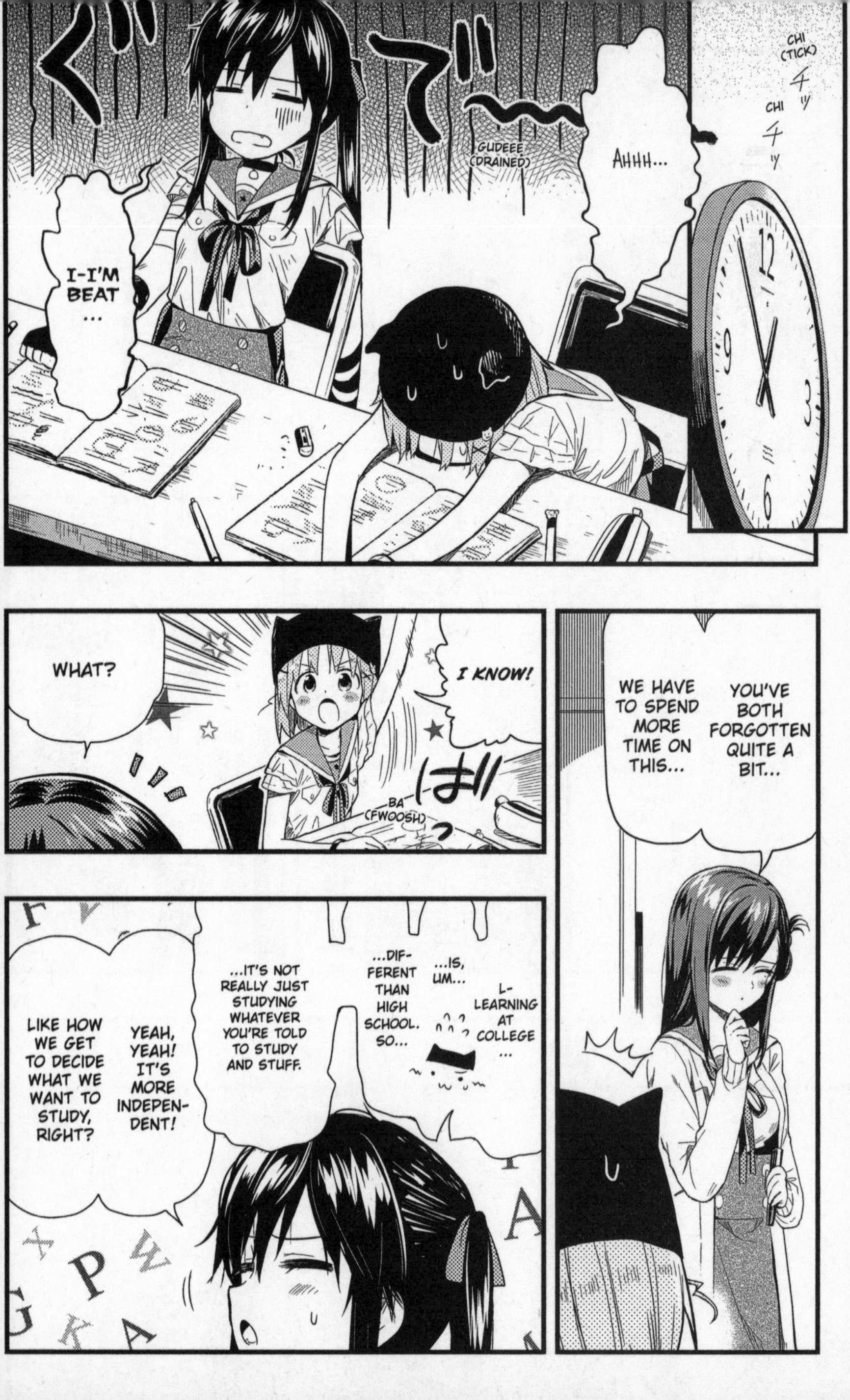
CHI (TICK)
チッ
CHI
チッ
AHHH...
GUDEEE (DRAINED)
I-I'M BEAT...
YOU'VE BOTH FORGOTTEN QUITE A BIT...
WE HAVE TO SPEND MORE TIME ON THIS...
I KNOW!
BA (FWOOSH)
ばっ
WHAT?
L-LEARNING AT COLLEGE...
...IS, UM...
...DIF-FERENT THAN HIGH SCHOOL. SO...
...IT'S NOT REALLY JUST STUDYING WHATEVER YOU'RE TOLD TO STUDY AND STUFF.
YEAH, YEAH! IT'S MORE INDEPEN-DENT!
LIKE HOW WE GET TO DECIDE WHAT WE WANT TO STUDY, RIGHT?

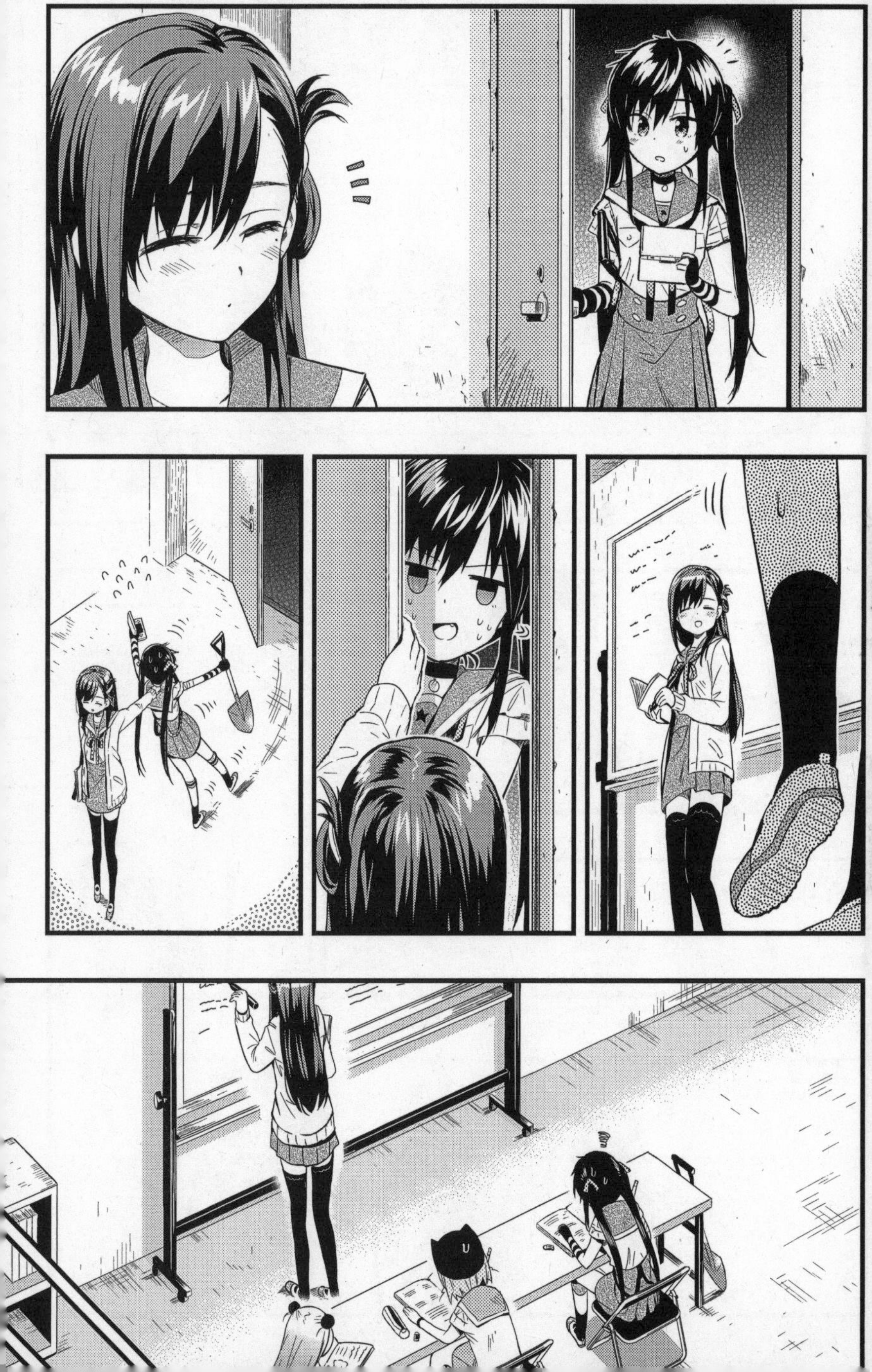

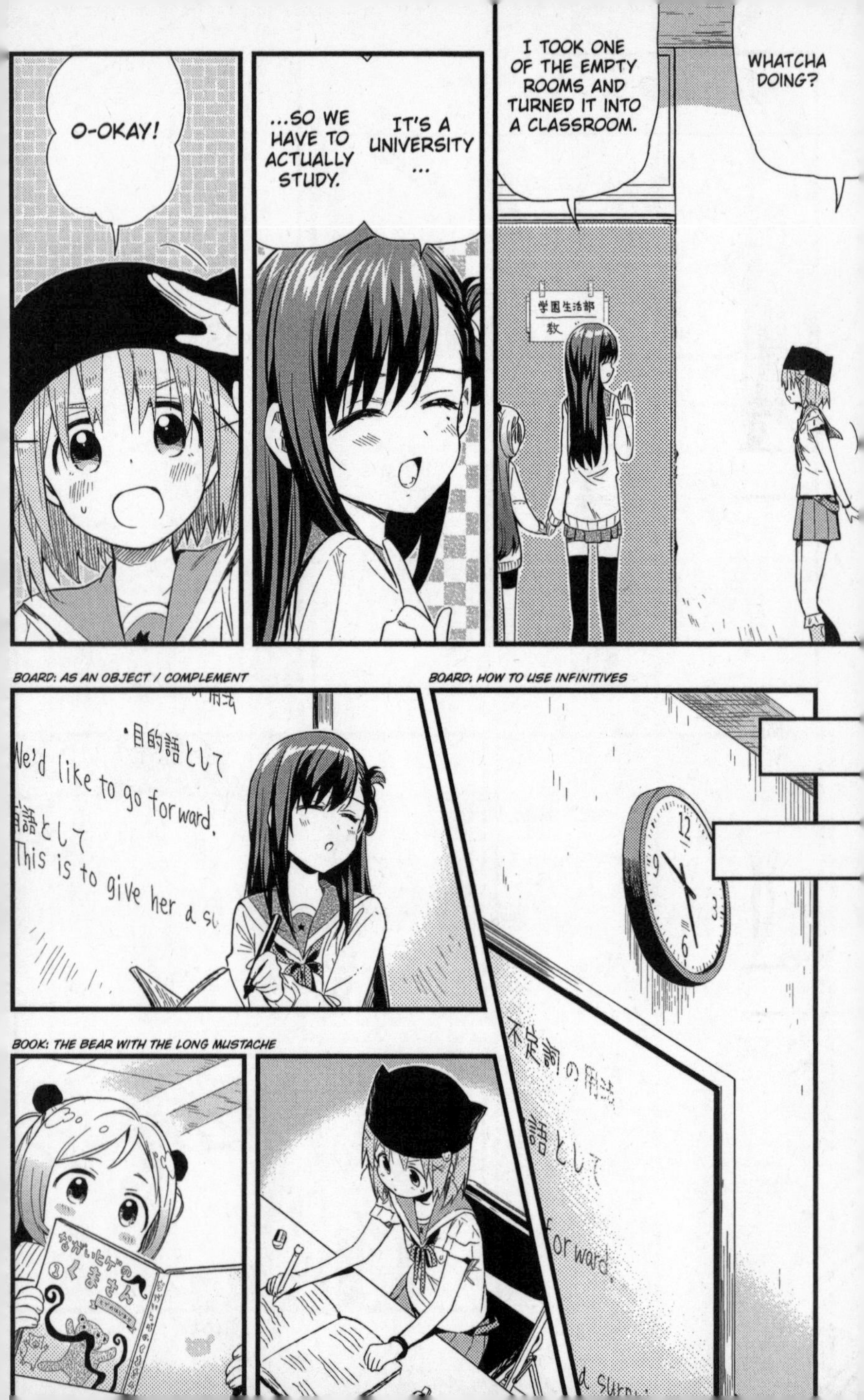
WHATCHA DOING?
I TOOK ONE OF THE EMPTY ROOMS AND TURNED IT INTO A CLASSROOM.
学園生活部
教
IT'S A UNIVERSITY ...
...SO WE HAVE TO ACTUALLY STUDY.
O-OKAY!
BOARD: HOW TO USE INFINITIVES
BOARD: AS AN OBJECT / COMPLEMENT
・目的語として
We'd like to go forward.
This is to give her a
BOOK: THE BEAR WITH THE LONG MUSTACHE

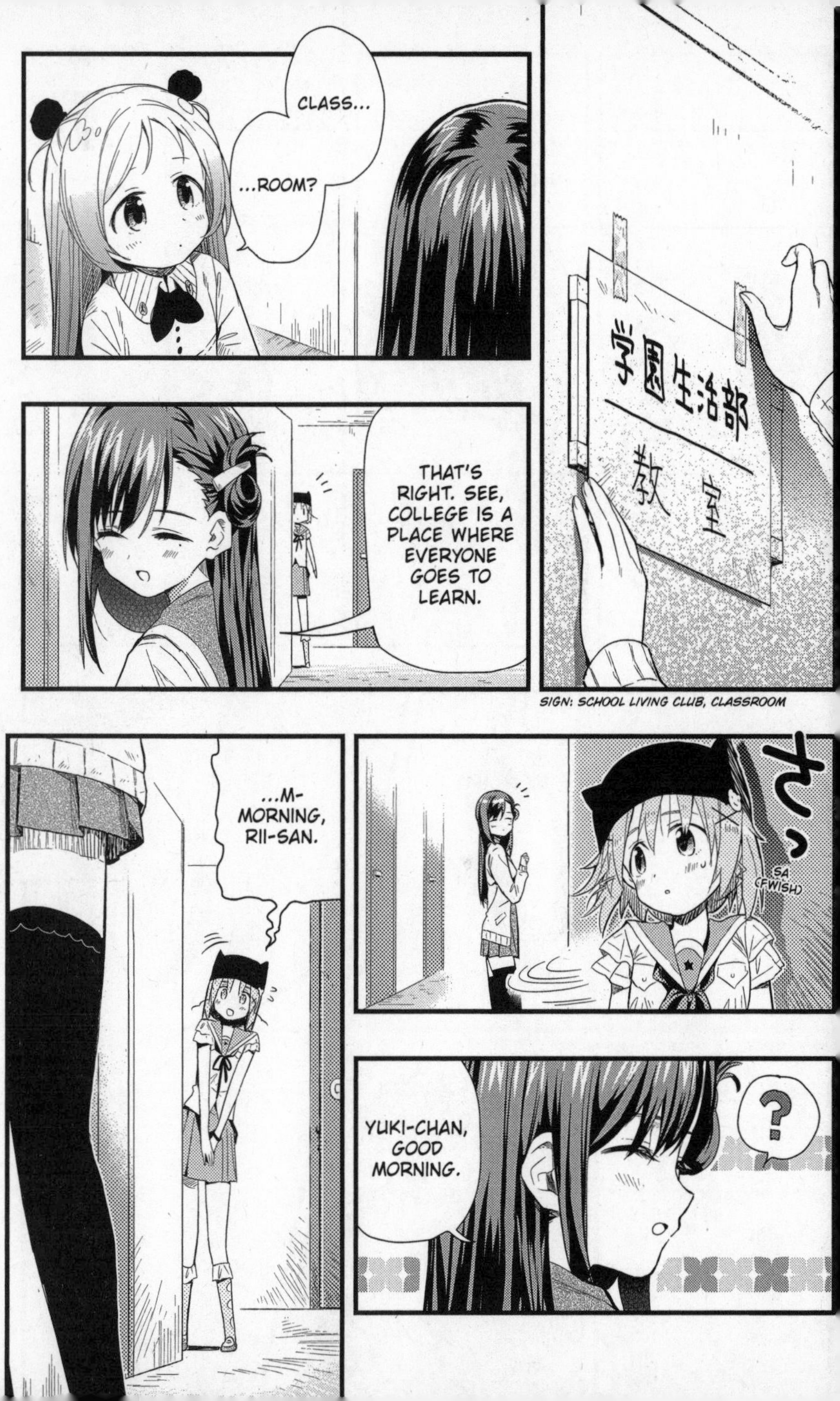
学園生活部
教室
SIGN: SCHOOL LIVING CLUB, CLASSROOM
CLASS...
...ROOM?
THAT'S RIGHT. SEE, COLLEGE IS A PLACE WHERE EVERYONE GOES TO LEARN.
さっ
SA (FWISH)
YUKI-CHAN, GOOD MORNING.
?
...M-MORNING, RII-SAN.

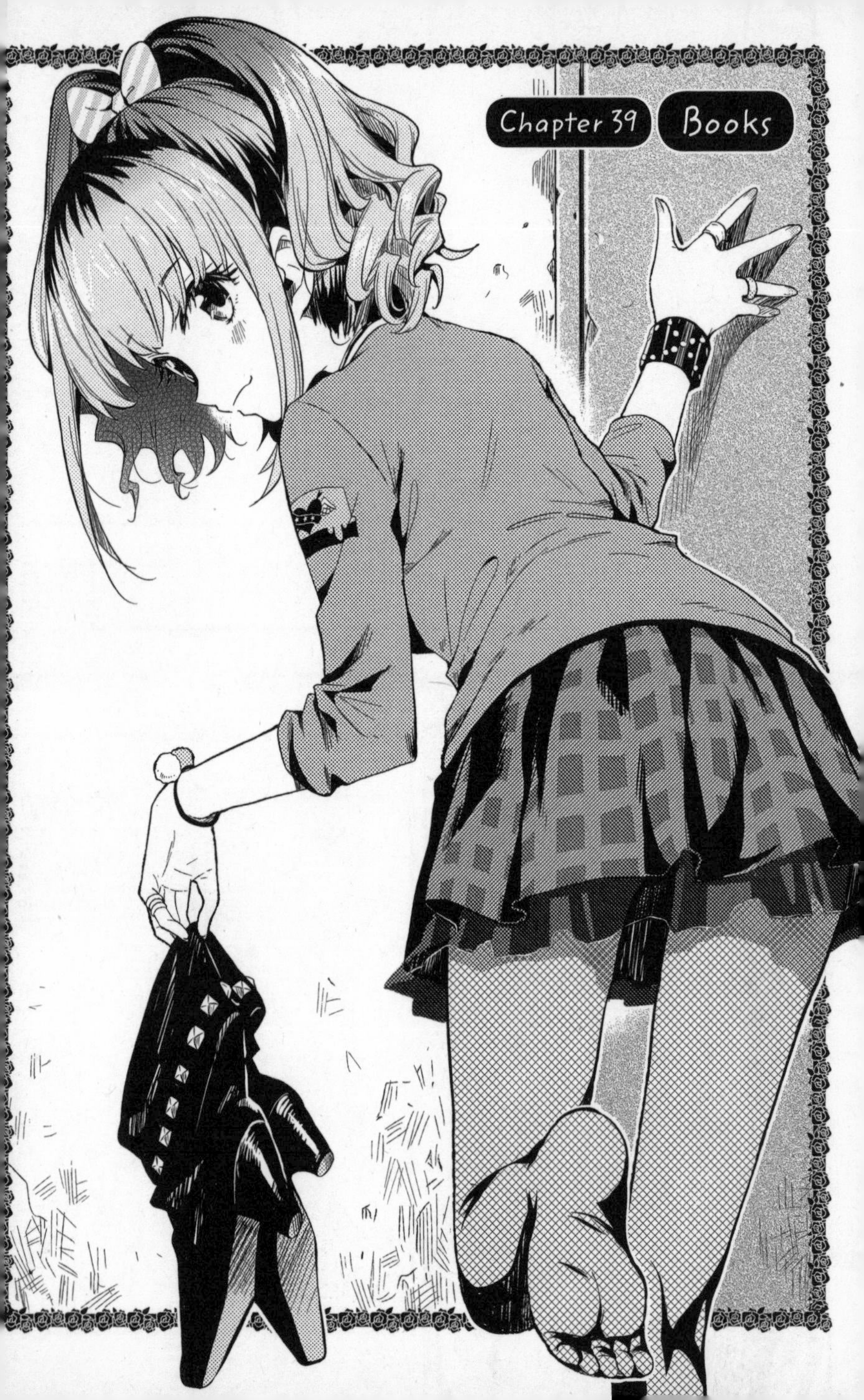
Chapter 39
Books

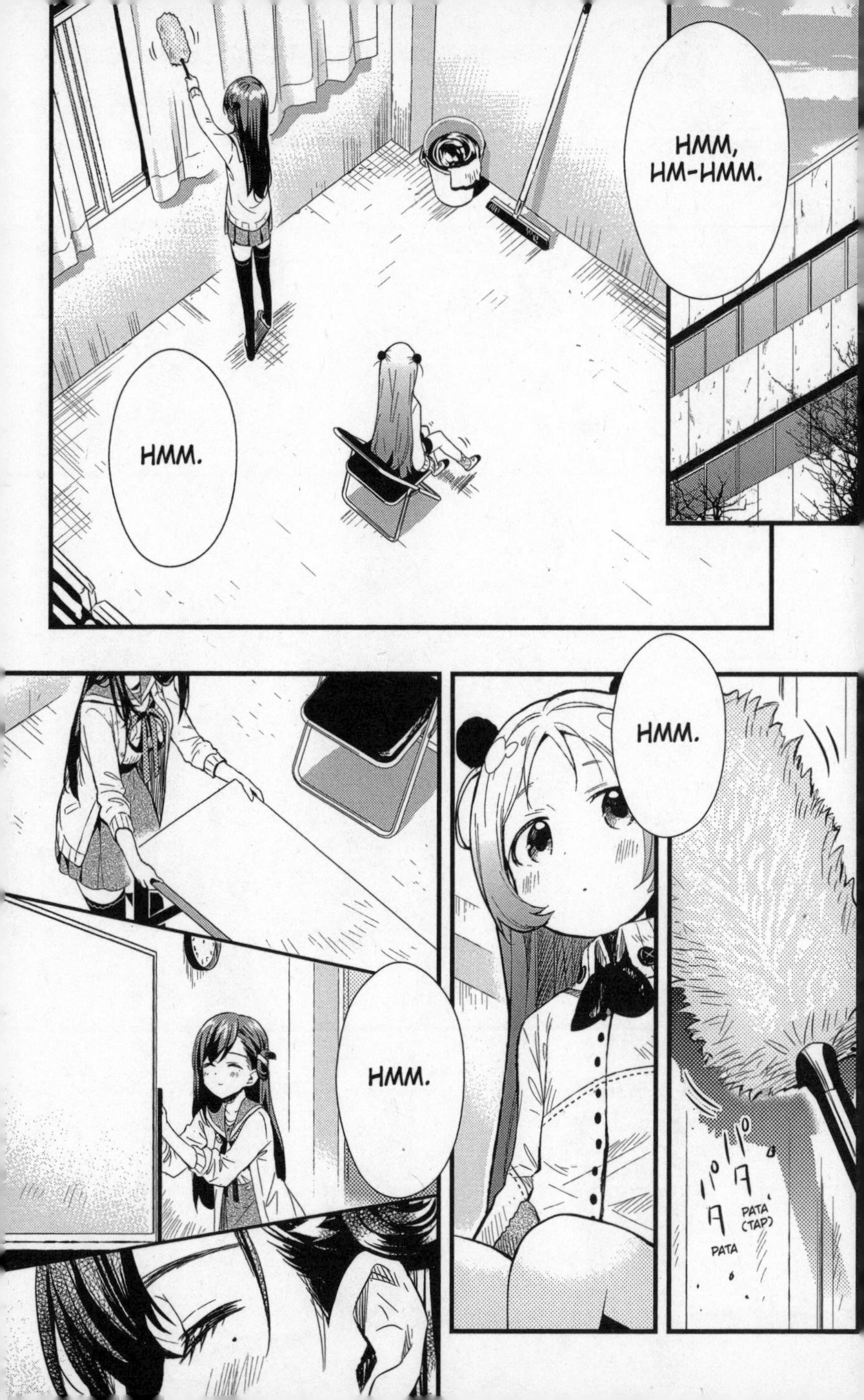
HMM, HM-HMM.
HMM.
HMM.
PATA PATA (TAP)
HMM.

SCHOOL-LIVE!

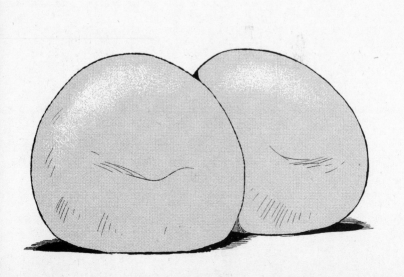

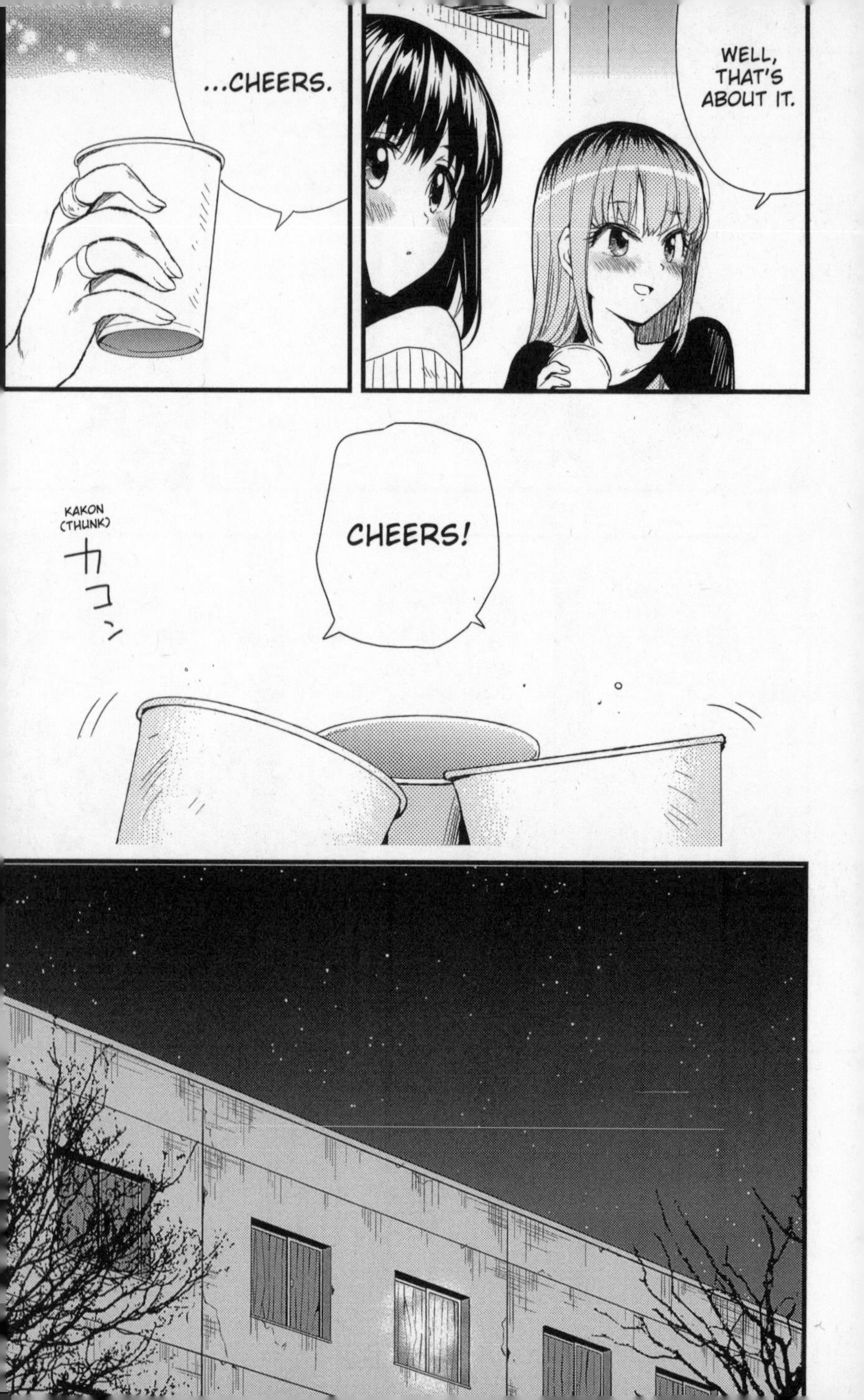
WELL, THAT'S ABOUT IT.
...CHEERS.
CHEERS!
KAKON (THUNK)
カコン

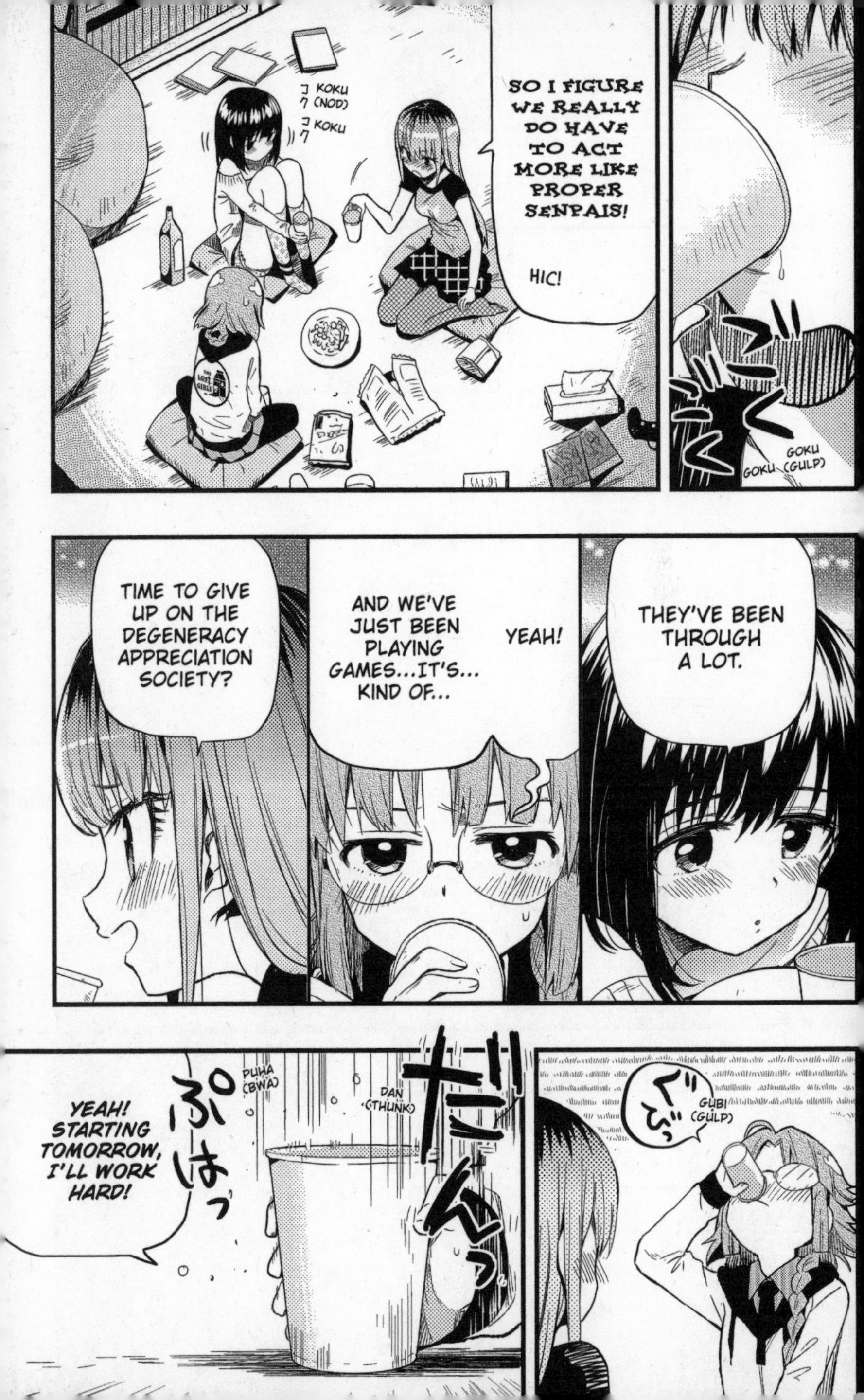
GOKU GOKU (GULP)
SO I FIGURE WE REALLY DO HAVE TO ACT MORE LIKE PROPER SENPAIS!
HIC!
コク KOKU (NOD)
コク KOKU
THEY'VE BEEN THROUGH A LOT.
YEAH!
AND WE'VE JUST BEEN PLAYING GAMES...IT'S... KIND OF...
TIME TO GIVE UP ON THE DEGENERACY APPRECIATION SOCIETY?
GUBI (GULP)
DAN (THUNK)
PUHA (BWA)
YEAH! STARTING TOMORROW, I'LL WORK HARD!

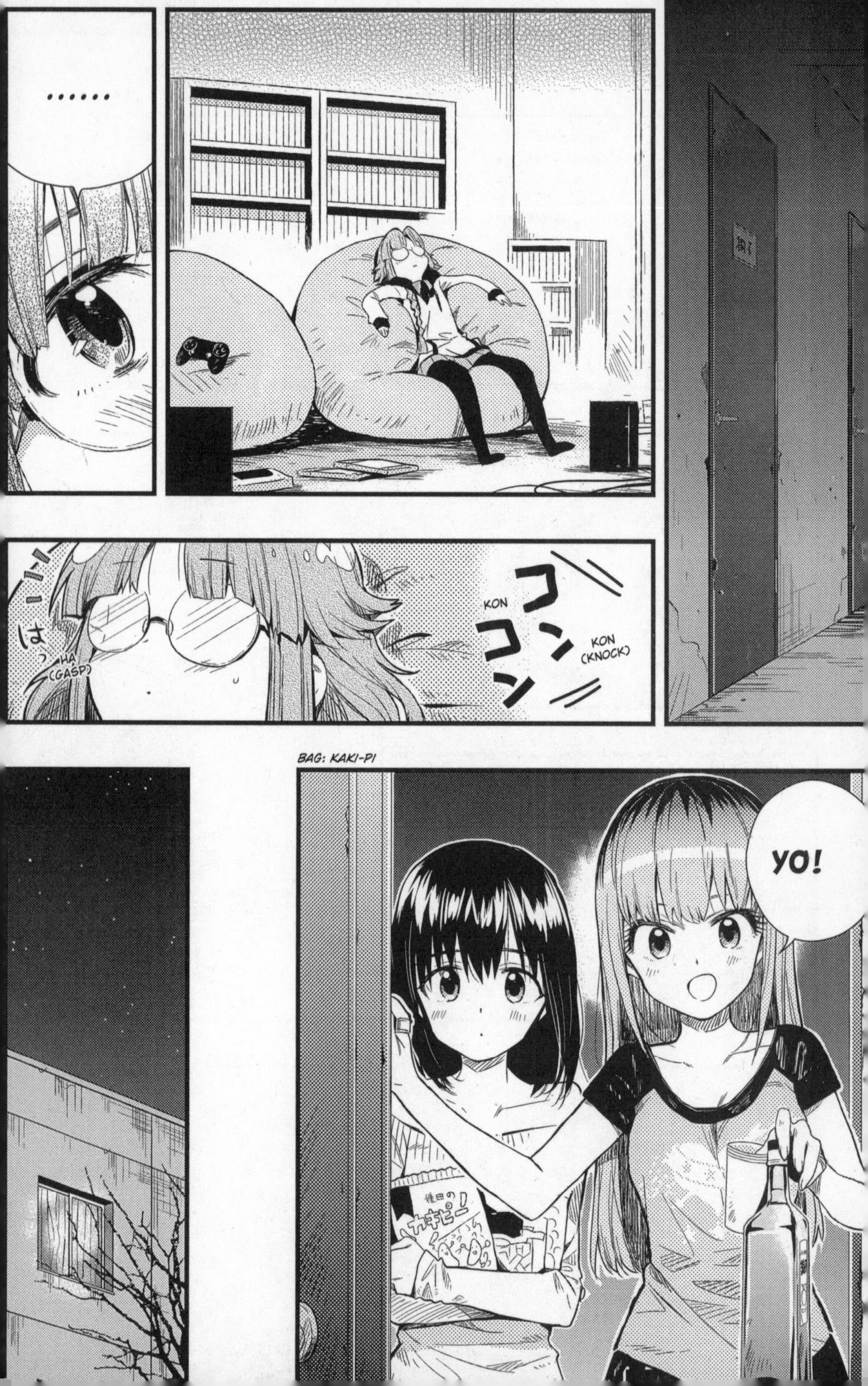

......
コンコン
KON KON (KNOCK)
はっ
HA (GASP)
BAG: KAKI-PI
YO!
カキピー!

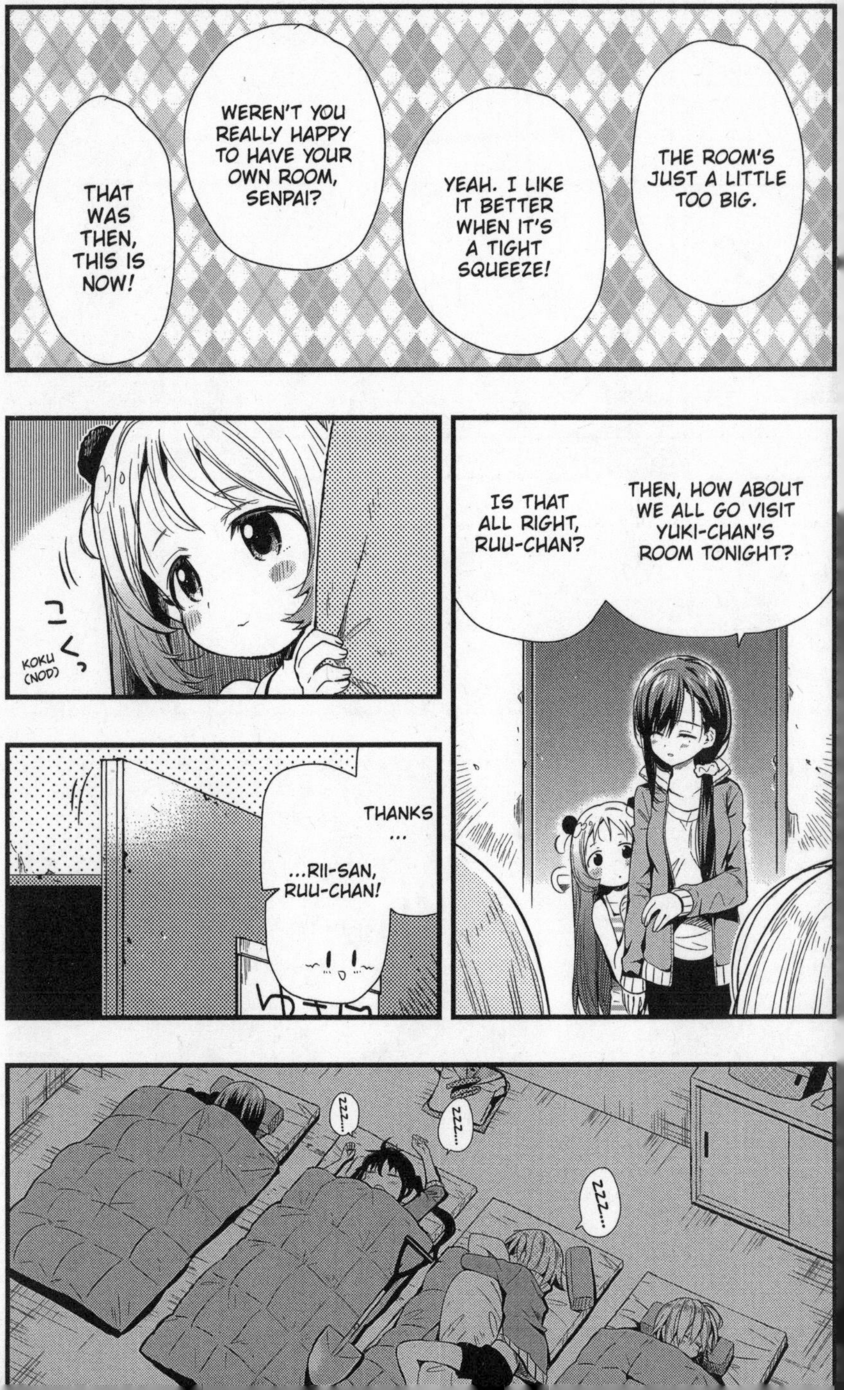
THE ROOM'S JUST A LITTLE TOO BIG.
YEAH. I LIKE IT BETTER WHEN IT'S A TIGHT SQUEEZE!
WEREN'T YOU REALLY HAPPY TO HAVE YOUR OWN ROOM, SENPAI?
THAT WAS THEN, THIS IS NOW!
THEN, HOW ABOUT WE ALL GO VISIT YUKI-CHAN'S ROOM TONIGHT?
IS THAT ALL RIGHT, RUU-CHAN?
こく
KOKU (NOD)
THANKS ...
...RII-SAN, RUU-CHAN!
ZZZ...
ZZZ...
ZZZ...

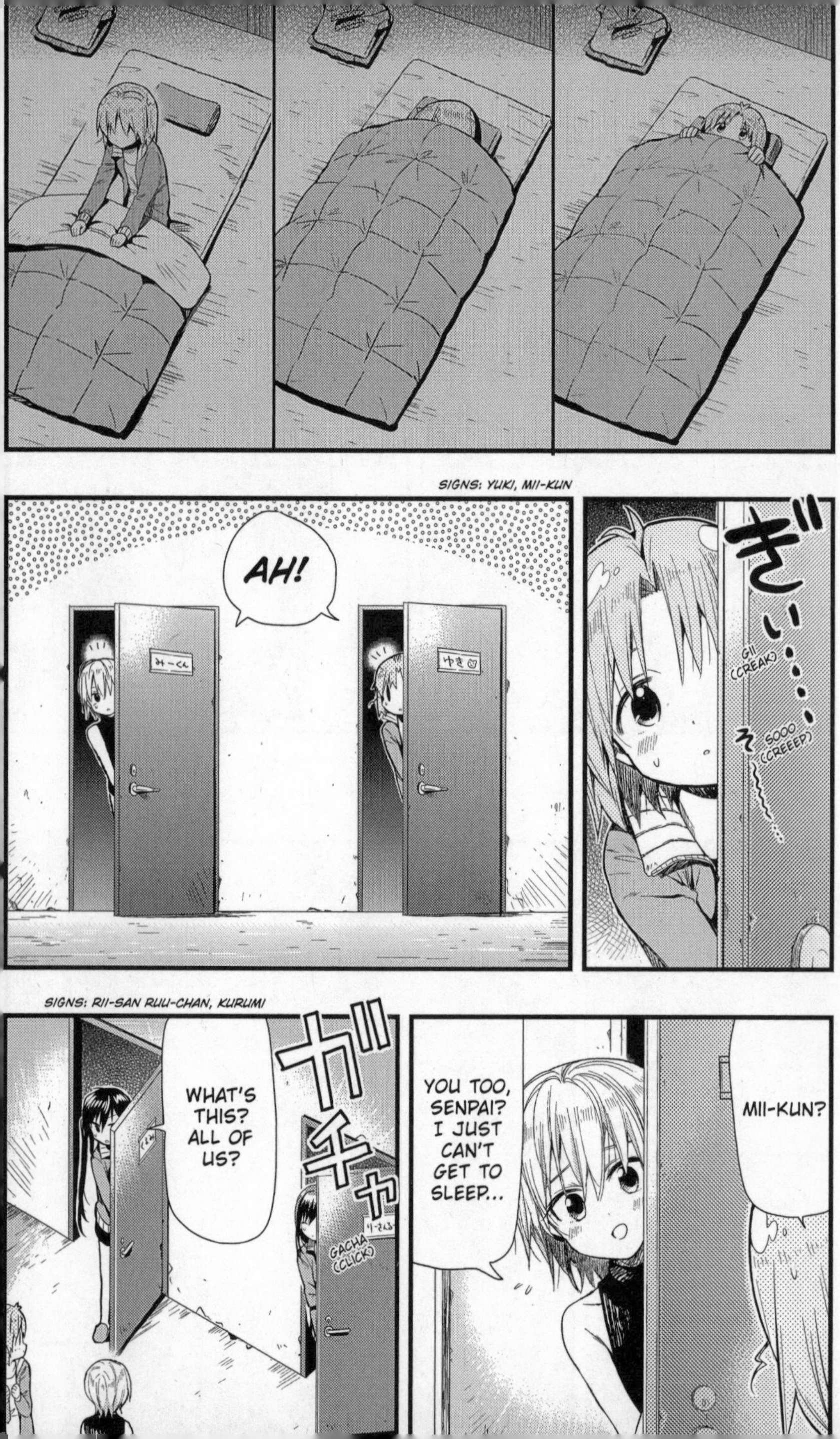
SIGNS: YUKI, MII-KUN
ぎぃ…
GII (CREAK)
そ～…
SOOO (CREEEP)
AH!
みーくん
ゆき
SIGNS: RII-SAN RUU-CHAN, KURUMI
MII-KUN?
YOU TOO, SENPAI? I JUST CAN'T GET TO SLEEP...
ガチャ
GACHA (CLICK)
WHAT'S THIS? ALL OF US?

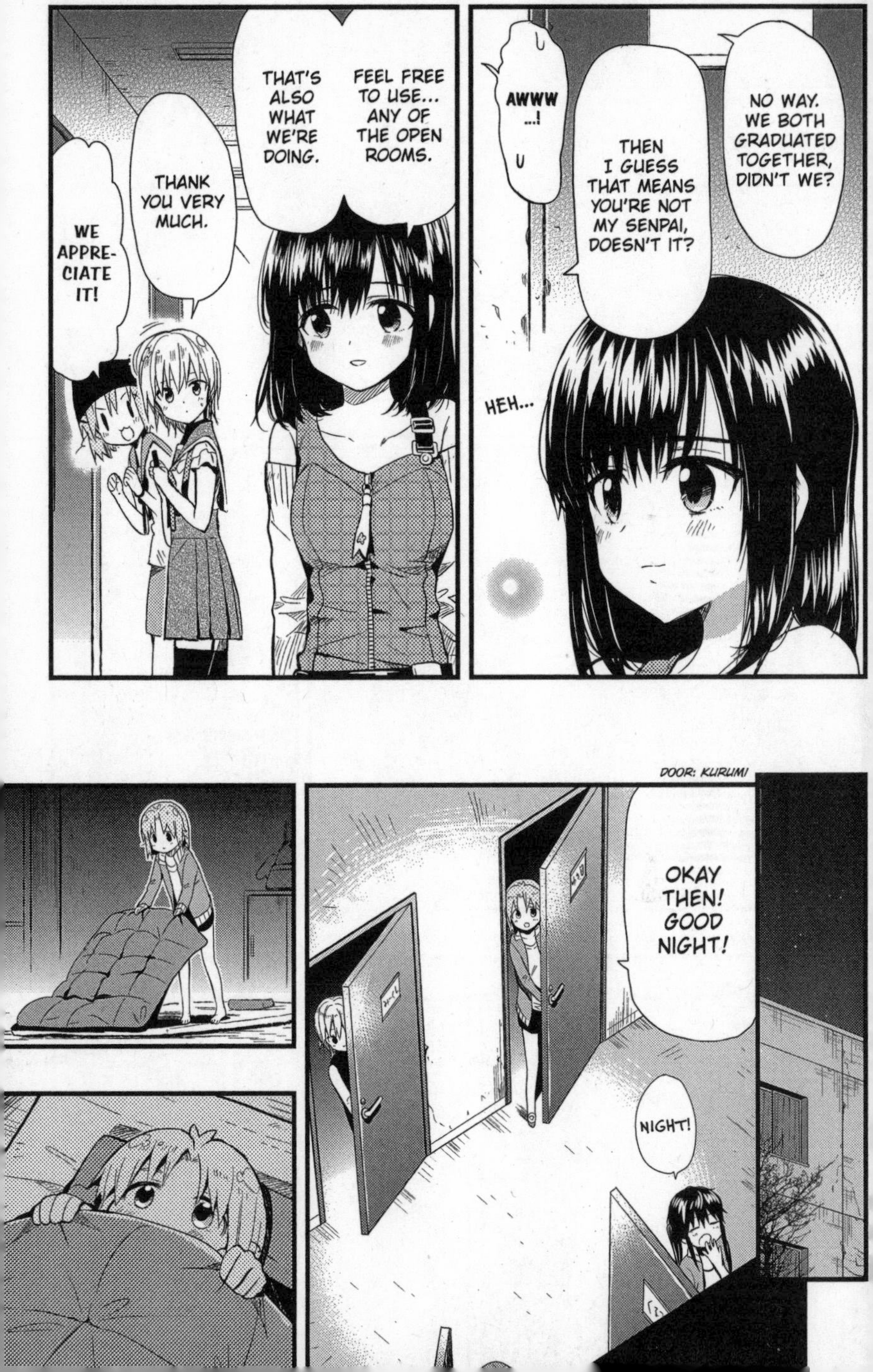
NO WAY. WE BOTH GRADUATED TOGETHER, DIDN'T WE?
THEN I GUESS THAT MEANS YOU'RE NOT MY SENPAI, DOESN'T IT?
AWWW...!
HEH...
FEEL FREE TO USE... ANY OF THE OPEN ROOMS.
THAT'S ALSO WHAT WE'RE DOING.
THANK YOU VERY MUCH.
WE APPRE-CIATE IT!
DOOR: KURUMI
OKAY THEN! GOOD NIGHT!
NIGHT!

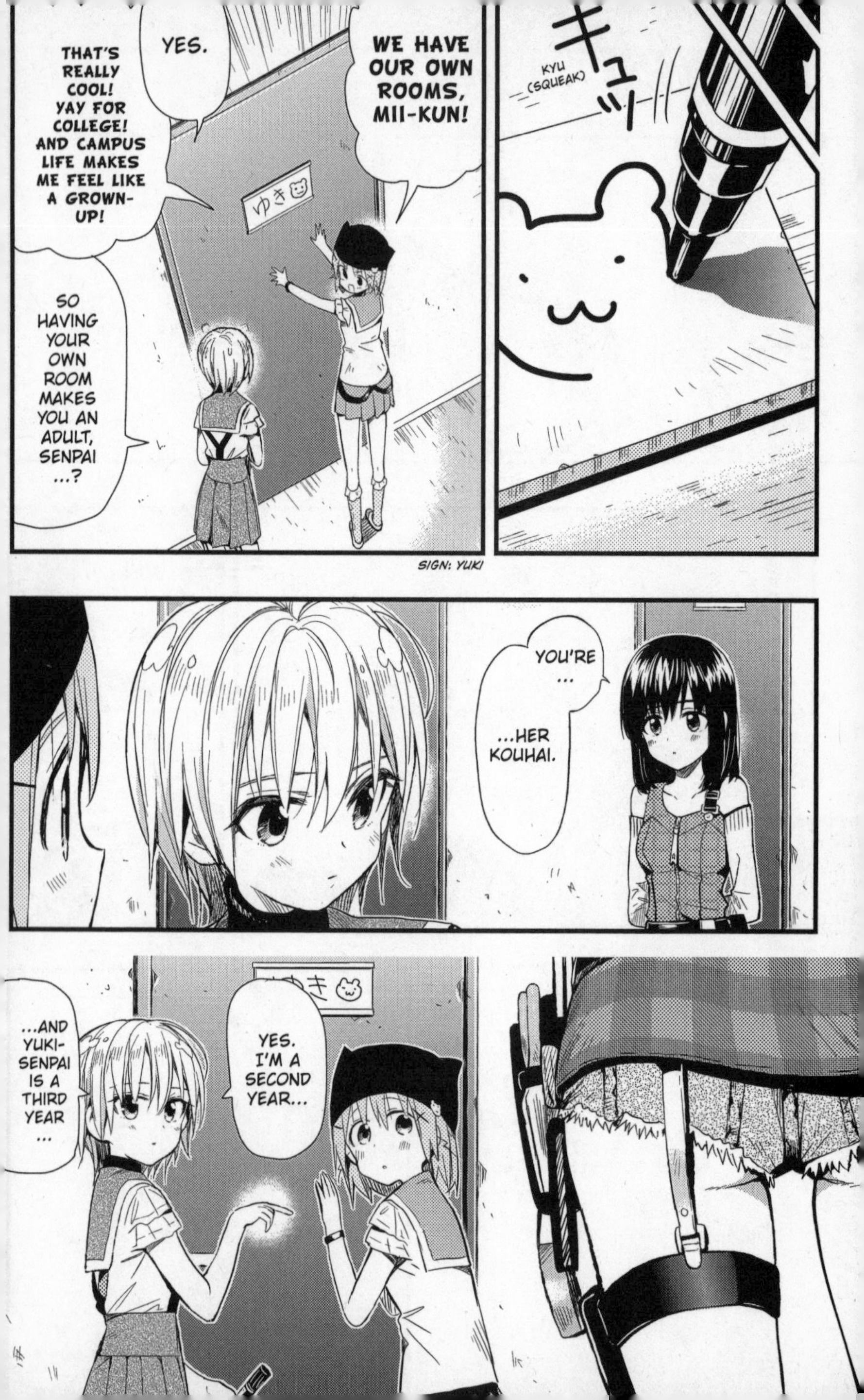
キュッ
KYU (SQUEAK)
WE HAVE OUR OWN ROOMS, MII-KUN!
YES.
THAT'S REALLY COOL! YAY FOR COLLEGE! AND CAMPUS LIFE MAKES ME FEEL LIKE A GROWN-UP!
ゆき
SO HAVING YOUR OWN ROOM MAKES YOU AN ADULT, SENPAI ...?
SIGN: YUKI
YOU'RE ...
...HER KOUHAI.
YES. I'M A SECOND YEAR...
...AND YUKI-SENPAI IS A THIRD YEAR ...

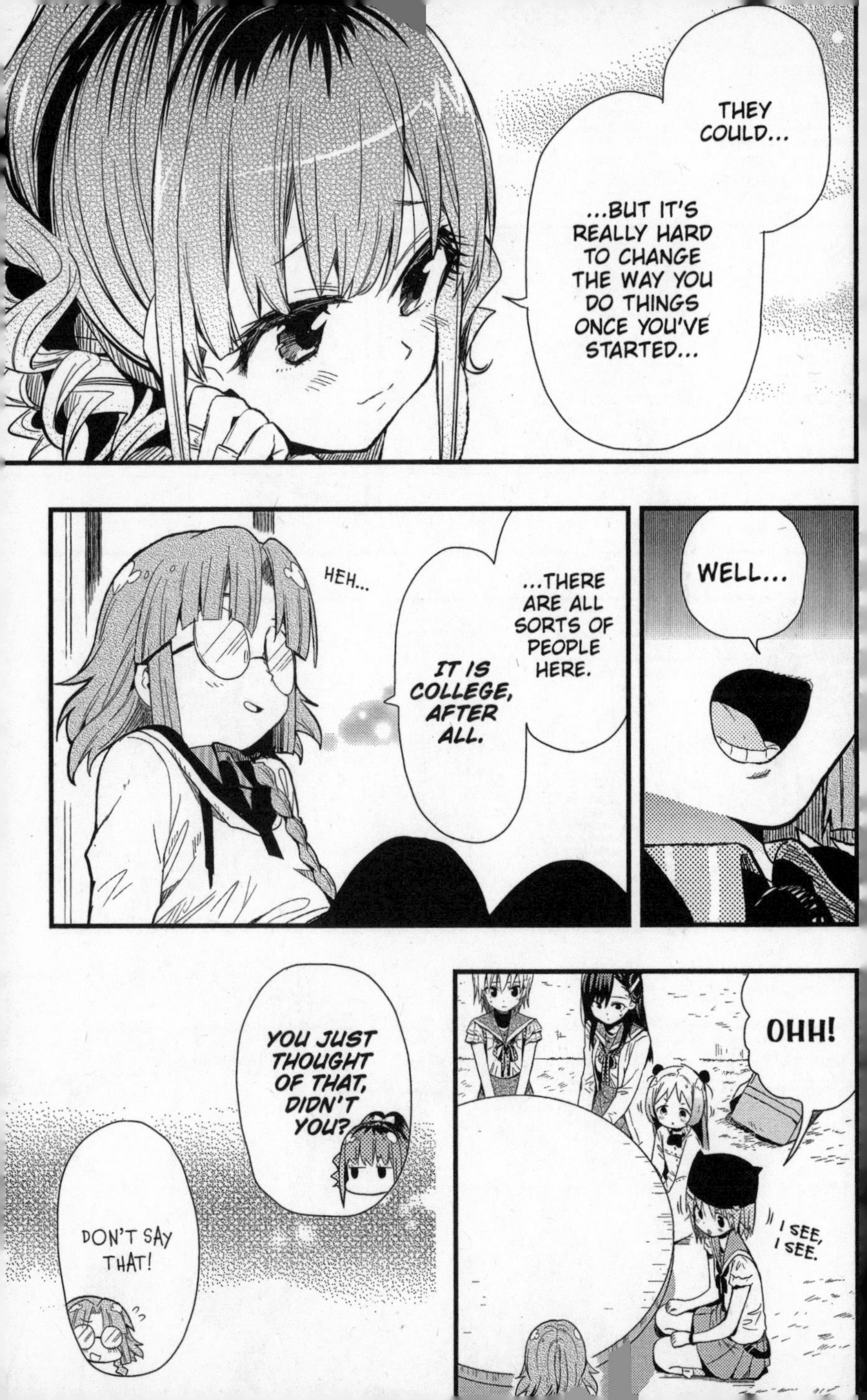
THEY COULD...
...BUT IT'S REALLY HARD TO CHANGE THE WAY YOU DO THINGS ONCE YOU'VE STARTED...
WELL...
...THERE ARE ALL SORTS OF PEOPLE HERE.
IT IS COLLEGE, AFTER ALL.
HEH...
OHH!
I SEE, I SEE.
YOU JUST THOUGHT OF THAT, DIDN'T YOU?
DON'T SAY THAT!

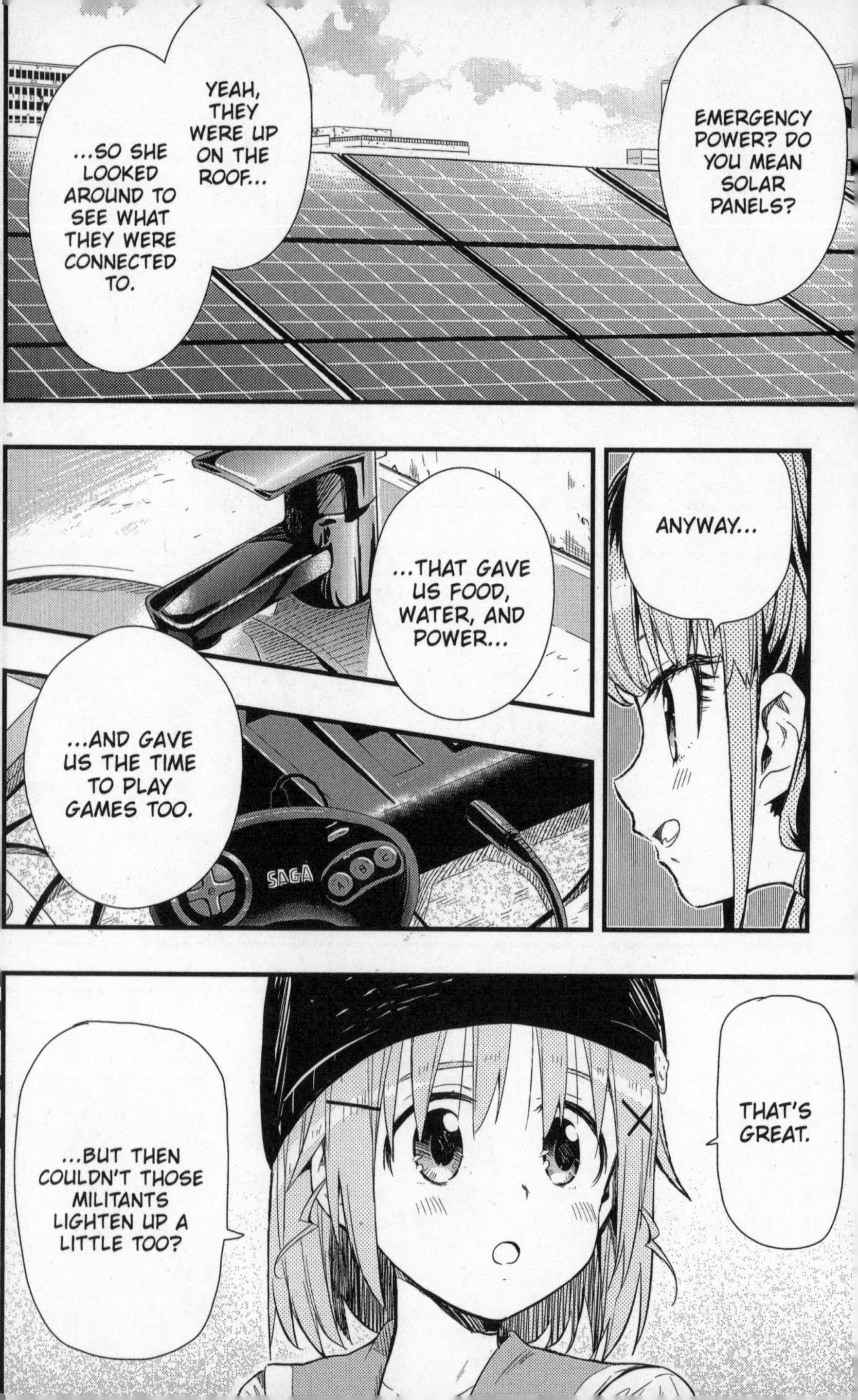
EMERGENCY POWER? DO YOU MEAN SOLAR PANELS?
YEAH, THEY WERE UP ON THE ROOF...
...SO SHE LOOKED AROUND TO SEE WHAT THEY WERE CONNECTED TO.
ANYWAY...
...THAT GAVE US FOOD, WATER, AND POWER...
...AND GAVE US THE TIME TO PLAY GAMES TOO.
SAGA
THAT'S GREAT.
...BUT THEN COULDN'T THOSE MILITANTS LIGHTEN UP A LITTLE TOO?

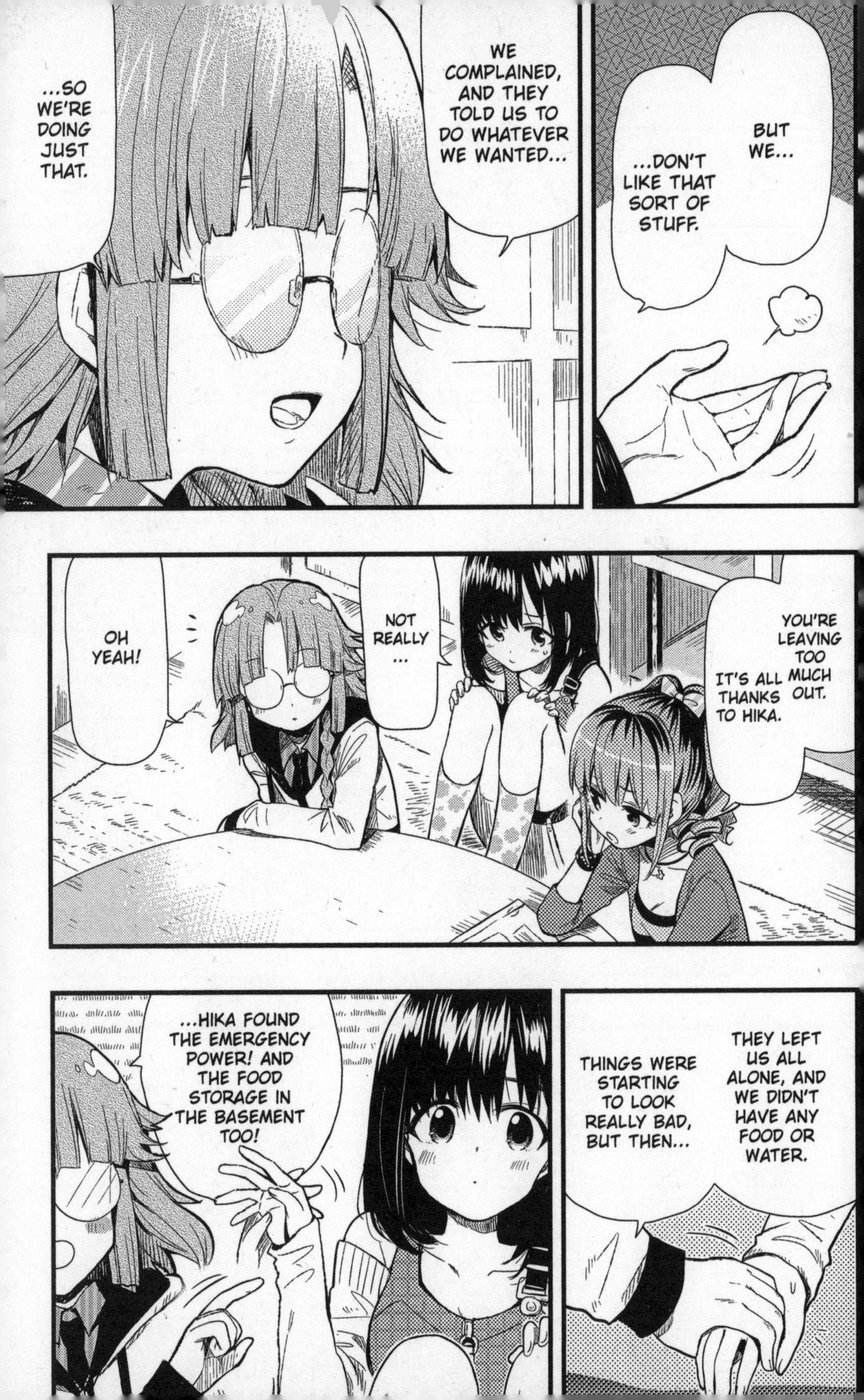
BUT WE...
...DON'T LIKE THAT SORT OF STUFF.
WE COMPLAINED, AND THEY TOLD US TO DO WHATEVER WE WANTED...
...SO WE'RE DOING JUST THAT.
YOU'RE LEAVING TOO MUCH OUT.
IT'S ALL THANKS TO HIKA.
NOT REALLY...
OH YEAH!
THEY LEFT US ALL ALONE, AND WE DIDN'T HAVE ANY FOOD OR WATER.
THINGS WERE STARTING TO LOOK REALLY BAD, BUT THEN...
...HIKA FOUND THE EMERGENCY POWER! AND THE FOOD STORAGE IN THE BASEMENT TOO!

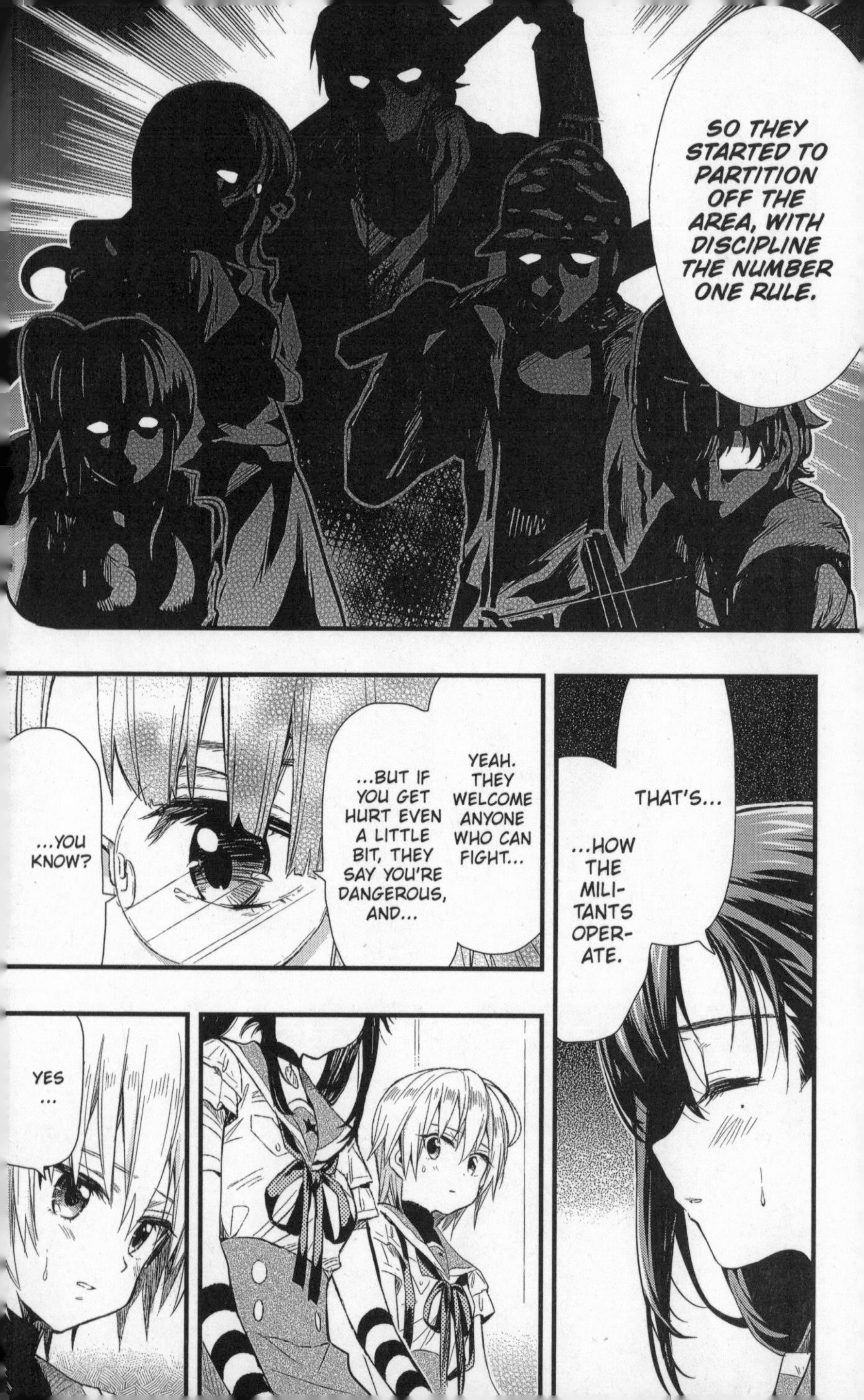
SO THEY STARTED TO PARTITION OFF THE AREA, WITH DISCIPLINE THE NUMBER ONE RULE.
THAT'S...
...HOW THE MILI-TANTS OPER-ATE.
YEAH. THEY WELCOME ANYONE WHO CAN FIGHT...
...BUT IF YOU GET HURT EVEN A LITTLE BIT, THEY SAY YOU'RE DANGEROUS, AND...
...YOU KNOW?
YES...

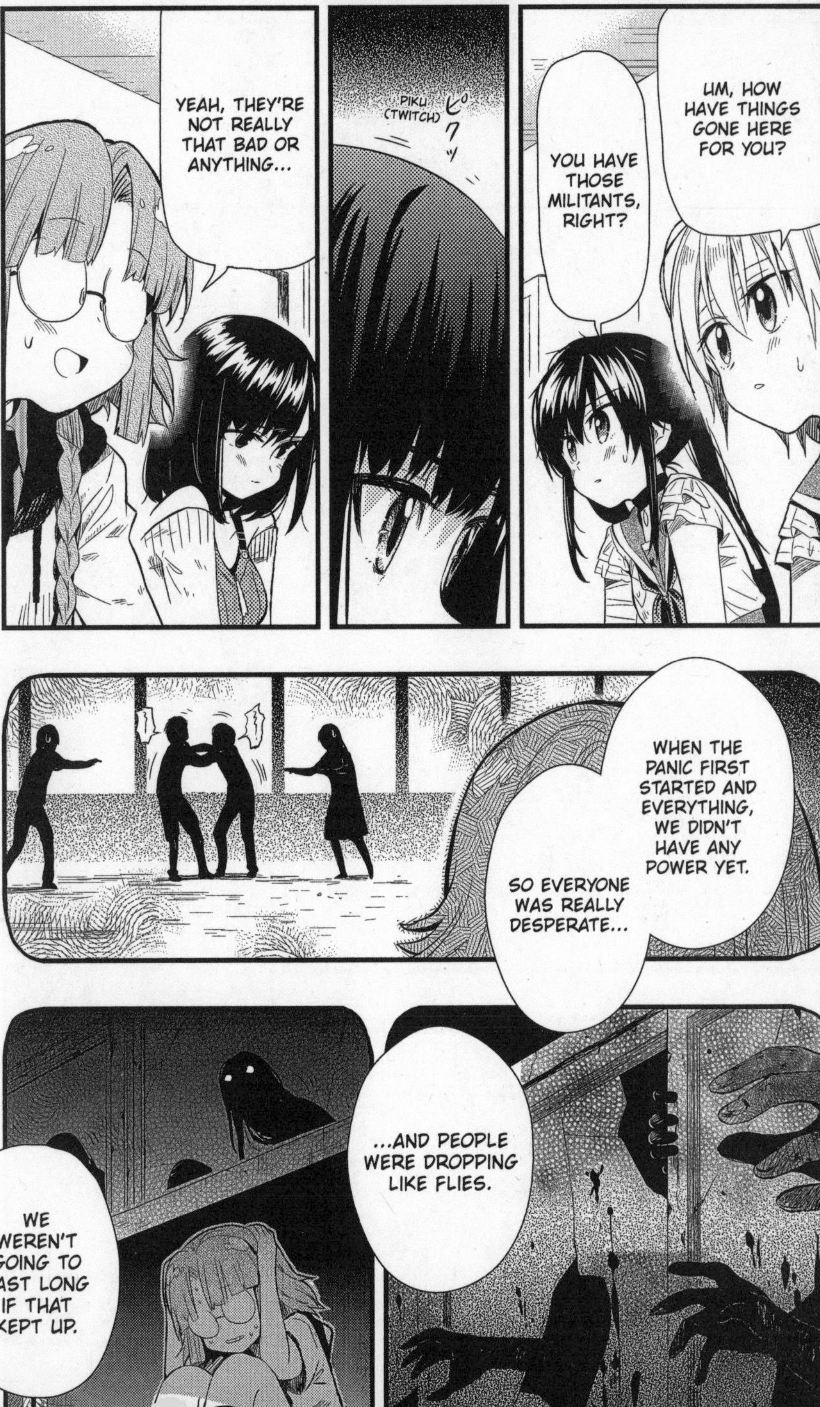
UM, HOW HAVE THINGS GONE HERE FOR YOU?
YOU HAVE THOSE MILITANTS, RIGHT?
PIKU (TWITCH) ピクッ
YEAH, THEY'RE NOT REALLY THAT BAD OR ANYTHING...
WHEN THE PANIC FIRST STARTED AND EVERYTHING, WE DIDN'T HAVE ANY POWER YET.
SO EVERYONE WAS REALLY DESPERATE...
...AND PEOPLE WERE DROPPING LIKE FLIES.
WE WEREN'T GOING TO LAST LONG IF THAT KEPT UP.

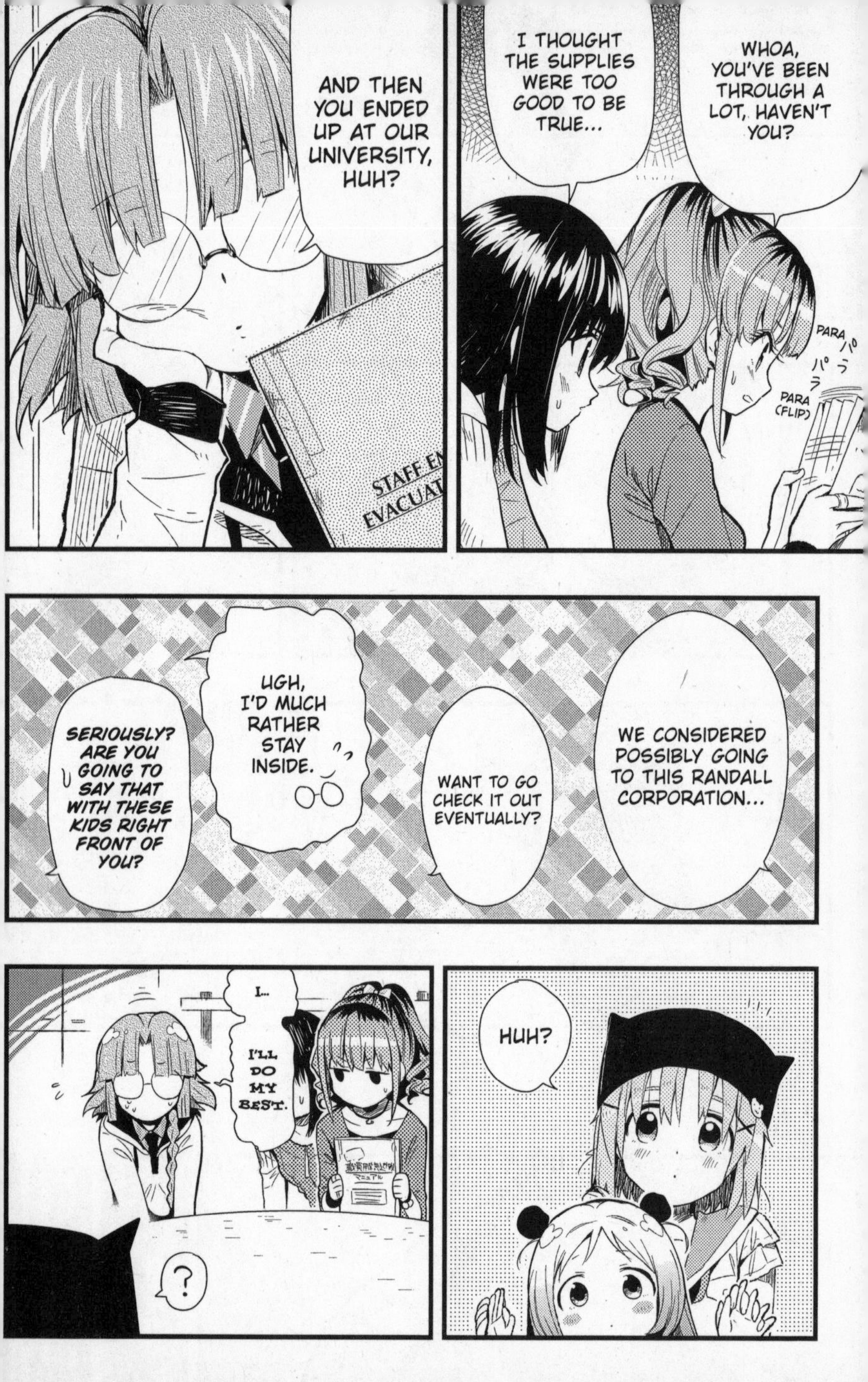
WHOA, YOU'VE BEEN THROUGH A LOT, HAVEN'T YOU?
I THOUGHT THE SUPPLIES WERE TOO GOOD TO BE TRUE...
PARA PARA (FLIP)
AND THEN YOU ENDED UP AT OUR UNIVERSITY, HUH?
WE CONSIDERED POSSIBLY GOING TO THIS RANDALL CORPORATION...
WANT TO GO CHECK IT OUT EVENTUALLY?
UGH, I'D MUCH RATHER STAY INSIDE.
SERIOUSLY? ARE YOU GOING TO SAY THAT WITH THESE KIDS RIGHT FRONT OF YOU?
HUH?
I...
I'LL DO MY BEST.
?

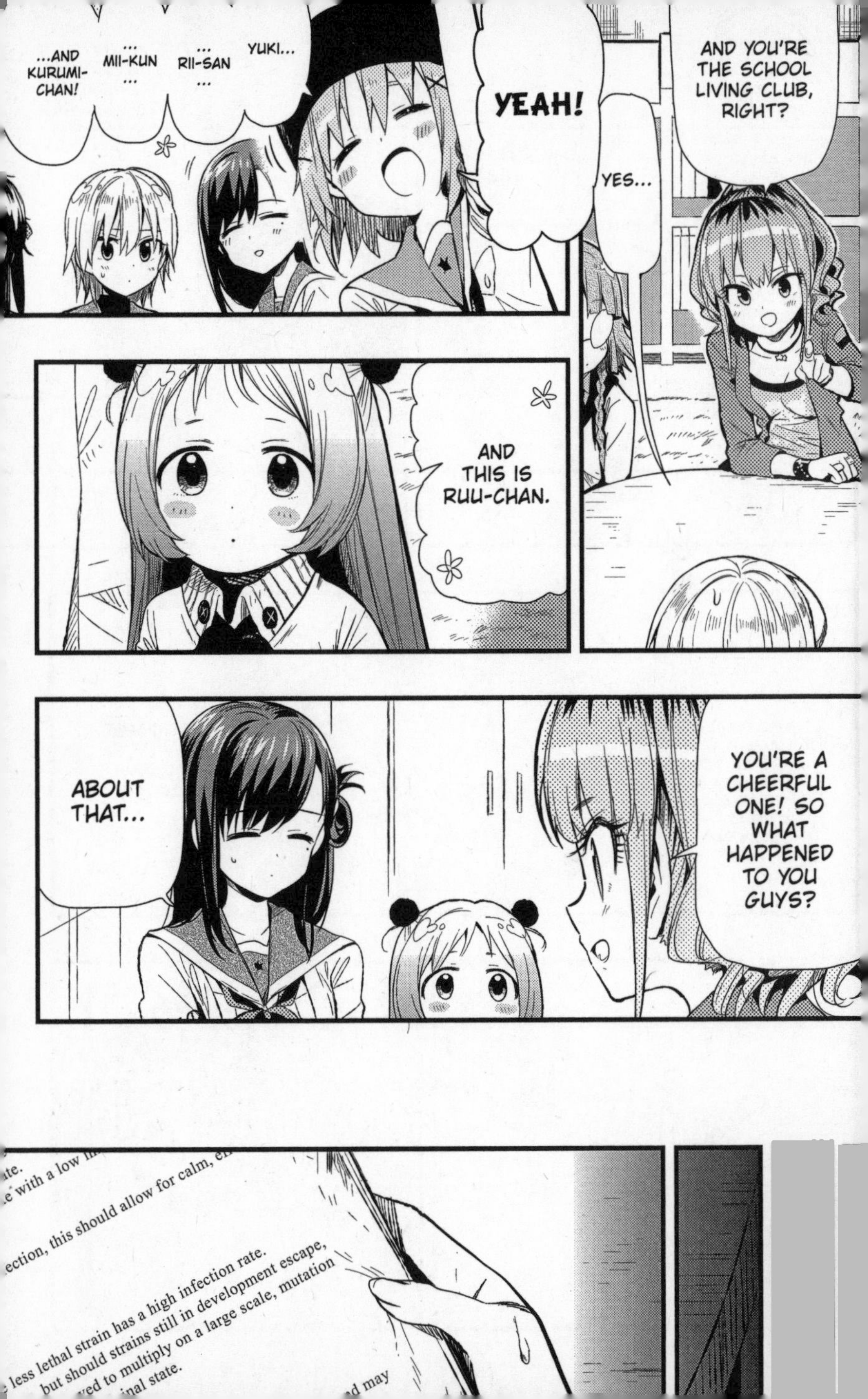
AND YOU'RE THE SCHOOL LIVING CLUB, RIGHT?
YES...
YEAH!
YUKI...
...RII-SAN...
...MII-KUN...
...AND KURUMI-CHAN!
AND THIS IS RUU-CHAN.
YOU'RE A CHEERFUL ONE! SO WHAT HAPPENED TO YOU GUYS?
ABOUT THAT...
ate.
with a low
ection, this should allow for calm,
ection rate.
less lethal strain has a high infection rate.
but should strains still in development escape,
wed to multiply on a large scale, mutation
inal state.
d may

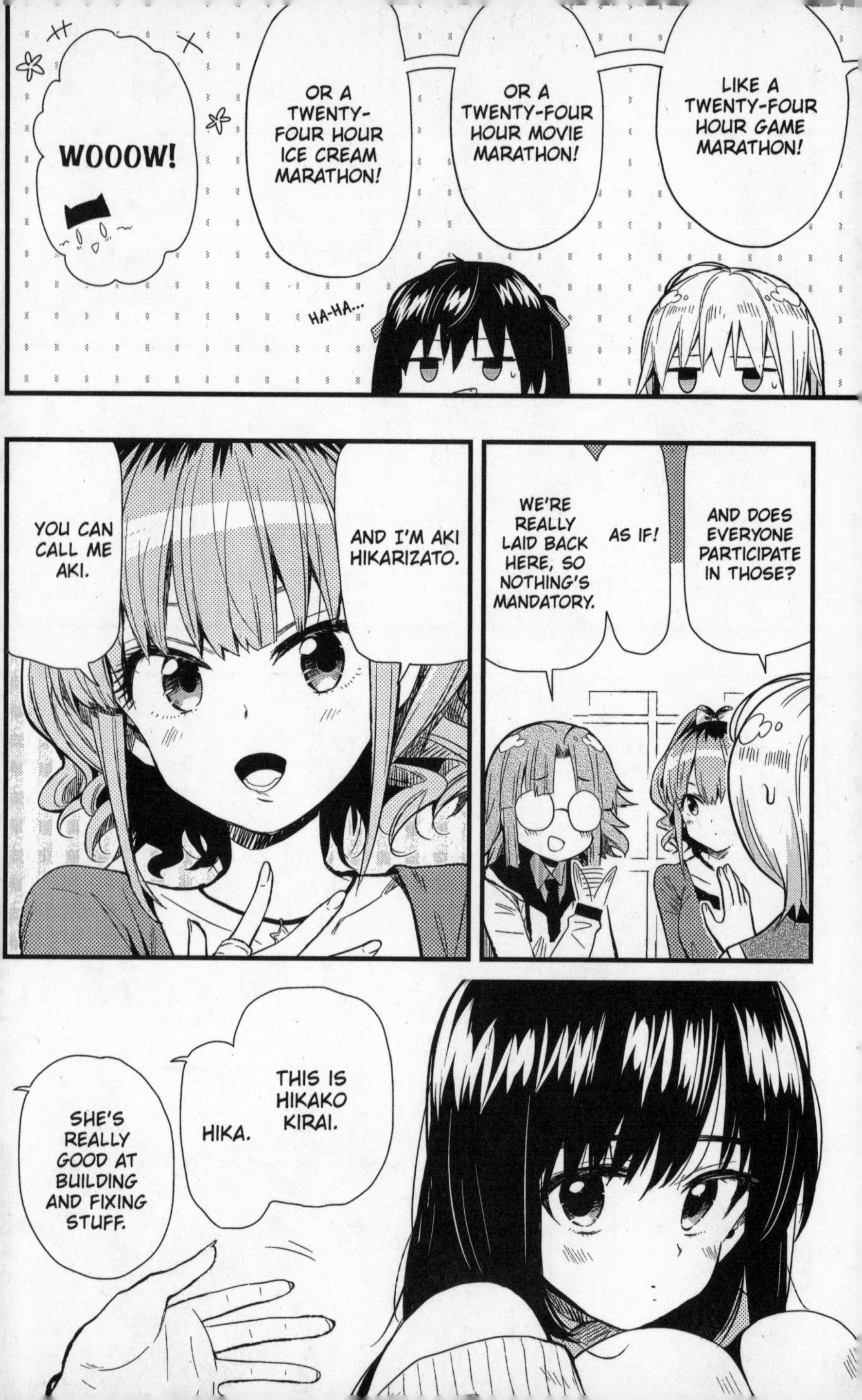
LIKE A TWENTY-FOUR HOUR GAME MARATHON!
OR A TWENTY-FOUR HOUR MOVIE MARATHON!
OR A TWENTY-FOUR HOUR ICE CREAM MARATHON!
WOOOW!
HA-HA...
AND DOES EVERYONE PARTICIPATE IN THOSE?
AS IF!
WE'RE REALLY LAID BACK HERE, SO NOTHING'S MANDATORY.
AND I'M AKI HIKARIZATO.
YOU CAN CALL ME AKI.
THIS IS HIKAKO KIRAI.
HIKA.
SHE'S REALLY GOOD AT BUILDING AND FIXING STUFF.

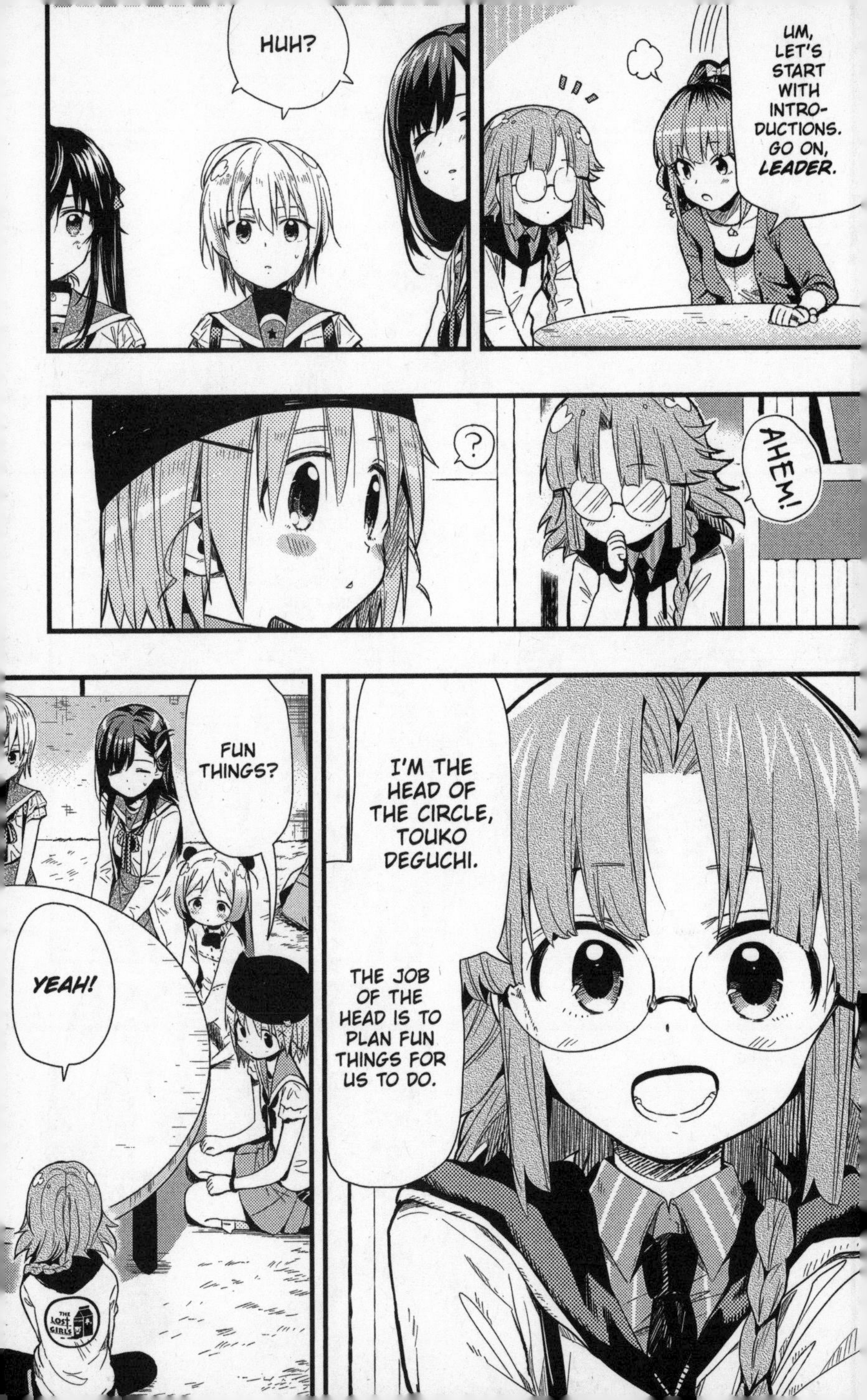
UM, LET'S START WITH INTRO-DUCTIONS. GO ON, ***LEADER***.
HUH?
AHEM!
?
I'M THE HEAD OF THE CIRCLE, TOUKO DEGUCHI.
THE JOB OF THE HEAD IS TO PLAN FUN THINGS FOR US TO DO.
FUN THINGS?
YEAH!
THE LOST GIRLS

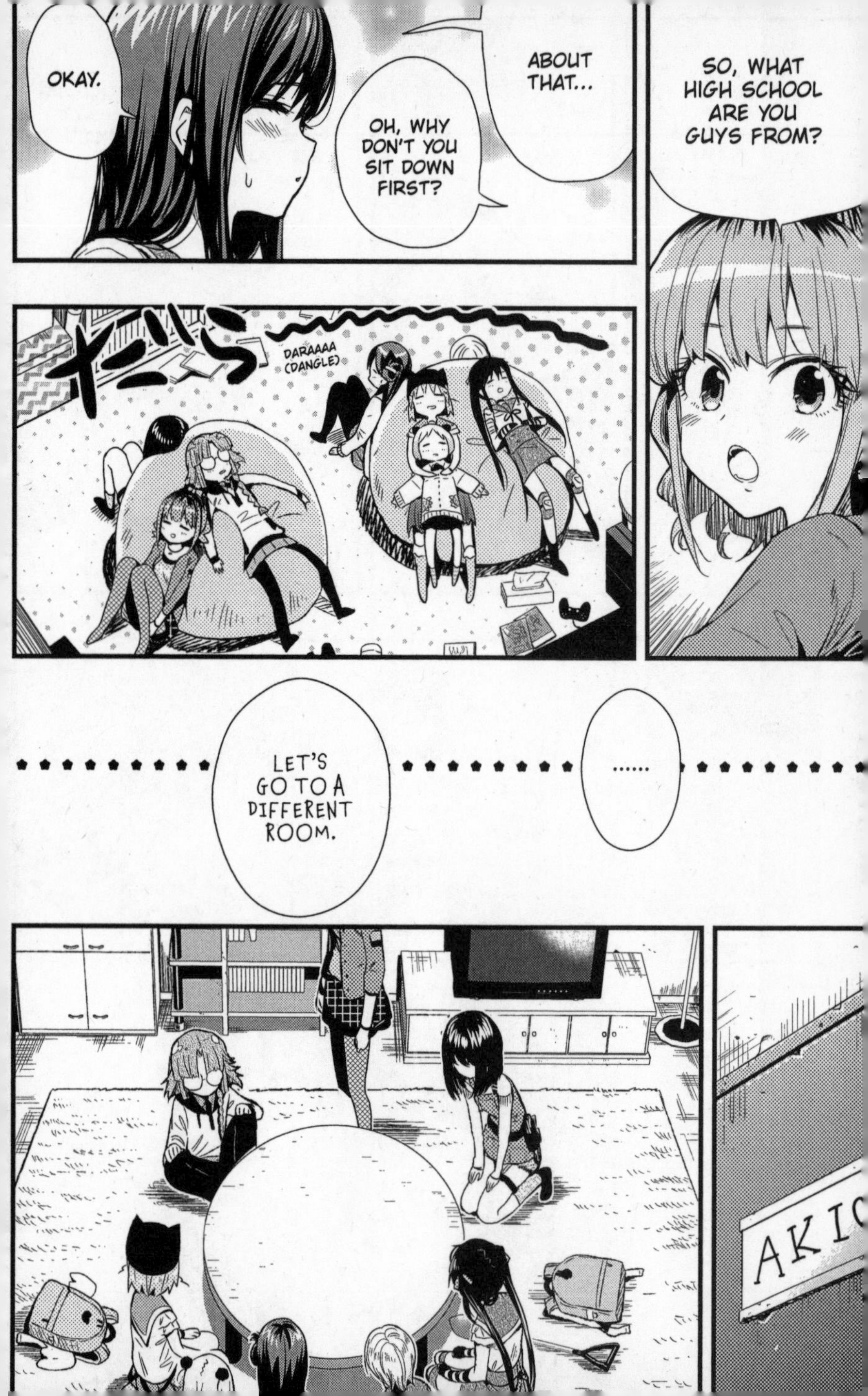
SO, WHAT HIGH SCHOOL ARE YOU GUYS FROM?
ABOUT THAT...
OH, WHY DON'T YOU SIT DOWN FIRST?
OKAY.
DARAAAA (DANGLE)
......
LET'S GO TO A DIFFERENT ROOM.
AKI

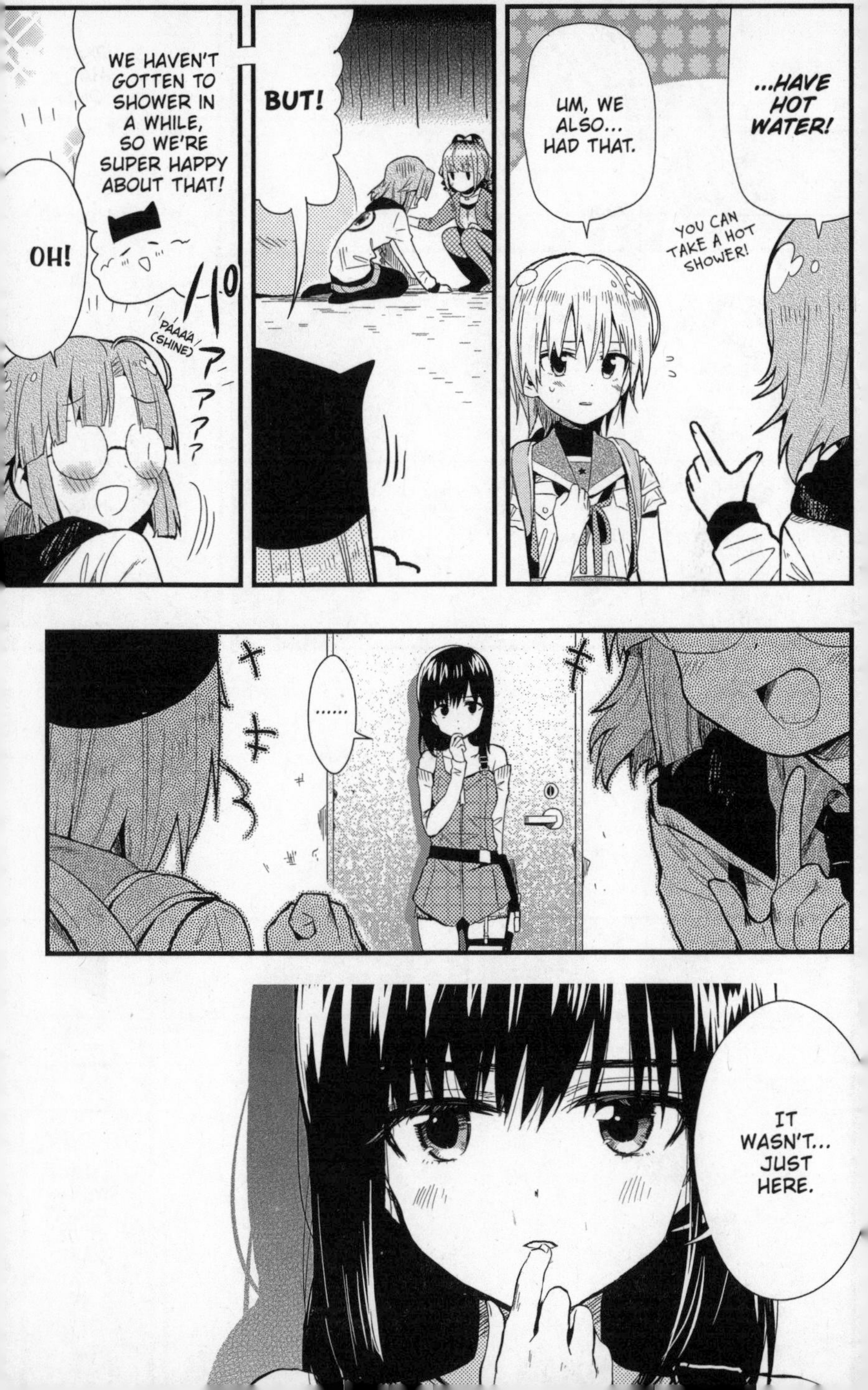
...HAVE HOT WATER!
YOU CAN TAKE A HOT SHOWER!
UM, WE ALSO... HAD THAT.
BUT!
WE HAVEN'T GOTTEN TO SHOWER IN A WHILE, SO WE'RE SUPER HAPPY ABOUT THAT!
PAAAA (SHINE)
OH!
......
IT WASN'T... JUST HERE.

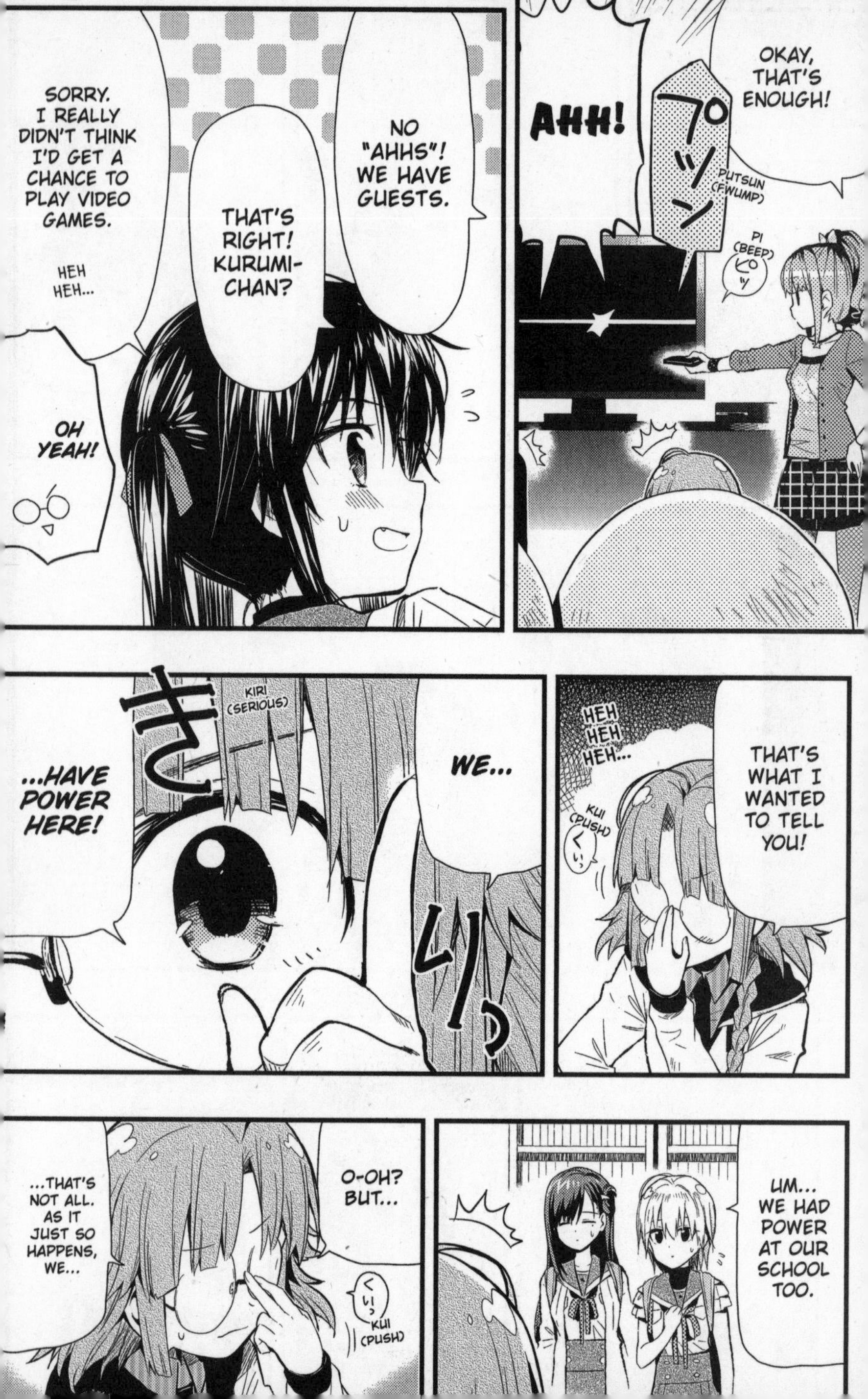
OKAY, THAT'S ENOUGH!
プツン
PUTSUN (FWUMP)
PI (BEEP)
ピッ
AHH!
NO "AHHS"! WE HAVE GUESTS.
THAT'S RIGHT! KURUMI-CHAN?
SORRY. I REALLY DIDN'T THINK I'D GET A CHANCE TO PLAY VIDEO GAMES.
HEH HEH...
OH YEAH!
HEH HEH HEH...
THAT'S WHAT I WANTED TO TELL YOU!
KUI (PUSH)
くいっ
WE...
KIRI (SERIOUS)
...HAVE POWER HERE!
UM... WE HAD POWER AT OUR SCHOOL TOO.
O-OH? BUT...
...THAT'S NOT ALL. AS IT JUST SO HAPPENS, WE...
くいっ
KUI (PUSH)

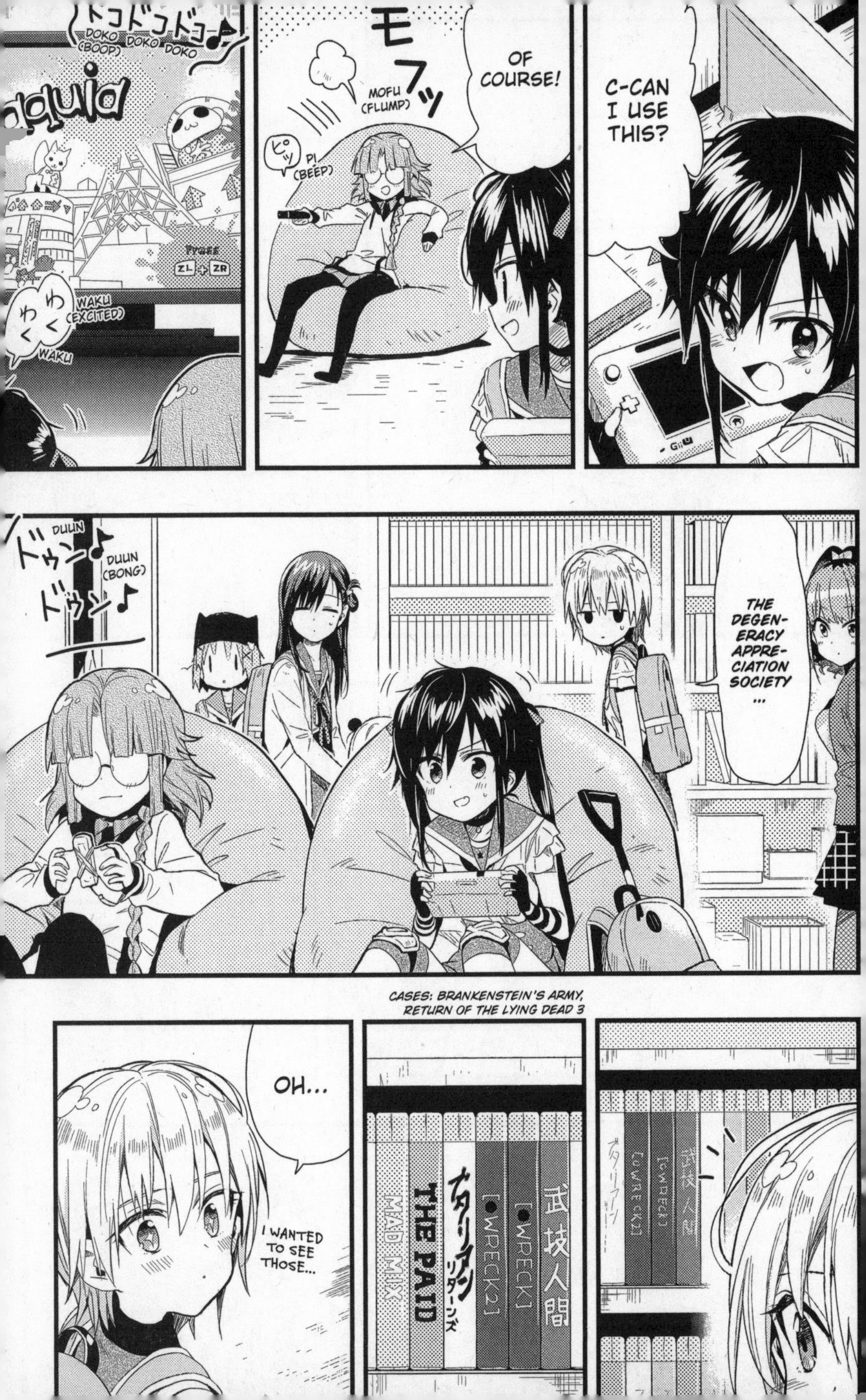
C-CAN I USE THIS?
OF COURSE!
モフッ MOFU (FLUMP)
ピッ PI (BEEP)
ドコドコドコ♪ DOKO (BOOP) DOKO DOKO
Press ZL + ZR
わくわく WAKU (EXCITED) WAKU
THE DEGENERACY APPRECIATION SOCIETY...
ドゥン♪ DUUN
ドゥン♪ DUUN (BONG)
CASES: BRANKENSTEIN'S ARMY, RETURN OF THE LYING DEAD 3
OH...
I WANTED TO SEE THOSE...
武抜人間
[WRECK]
[WRECK2]
オタリアン リターンズ
THE PAID
MAD MIX

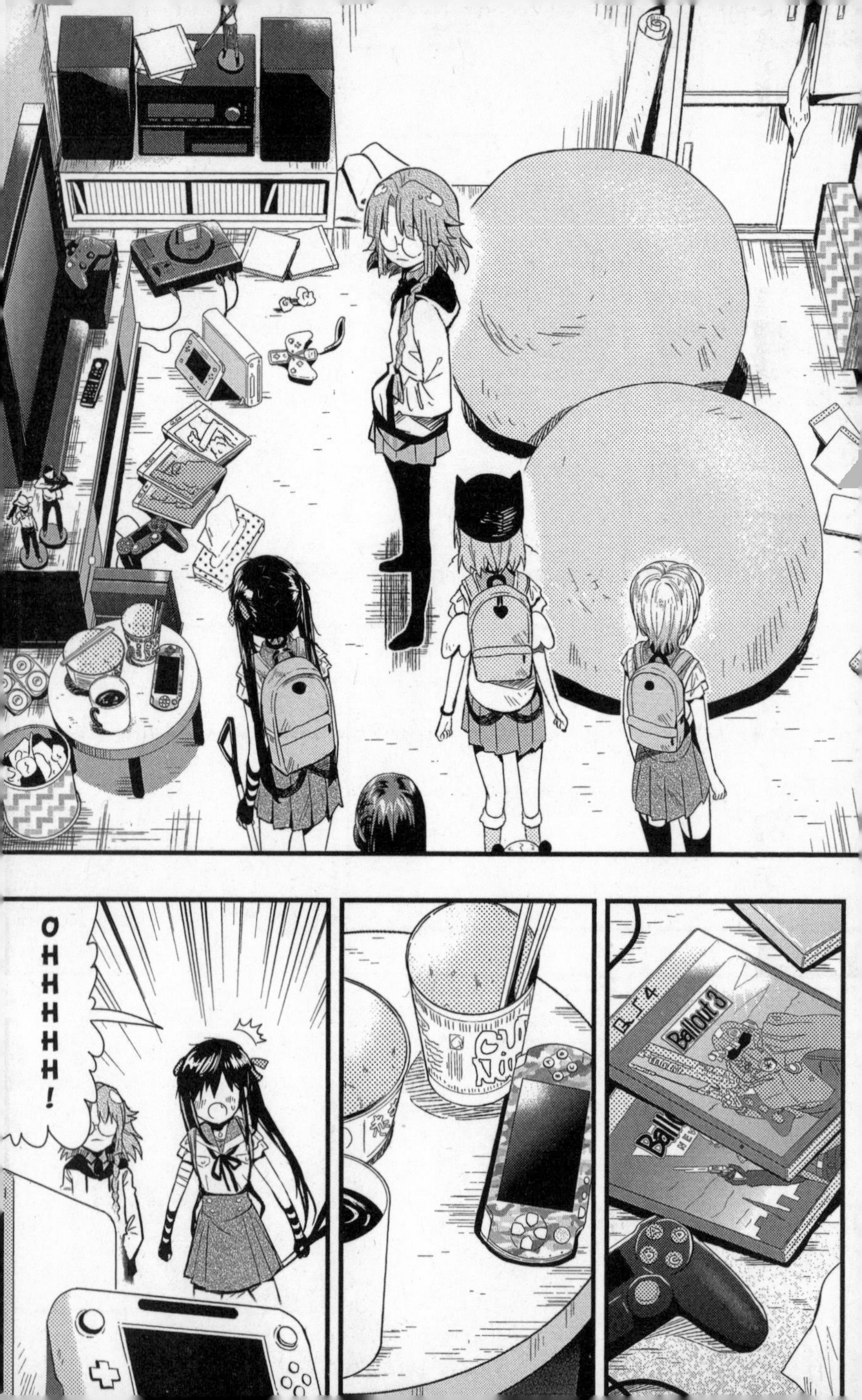
Ballout 3
OHHHHHH!

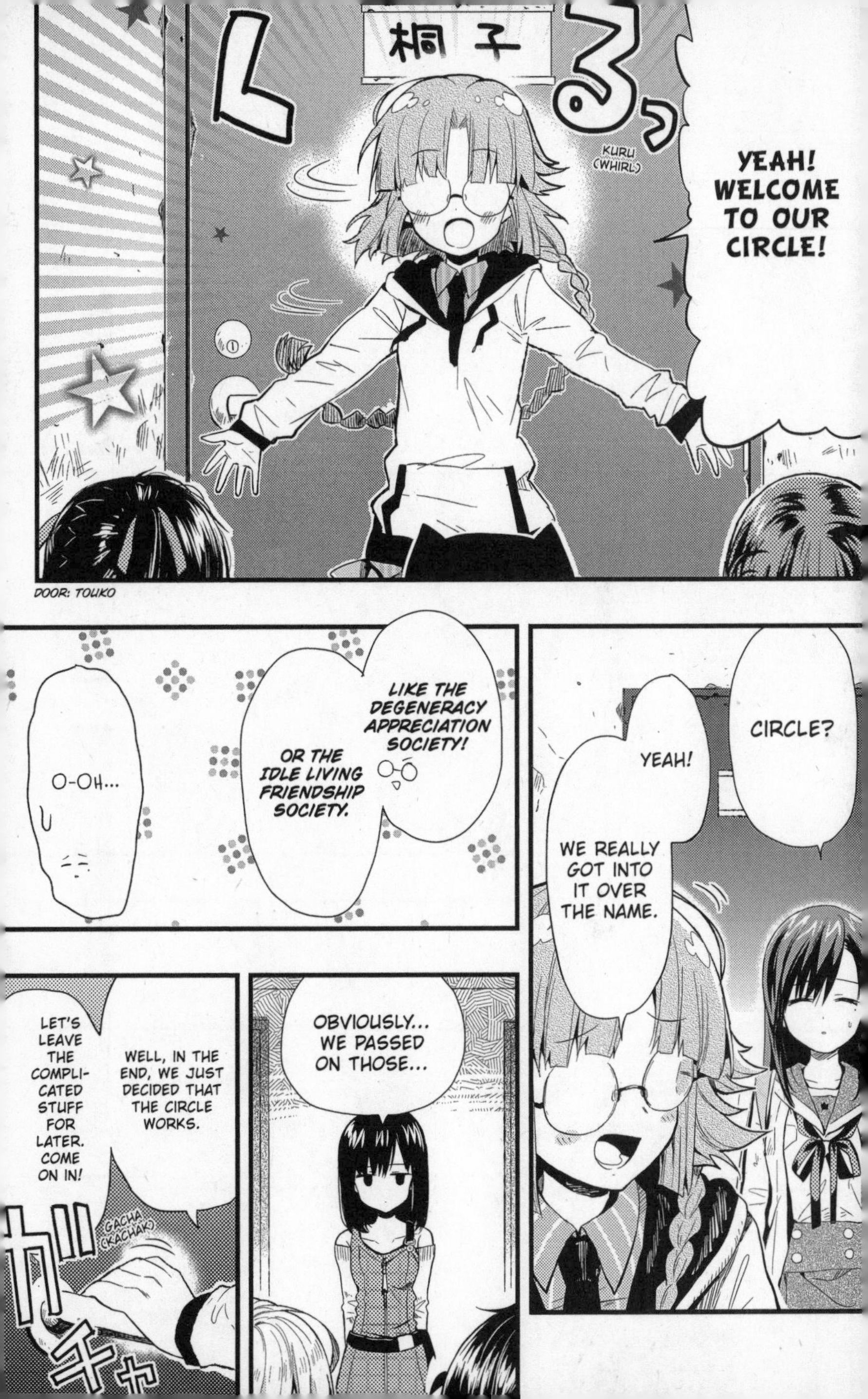
桐子
くるっ
KURU (WHIRL)
YEAH! WELCOME TO OUR CIRCLE!
DOOR: TOUKO
CIRCLE?
YEAH!
WE REALLY GOT INTO IT OVER THE NAME.
LIKE THE DEGENERACY APPRECIATION SOCIETY!
OR THE IDLE LIVING FRIENDSHIP SOCIETY.
O-OH...
OBVIOUSLY... WE PASSED ON THOSE...
WELL, IN THE END, WE JUST DECIDED THAT THE CIRCLE WORKS.
LET'S LEAVE THE COMPLICATED STUFF FOR LATER. COME ON IN!
ガチャ
GACHA (KACHAK)

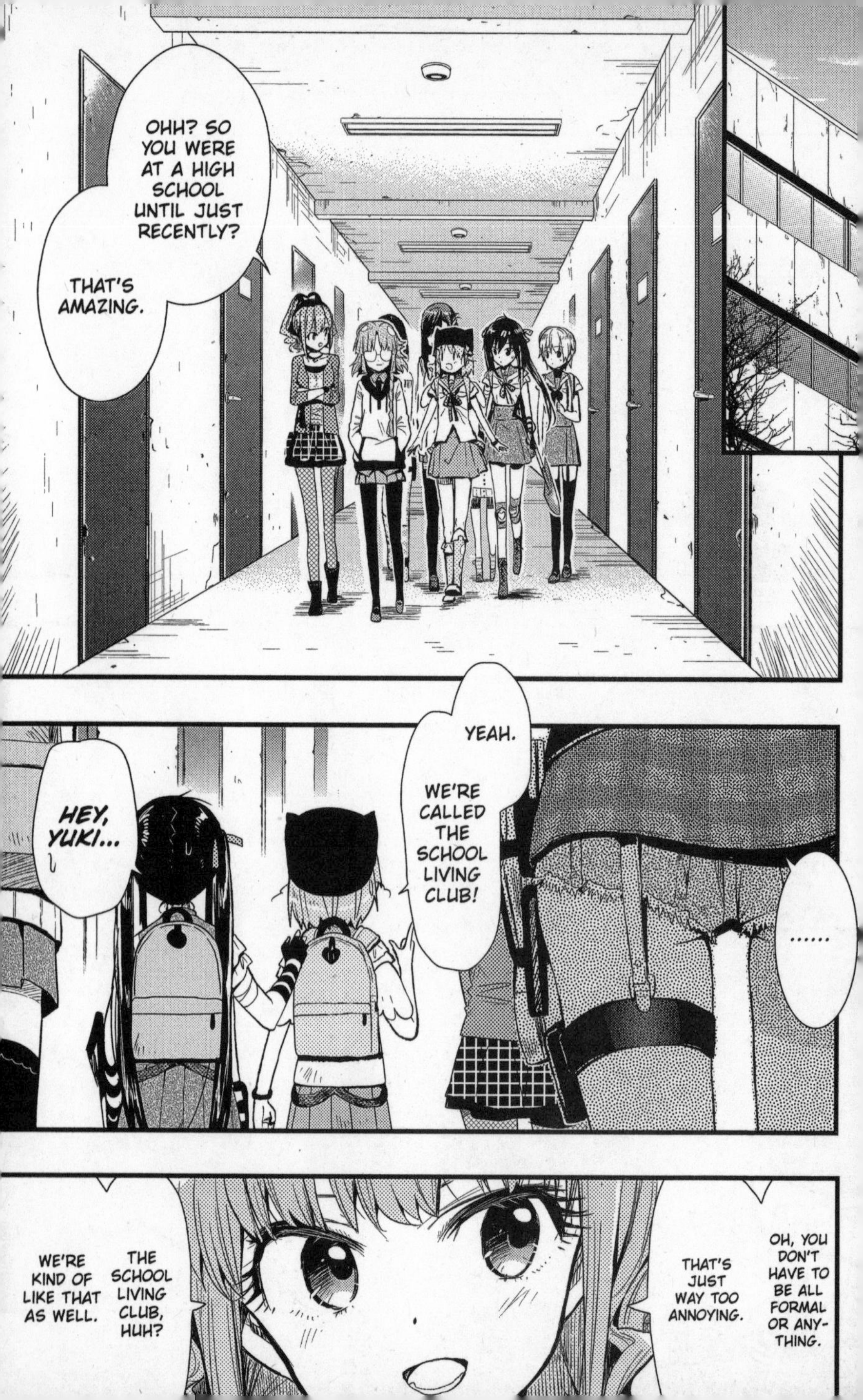
OHH? SO YOU WERE AT A HIGH SCHOOL UNTIL JUST RECENTLY?
THAT'S AMAZING.
......
YEAH.
WE'RE CALLED THE SCHOOL LIVING CLUB!
HEY, YUKI...
OH, YOU DON'T HAVE TO BE ALL FORMAL OR ANY-THING.
THAT'S JUST WAY TOO ANNOYING.
THE SCHOOL LIVING CLUB, HUH?
WE'RE KIND OF LIKE THAT AS WELL.

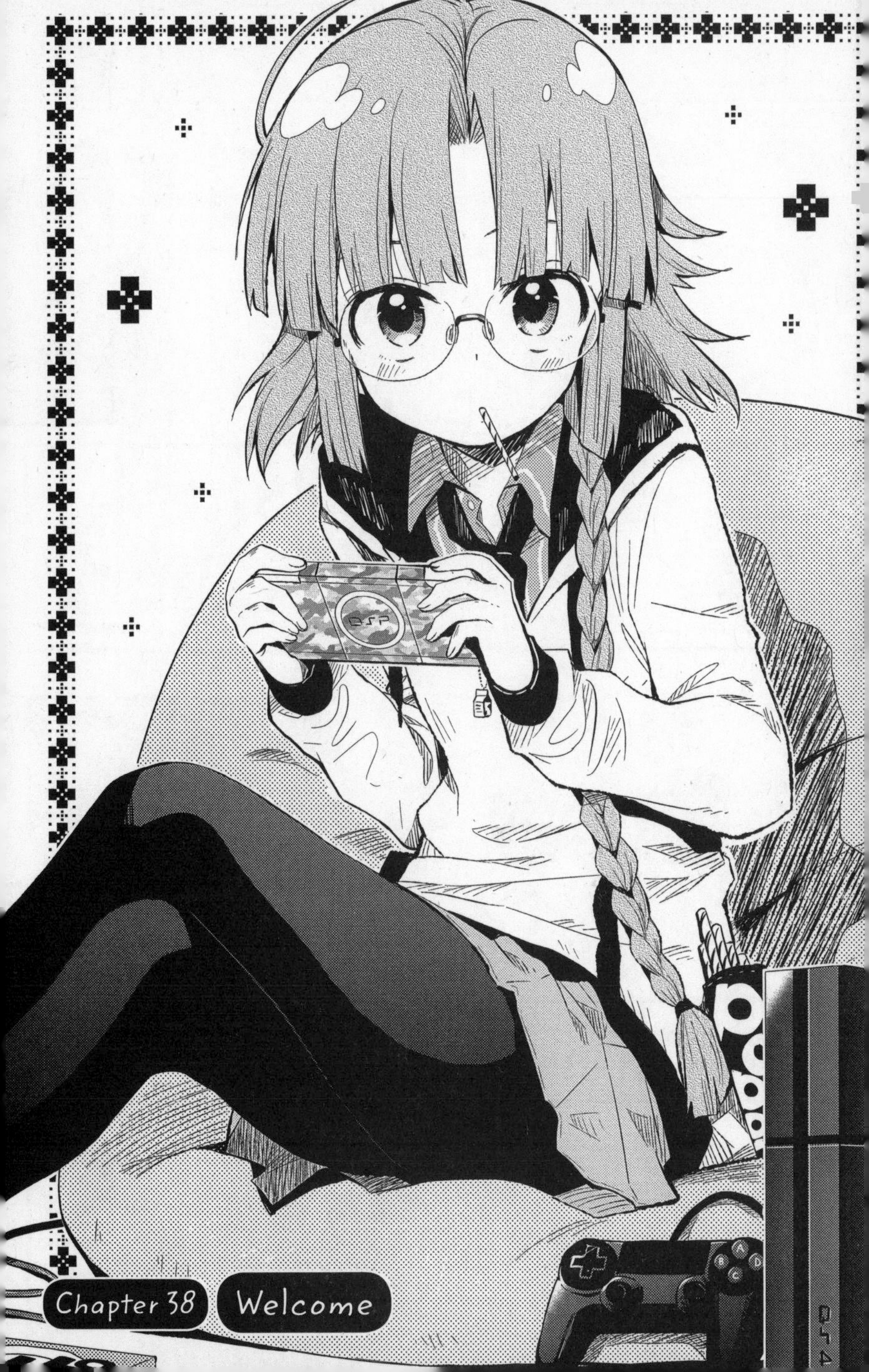
Chapter 38
Welcome

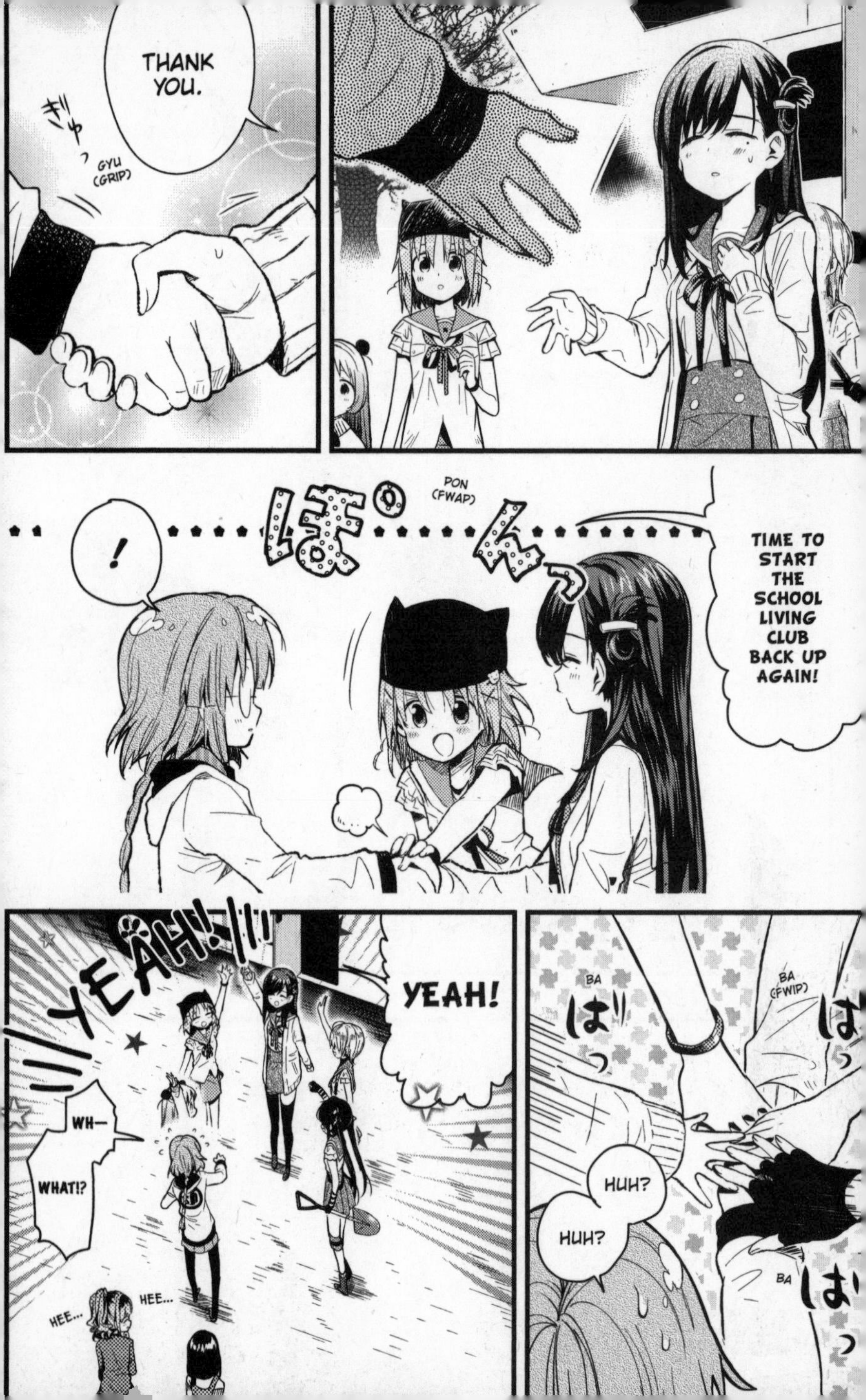
THANK YOU.
ぎゅっ
GYU (GRIP)
TIME TO START THE SCHOOL LIVING CLUB BACK UP AGAIN!
PON (FWAP)
ぽん
!
...
BA (FWIP)
はっ
BA
はっ
BA
はっ
HUH?
HUH?
YEAH!
YEAH!!!
WH—
WHAT!?
HEE...
HEE...

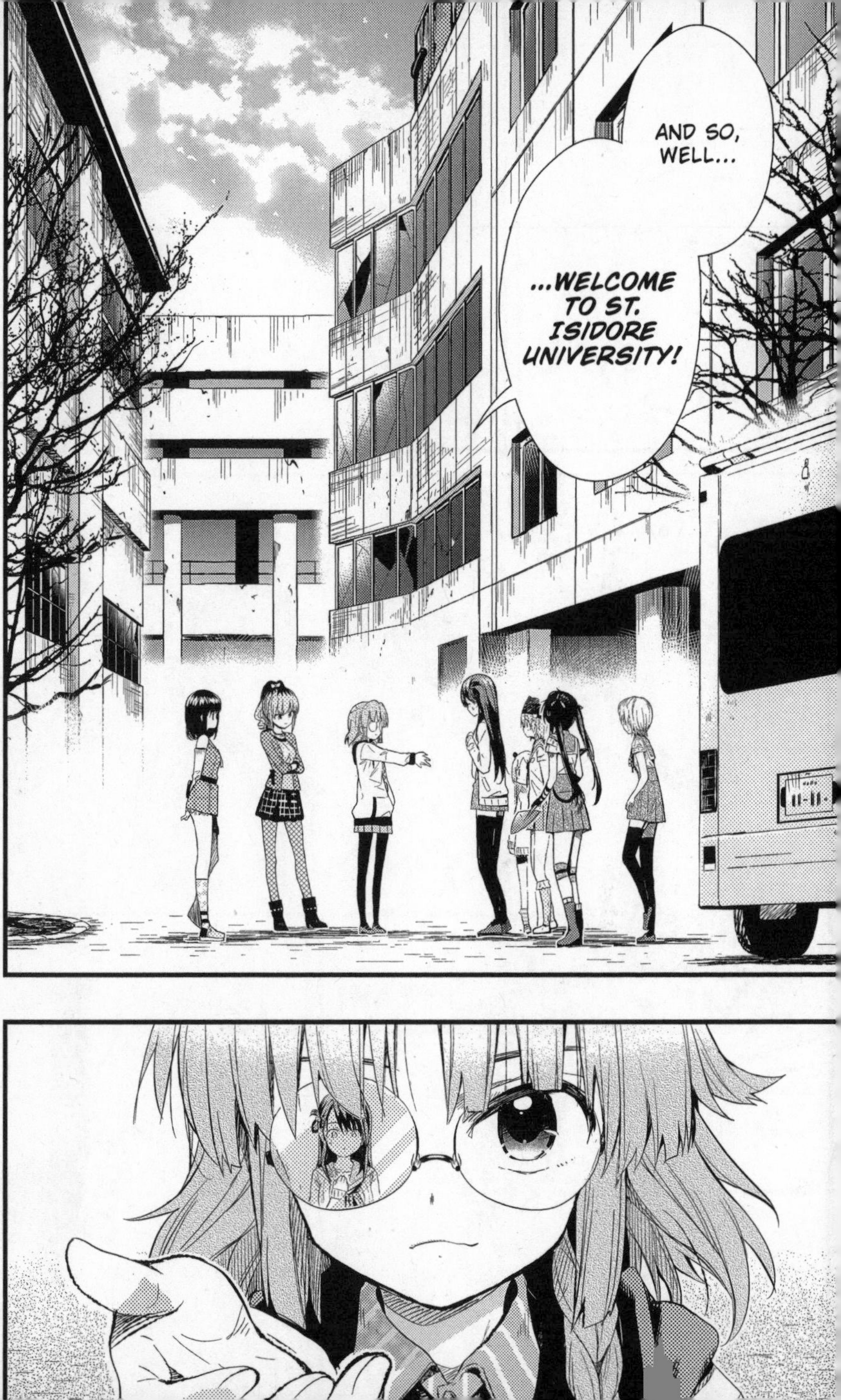
AND SO, WELL...
...WELCOME TO ST. ISIDORE UNIVERSITY!

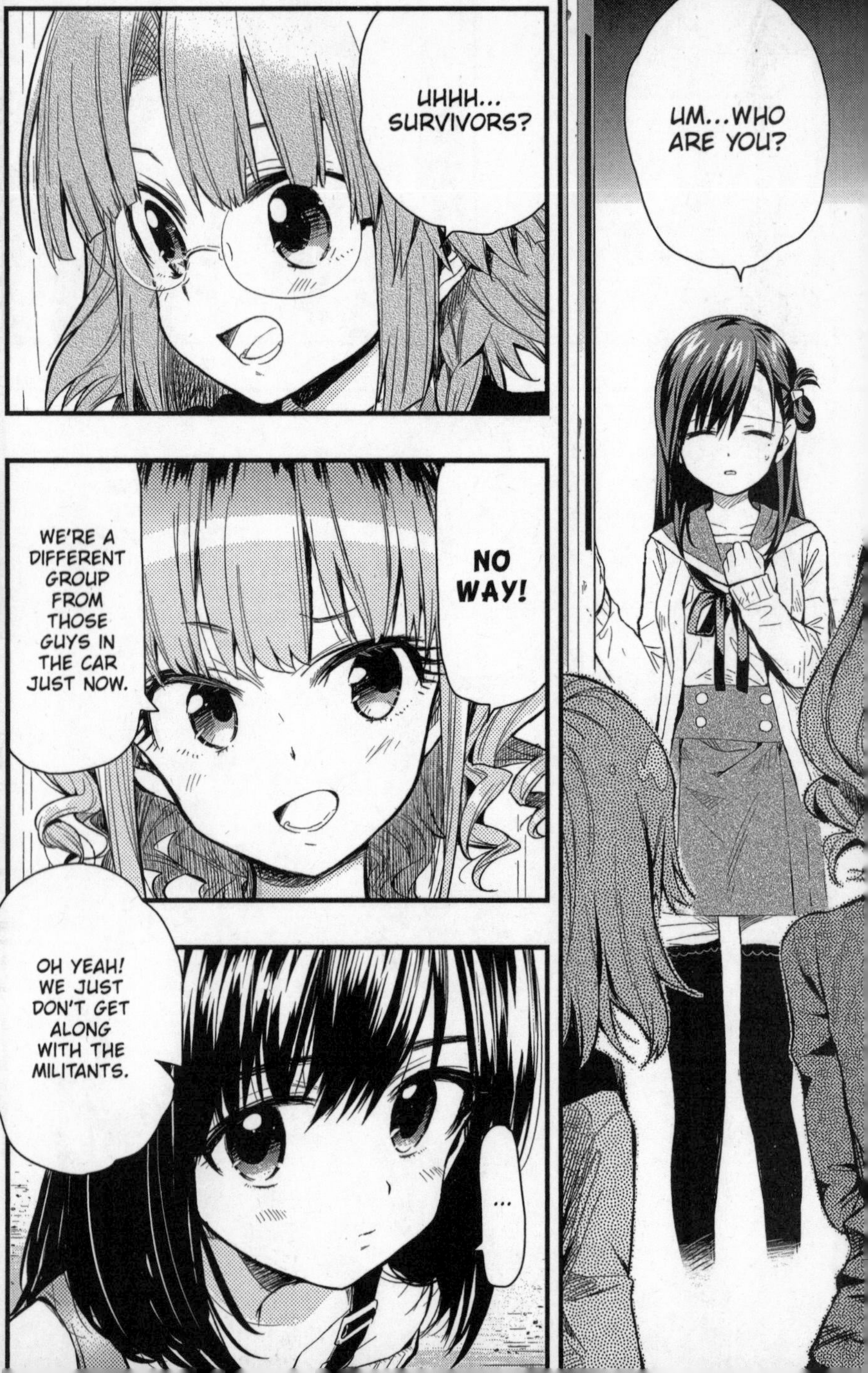
UM...WHO ARE YOU?
UHHH... SURVIVORS?
NO WAY!
WE'RE A DIFFERENT GROUP FROM THOSE GUYS IN THE CAR JUST NOW.
...
OH YEAH! WE JUST DON'T GET ALONG WITH THE MILITANTS.

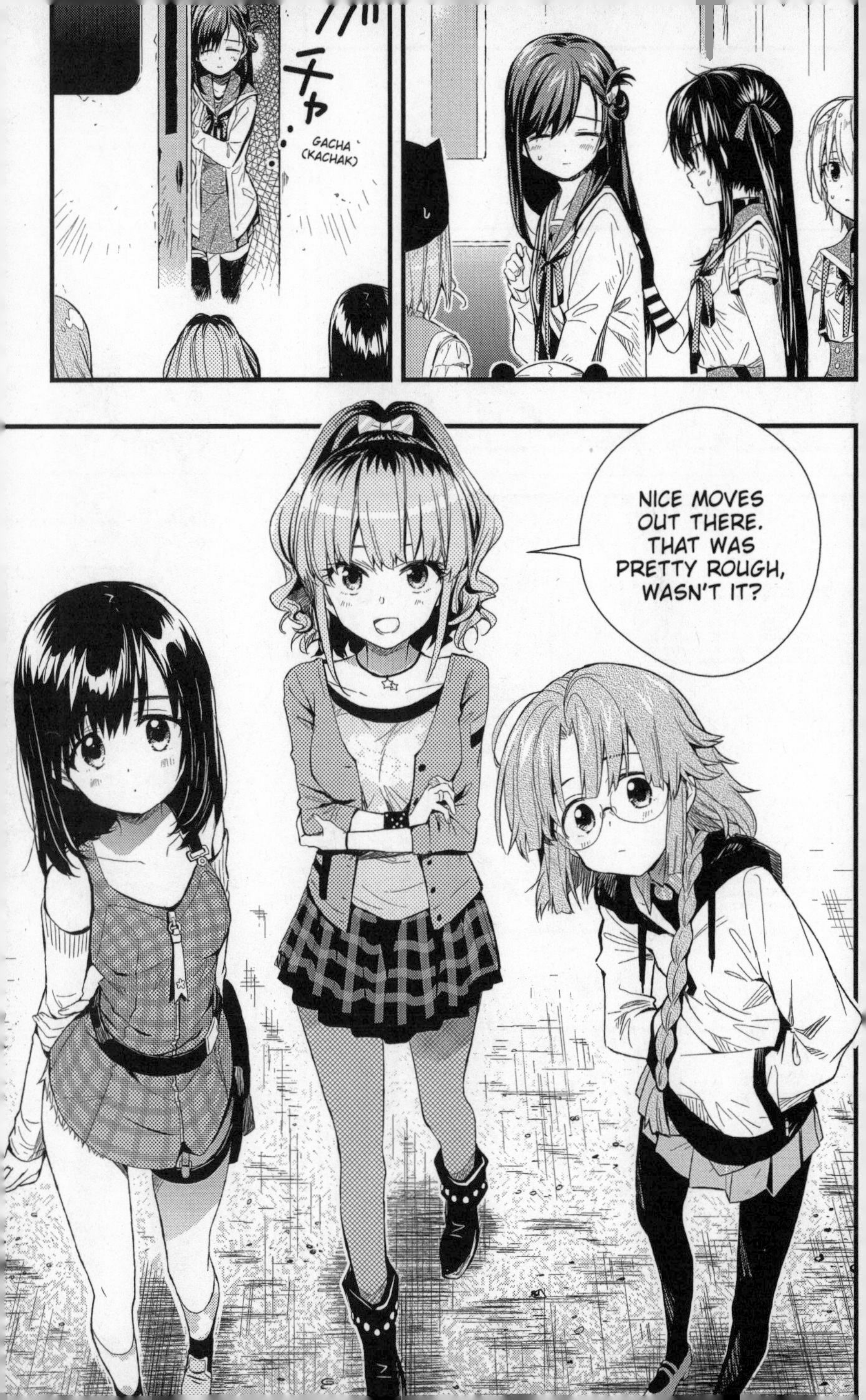
ガチャ
GACHA (KACHAK)
NICE MOVES OUT THERE. THAT WAS PRETTY ROUGH, WASN'T IT?

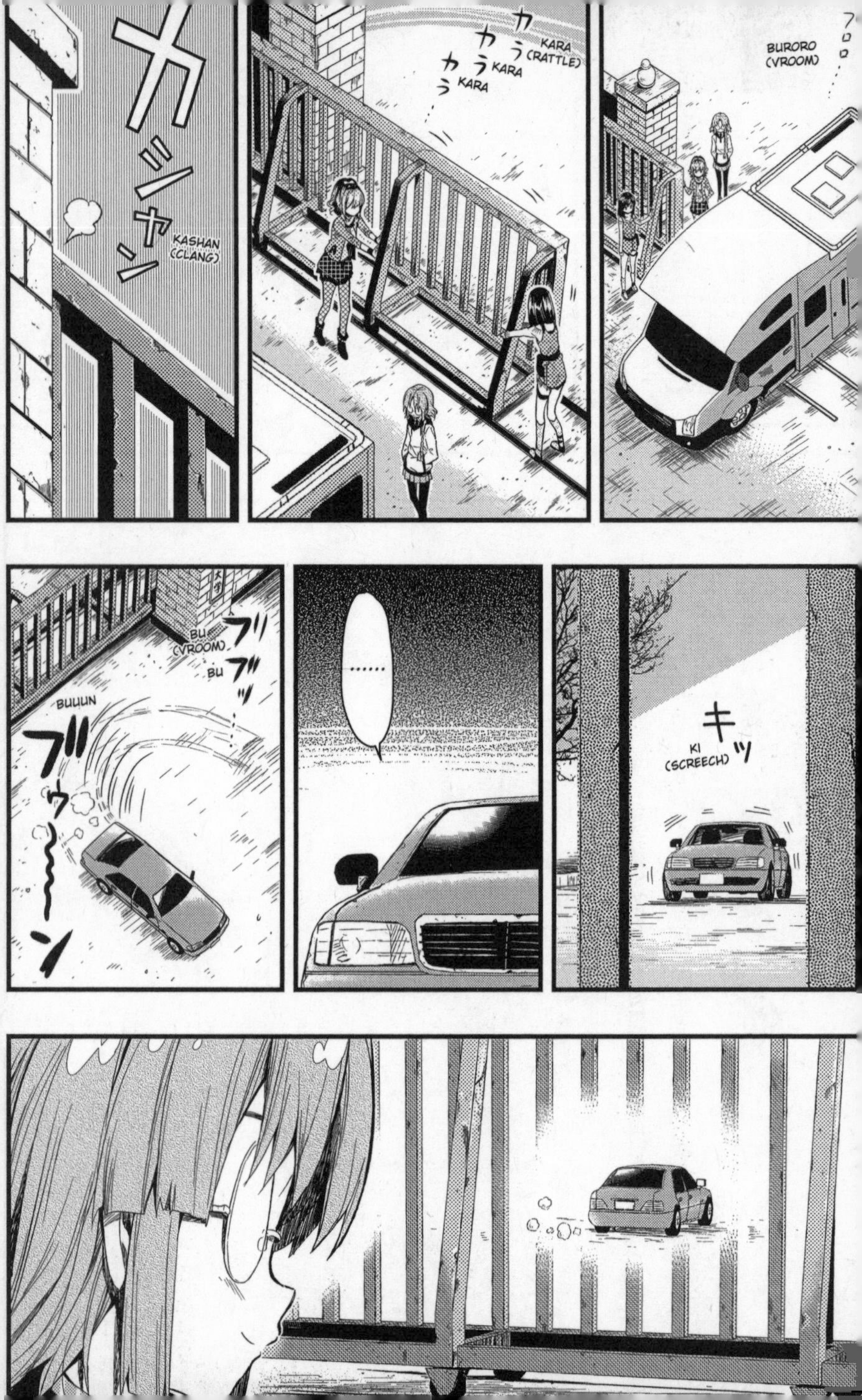
ブロロ…
BURORO (VROOM)
カラカラカラ…
KARA (RATTLE) KARA KARA
カシャン
KASHAN (CLANG)
キッ
KI (SCREECH)
……
ブブッ…
BU (VROOM) BU
ブゥーーン
BUUUN

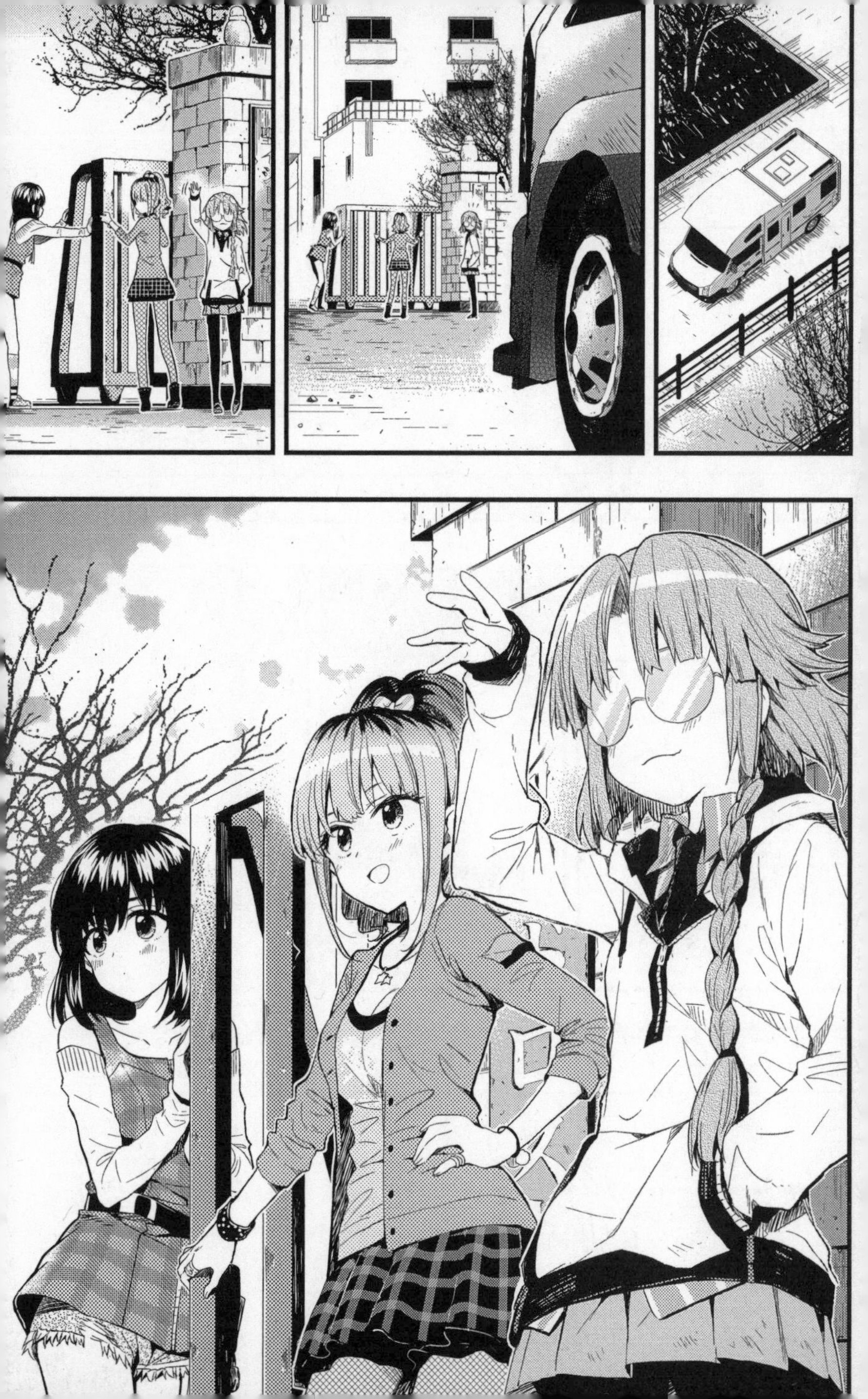

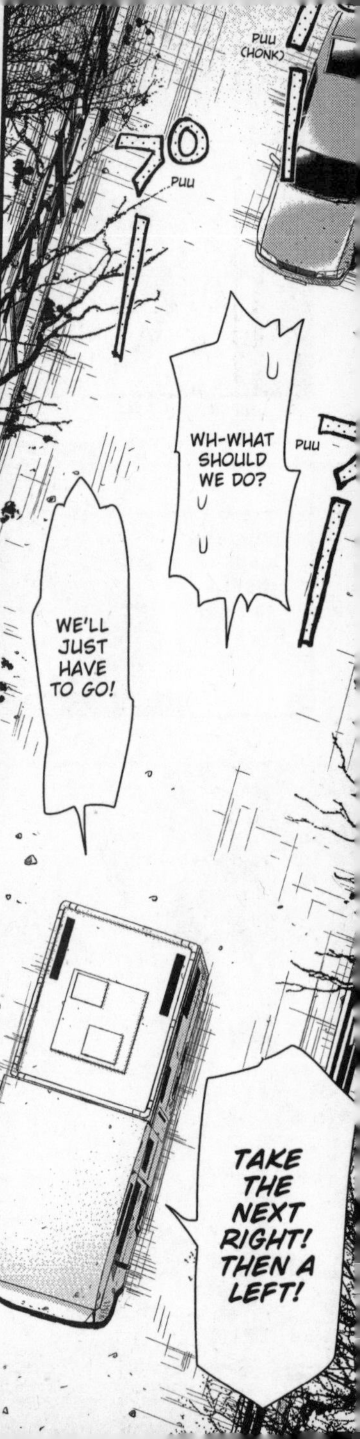
PUU
(HONK)
PUU
WH-WHAT SHOULD WE DO?
PUU
WE'LL JUST HAVE TO GO!
TAKE THE NEXT RIGHT! THEN A LEFT!

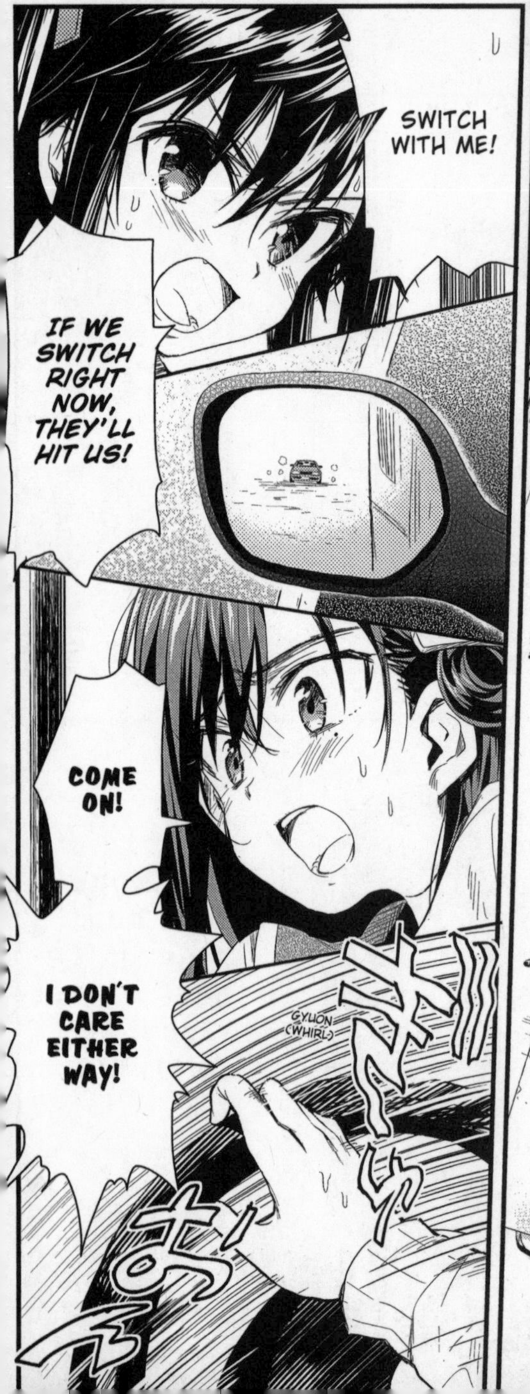
SWITCH WITH ME!
IF WE SWITCH RIGHT NOW, THEY'LL HIT US!
COME ON!
I DON'T CARE EITHER WAY!
GYUON
(WHIRL)

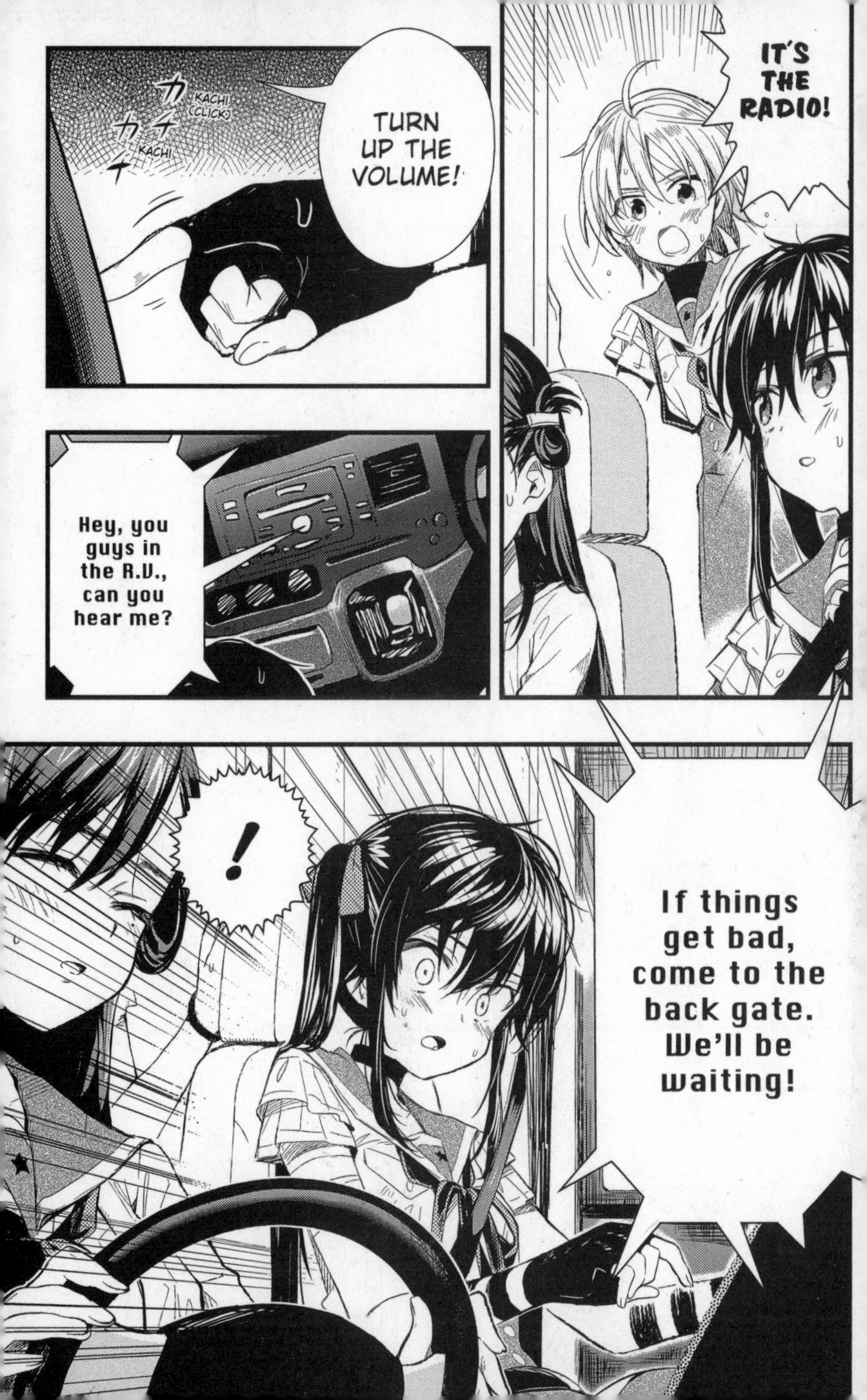
IT'S THE RADIO!
カチ KACHI (CLICK)
カチ KACHI
TURN UP THE VOLUME!
Hey, you guys in the R.V., can you hear me?
If things get bad, come to the back gate. We'll be waiting!
!

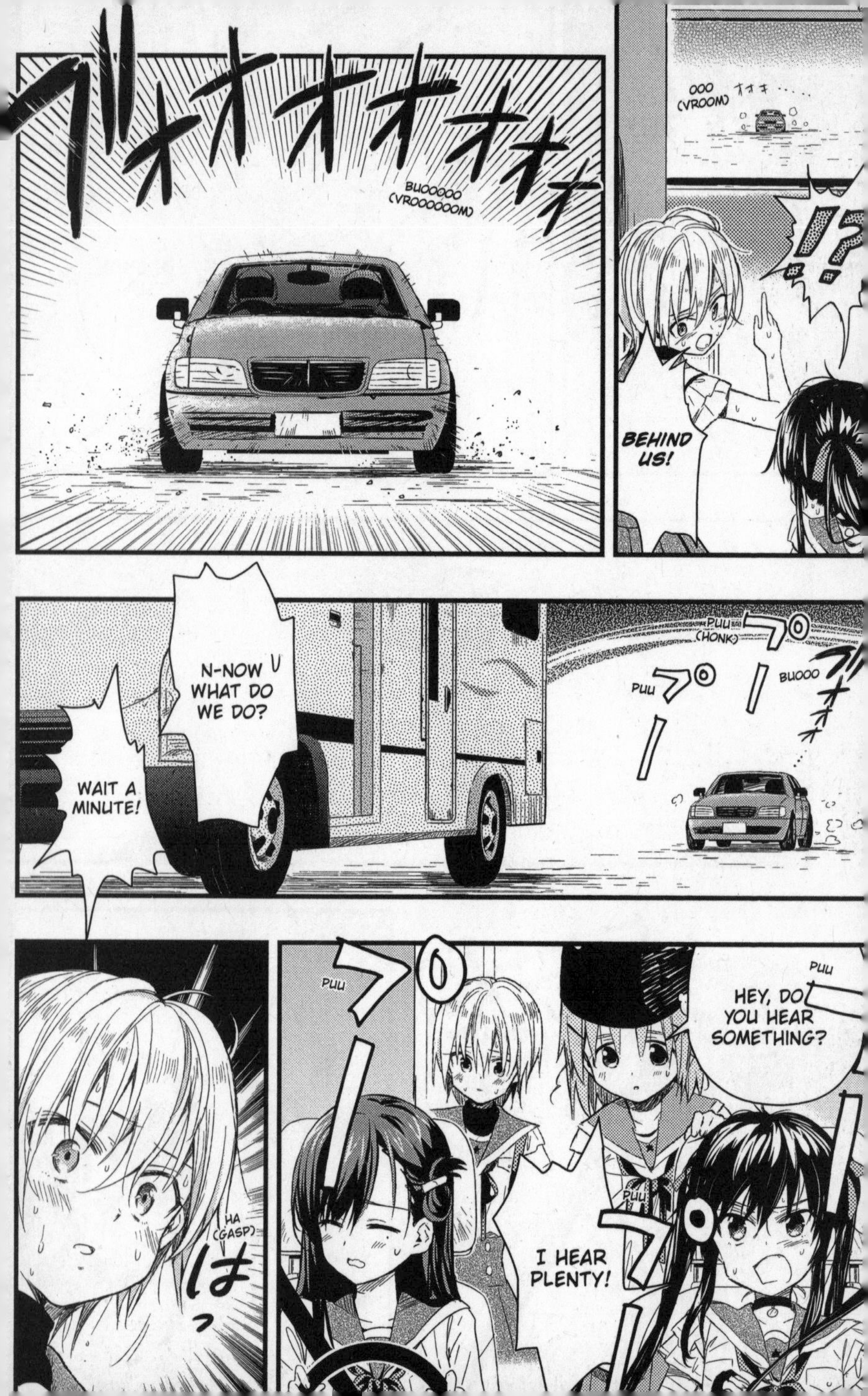
OOO (VROOM)
オオオ・・・
!?
BEHIND US!
ブォオオオオオ
BUOOOOO (VROOOOOOM)
PUU (HONK)
プー
BUOOO
ブォオオ
PUU
プー
N-NOW WHAT DO WE DO?
WAIT A MINUTE!
PUU
HEY, DO YOU HEAR SOMETHING?
PUU
プー
PUU
プー
I HEAR PLENTY!
HA (GASP)
はっ

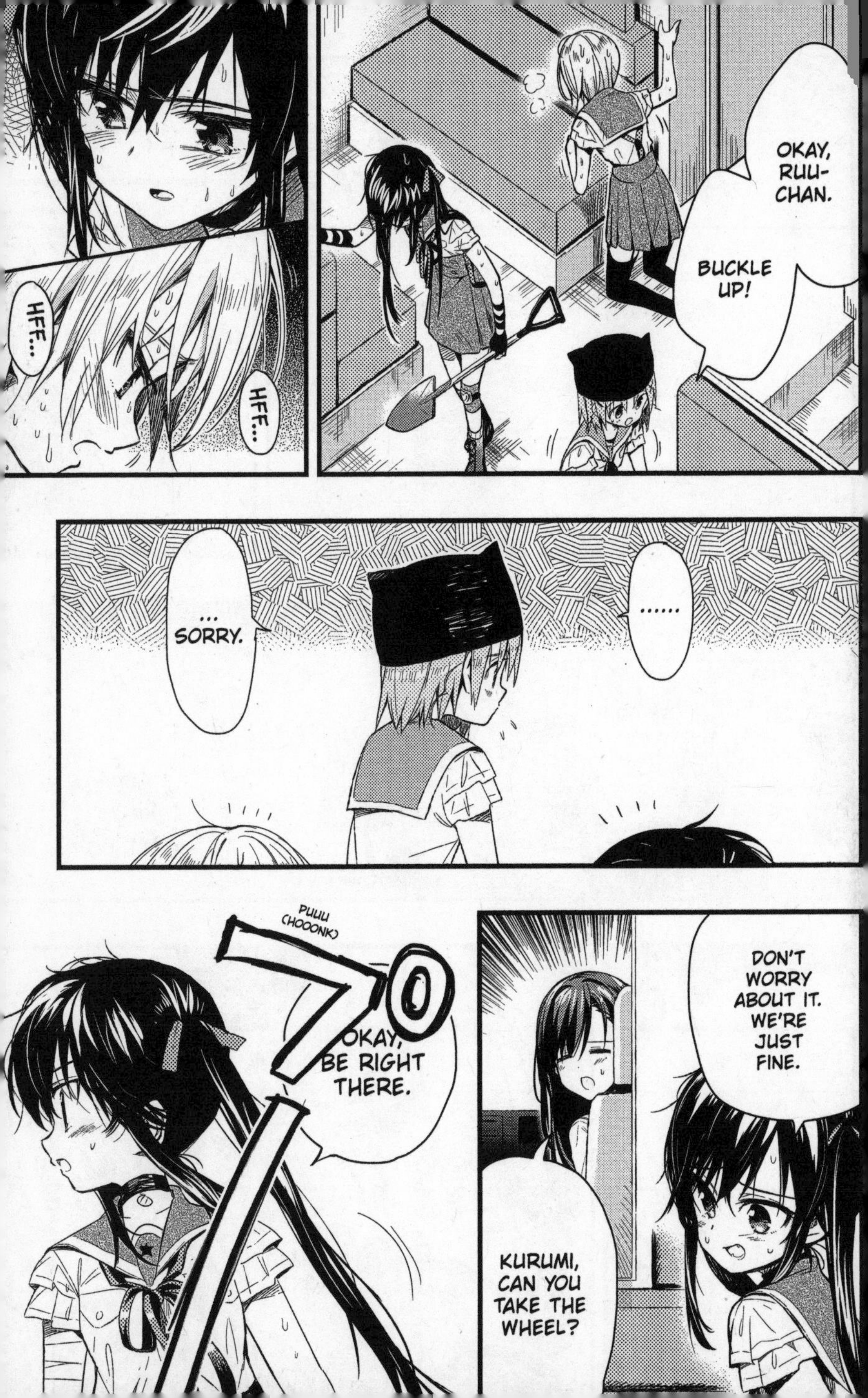
OKAY, RUU-CHAN.
BUCKLE UP!
HFF...
HFF...
......
... SORRY.
DON'T WORRY ABOUT IT. WE'RE JUST FINE.
KURUMI, CAN YOU TAKE THE WHEEL?
PUUU (HOOONK)
OKAY, BE RIGHT THERE.

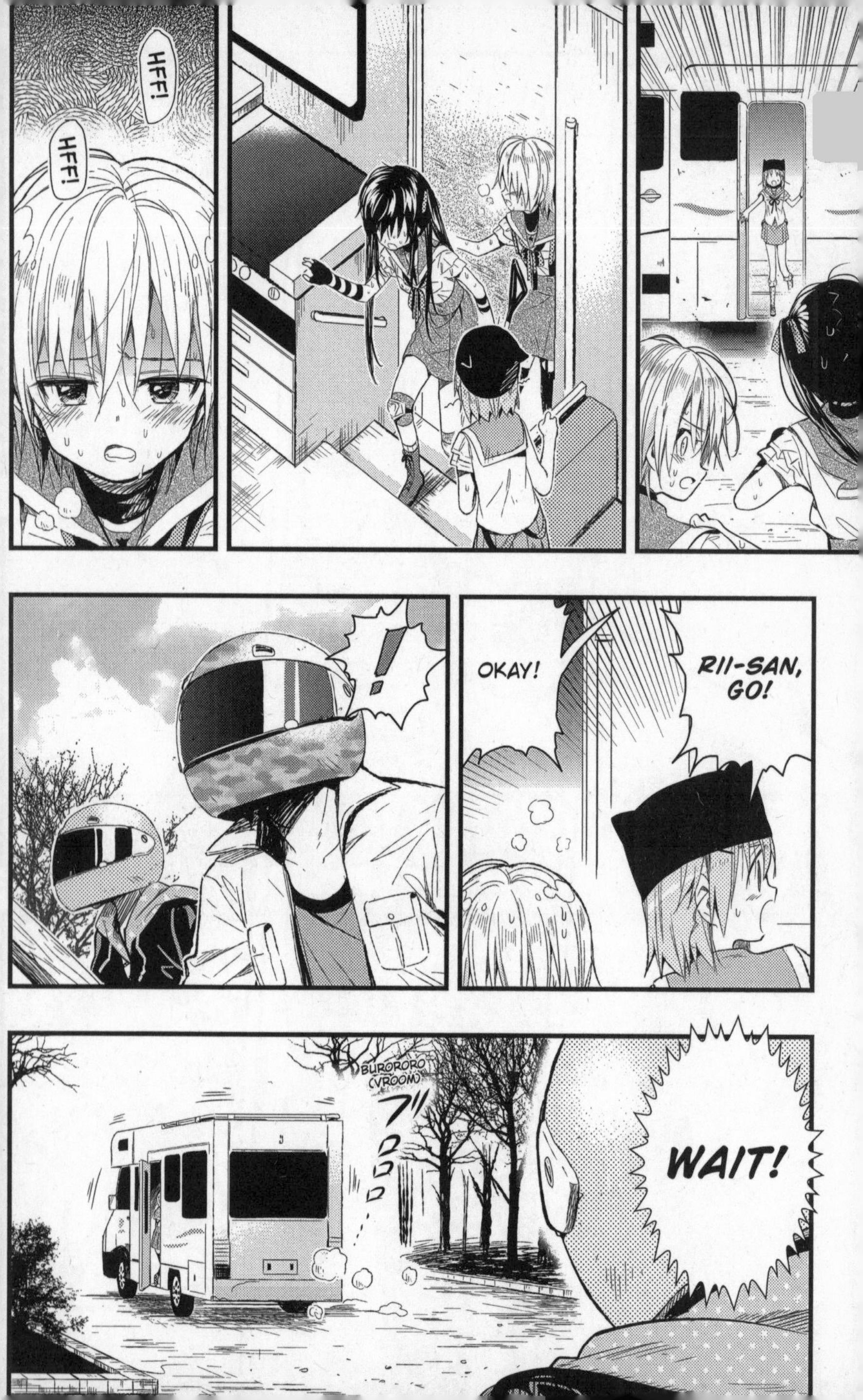
HFF!
HFF!
RII-SAN, GO!
OKAY!
!
WAIT!
BUROROROO (VROOM)

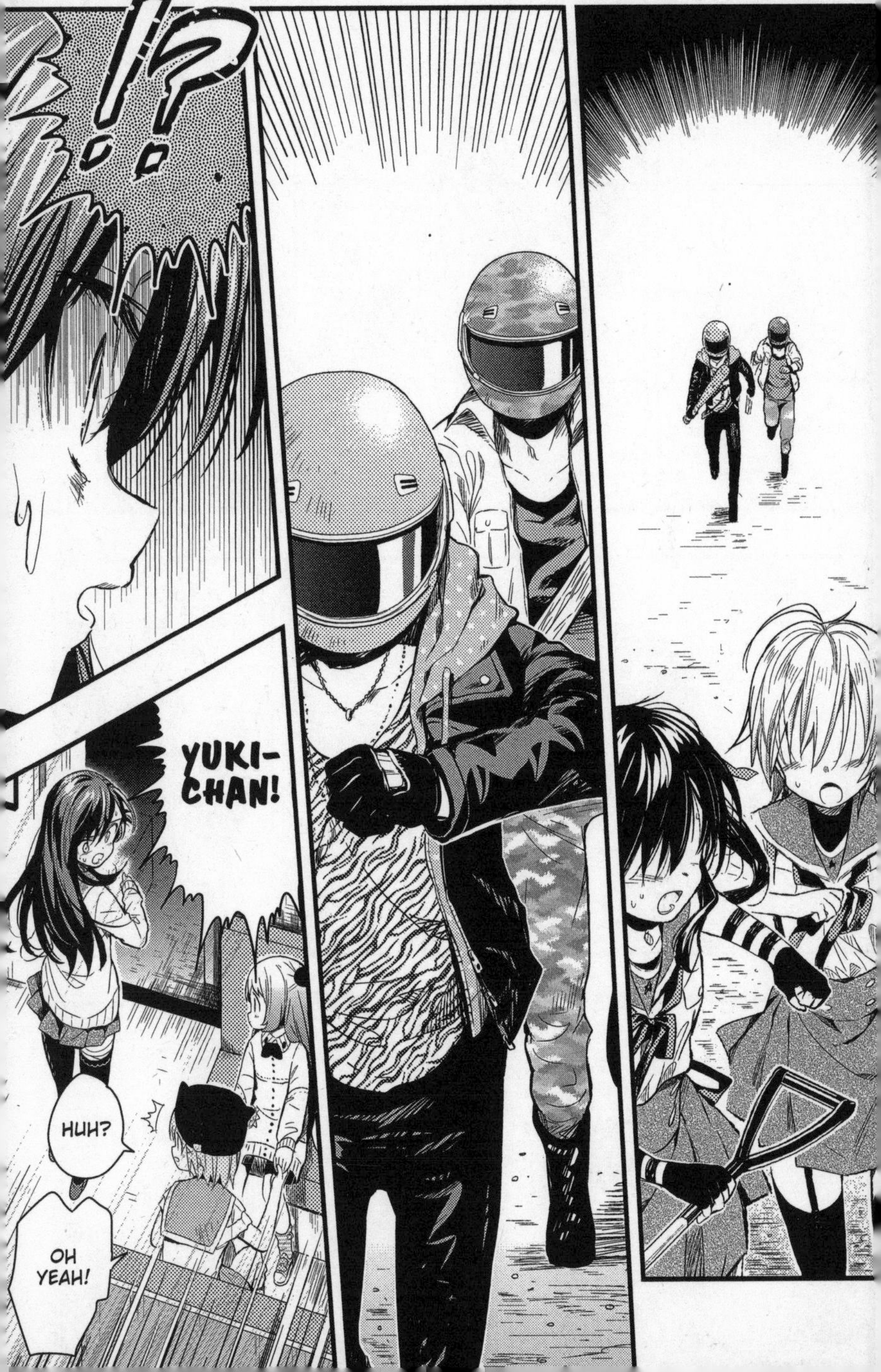
!?
YUKI-CHAN!
HUH?
OH YEAH!

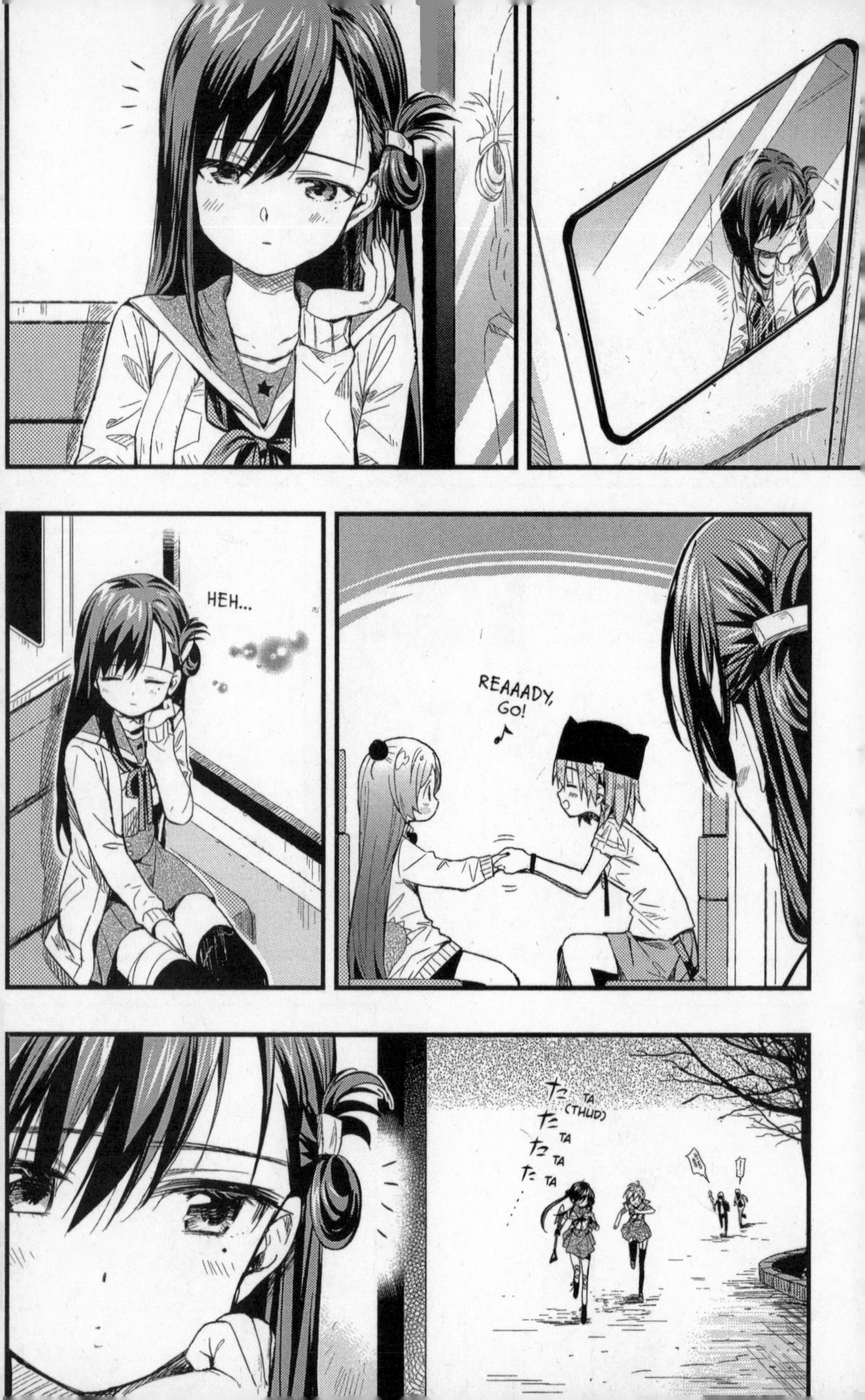
REAAADY, GO! ♪
HEH...
た TA
(THUD)
た TA
た TA
た TA

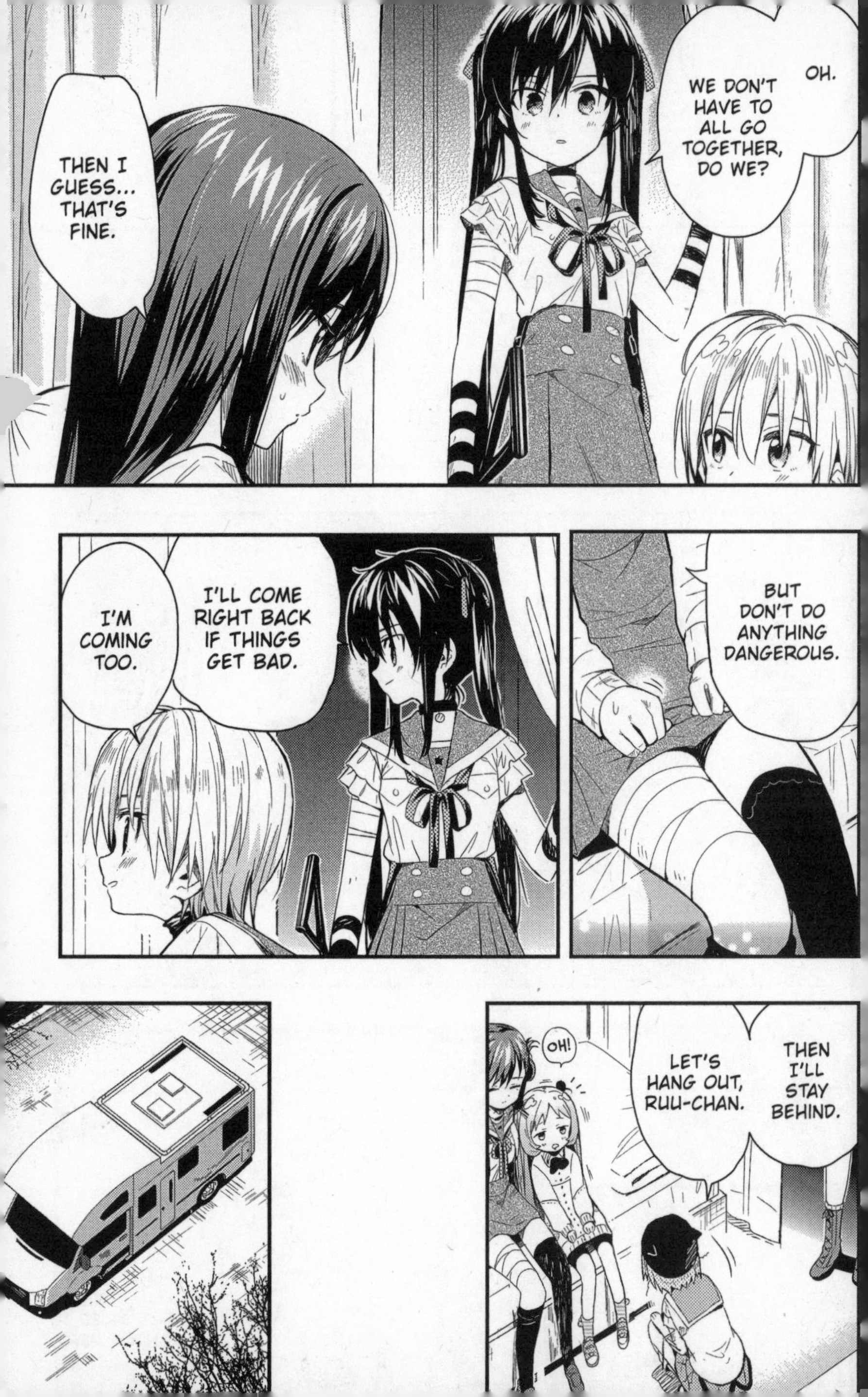
OH.
WE DON'T HAVE TO ALL GO TOGETHER, DO WE?
THEN I GUESS... THAT'S FINE.
BUT DON'T DO ANYTHING DANGEROUS.
I'LL COME RIGHT BACK IF THINGS GET BAD.
I'M COMING TOO.
THEN I'LL STAY BEHIND.
LET'S HANG OUT, RUU-CHAN.
OH!

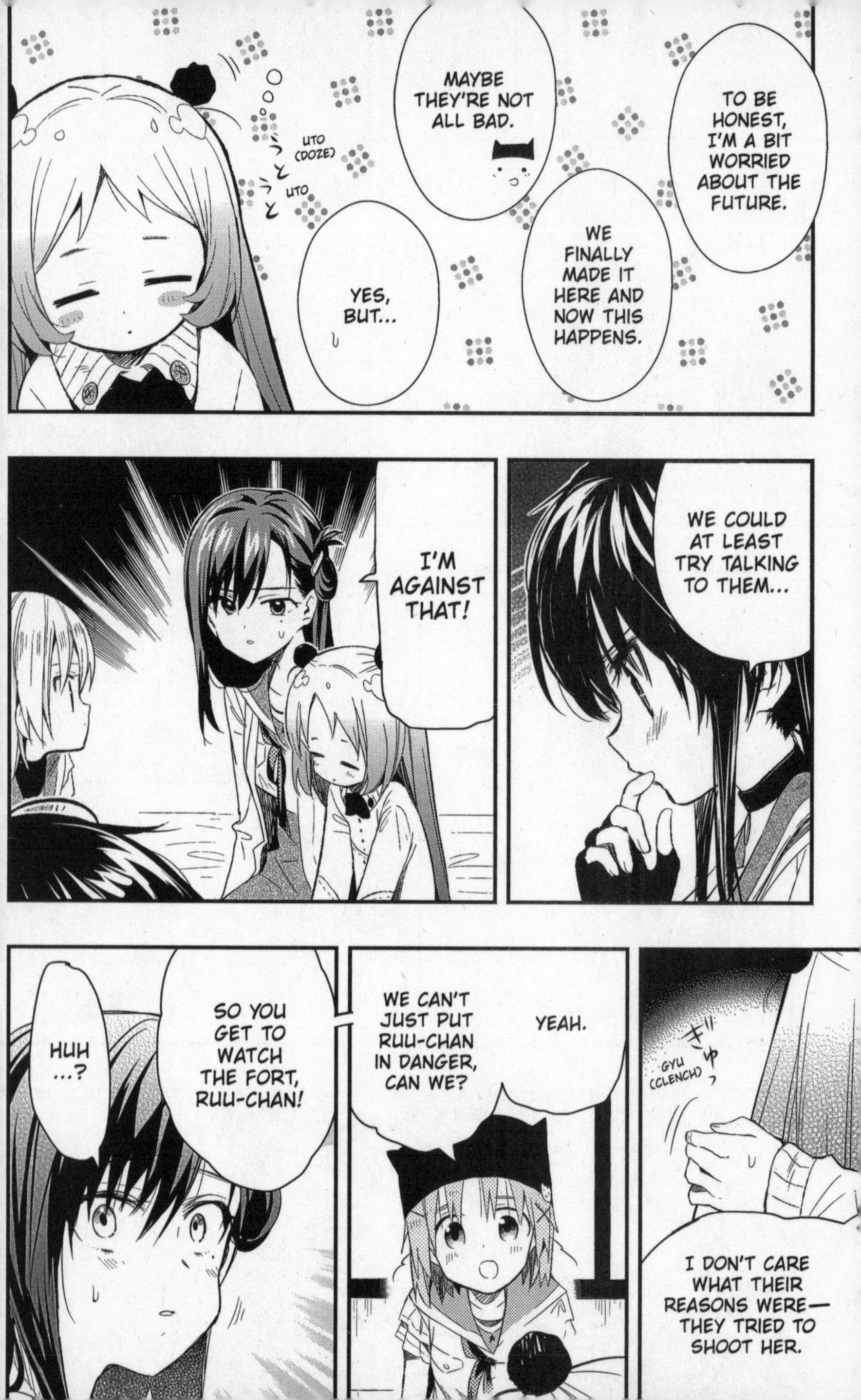
TO BE HONEST, I'M A BIT WORRIED ABOUT THE FUTURE.
MAYBE THEY'RE NOT ALL BAD.
WE FINALLY MADE IT HERE AND NOW THIS HAPPENS.
YES, BUT...
UTO (DOZE)
UTO
WE COULD AT LEAST TRY TALKING TO THEM...
I'M AGAINST THAT!
GYU (CLENCH)
I DON'T CARE WHAT THEIR REASONS WERE—THEY TRIED TO SHOOT HER.
YEAH.
WE CAN'T JUST PUT RUU-CHAN IN DANGER, CAN WE?
SO YOU GET TO WATCH THE FORT, RUU-CHAN!
HUH ...?

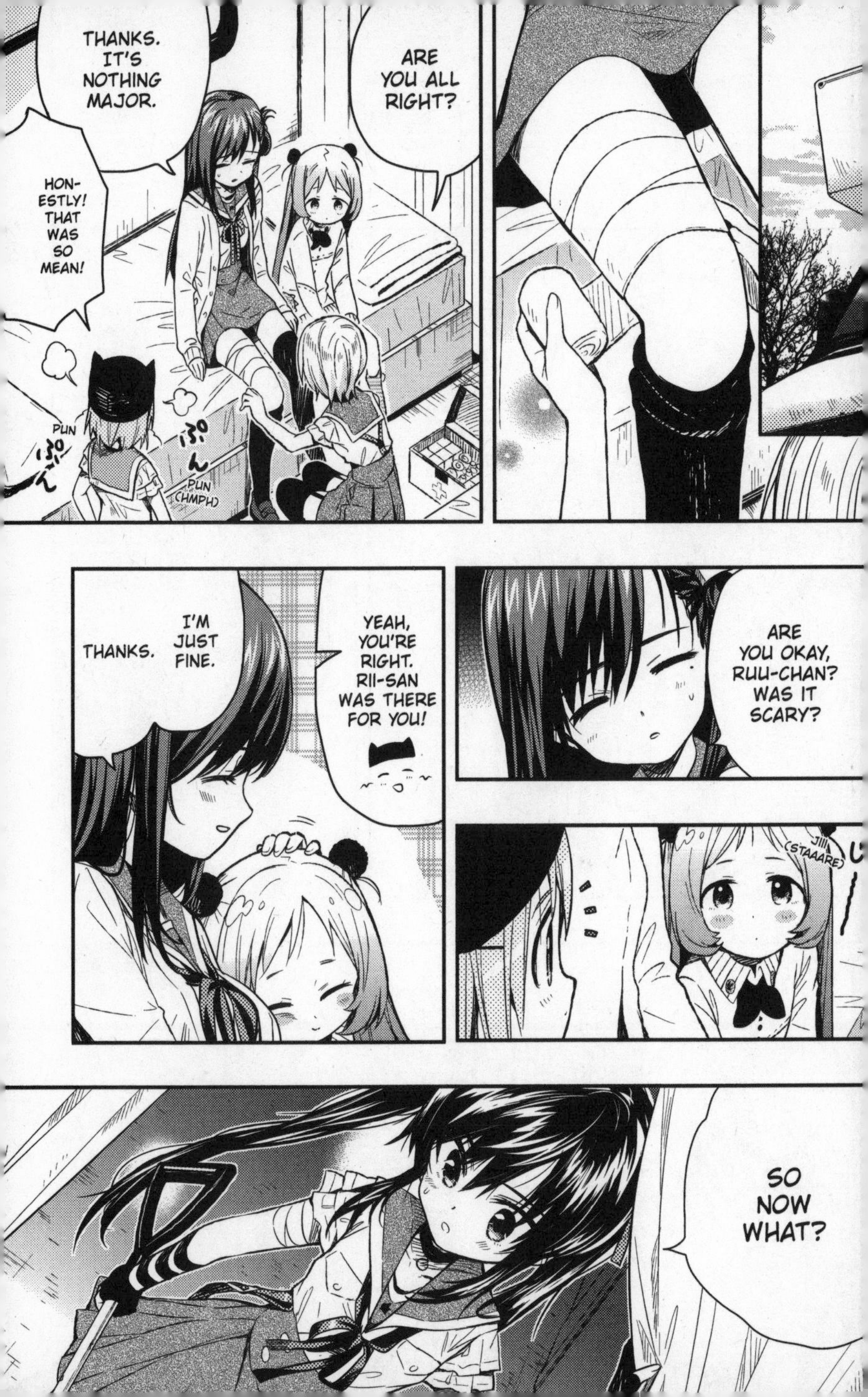
ARE YOU ALL RIGHT?
THANKS. IT'S NOTHING MAJOR.
HON-ESTLY! THAT WAS SO MEAN!
ぷん
PUN (CHMPH)
ぷ~ん
PUN
ARE YOU OKAY, RUU-CHAN? WAS IT SCARY?
じ~~
JIII (STAAARE)
YEAH, YOU'RE RIGHT. RII-SAN WAS THERE FOR YOU!
I'M JUST FINE.
THANKS.
SO NOW WHAT?

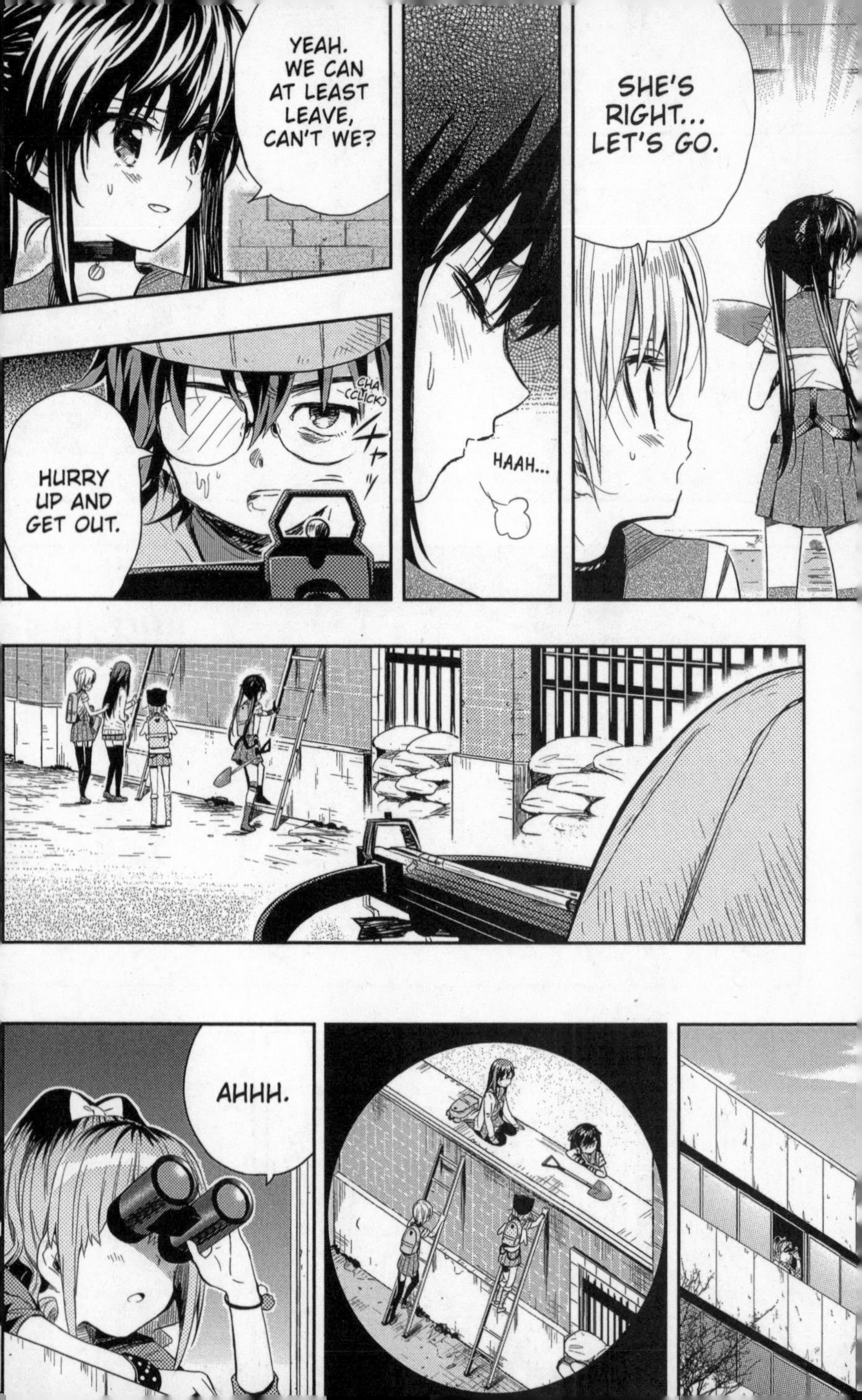
SHE'S RIGHT... LET'S GO.
HAAH...
YEAH. WE CAN AT LEAST LEAVE, CAN'T WE?
CHA (CLICK)
HURRY UP AND GET OUT.
AHHH.

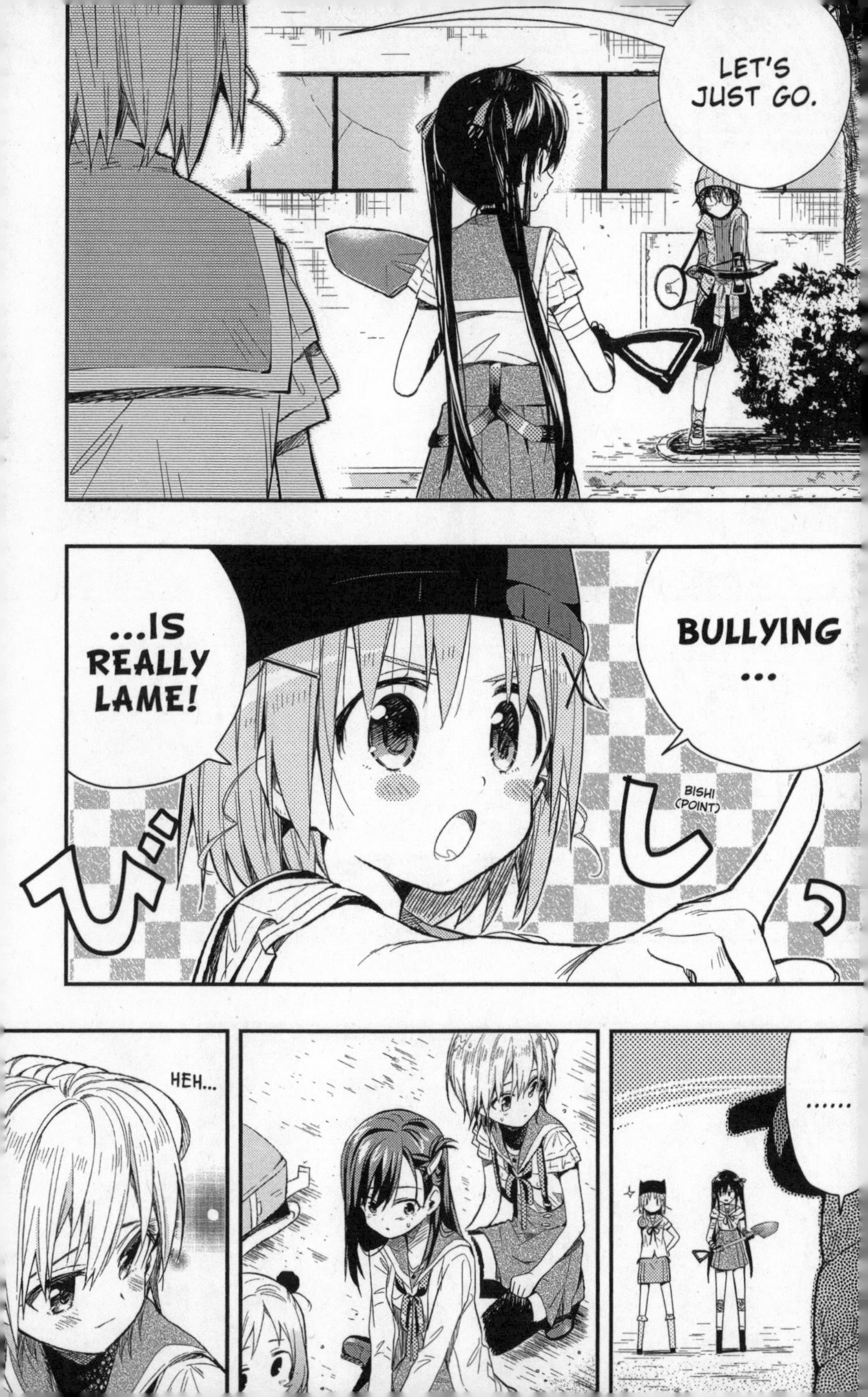
LET'S JUST GO.
BULLYING ...
...IS REALLY LAME!
BISHI (POINT)
......
HEH...

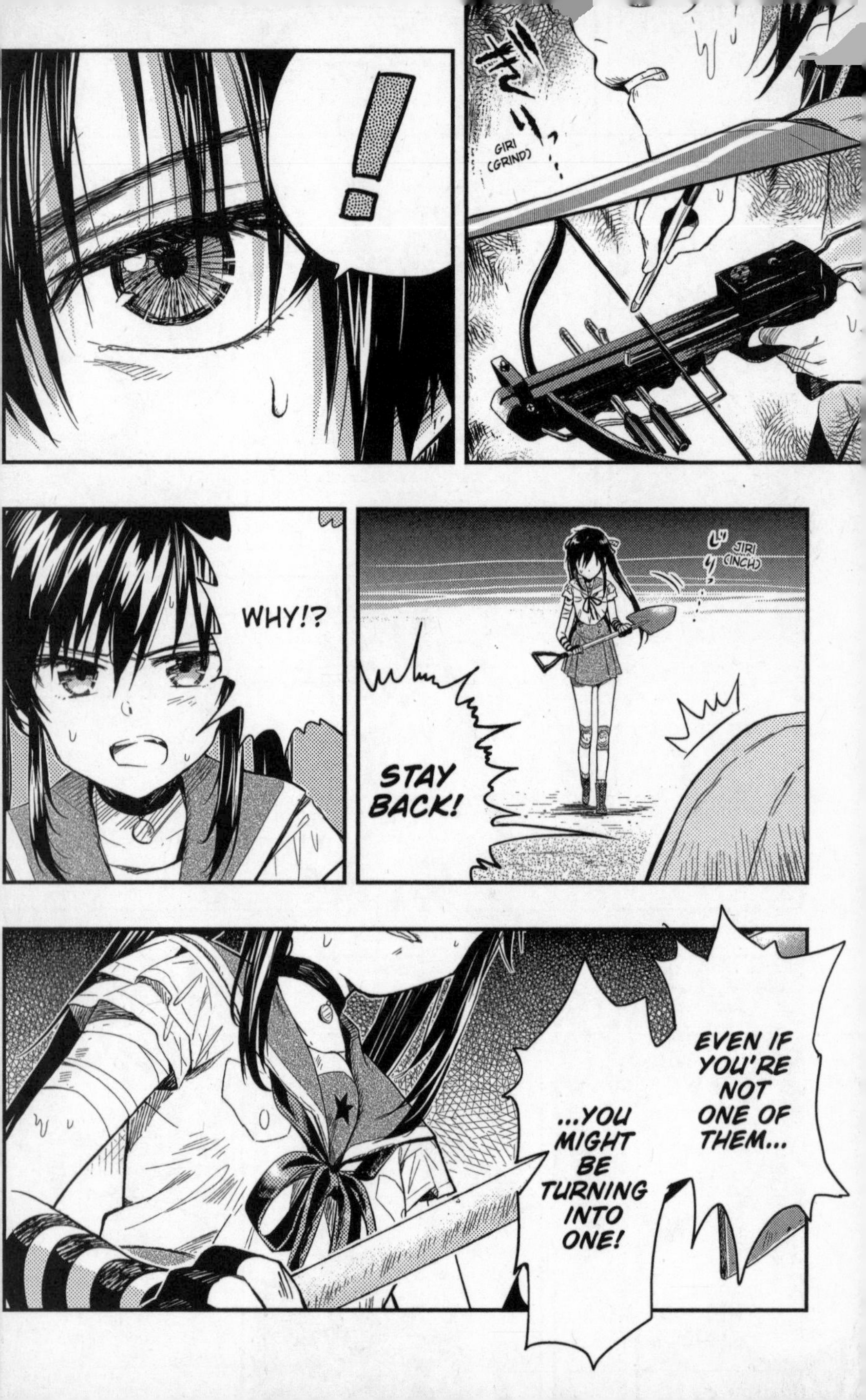
GIRI (GRIND)
!
JIRI (INCH)
STAY BACK!
WHY!?
EVEN IF YOU'RE NOT ONE OF THEM...
...YOU MIGHT BE TURNING INTO ONE!

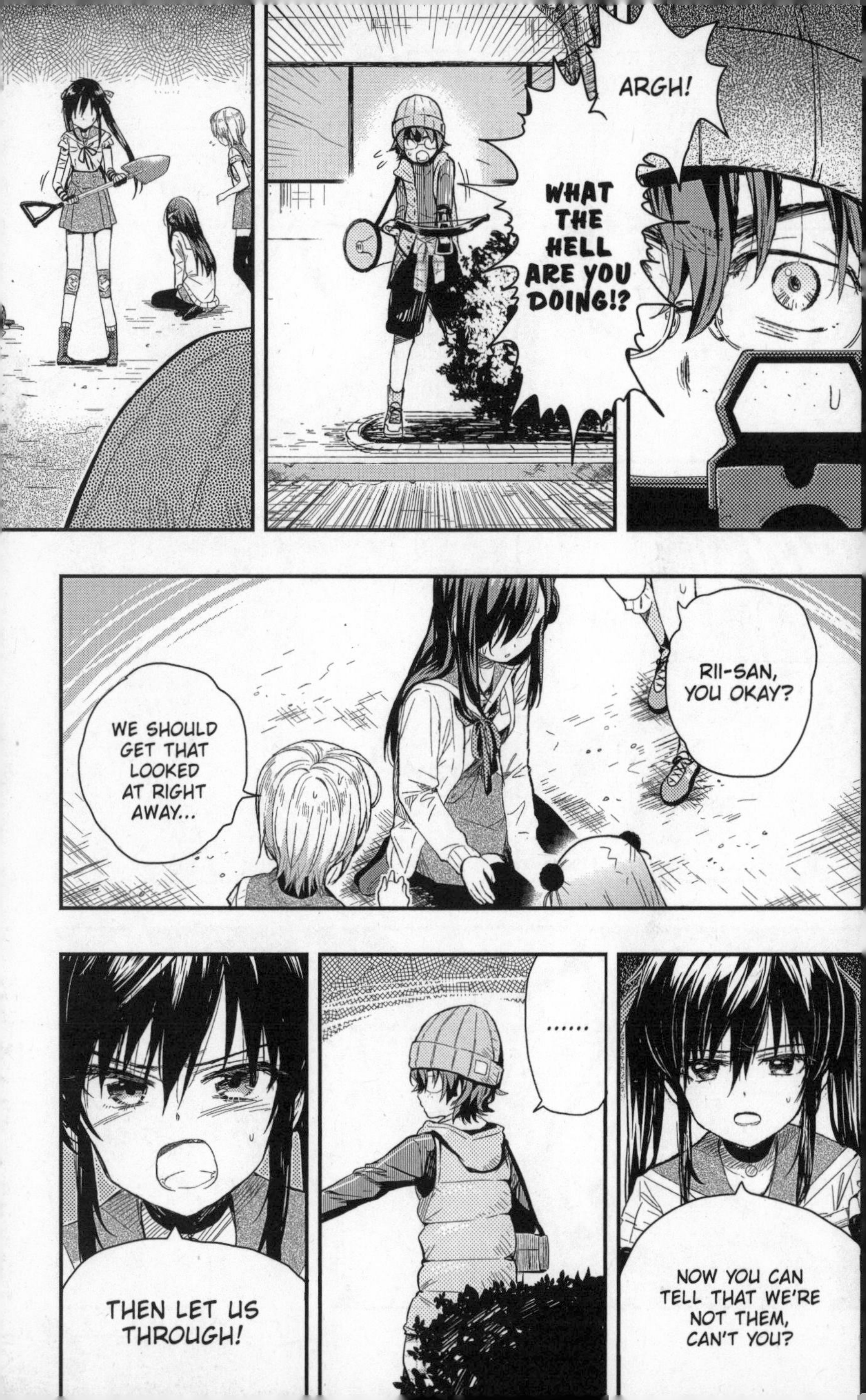
ARGH!
WHAT THE HELL ARE YOU DOING!?
RII-SAN, YOU OKAY?
WE SHOULD GET THAT LOOKED AT RIGHT AWAY...
NOW YOU CAN TELL THAT WE'RE NOT THEM, CAN'T YOU?
......
THEN LET US THROUGH!

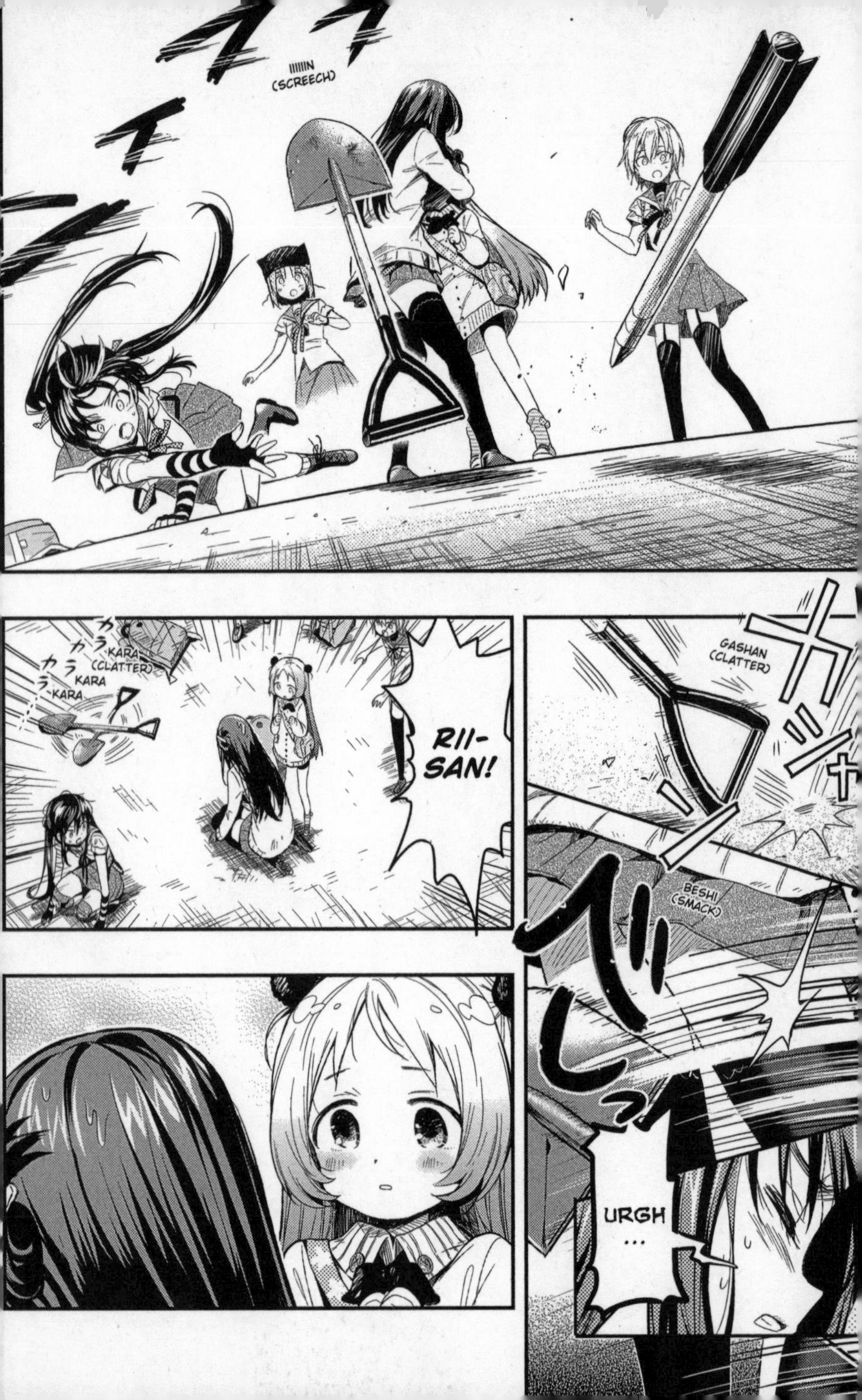
IIIIIIN
(SCREECH)
GASHAN
(CLATTER)
BESHI
(SMACK)
URGH
...
KARA
(CLATTER)
KARA
KARA
RII-
SAN!

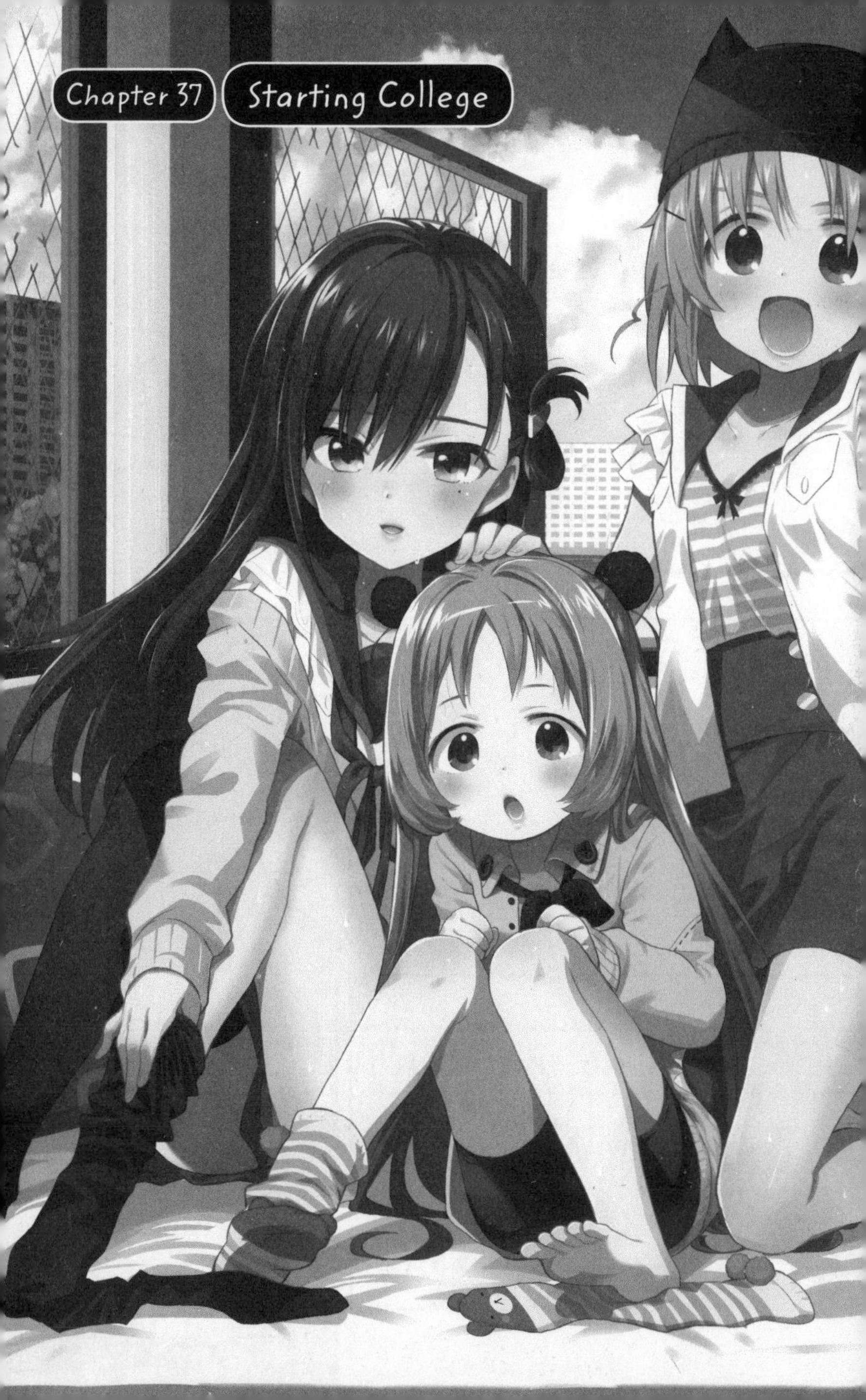
Chapter 37
Starting College

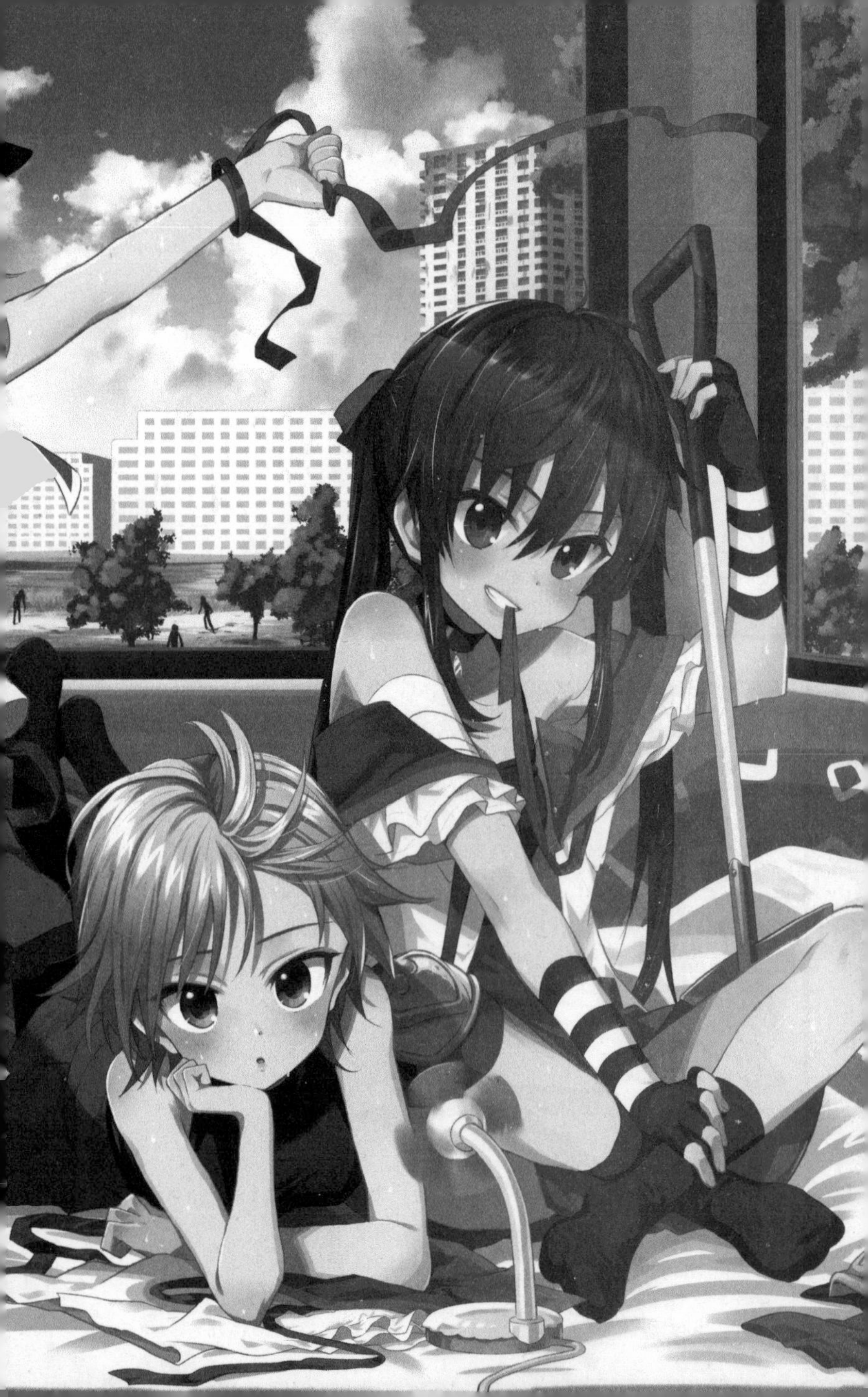

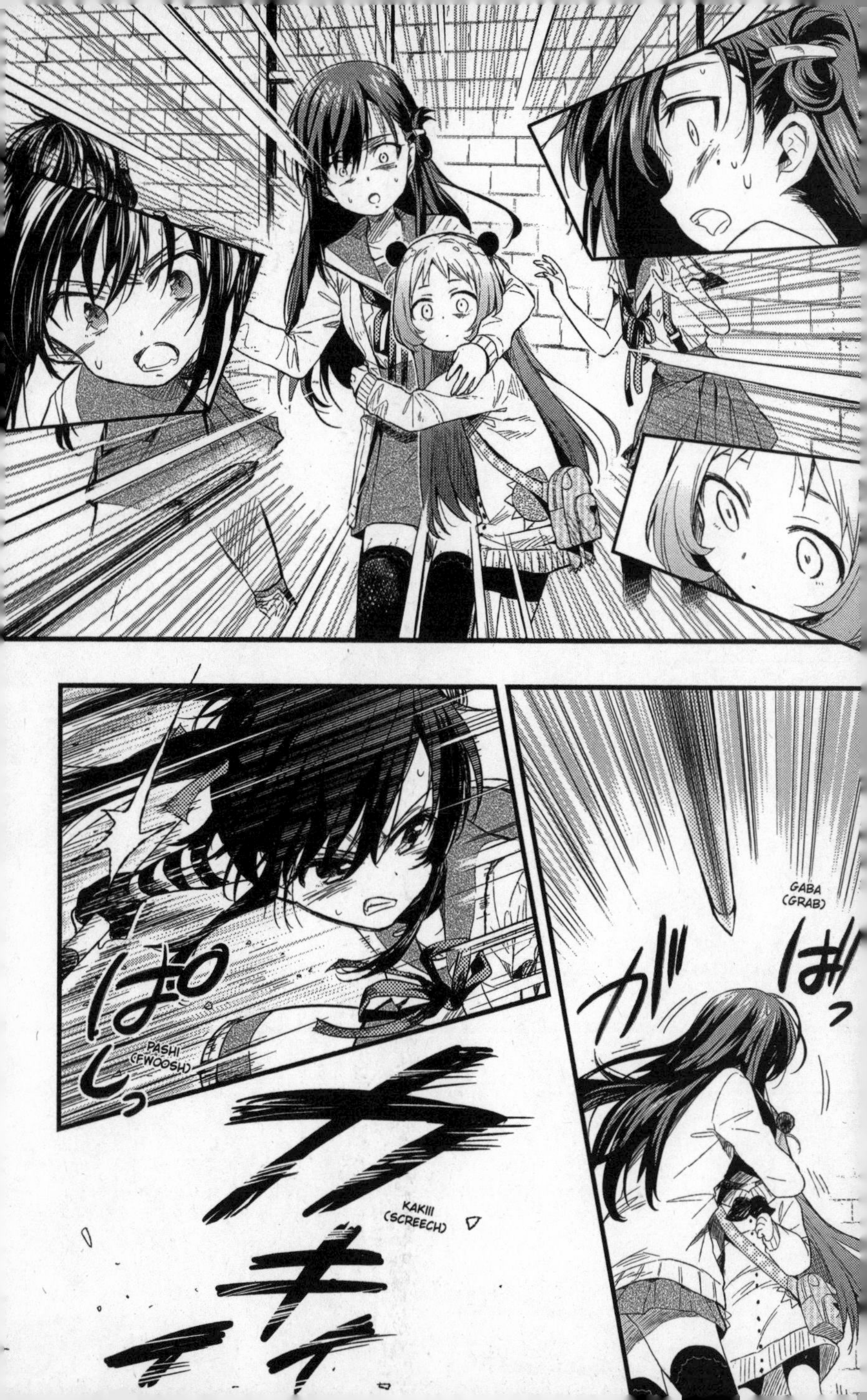
GABA
(GRAB)
PASHI
(FWOOSH)
KAKIII
(SCREECH)

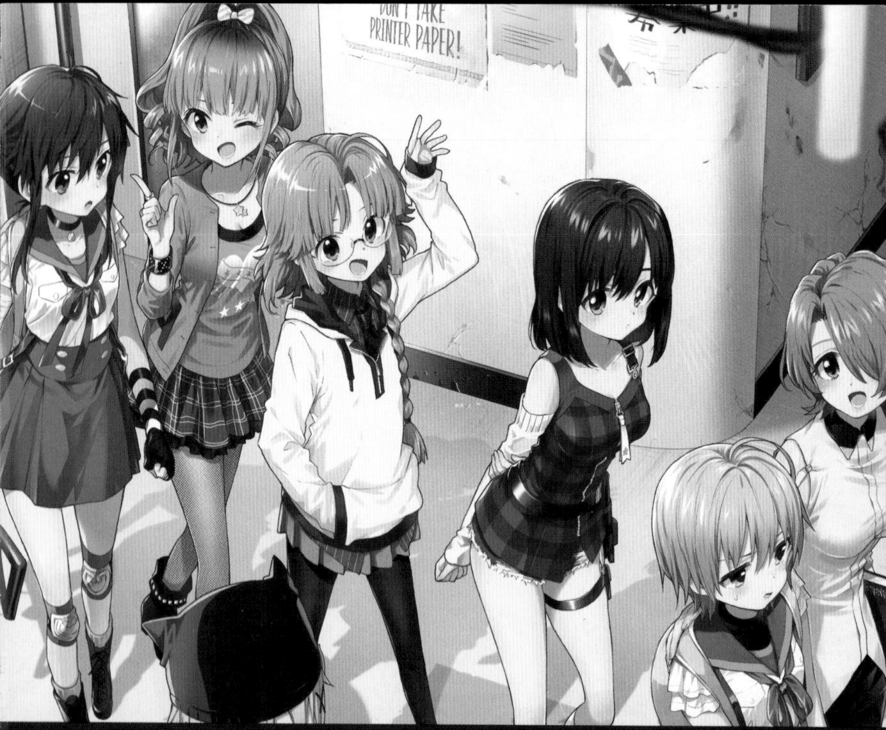
PRINTER PAPER!

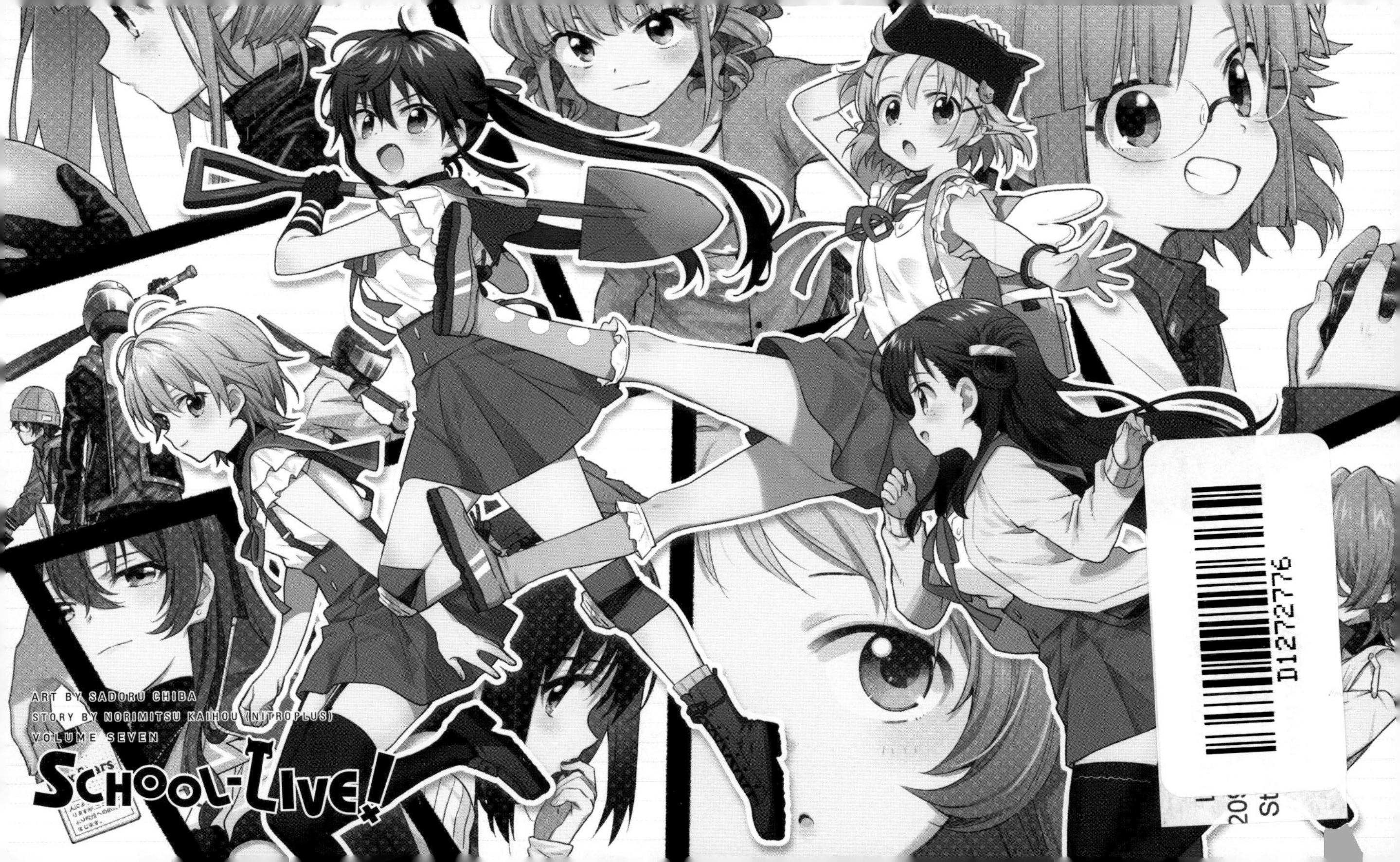
ART BY SADORU CHIBA
STORY BY NORIMITSU KAIHOU (NITROPLUS)
VOLUME SEVEN
SCHOOL-LIVE!